# Sport in Society

# Other books by Richard E. Lapchick

*The Politics of Race and International Sport:*
*The Case of South Africa*

*Oppression and Resistance:*
*The Saga of Women in Southern Africa*

*Broken Promises:  Racism in American Sports*

*Fractured Focus:  Sport as a Reflection of Society*

*On the Mark:  Putting the Student Back in the Student-Athlete*

*Rules of the Game:  Ethics in College Sport*

*Five Minutes to Midnight:  Race and Sport in the 1990s*

# Sport in Society

## Equal Opportunity or Business as Usual?

## Richard E. Lapchick

EDITOR

**SAGE** Publications
*International Educational and Professional Publisher*
Thousand Oaks   London   New Delhi

*For information address*:

 SAGE Publications, Inc.
2455 Teller Road
Thousand Oaks, California 91320
E-mail: order@sagepub.com

SAGE Publications Ltd.
6 Bonhill Street
London EC2A 4PU
United Kingdom

SAGE Publications India Pvt. Ltd.
M-32 Market
Greater Kailash I
New Delhi 110 048 India

Printed in the United States of America

**Library of Congress Cataloging-in-Publication Data**

Main entry under title:

Sport in society: Equal opportunity or business as usual? / edited by
  Richard E. Lapchick
       p.   cm.
    Includes bibliographical references and index.
    ISBN 0-8039-7280-6 (cloth). — ISBN 0-8039-7281-4 (pbk.)
    1. Sports—Social aspects—United States.   2. Discrimination in
  sports—United States.   3. Sex discrimination in sports—United
  States.   4. Mass media and sports—United States.   5. College
  sports—Social aspects—United States.   I. Lapchick, Richard
  Edward.
  GV706.5.S7338   1995
  306.4′83—dc20                                    95-35477

This book is printed on acid-free paper.

96   97   98   99   10   9   8   7   6   5   4   3   2   1

Sage Production Editor:  Astrid Virding
Sage Copy Editor:  Linda Gray
Sage Typesetter:  Janelle LeMaster

For my good friends, Northeastern University President Jack Curry and Chairman of the Board George Matthews, whose lives have inspired me to fight for a better world and whose professional leadership and personal faith in me have helped me to stay in the fight.

# Contents

# Introduction

In 1984, I helped found Northeastern University's Center for the Study of Sport in Society. The center was formed, in part, to study the effect of sport on society. With our premise being that sport reflects society as opposed to being a remedy for its ills, we set out to examine the feasibility of using athletes as agents for social change. One of our first items of business was to embrace the *Journal of Sport & Social Issues (JSSI),* which was created to provide an alternative voice for scholars to go beyond analysis of sport traditions and historical values. It was originally created by ARENA, the Institute for Sport and Social Analysis.

*JSSI* remains the official publication of the center and is now being published by Sage Publications. It has brought together leading journalists, historians, sociologists, anthropologists, and activists to critically examine and identify the problem areas within sport.

The purpose of *Sport in Society: Equal Opportunity or Business as Usual?* is to indicate current and potential problems that accompany the increasing popularity of sport within our culture and to establish an understanding of the effective use of sport to improve the social fabric of society. The book relies on a mix of previously published articles, some of which have appeared in *JSSI,* as well as on new articles written in the spirit of the journal.

I must emphasize that my own writings reflect my belief, dating back to when the center opened in 1984, that the world of sport had been pervaded by problems of racism; sexism; the exploitation of student-athletes; stereotypes of student-athletes, coaches, and sports officials; and a media that refused to effectively address the issues that encircled the sport world. The articles in *Sport in Society* reflect those problems as well as developments in the decade following the center's opening that helped to begin to improve sport in America.

Sport captures people's imaginations—including both positive and negative passions. Even the negative stories about sport serve to educate the public because we do pay attention to what is going on in sport. Millions had died, were imprisoned, or tortured in South Africa, yet there were few reports anywhere in the United States until stories regarding the sports boycott revealed the horrors of life under apartheid. Society called cocaine "recreational" until Len Bias's death showed us it was lethal and that there were 2 million addicts in America. There were few stories on America's 8 million gambling addicts until Pete Rose's involvement woke us up.

America's annual 1.5 million assaults were buried in the metro sections of newspapers until the attacks on Monica Seles and Nancy Kerrigan became front-page news. Thousands of nightmares in Bosnia were disappearing on inner pages until the death of 20 soccer players took Bosnia back to the front page. The AIDS plague was the property of gay men and intravenous drug users when Magic Johnson and Arthur Ashe made it mainstream.

Who knew that 25% of college women face rape in college until reports of athletes raping women uncovered this hidden campus issue? Stories about athletes brought attention to the issue. Sexual abuse is a serious problem on campus and in America. No group of people is immune: not athletes, fraternity brothers, friends at the neighborhood bar—not even priests, naval commanders, and scoutmasters. However, even with the stories about athletes, it took the O. J. Simpson case to truly force America to confront the fact that more than 3 million women each year are the victims of gender violence.

The well-publicized scandals involving college sports in the early 1980s and the revelation of the low graduation rates of student-athletes were strong indicators that the exploitation of athletes was an area in need of significant attention. In particular, black athletes were failing to graduate while continuing to believe they could overcome the 10,000 to 1 odds against making a professional team. But the worst news about the graduation rates was that black student-athletes were graduating at a higher rate than black students in general.

In an attempt to empower student-athletes, the center established the National Consortium for Academics and Sports in 1985. In an effort to keep the "student" in *student-athlete,* the consortium was founded with 11 universities that agreed to bring back former student-athletes who participated in revenue-producing sports without completing their degree. In exchange for a tuition-free opportunity, the 7,000 returning student-athletes were required to participate in school and community outreach programs. Over 10 years, they have served more than 2,300,000 youth. Now 117 colleges and universities are members of the consortium.

A decade of research and experience has taught us that sport has the capacity to do more than simply mirror society. It can, in fact, cause it to change. By 1995, the center was recognized as the nation's leading creator of programs that use athletes to improve social conditions in society. With four regional offices located throughout the country, the center and the consortium successfully use sport to address job discrimination based on race and sex, violence against women, racial tension, and poor graduation rates among student-athletes.

The center's flagship program, Project TEAMWORK, was formed in 1990. Seeing the influence of athletes who worked in their respective communities as part of the degree completion program, the center assembled a team of former athletes to educate students on the subjects of racism, gender discrimination, and conflict resolution. In 1993, Project TEAMWORK received the Peter F. Drucker Award for being the nation's most innovative nonprofit program in the social sector; it was also named by Lou Harris as "the nation's most successful violence prevention program."

For the most part, *Sport in Society: Equal Opportunity or Business as Usual?* focuses on the issues of race, gender, student-athletes, stereotypes and myths, and the media's filter on sports. There is also a section on international sports.

The center's annual Racial Report Card has become a critical tool in improving job opportunities for minorities in the front offices of professional sports teams. In 1987, the statements on ABC's *Nightline* by Los Angeles Dodger executive Al Campanis revealed some of the stereotypes about blacks that were preventing their advancement within team administrations. Beginning in 1988, the center published the report to emphasize the discrepancy between the number of blacks and Hispanics performing on the field of play and their virtual absence in management positions.

By 1994, there was a noticeable increase in the willingness of professional teams to hire blacks for top managerial positions. Equally significant, two of the National Basketball Association's (NBA) most prominent players in the 1980s—Isiah Thomas and Earvin "Magic" Johnson—became part-owners of NBA teams after their retirement. Furthermore, the Jacksonville Jaguars, Carolina Panthers, and Toronto Raptors—all expansion teams in the National Football League (NFL) and NBA, respectively—have either African American part-owners or African Americans employed in the highest management position in terms of player personnel matters. Although there have been improvements in this area, there is still a great deal of work to do.

With strong evidence supporting its conviction that sport has the capacity to bring about important social change, the center created various proactive programs intended to use organized athletics for intervention and prevention. The center's Mentors in Violence Prevention (MVP) program is a unique attempt to take advantage of athletes' influence in society to prevent acts of violence against women. Using college athletes as peer educators, MVP works to reduce the frequency of violence against women on college campuses. Sexual and physical violence against women has generally been considered by many to be a "women's issue," thus relieving men from actively opposing it. The center employs former male athletes to train male college student-athletes as peer educators and role models in their communities.

In addition to the increased awareness of abuse against women, we are witnessing a continuing rise in the number of youth falling prey to the affects of substance abuse. In sport, the NBA, NFL, Major League Baseball, and the National Collegiate Athletic Association (NCAA) have invested a significant amount of money and time to educate athletes about substance abuse and to provide proper treatment to athletes who suffer its affects. Yet the public is frequently reminded that players sometimes struggle with drug and alcohol abuse. The banning of Dwight Gooden from baseball after repeated failed drug tests is only the most recent case that proves that successfully halting an addiction is far more difficult than reducing substance abuse through preventive education.

As *Sport in Society: Equal Opportunity or Business as Usual?* was being completed early in 1995, one could not help being struck by two things in sport. The first was the explosion of the issue of violence in sport. The second was the forced ending of any remaining illusion prevalent among fans that sport was not a huge business enterprise infused with the same drive of corporate America to earn as much revenue as possible.

Two of the most notable news stories linked to sport were the double murder charges filed against O. J. Simpson and the assault of Nancy Kerrigan preceding the Olympics. Although the nature of these two crimes differed considerably in seriousness and in their relationship to sport, both underline the ever increasing violent trend within our society.

The unprecedented media attention afforded to the case against Simpson finally brought the problem of gender violence to the forefront of America's social agenda. It has also called the concept of "sports hero" into question and has increased the degree of cynicism regarding athletes as role models.

Unlike the tragedy in Los Angeles, the attack on Kerrigan had a direct link to competitive sports. In an attempt to ensure victory, people associated with Kerrigan's main competitor, Tanya Harding, orchestrated the plan to have Kerrigan clubbed after exiting from the ice. The criminal convictions that followed were an indication of the loss of perspective that can result when the stakes associated with winning are so high.

Similarly, the World Cup was tarnished by the assassination of Colombia's star player, Escobar. He had accidentally deflected the ball into his own goal, resulting in Colombia's elimination from the tournament. After returning to his country, he was shot by four assassins who reportedly killed him because of his play on the field.

Consistent with the rising stakes connected to competitive sports is the increasing prevalence of games being replaced by labor strife between players and owners. At one point, it appeared that we might see the competitive seasons in three sports—the NBA, where a strike was contemplated; Major League Baseball, which was on strike; and the National Hockey League (NHL), which was involved in a lockout—come to a complete halt. The year 1994 will long be remembered as the first year a World Series was canceled in nearly a century. The inability of negotiators to resolve the dispute between owners and players has soured the taste of fans and jeopardized the future of the game. Members of Congress proposed to draft legislation that would amend a Supreme Court decision from 1922 that exempts baseball from the interstate commerce clause. Senator Daniel Patrick Moynihan introduced the National Pastime Preservation Act to repeal baseball's exemption from anti-trust laws and ultimately return the game to the fans. President Clinton finally stepped into the fray early in 1995.

Similarly, the NHL, after experiencing its most successful season in league history, was unable to reach a collective bargaining agreement prior to the start of the 1994 season. Ultimately, a lockout went into effect that led to the cancellation of half of the regular season. With a similar threat facing the NBA, a last-minute compromise enabled the league and the Players Association to play a full season. If they had ever doubted it, fans now had to recognize the extent to which sport has become a major corporate enterprise.

Despite these major challenges produced by the rising popularity of sport and increased scrutiny by the press, organized athletics has also become a refreshing tool with powerful influence to rectify issues of both domestic and international importance. In 1993, the Rainbow Commission for Fairness in Athletics and the Coalition for Equality in Sport were both formed to reduce racial and gender barriers in the hiring practices of professional sport teams. These organizations brought together civil rights activists, players, coaches, and government officials to improve opportunities for racial minorities and women, who had historically been discriminated against by the sports industry.

Although this book does not address all the current issues relating to sport, it does deal with challenges to some of the more pressing problems that sport is confronting. Clearly, the domestic challenges that confront America in the coming decade can be partially reduced by using the resources of sport to effect change. This collection of articles leads readers into a new era in sport in which the unprecedented popularity of organized athletics will present unique challenges to the sports world as well as new opportunities to influence society.

Most of the contributors to this book have had extensive experience working in or studying the sport industry and therefore possess strong views in their articles. Many of these individuals have dedicated a significant portion of their professional lives to improving the equity and integrity of sport. I have selected articles that bridge a gap between the problems we faced and addressed in the 1980s and the challenges that await us as we approach the 20th century. It should be noted that the data in previously published articles was not updated for *Sport in Society*. The data in original articles was updated through January 1, 1995.

Beginning with a focus on racism, particular attention is given to the progress that has been made by blacks in the area of team administration and head coaching positions. Although the number of black players continues to far exceed the number of blacks employed in management, there has been notable effort made in the professional leagues to extend opportunity to people of color who were previously excluded.

Furthermore, the first section looks at the issue of black student-athletes whose transition to predominantly white campuses remains inadequately addressed. College campuses continue to be environments that do not resemble the backgrounds of many African American students who are entering as freshman. Articles presented here examine problems for black players and black coaches. Finally, this section considers the use of racially and ethnically sensitive names for team mascots.

Sport has been as slow to improve opportunities for women and girls playing and working in the world of sport as in other sections of society. The section on Gender in Sport features articles on the many barriers faced by women who desire employment in the field of athletics as well as on the disproportionate allocation of funds that typically favor male college student-athletes. It also examines the concepts of masculinity in sport and the way male athletes view women and how that treatment is reflected in both words and actions.

An issue that has always attracted sharp criticism is the abuse of student-athletes by educational institutions. In the section on Uses and Abuses of Sport, authors examine the tremendous pressure to attract physically gifted high school and college athletes. Grades often suffer along with facets of their social lives. There is a historical piece about the public's "discovery" of the problem in the 1980s. Various writers, including four award-winning journalists, provide provocative views of athletics that can easily lead to very damaging results on the overall well-being of student-athletes. The section concludes with an optimistic survey of high school student-athletes and with a report recommending change produced by a blue-ribbon commission.

One of the most controversial issues in sport today is covered in the section on Stereotypes, Myths, and Realities About Athletes. It considers athletes as role models, the apparent increase in on-the-field violence, and perceptions that students and the public have toward the intelligence of student-athletes, along with the perception of the role of coaches.

The media's role in sport has been the single most powerful vehicle in forming the popular images of athletes in our culture. The section on the media looks at the lack of representation of people of color and women in the sports media and the consequences. It examines the different quality and quantity of coverage of men's and women's sporting events. Finally, it raises ethical conflicts of interest for sports editors and writers.

The Sport in the International Arena section demonstrates the significant effect that sport has played in forcing change in the nation of South Africa. Recent articles feature the inauguration of Nelson Mandela as president and the NBA's recent involvement in South Africa. In 1993, the NBA sent an envoy of players and coaches to South Africa in an effort to provide facilities for the nation's children and to teach basketball skills. This was part of the Center for the Study of Sport in Society's TEAMWORK: South Africa program. A second contingent returned a year later—led by Patrick Ewing, Alonzo Mourning, Dikembo Mutombo, and John Crotty—to conduct a goodwill tour shortly after Mandela's election.

Finally, this section contains an in-depth examination of the history of the Olympics and the political controversies that have plagued the games in the modern era.

I have chosen to conclude *Sport in Society: Equal Opportunity or Business as Usual?* on a positive note by sharing the stories of people who have entertained us on the playing field while making a much larger contribution to society. A series of inspiring tributes recognizing their lives offers a richness and a sense of extraordinary commitment in stark contrast to the typical negativism that is attributed to sport through the popular press. They are what sport should be all about.

Although the articles in *Sport in Society: Equal Opportunity or Business as Usual?* focus on current issues, the reader is exposed to the history of the existing state of sport. It is hoped that the book will increase the reader's understanding of complex social issues that involve sport and encourage the use of sport as a mechanism for positive change.

I have had the privilege of being a witness to men and women across the country who are associated with athletics and use its broad appeal to better our nation. From small towns in the Midwest to the halls of Congress, these individuals have used the positive aspects of sport to bring about change that often goes unmentioned but surely not unrecognized by the many who reap the benefits.

Richard E. Lapchick<br>Center for the Study of Sport in Society

# Acknowledgments

W hen this project was conceived with Sage Publications, I was going to do this book with assistance from Jeffrey Benedict, the director of research at Northeastern University's Center for the Study of Sport in Society. Jeff helped select the articles, contacted authors, and helped write the introductions to each section. Since Jeff's views on some of the issues differ significantly from my own, he provided an important sounding board. His directness and candor were invaluable. This book would not have been possible without Jeff.

The overwhelming majority of articles in *Sport in Society* come from either the *Journal of Sport & Social Issues* or *The Sporting News*. Therefore, the first people I would like to thank are the succession of editors at the *Journal of Sport & Social Issues* and John Rawlings, the managing editor at *The Sporting News*. Jim Frey, chairman of the Department of Sociology at the University of Nevada at Las Vegas, served as the editor of *Journal of Sport & Social Issues* from 1978 to 1983. Leon Chorbajian and Jordan Gebre-Mehdin were coeditors from 1984 to 1988 when the Center for the Study of Sport in Society took over the publication of the journal from ARENA, the Institute for Sport and Social Analysis. Michael Malec, a sociologist at Boston College was editor from 1988 to 1992, when the University of San Francisco's Lawrence Wenner became the current editor. Under Larry' stewardship Sage purchased the journal and, later, contracted for this book.

John Rawlings has given me a free hand with my column for *The Sporting News*. He has encouraged me to write from my own vantage point, and I have tried to bring that perspective to the column.

Sage's Sophy Craze has been refreshingly flexible about deadlines and encouraging about content. That content has been blessed with original contributions by some of the nation's leaders in sport: Donna Lopiano, Ron Thomas, Mary Schmitt, Sandy Padwe, Byron Hurt, and Jackson Katz. We are also grateful for the use of previously published articles by scholars Donald Siegel,

Dean Anderson, Stanton Wheeler, Raymond Yasser, Lawrence Wenner, Gary Sailes, Bethany Shifflett, and Rhonda Revelle and by journalists Alison Bass of the *Boston Globe,* Debra Blum of the *Chronicle of Higher Education,* Ed Sherman and Barry Temkin of the *Chicago Tribune,* and Shelly Sanford and Suzanne Halliburton of the *Austin American-Statesman.* Finally, the Knight Commission of Intercollegiate Athletics allowed us to include their latest report.

We received valuable research information from the National Collegiate Athletic Association, the Black Coaches Association, the Rainbow Commission for Fairness in Athletics, John Hoberman, and John Powers.

I want to thank the entire staff of the Center for the Study of Sport in Society. Each person participated in some manner. Bob McCabe and Lee Durocher helped with some new research. Sarah Sokol, our communication coordinator, was particularly helpful with final edits.

But I could never have completed *Sport in Society* without Mary Frances Anderson, who played a critical role as an editor, researcher, and writer in the final months of development.

# PART I

# Race in Sport

## Introduction

Since Jackie Robinson broke the color barrier in baseball, no industry or business has equaled professional sports with respect to advancing opportunities for minorities. Sport, once the exclusive domain of whites, has served as a vehicle for integrating people of color, particularly blacks, based on the merits of their performance. Its success has demonstrated that people of different racial backgrounds can perform as teammates and as equals.

Due to the overwhelming popularity of athletics in American culture, sport has also proven to be an effective forum for addressing more subtle forms of racism. Institutionalized bias has been more slow to erode. Decades after blacks were granted access to the playing field, team owners remained resistant to offering them the opportunity to function as managers and executives. At least some of the reluctance was due to stereotypical beliefs that blacks possessed inferior leadership skills and thinking capacities. In addition, the so-called old boys network played a major part. The tremendous success of the handful of African American and Latino coaches, managers, and administrators in professional sports has helped explode the lingering myth that blacks and those from other minority groups lack the leadership skills to succeed in a predominantly white society.

These widely held stereotypes began to diminish as teams gradually afforded former players who are black the opportunity to become assistant coaches and, eventually, head coaches and managers. In the 1990s, it has become commonplace for black coaches to display the kind of consistent managerial and coaching success that lands them at the top of their profession. In a 1-year span, the University of Arkansas won the National Collegiate Athletic Association (NCAA) men's basketball championship, resulting in head coach Nolan Richardson's being named Coach of the Year; the Toronto Blue Jays won the World Series, making manager Cito Gaston the first black manager to win consecutive baseball championships; and both Lenny Wilkens of the National Basketball Association's (NBA) Atlanta Hawks and Dusty Baker of Major League Baseball's San Francisco Giants were named Coach of the Year.

Perhaps the most notable milestone of all occurred at the start of the 1994-95 NBA season when legendary Celtics coach Red Auerbach saw his seemingly untouchable record of 795 regular-season coaching victories surpassed by Lenny Wilkens. It was Auerbach who named Bill Russell as the first black head coach in league history.

There are also significant disparities between blacks and whites in other crucial areas. It remains very difficult for people of color seeking ownership and financial roles on teams. Nearly 45 years after Robinson's first season with the Dodgers, Peter Bynoe and Bertram Lee purchased the Denver Nuggets in the late 1980s and became the first black owners of a professional sports franchise. The formation of expansion teams in both the National Football League (NFL) and Major League Baseball has contributed to a breakthrough for minorities in terms of ownership opportunities. Both of the NFL's newest teams are owned in part by blacks. In addition, Isiah Thomas purchased a portion of the Toronto Raptors and Earvin "Magic" Johnson purchased nearly 10% of the Los Angeles Lakers.

The slow progress of people of color in coaching and management of professional team sports has been paralleled in many college athletic administrations. The ever increasing number of black student-athletes are met by few people of color working as presidents, administrators, professors, academic advisers, coaches, or athletic directors when they are recruited by predominantly white institutions. The resignation of the University of Colorado's football coach, Bill McCartney, during the 1994 season signified how volatile this issue has become.

The subsequent search for a replacement resulted in McCartney's longtime assistant Bob Simmons, who is black, being passed over for a younger, less experienced coach, Rick Neuheisel. The Reverend Jesse Jackson and the Rainbow Commission for Fairness in Athletics pointed to Colorado's decision as a prime example of qualified black coaches in college sport being repeatedly overlooked for advancement while schools continue to field teams dominated by black talent. Simmons left Colorado when he was offered the head coaching position at Oklahoma State. Stanford University and Louisville hired black head coaches. By January 1, 1995, there were five black head coaches among the 107 Division I-A[1] programs in the country. Despite these hirings, the football arm of the Black Coaches Association vowed to take a more aggressive approach to increase the number of black coaches being considered for head coaching openings.

On the heels of the Colorado incident, Reverend Jackson revealed a new initiative called a "fairness index" that will track minority hiring and graduation rates for athletes at institutions that have a large number of black athletes performing in basketball and football. He suggested that institutions with a poor record of hiring blacks and graduating black student-athletes will be targeted as part of an effort to discourage black high school athletes from attending them. Arkansas's coach Nolan Richardson reiterated a similar theme and insisted that the Black Coaches Association was going to actively steer black athletes away from schools that didn't have the player's best interest at heart.

This section opens with Richard Lapchick's comprehensive examination of where college sport is going in dealing with racism. The chapter discusses previous injustices that have slowed the progress of black student-athletes and identifies conditions in college athletics that are particularly detrimental.

Donald Siegel's chapter, "Higher Education and the Plight of the Black Male Athlete," considers the continuing disparity between the graduation rates of white and black football players at elite Division I schools across the country. Some have suggested that one of the leading contributors to the academic struggles of black student-athletes is the difficult transition that takes place when they move from predominantly black neighborhoods to campuses that have virtually no black professors, athletic administrators, or coaches.

Dean Anderson, in his chapter, "Cultural Diversity on Campus: A Look at Intercollegiate Football Coaches," investigates the lack of racial diversity in college football administrations. He offers a critique of the conflicting vertical movement of black athletes on the playing field and the horizontal movement of coaches who are black.

With the recent stands taken by the Black Coaches Association, college basketball has become a fertile place to focus on the quality of opportunities for young black athletes entering college. In his chapter, "A Step in the Right Direction: The Presidents Meet the Black Coaches," Lapchick discusses the often overlooked goals and struggles of the black coaches throughout college basketball as well as the reasons behind their threats to boycott games.

In "The 1994 Racial Report Card," Richard Lapchick examines how professional sports provide opportunities for people of color. The latest version of the Center for the Study of Sport in Society's annual Racial Report Card pays particular attention to advancements of minorities in front office positions. Initially motivated by the notorious statements by Al Campanis in

1987 on ABC's *Nightline,* the center began tracking the number of people of color employed in front office positions in professional sport. Over the ensuing 6 years, there have been some gains in the areas of head coaches and managers, assistant coaches, and general managers. Yet there continues to be a disappointing absence of blacks and Latinos in many professional positions, such as team doctors, lawyers, accountants, and chief executive officers.

Lapchick also discusses the effect that activist groups have had on encouraging professional sports to expand opportunities for minorities. His article, "There Is Gold at the End of This Rainbow: Jesse Jackson Steps Up to the Plate," shows how Jackson's Rainbow Commission has become a significant player in the advancement of minorities by using affirmative actions policies to ensure greater representation. Jackson's recent involvement has coincided with the expanding voice of the Black Coaches Association.

In addition to the racial issues most frequently raised by sports, a significant amount of attention has been paid to college and professional teams maintaining nicknames or mascots that are considered by some to be racially degrading. Protests against offensive names have caused some schools to change their logos. Richard Lapchick discusses how the insistence on using racially degrading team names only facilitates prejudicial stereotypes.

With all the issues of race that remain to be resolved, Lapchick concludes this section with an article on the transformation that took place in LaGrange, Georgia, when a group of athletes were brought there from various emerging nations. LaGrange had been Klan country, but these athletes did the best that sport can do by bringing people of different cultures together in an open and positive way.

## NOTE

1. The divisions of the National Collegiate Athletic Association are set up as follows:

| | |
|---|---|
| Division I: | Approximately 300 schools that offer the full allotment of scholarships. |
| Division I-A: | A subcategory under the Division I rubric. This classification is generally used to distinguish between football programs. It is based on scheduling, the number of seats in home stadiums, and the average paid attendance at home games. |
| Division I-AA: | A subcategory under the Division I rubric. Football programs that fall into this classification have a lower number of seats in their home stadiums, a lower average paid attendance, and schedules that are considered less difficult. |
| Division I-AAA: | A subcategory under the Division I rubric. No football programs are present in this classification. |
| Division II: | Fewer athletic scholarships are offered by schools in this category. |
| Division III: | No athletic scholarships are offered by schools in this category. |

# 1

# Race and College Sports
## A Long Way to Go

Richard E. Lapchick

As America confronts yet another racial crisis in the 1990s, the expectation remains that sports, nearly 45 years after Jackie Robinson broke baseball's color barrier, can lead the way. College sports, in particular, has been portrayed as a beacon for democracy and equal opportunity.

This perception is taking place at a time when 75% of high school students indicated to public opinion analyst Lou Harris that they had seen or heard a racial act with violent overtones either very often or somewhat often in the previous 12 months. In all, 54% of black high school students reported that they had been a victim of a racial incident (Louis Harris & Associates, 1993, p. 2).

One in three students said that they would openly join in a confrontation against another racial or religious group if they agreed with the instigators. Another 17%, although they would not join, said they would feel that the victims deserved what they got (Louis Harris & Associates, 1990, p. 2).

According to Harris, the nation's leading opinion analyst, too many of our children have learned how to hate. He concluded that

> America faces a critical situation. Our findings show that racial and religious harassment and violence are now commonplace among our young people rather than the exception. Far from being concentrated in any one area, confrontations occur in every region of the country and in all types of communities. (Louis Harris & Associates, 1990, p. 2)

One of the most hallowed assumptions about race and sports is that athletic contact between blacks and whites will favorably change racial perceptions. However, for this change to take place, coaches must be committed to helping guide players' social relations. The *Racism and Violence in American High Schools* survey conducted by Louis Harris for Northeastern University in 1993 showed that 70% of high school students reported that they had become friends with someone from a different racial or ethnic group through playing sports. Among blacks, a 77% majority reported this result; the comparable majority was 68% among whites and 79% among Hispanics. That, indeed, was encouraging news.

## BLACK STUDENT-ATHLETES ON
## PREDOMINANTLY WHITE CAMPUSES

However, on predominantly white campuses, as in corporate boardrooms, the atmosphere naturally reflects the dominant white culture. Most campuses are not equal meeting grounds for white and black students, whether from urban or rural America.

American public opinion of college sports reached its nadir in the mid 1980s. In an attempt to create meaningful reform, many measures were passed. Among them were Propositions 48, 42, and 16. The wide-ranging debate and protest against Proposition 42 placed the issue of race among the central ethical issues in college sports in the 1990s. Proposition 42 would have prevented athletes who did not achieve certain academic standards from receiving a scholarship. The new debate over Proposition 16 in 1994-95 has again raised the racial specter in college sports to a new level. (For a more complete discussion on these propositions, see Chapter 4.)

The American Institutes for Research (AIR) produced a study for the National Collegiate Athletic Association (NCAA) in 1989 suggesting that there are low academic expectations for black athletes. Only 31% of the black athletes surveyed for the AIR study indicated that their coaches encouraged good grades. The study also suggested that black student-athletes are not receiving the education promised by colleges in that they graduate at a significantly lower rate than do whites. They have few black coaches or faculty members on campus to model themselves after (AIR, 1989). All of this is drawing public attention and pressure. The Reverend Jesse Jackson founded the Rainbow Commission for Fairness in Athletics to change such imbalances.

Although less than 6% of all students at Division I-A institutions are black, 60% of the men's basketball players, 37% of the women's basketball players, and 42% of the football players at those schools are black (NCAA, 1994a).

All colleges and universities have some form of "special admittance" program in which a designated percentage of students who do not meet the normal admission standards of the school are allowed to enroll. According to the NCAA, about 3% of all students enter as "special admits." Yet more than 20% of football and basketball players enter under such programs. Thus, many enter with the academic odds already stacked against them.

The 1989 NCAA AIR study presented a wealth of data. Those familiar with college athletics were not surprised by the study's findings, which indicated that black athletes feel racially isolated on college campuses, are overrepresented in football and basketball, have high expectations of pro careers, and are uninvolved in other extracurricular activities. However, the results of the NCAA study stood in stark contrast to the findings published by the Women's Sports Foundation (1989). It was the first major study of minorities playing high school sports. It clearly established that in comparison to black nonathletes, black high school student-athletes feel better about themselves, are more involved in extracurricular activities other than sports, are more involved in the broader community, aspire to be community leaders, and have better grade point averages and standardized test scores. Almost all those results contradict the view that most of white society has about the black athlete.

According to Lou Harris and Associates (1993), it is apparent that most varsity athletes believe that their participation in high school team sports has helped them to become better students and citizens and to avoid drugs:

> It is especially significant to note that the value of playing sports in all these areas was significantly higher for African-American student-athletes in particular and for football and basketball players in general. It merits considerable attention by colleges and universities where the experience of African-American student-athletes as well as their football and basketball players is significantly different and appears much more negative.[1]

The primary question that now must be asked is what happens to black athletes, and black students in general, between high school and college that seems to totally change how they perceive themselves. Among other things, many black students leave a high school that is either overwhelmingly black or at least partially integrated. If students are from an urban area, they leave behind a core of black teachers and coaches. If students live on campus or go to school away from home, they leave behind whatever positive support network existed in the community in which they were raised and possible black role models who are not exclusively athletes.

Students arrive at college to discover that the proportion of black students at Division I-A schools is approximately 6%. Furthermore, less than 2% of the faculty positions at colleges and universities are held by blacks. Finally, the athletic departments hire just a few more blacks than the number of blacks on the faculty and actually hire fewer blacks than do the professional sports teams.

A great deal of emphasis has been placed on racial discrimination in professional sports, especially in the hiring practices of professional franchises. In fact, a great deal of the research done at the Center for the Study of Sport in Society is devoted to the publication of the annual *Racial Report*

*Card.* (The 1994 *RRC* appears as Chapter 5 in this book.) However, a look at the number of available employment positions in our colleges and universities indicates that it is less likely for blacks to be hired in higher education than in professional sports.

Although the militancy and struggle of the 1960s and 1970s have reduced the negative self-perceptions of most young blacks, the stereotypes—and all the taboos that go with them—still exist for many whites. White and black athletes can meet on campus carrying a great deal of racial baggage. Their prejudices won't automatically evaporate with the sweat as they play together on a team. The key to racial harmony on a team is the attitude and leadership of the coach.

He or she must be committed to equality and clearly demonstrate this to the team. The history of young athletes, and students in general, makes it an uphill task. Chances are that competition at the high school level bred some animosity; usually, white teams play against black teams, reflecting urban residential housing patterns. There is virtually no playground competition between blacks and whites because few dare to leave their neighborhoods.

On a college team, blacks and whites compete for playing time, while in the society at large, black and white workers compete for jobs, public housing, and even welfare. A primary difference is that whites are apt to accept blacks on the team because they will help the team win more games and perhaps get the white athletes more exposure.

It is easy for white athletes, no matter what their racial attitudes, to accept blacks on their teams for two other reasons. First, they need not have any social contact with black teammates. Sports that blacks dominate are not sports like golf, tennis, and swimming where socializing is almost a requirement for competition. Players need not mingle after basketball, baseball, or football. More important, black male players need not mingle with white women after those games. Housing on campus, and social discrimination through fraternities and sororities, further isolates black athletes. Whether in high school or college, the black student-athlete faces special problems as an athlete, a student, and a member of the campus community.

Most of white society believed we were on the road to progress until Al Campanis and Jimmy "the Greek" Snyder made us challenge our perceptions. Their statements on national television that blacks and whites are physically and mentally different were repugnant to much of the country and led to widespread self-examination. Like many whites who accept black dominance in sports, Campanis believed that blacks had less intellectual capacity. It makes things seem simple to people like Campanis: Blacks sure can play, but they can't organize or manage affairs or lead whites. Marge Schott, speaking in private, reopened the wounds in 1992 when her remarks about blacks and Jews again stunned the world of sports.

Many people wouldn't see much to contradict this view if they looked to society at large. In 1995, white men and women were twice as likely as black men to hold executive, administrative, and managerial positions. At the same time, blacks were twice as likely as whites to hold positions of manual labor. Decades of viewing this pattern could easily reinforce the Campanis viewpoint: Whites are intelligent and blacks are physically powerful.

After 50 years of trying to determine the genetic superiority of blacks as athletes, science has proved little. Culture, class, and environment still tell us the most. Instead of developing theories about why black Americans excel in sports, perhaps more time will now be spent on the achievement of black Americans in human rights, medicine, law, science, the arts, and education who overcame the attitudes and institutions of whites to excel in fields where brains dictate the champions.

## COACHES: A STUDY IN BLACK AND WHITE

The coach becomes the black student-athlete's main contact, and the court frequently becomes the home where he or she is most comfortable. Nonetheless, some black athletes feel that their white coaches discriminate against them and that their academic advisers give them different counseling. This may reflect a general distrust of whites or a strong perception that racism is the cause of certain events. Even well-intentioned acts can be interpreted by blacks as being racially motivated.

Over the years, black student-athletes have made a series of similar complaints irrespective of their campus location: subtle racism evidenced in different treatment during recruitment, poor academic advice, harsh discipline, positional segregation on the playing field and social segregation off it, blame for situations for which they are not responsible. There are also complaints of overt racism: racial abuse, blacks being benched in games more quickly than whites, marginal whites being kept on the bench while only blacks who play are retained, summer jobs for whites and good jobs for their wives.

To say that most or even many white coaches are racist is a great exaggeration. But most white coaches were raised with white values in a white culture. The norm for them is what is important for a white society.

## STEREOTYPES OF THE BLACK ATHLETE

If white coaches accept stereotypical images of what black society is and what kind of people it produces, they may believe that blacks are less motivated, less disciplined, less intelligent (53% of all whites believe blacks are less intelligent), and more physically gifted. They may think that all blacks are raised in a culture bombarded by drugs, violence, and sexuality and that they are more comfortable with other blacks.

They might believe those characteristics are a product of society or simply that they are the way God chose to make them. They might recognize themselves as racist, disliking blacks because of perceived negative traits. More than likely, however, they view themselves as coaches trying to help. In either case, if they act on these images, their black players are victimized.

In one of the most important scandals of the 1980s, Memphis State, a 1985 NCAA Final Four participant, fell into disgrace. There were many allegations about the improprieties of the school and its coach, Dana Kirk.

One that could not be disputed was the fact that 12 years had gone by without Memphis State's graduating a single black basketball player. Like several other urban institutions, Memphis State built a winning program with the talents of fine black athletes. The fact that none had graduated brought back memories of Texas Western's NCAA championship team, which failed to graduate a single starter, all of whom were black. But this went on at Memphis State for more than a decade. The National Association for the Advancement of Colored People (NAACP) sued the school. Publicity finally led to the dismissal of Kirk. Indications are that Larry Finch, who replaced Kirk, has run a clean program. Perhaps the fact that Finch is black has resulted in a different approach to black players. In 1995, Memphis State has one of the nation's most open-minded and progressive presidents in Lane Rawlings.

I do not mean to single out Memphis State. In the 10 years since Dana Kirk was fired, I have been on more than 75 campuses. The pattern is frequently similar: The academic profile of black football and basketball players and their treatment as students is different from whites, and their graduation rate is lower.


## POSITIONAL SEGREGATION IN COLLEGE

The issue of positional segregation in college is becoming less of a factor. For years, whites played the "thinking positions." The controlling position in baseball is the pitcher; in football, it is the quarterback. Everyone loves the smooth, ballhandling guard in basketball. These are the glamour positions that fans and the press focus on. These have largely been white positions. College baseball still poses the greatest problem at all positions, as fewer and fewer blacks play college baseball. Less than 3% of Division I-A college baseball players are black (personal interview with Stanley Johnson of the NCAA, January 31, 1993).

However, in a major shift in college football, large numbers of black quarterbacks have been leading their teams since the late 1980s. Between 1960 and 1986, only 7 black quarterbacks were among the top 10 candidates for the Heisman Trophy, and none finished higher than fourth. In 1987, 1988, and 1989, black quarterbacks Don McPherson (Syracuse), Rodney Peete (University of Southern California), Darien Hagan (Colorado), Reggie Slack (Auburn), Tony Rice (Notre Dame), Stevie Thompson (Oklahoma), and Major Harris (West Virginia) all finished among the top 10 vote getters. In 1989, Andre Ware (Houston) became the first black quarterback to win the award. Florida State's Charlie Ward won it in 1993. In 1994, Nebraska won the national championship with a dramatic Orange Bowl victory behind the leadership of quarterback Tommie Frazier. Coach Osborne inserted Frazier into the starting lineup after Frazier missed nearly the entire season with a blood clot.

In basketball, more top point guards coming out of college are black. Recent stars such as Kenny Anderson, Tim Hardaway, Anfernee Hardaway, and Jason Kidd are just a few of the more prominent black point guards. Perhaps this bodes well for an end to positional segregation in college sports in the near future. (Positional segregation in professional sports is discussed in depth in Chapter 5.)

## CAN BLACK ATHLETES SPEAK OUT?

The coach is the authority. Historically, athletes have rarely spoken out. This creates problems for all coaches who come up against an outspoken player. When the player is black and not a superstar, that player will often be let go. Only the superstars such as Bill Russell, Kareem Abdul-Jabbar, and Muhammad Ali can securely remain because no one can afford to let them go. But even the greatest ones paid heavy prices for many years after their outspokenness.

Muhammad Ali, who had refused to go into the army, knew that you had to be at the top to speak out if you were black. Ultimately, Ali had the money and influence to go all the way to the Supreme Court. Most blacks have neither the money nor the influence to make the system work.

In 1992, Craig Hodges spoke out about the Rodney King case in Los Angeles. Hodges was a great shooter but was a peripheral player on the National Basketball Association (NBA) championship team, the Chicago Bulls. He had won the three-point contest at the NBA All-Star Game. After his remarks, he was cut by the Bulls and not one team picked him up.

Tommy Harper's case is also instructive. His contract was not renewed by the Boston Red Sox in December of 1985. The Red Sox said he was let go because he was not doing a good job as special assistant to the general manager. Harper, however, charged that he was fired because he spoke out against racist practices by the Red Sox. Earlier in 1985, he said that the Sox allowed white players to receive passes to the whites-only Elks Club in Winter Haven, Florida, where they held spring training. (The Sox later stopped the tradition.) Harper sued and the Equal Employment Opportunity Commission ruled that the firing was a retaliatory action against Harper because he spoke out against discrimination. It took him a while to get back into baseball. As of this writing, he is a coach for the Montreal Expos.

There are positive examples as well. It did not go unnoticed that a group of black athletes at Auburn asked the president of the university to get a Confederate flag removed from a dormitory; it was removed. In 1987, the Pittsburgh basketball team wore ribbons as a protest against their school's investments in South Africa. In 1990, black athletes at the University of Texas at Austin led a protest against racism on campus. They had even been encouraged by members of the athletic department. Whether or not this will become a trend is hard to see, but the positive and widespread media coverage of their actions stood in dramatic contrast to early reactions to Russell, Ali, and Abdul-Jabbar.

In 1969, 14 black players on the University of Wyoming football team informed their athletic department of their intention to wear black armbands during their upcoming game against Brigham Young University. The players' intent was to bring attention to the doctrinal position of the Church of Latter Day Saints that prevented blacks from holding the priesthood. After hearing of the players' plan, Wyoming's head football coach cited a long-standing team policy that prevented players from engaging in protests of any kind. When the players showed up at his office wearing the arm bands just 1 day before the game, the coach interpreted their action as in defiance of the rule and a direct threat to his authority. He summarily dismissed all 14 players from the football team.

Although this incident remained a sore spot in the history of Wyoming athletics for nearly 24 years, the university held ceremonies to honor the players on September 24, 1993. The event was the result of the African American Studies Department working in conjunction with the school's administration to recognize the former players, signaling a new era in communication between student-athletes and the administration.

## INTERRACIAL DATING
## AND SEXUAL STEREOTYPES

The image of the black male involved with sex and violence took a profound turn in 1994 after O. J. Simpson was charged with a brutal double murder. Looking beyond the horror of the murders, the case once again brought out the fact that interracial dating is still a volatile issue in the 1990s. There is no question that it is far more common in the mid-1990s than it was in 1970 or even 1980 when Howie Evans, then a black assistant coach at Fordham and a columnist for the *Amsterdam News,* told me of when he used to work at a black community center in New York. Recruiters from predominantly white southern schools would come there to recruit black women for their schools. Those coaches seemed to think that they understood the powerful sexual drives of black men, so they went out to get them some "safe" women friends from the North.

When I talk to black athletes after a lecture, I try to ask them about this. It doesn't matter where I am—Los Angeles, Denver, New York, Nashville, or Norfolk—almost everyone says there is pressure, now usually very subtle, not to date white women. It doesn't matter how big the star is.

Black athletes also tell me that the assumption on campus is that they want white women more than black women. Not that blacks say they do but that whites believe they do. If a white student wants to sleep with a coed, that's part of college life in our times. If a black student wants to do the same, that's the primal animal working out his natural instincts. Stereotypes of blacks in the media are, of course, perpetuated by the virtually all-white sports media. Chapter 31 deals with this in greater depth.

## THE OPTIONS FOR BLACK
## ATHLETES CHOOSING A COLLEGE

The effects of the actions of white coaches who act on stereotypical images of black athletes are not dissimilar. Study after study has shown the devastating consequences to a person's psyche. As long as the act is perceived as being racially motivated—even if it is a well-intentioned act—the end result is the same.

Black student-athletes with professional aspirations seem to have three choices, none of which are equal. They can choose to attend a historically black college, a predominantly white school with a black head coach, or a predominantly white school with a white head coach.

So what should black athletes do? Should they attend a historically black college? After all, black colleges have turned out great pro athletes for years. But black college athletic programs started to decline when the white schools began to integrate. They don't have million-dollar booster clubs to compete with white schools to get star black athletes. Division I-A schools also offer the lure of bowl games, television coverage, and a "good education."

NBA Players Association Director Charles Grantham told me that the black athlete who wants to turn pro has little realistic choice. "Exposure on TV means the scouts will see you and, if they like you, a higher position in the draft. That means more money, much more money" (personal communication, September 1993).

The Southwestern Athletic Conference, which included Grambling, Jackson State, and Southern, used to provide 35 to 40 players a year to the National Football League (NFL) in the early 1970s. By the 1990s, the numbers were between 6 to 10 in a big year.

Grambling's Eddie Robinson is the winningest coach in college history and has sent more players to the NFL than any coach. Could Eddie Robinson coach at Michigan or in the NFL? He has never had the opportunity to turn down a Division I-A job. Eddie Robinson is black; he became a coach before white institutions were ready for him.

Playing for a black coach at a predominantly white institution is another option for the black student-athlete. Many of today's black players would like to attend schools that have black coaches. For Division I basketball players, that amounts to 45 schools, excluding the 16 historically black institutions (personal interview with Deb Kruger of the Black Coaches Association, January 15, 1995). The NCAA has 302 Division I schools with approximately 13 players per basketball team. Therefore, of the 3,926 slots for men's basketball players, approximately 793 fall under black basketball coaches.[2] The slots are far fewer in college football where there was only five black head coaches at the Division I level at the close of the 1994 season. Finally, in Division I college baseball, there is not a single black manager (personal interview with the Black Coaches Association, February 1995). (See Table 1.1 for a breakdown of the percentages of Black employees in NCAA member institutions.)

The NCAA's 1994 Men's Final Four featured four teams with a total of 54 players; 29 were black (54%), 24 were white (44%), and one was Hispanic. On the other hand, alongside the court there were 39 coaches; 85% were white. There was not a single person of color on any of the four teams' medical staffs. The 15 athletic directors and associate athletic directors were all white. Of the 54 basketball administrators, only 5 were black (9%). Of the 186 basketball support staff positions, whites occupied 174 (94%). Even the media covering the game were overwhelmingly white. Twelve of the 13 local radio and television broadcasters were white as well as 145 of the 150 local newspaper reporters.[3]

The 1995 National Championship game in football, played at the Orange Bowl, was no different. Table 1.2 demonstrates the combined racial breakdown of the University of Nebraska and University of Miami football programs. Although nearly 63% of the players were black, 100% of the presi-

**TABLE 1.1**  Percentage of Black Employees in NCAA Member Institutions

| | |
|---|---|
| Athletic administration | 6.2 |
| Athletic directors | 3.6 |
| Associate athletic directors | 4.5 |
| Assistant athletic directors | 4.9 |
| Head coaches | 3.9 |
| Revenue-sports head coaches | 12.9 |
| Assistant head coaches | 9.8 |

SOURCE: National Collegiate Athletic Association (1994b).

dents, athletic directors, head coaches, associate athletic directors, sports information directors, and medical staff were white.

There are many potential jobs available for blacks in coaching and in athletic departments. There are 906 NCAA members in all divisions, with an average of 15.8 teams per school (personal interview with NCAA spokesperson, Phyllis Ton, January 25, 1995). That amounts to 14,315 teams. The National Association of Intercollegiate Athletics (NAIA) has 391 members with an average of 9.5 teams per school. That's another 3,715 teams. With an average of 2.5 coaches per team, college sports has approximately 45,075 coaching jobs. That excludes junior and community colleges.

When so very few coaching positions are held by black Americans, there should be little wonder that black student-athletes feel isolated on campus. Pressure needs to be placed here to change these percentages. The coaches are available. According to the Black Coaches Association, it has 3,000 members. If there is to be a more promising future for the black student-athlete, then more black coaches and assistants will have to be hired.

How do present-day black coaches fare? In 1985, Nolan Richardson was hired by Arkansas and became the Southwest Conference's first black head basketball coach. When his first two teams lost 30 games, Arkansas newspapers wrote him off. When he led the team to the Final Four in 1990, Richardson was elevated to sainthood in the Arkansas media. When Arkansas won the 1994 National Championship, Richardson was clearly a star in the state. People were saying that his presence, and especially his success, was leading to improved race relations in northern Arkansas.

Georgetown's John Thompson made many people angry when he became the first black coach to win the national championship in 1984. This was especially true of some media figures who said he was arrogant and abrasive and kept his team insulated from the public. They said his team was overly aggressive. The intensity of the attack varied but was prolonged over a decade. His personal leadership as the outspoken elder statesman of America's black coaches has enhanced his status in the black community and alienated many in the white community.

**TABLE 1.2** 1995 College Football National Championships: Racial Breakdown of Participants

| Presidents/Chancellors[a] | | | Sports information director | | |
|---|---|---|---|---|---|
| White | 3 | (100%) | White | 2 | (100%) |
| Total | 3 | | Total | 2 | |
| | | | | | |
| Athletic directors | | | Assistant coaches | | |
| White | 2 | (100%) | White | 29 | (78%) |
| Total | 2 | | Black | 7 | (19%) |
| | | | Latino | 1 | (3%) |
| Head coaches | | | Total | 37 | |
| White | 2 | (100%) | | | |
| Total | 2 | | Medical staff | | |
| | | | White | 18 | (100%) |
| Associate athletic director | | | Total | 18 | |
| White | 5 | (100%) | | | |
| Total | 5 | | Nonplaying staff | | |
| | | | White | 167 | (89%) |
| Assistant athletic director | | | Black | 16 | (8.5%) |
| White | 5 | (71%) | Latino | 5 | (2.5%) |
| Black | 2 | (29%) | Total | 188 | |
| Total | 7 | | | | |
| | | | | | |
| Players | | | | | |
| White | 49 | (36%) | | | |
| Black | 85 | (62.5%) | | | |
| Latino | 2 | (1.5%) | | | |
| Total | 136 | | | | |

SOURCE: Rainbow Commission for Fairness in Athletics, January 1995.[4]
a. The University of Nebraska has both a president and a chancellor.

Thompson was breaking all the molds shaped by a stereotyping public. First, he was a big winner with a lot of black recruits coming to an increasingly multicultural campus. Second, these black players were not a freewheeling, footloose team but, rather, one of the more disciplined teams in the country. Even more important, at a time of great negative publicity concerning the academic abuse of college athletes, Thompson's players had one of the highest graduation rates in America. Was there some jealousy involved in the attacks? Didn't these same writers call aggressive white teams "hustling teams?" White coaches like John Wooden were called fatherly figures when they kept the press at arm's length from their teams.

Even if you accept the fact that Thompson's style was a tough one for the public to grapple with, this still doesn't explain the degree of the attacks against him. The racial issue seemed, once again, to be a factor. Although several national writers write balanced pieces on John Thompson and Georgetown, too many others clearly show us how far we have to go.

For now, most black athletes will have to play for white coaches, and many may have the problems mentioned. Academically, black athletes may enter college at a disadvantage, one artificially maintained because they might be steered into easier courses. They are less likely to get a degree. With prevailing stereotypes, some coaches will make assumptions about them they would never make about whites. Socially, they will be in an alien world, segregated in student housing, off-campus housing, and on road trips. Increasingly, they will be forced to withdraw into the safer athletic subculture, becoming isolated from both black and white nonathletes.

The odds are surely not in favor of black student-athletes. If, after enduring all these problems, they don't get a degree, then why do they subject themselves to all of this in the first place? The answer is simple. They assume that sports is their way out of poverty. How prevalent is this belief? The NCAA AIR study on the black college athlete showed that in 1989, approximately 45% of black basketball and football players at predominantly white schools think they will make the pros (AIR, 1989). Less than 1% will. The Northeastern University study conducted by Lou Harris in 1993 showed that 51% of black high school student-athletes think they can make the pros.

Sport has been promoted as the hope of black people. But too often that hope is empty. If black athletes do not emphasize their studies, they will slip farther and farther toward the bottomless pit of functional illiteracy. Black athletes become involved in a cycle that trades away their education for the promise of stardom, a promise that is very unlikely to ever be real. A black high school student has a better chance of becoming a doctor or an attorney than of becoming a professional athlete. But those civic role models are not as visible as black athletes. For black high school students, the professional athlete seems like the best model.

Unfortunately, some schools "pass" certain students-athletes to the next level without regard to academic achievement. They are conditioned to believe that academic work is not as necessary as working on their bodies. The promise of the pros is the shared dream, no matter how unrealistic.

As noted elsewhere in the book, the media is now reporting more on the problems. The NCAA has paid far greater attention to the racial issue in college sports. In the last 10 years, things have gotten markedly better for black student-athletes. Their graduation rates have improved by more than 10%. The number of black coaches has increased. Public pressure for change, especially that coming from the Rainbow Commission for Fairness in Athletics founded by the Reverend Jesse Jackson, has finally been sustained over time.

Nonetheless, college sports has a long way to go before it fulfills its promise as a beacon of democracy and equal opportunity.

## NOTES

1. Quotation taken from unpublished data from the 1993 Louis Harris survey. Available from the Center for the Study of Sport in Society, 360 Huntington Ave., 161 CP, Boston, MA 02115.

2. This number is an estimate arrived at by multiplying the number of Division I schools by the number of roster spots on a basketball team, then dividing the sum by the number of schools with black coaches.

3. See the April 1994 press release from the Rainbow Commission for Fairness in Athletics. Available from the National Rainbow Coalition, P.O. Box 27385, Washington, DC 20005.

4. Data for Table 1.2 available from the National Rainbow Coalition, P.O. Box 27385, Washington, DC 20005.

## REFERENCES

American Institutes for Research. (1989). *The experiences of black intercollegiate athletes at NCAA Division I institutions* (Report No. 3). Palo Alto, CA: Center for the Study of Athletics.

Louis Harris & Associates, Inc. (1990, October). *High school students: Attitudes on human rights, community activity and steps that might be taken to ease racial, ethnic and religious prejudice.* (Available from the Center for the Study of Sport in Society, 360 Huntington Ave., 161 CP, Boston, MA 02115)

Louis Harris & Associates, Inc. (1993). *Racism and violence in American high schools: Project TEAMWORK responds.* (Available from the Center for the Study of Sport in Society, 360 Huntington Ave., 161 CP, Boston, MA 02115)

National Collegiate Athletic Association. (1994a, June). *1994 NCAA Division I graduation rates report.* (Available from the National Collegiate Athletic Association, 6201 College Boulevard, Overland Park, KS 66211)

National Collegiate Athletic Association. (1994b). *The NCAA minority opportunities and interests committee's four-year study of race demographics of member institutions, 1994.* (Available from the National Collegiate Athletic Association, 6201 College Boulevard, Overland Park, KS 66211)

Women's Sports Foundation. (1989, August). *Minorities in sports: The effect of varsity sports participation on the social, educational, and career mobility of minority students.* (Available from the Women's Sports Foundation, Eisenhower Park, East Meadow, NY 11554)

# 2

## Higher Education and the Plight of the Black Male Athlete

Donald Siegel

$W$hile watching the "Sweet 16" in the National Collegiate Athletic Association's (NCAA) basketball championships, Lipsyte (1992) recently pondered, "Does it make much sense that 16 colleges whose student bodies are more than 90 percent White will be offering up teams that are 80 percent Black?" (p. B12). He went on to make the observation that, among the schools involved at that point in the tournament, the average proportion of Black students was 5.6% (approximately half of whom were females).

Lipsyte's casual observation was not a statistical aberration of unique happenings in the tournament. As reported by Lederman (1992), Black males make up approximately 22.2% of all scholarship athletes in Division I (i.e., schools that award athletic scholarships), 60% of those in men's basketball, and 43% of those in football. Yet across Division I, approximately 6% of all students (male and female) are Black. At 100 of the 245 colleges in Division I[1] during 1993, 20% of the Black male student body were athletes, and that figure was more than 50% at 21 of these schools. At Boise State University during 1990-91, 35 of 40 Black male students were athletes.

The highly disproportional representation of Black male athletes in collegiate revenue-producing sports appears to be an anomalous phenomenon, considering that it was only after World War II that barriers to athletic segregation began to dissipate. With only a few exceptions and isolated cases such as those of Paul Robeson, Frederick Pollard, De Hart Hubbard, Eddie Tolan, Ralph Metcalfe, Jesse Owens, and Jackie Robinson, Black collegiate athletes before the 1950s played predominantly at Black colleges that participated in Black conferences (Chalk, 1976; Grundman, 1986). During the 1950s and 1960s, things began to change. Eitzen and Sage (1986) illustrate the dramatic rise of the Black collegiate athlete in the following comparisons: (a) In 1948, 10% of college basketball teams had at least one Black member, but by 1962, 45% had at least one Black and by 1975, 92% had at least one Black member;

(b) from 1882 to 1945, there were only four Black lettermen in football and none in basketball at the University of Michigan, but from 1945 to 1972 there were 71 Black lettermen in football and 21 in basketball. They went on to report that the last major athletic conference to integrate was the Southeast Conference (SEC) when, in 1966, the University of Tennessee signed a Black defensive back and Vanderbilt University signed a basketball player. Yet by 1983, 44 of the SEC's 50 starting basketball players were Black. During the 1991-92 season, 57% of the football players[2] and 64% of the basketball players in the conference were Black (Reed, 1991).

At face value, the acceptance of Black athletes by colleges, along with their preeminence in the visible revenue-producing sports of basketball and football, appears to be a case study in equal opportunity and upward mobility. In no other area in American life, with the possible exception of the entertainment industry, has merit been so important in recruitment or have Blacks risen so quickly and been so successful. Because of athletic prowess, it appears that young Black men, who for various social and economic reasons might not have had an opportunity to attend college, now have a chance to do so. In return, colleges and universities expect dedication from recruits. They also expect them to produce successful athletic teams that win league titles and appear in national tournaments.

Nonetheless, the nature of the contract between athletes and colleges regarding education is somewhat nebulous. In the recruitment process, institutions typically promote such things as the extensiveness of educational opportunities, supportiveness of academic and social environments, and importance of leaving college with a degree. But recruiters also do not neglect to convey to prospective student-athletes the value of playing in high-profile programs with national exposure.

Reconciling the apparent conflict between obtaining a high-quality education while practicing between 2 and 4 hours a day, dealing with the emotional and physical pressures associated with sports performance, and traveling around the nation[3] while classes are in session are seemingly not major concerns. Interestingly, this dilemma has been around for quite a while without resolution. As far back as 1929, the prestigious Carnegie Foundation (Savage, Bentley, McGovern, & Smiley, 1929) concluded that inferior academic achievement by athletes was not a consequence of their academic ability but of the very hard training and long practice hours that limited the time and energy athletes could devote to course work.

Although the conflict between athletics and academics exists for athletes in general, the pressure to succeed as athletes is greater for Blacks. For years, Edwards (1986) has argued that because Blacks have fewer opportunities in other fields, Black culture has embraced athletic excellence as a symbol of high status and sports as an endeavor through which individuals can achieve

upward social and economic mobility. Accordingly, he claimed that a disproportionate number of talented and motivated Black males are channeled into
a few sports having a relatively small number of professional positions while
their White peers distribute themselves across a variety of occupations in
which real employment opportunities exist. Edwards (1988) estimated that of
all the Black athletes who play collegiate football, basketball, or baseball, only
1.6% will ever sign a professional contract and that, within $3\frac{1}{2}$ years, "over
60 percent of those who do sign such contracts are out of professional sports,
more often than not financially destitute or in debt, and on the streets without
either the credentials or skills to make their way productively" (p. 140).

Ashe (1977) also felt a need to warn Blacks about investing themselves too
heavily in sports. He urged Black parents to instill in their children a desire
for learning along with the aspiration to become athletes. His proposal was
for parents to require children to spend 2 hours in the library for every hour
they spent on the playing field so that if they were unsuccessful in sports,
Black youth would have other options. In a recent teleconference (Lederman,
1990), Ashe, Edwards, and Lapchick concluded that the major factors reinforcing Blacks to pursue athletics at the expense of education included
(a) Black parents who drive their children toward athletic careers, (b) media
coverage that glorifies professional athletes, (c) coaches who overemphasize
the importance of sports, and (d) colleges that admit Black athletes who have
little chance of succeeding academically. Because of the vast numbers of
Black youth who vie for the relatively few college and fewer professional
positions, Edwards (1986) observed that, for most Black adolescents who
neglect academic opportunities, the option of sports becomes "a tread-
mill to oblivion rather than the escalator to wealth and glory it was believed
to be" (p. 33).

## GRADUATION RATES AND THE BLACK ATHLETE

Clearly, Black collegiate athletes are being used to bring recognition and
wealth to the institutions for which they play, but it is unclear whether they
are getting degrees in numbers that reflect true reciprocity in the basic
contract: "I give you my athletic ability for four years, and you give me the
opportunity to obtain a college education." To address the issue of creating
better balance in the student-athlete equation, in 1990, at the urging of
Congress, the NCAA legislated public disclosure of graduation rates. Although graduation rate may be only one of many indexes used to assess the
extent to which athletes are able to fulfill their role as students,[4] it has become
a standard and is believed to be a common denominator for assessing institutional accountability to student-athletes. As implied by Cross (1993), the

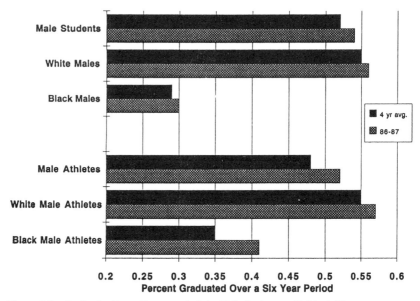

**Figure 2.1.** Graduation Rates (6-year period) for Male Students and Male Athletes

publication of graduation rates also produces a database of information that can be a powerful stimulus for fostering institutional competition in the area of social and racial change. Presumably, those athletic prospects who have a dream of upward mobility through educational attainment may, because of such information, have a better indication of the institutions to which they should be applying. Concomitantly, institutions that have dismal graduation rates not only will suffer antipathy from their peers and the public but presumably will find it harder to recruit athletic talent.

The most recent report compiled by the NCAA on graduation rates of Division I schools ($N = 298$) was released in June of 1993 (Benson, 1993). It encompassed information on graduation rates for individuals who were freshmen during 1986-87 and graduated within a 6-year period. A combined 4-year average of those rates representing the freshman classes of 1982-83, 1983-84, 1984-85, and 1985-86 was computed as well to provide a basis of comparison. Data were also broken down by race and sport.

The 4-year average data place the mean graduation rate for all males at 52%. Figure 2.1 shows that, when the data are broken down by race, Whites graduated at a rate nearly twice that of Blacks (55% vs. 29%). Also, White athletes graduated at the same rate as did the White male student body, whereas Black athletes surpassed the graduation rate of their Black cohorts by 6%. White athletes graduated at a rate 20% higher than did Black athletes. In all instances, freshmen during 1986-87 graduated with a higher rate than

**TABLE 2.1** Male Graduation Rates for Top 25 NCAA Division I Universities

| Rank | University | Overall 1986-87 Cohorts | White 1986-87 Cohorts | Black 1986-87 Cohorts | Overall 4-Year Average | White 4-Year Average | Black 4-Year Average |
|---|---|---|---|---|---|---|---|
| 1 | Harvard | 97 | 98 | 89 | 95 | 96 | 86 |
| 2 | Princeton | 95 | 96 | 86 | 95 | 95 | 82 |
| 3 | Yale | 96 | 96 | 89 | 95 | 95 | 88 |
| 6 | Stanford | 92 | 92 | 87 | 91 | 92 | 82 |
| 7 | Duke | 93 | 94 | 76 | 92 | 93 | 76 |
| 8 | Dartmouth | 94 | 96 | 84 | 94 | 96 | 81 |
| 10 | Cornell | 90 | 91 | 71 | 87 | 89 | 70 |
| 11 | Columbia | 79 | 81 | 74 | 87 | 89 | 83 |
| 12 | Brown | 92 | 93 | 81 | 93 | 93 | 84 |
| 13 | Northwestern | 89 | 89 | 68 | 87 | 88 | 74 |
| 14 | Rice | 86 | 87 | 71 | 84 | 84 | 75 |
| 16 | Pennsylvania | 90 | 91 | 62 | 89 | 90 | 64 |
| 17 | Georgetown | 92 | 93 | 84 | 90 | 91 | 75 |
| 19 | California—Berkeley | 76 | 82 | 47 | 72 | 77 | 47 |
| 20 | Vanderbilt | 81 | 81 | 85 | 78 | 79 | 62 |
| 21 | Virginia | 92 | 93 | 82 | 90 | 92 | 71 |
| 22 | UCLA | 73 | 81 | 46 | 69 | 77 | 43 |
| 23 | Michigan | 83 | 85 | 59 | 81 | 83 | 57 |
| 25 | Notre Dame | 94 | 95 | 81 | 92 | 93 | 71 |
| | Mean | 88.6 | 90.2 | 74.8 | 87.4 | 89.1 | 72.2 |
| | Standard deviation | 7.0 | 5.7 | 13.3 | 7.6 | 6.2 | 12.7 |

did freshman classes averaged over the previous 4 years. The largest improvement appeared to be for athletes (4%) and Black athletes (6%).

Although these graduation rates do not seem overly impressive across all categories, it is difficult to know what rate may be considered good. As a basis of comparison, graduation data from universities ranked by *U.S. News & World Report* ("America's Best Colleges," 1993) as being in the top 25 in the country[5] and included in the NCAA survey are listed in Table 2.1. As can be seen, the average 4-year graduation rate for these institutions was considerably higher than that for all schools in Division I (85% vs. 52%). White males (88%) graduated at a rate 33% higher than that at the average Division I school (55%), whereas Black males graduated at a considerably higher rate (68%) than did Black males across all Division I schools (29%). In contrast to the analysis on all schools, the 1986-87 data for these elite institutions did not appear to differ very much from their 4-year average. Finally, White males had graduation rates that exceeded those of Blacks by 20%. It appeared that the average Division I school has a rather low graduation rate compared to those of the elite institutions in Division I.

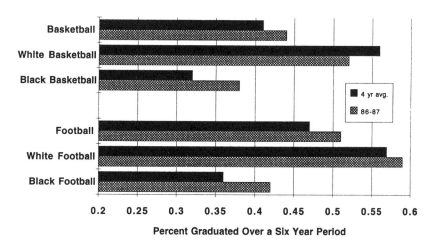

**Figure 2.2.**   Graduation Rates (6-year period) for Basketball and Football Players

As noted previously, a great deal of debate has ensued regarding the potential conflict between academics and athletics, especially in the revenue-producing sports of football and basketball. The recruitment of underqualified students who are subjected to intense emotional and physical pressures while having limited amounts of time to study has been identified as a major factor working against athletes achieving academic success. Figure 2.2 presents graduation rates for these sports. As can be seen, football players (47%) graduated at a rate 5% less than that of male students in general (52%). Breaking down the data by race, one finds that White football players (57%) surpassed the graduation rate of White male students (55%), whereas Black football players (36%) surpassed the graduation rate of Black male students (29%). On the other hand, Black football players trailed their White teammates' graduation rate by 21%. Again, the data showed improvement between the freshman class of 1986-87 and the previous 4-year averages.

Basketball players tended to graduate at a lower rate (41%) than did males in general (52%) and football players. A racial breakdown showed White players (56%) surpassing White males by 1%. Black basketball players (32%) exceeded the graduation rate of Black males by 3% but were 24% behind that of their White teammates. Only in the case of White basketball players did the 1986-87 graduation rate decrease when compared to the average of the previous 4 years.

**TABLE 2.2**  Graduation Rates of Athletes From Elite Institutions (4-year average)

| | | | | | Basketball | | Football | |
|---|---|---|---|---|---|---|---|---|
| Rank | University | Athletes | White | Black | White | Black | White | Black |
| 6 | Stanford | 82 | 83 | 63 | 67 (b) | 75 (a) | 78 (e) | 64 (c) |
| 7 | Duke | 89 | 91 | 83 | 100 (a) | 67 (b) | 86 (e) | 86 (e) |
| 13 | Northwestern | 80 | 80 | 75 | 100 (b) | 100 (a) | 75 (e) | 70 (e) |
| 14 | Rice | 67 | 64 | 76 | 46 (c) | 67 (b) | 62 (e) | 71 (e) |
| 17 | Georgetown | 89 | 91 | 84 | NWP | 80 (c) | n.a. | n.a. |
| 19 | California— | | | | | | | |
| | Berkeley | 55 | 60 | 46 | 20 (a) | 43 (b) | 68 (e) | 59 (e) |
| 20 | Vanderbilt | 72 | 75 | 57 | 80 (b) | 75 (a) | 77 (e) | 57 (e) |
| 21 | Virginia | 79 | 85 | 63 | 80 (a) | 44 (b) | 76 (e) | 71 (e) |
| 22 | UCLA | 57 | 66 | 41 | 67 (a) | 25 (b) | 76 (e) | 40 (e) |
| 23 | Michigan | 62 | 66 | 52 | 83 (b) | 33 (b) | 71 (e) | 56 (e) |
| 25 | Notre Dame | 83 | 82 | 85 | 67 (b) | 67 (b) | 82 (e) | 90 (e) |
| Mean | | 74.1 | 76.6 | 65.9 | 71.0 | 61.5 | 75.1 | 66.4 |
| Standard deviation | | 12.3 | 11.1 | 15.7 | 24.2 | 22.5 | 6.8 | 14.7 |

NOTE: Letters in parentheses indicate number of athletes in each sample: (a) = 1-5; (b) = 6-10; (c) = 11-15; (d) = 16-20; (e) = greater than 20; NWP = no white players; n.a. = no team.

Again, as a basis of comparison, graduation rates of athletes from the nation's best institutions were used to provide a standard against which other schools were evaluated. Unfortunately, eight of these schools—those in the Ivy League—are not required by the NCAA to report graduation rates for athletes because they do not award scholarship aid on the basis of athletic prowess. Consequently, Table 2.2 consists of data for athletes from the remaining 11 institutions. The summary results indicate a 9% difference in graduation rates between the average 4-year rate for all males (82%) and that for athletes (73%). White athletes (76%) were 10% lower than White students (86%), whereas Black athletes (64%) were 3% higher than Black students (61%).

An analysis of revenue-producing sports[6] resulted in football players (71%) graduating at a rate 11% lower than that of males in general. White football players (75%) were 7% behind all males and trailed White male students by 11%. Blacks (64%) were 18% behind all males but 3% higher than Black male students. Black football players trailed their White counterparts by 11%. Basketball players (63%) were 19% behind all males. Furthermore, White basketball players (73%) were 13% behind White males, and Black basketball players (58%) were 3% behind their Black male cohorts. White basketball players at these institutions graduated at a rate 15% higher than that of their Black peers.

## DISCUSSION

It appears that graduation rates fluctuate greatly among Division I institutions. Furthermore, there appears to be a tendency for athletes across Division I to graduate at a slightly lower percentage than that of the general student population. Yet White athletes approximate the overall graduation rate of White males across Division I. In contrast to popular belief, Black athletes tend to graduate at a slightly higher rate than that of Blacks in general. There also seems to be a pattern across racial groupings in which football players graduate at a slightly higher rate than do basketball players.

At the elite institutions, the overall pattern is for the general population of students to surpass the graduation rates of athletes. When the data are broken down by racial grouping, it appears that White athletes do significantly worse than their White cohorts, whereas Black athletes graduate at a slightly higher rate than their Black peers. Also, football players have only a marginal advantage in graduation rate over basketball players. Nonetheless, White football players trail their White peers by a fairly large margin, whereas Black football players graduate at about the same rate as do Blacks in general. In these institutions, both White and Black basketball players trail their respective nonathletic cohort groups, with the margin of difference being greater for Whites than it is for Blacks.

Even though Blacks underperform Whites in graduation rate across all categories, it appears that rather dramatic increases occur for both Blacks and Whites who attend elite schools. For example, Black athletes at the elite schools (64%) outperform by 29% Black athletes across Division I (35%) institutions. The data for Black basketball and football players also show rather dramatic differences for those attending elite institutions. Basketball players (58%) have a 26% advantage over their peers distributed across all schools (32%), whereas football players (64%) hold a 29% advantage over their peers (35%). Interestingly, this trend was also evident for White athletes with individuals at elite institutions (76%) exceeding the graduation rate of their peers (55%) by 21%. White basketball players have a 17% advantage over their peers across Division I, whereas football players have an 18% advantage.

The picture seems to indicate that graduation rates across racial groupings for all students and athletes (including those in revenue-producing sports) are significantly greater in institutions with better academic reputations. But it also appears, contrary to popular belief, that participation in revenue-producing sports at the average Division I institution is not associated with poorer graduation rates. Indeed, Blacks appear to benefit somewhat by such involvement. On the other hand, at the elite institutions, participation in revenue-producing athletics is associated with poorer graduation rates, but this phenomenon is predominantly a function of White athletes underperforming their White cohorts. Black athlete graduation rates again surpass, by a small margin, the graduation rates of their Black peers.

From this analysis, it appears that race and academic reputation of an institution are much more important factors in determining graduation rate than is whether a student participates in athletics. Across Division I, the difference in graduation rates between Whites and Blacks is 26% for students overall and 20% for athletes. At elite institutions, the difference between Whites and Blacks is 25%[7] for students overall, and Whites surpass Blacks by 12% for athletes. Furthermore, Whites at elite schools graduate at a rate 31% greater than that of Whites at the typical Division I school, whereas White athletes at these elite schools have a 21% advantage over White athletes across Division I. For Blacks, differences are comparable, with typical students at elite schools enjoying a 32% advantage, whereas athletes at these schools graduate at a rate 29% higher than the Division I average. Surprisingly, it appears that if there is a problem to be addressed, it should focus on the reasons for these racial and institutional disparities rather than on whether an individual is an athlete.

## What Factors Account for
## Differences in Graduation Rates?

Such issues are of major concern to society at large, and the athletic community has been under considerable pressure to report and improve the graduation rates of athletes. From an ongoing series of studies by the NCAA (1991, 1993), it has become fairly well established that the best predictors of college graduation are precollege test scores (i.e., Scholastic Aptitude Tests [SATs] or American College Tests [ACTs]) and high school grade point average (GPA). When combined, tests and GPA account for between 11% and 15% of the variance in graduation rate. These measures have also been found to be accurate in predicting graduation rates across races, genders, and institutions.

Seemingly, the divergent admission standards for these variables between elite Division I schools and the rest of Division I might partially account for differential graduation rates. Although data that break down these measures by institution, race, gender, and athletic status are not available, an overall analysis of the SAT scores of athletes at the elite schools listed in Table 2.2 yields a combined 3-year average (1990-1992) of 1019. Football players had a mean SAT of 951, and basketball players averaged 899. Across Division I schools, the combined 3-year average for all athletes was 905, with football players having an average SAT of 858 and basketball players an average SAT of 836. High school GPAs followed a similar pattern. Athletes at elite schools had an average high school GPA of 3.13. Football players averaged 3.01, and basketball players had a mean of 2.95. By contrast, the average GPA for all athletes listed in Division I institutions was 2.78, with football players averaging 2.68 and basketball players averaging 2.65. These indexes, as anticipated, tend to mirror observed graduation rates. Consequently, if SATs and GPAs for Black athletes follow the same trend, differences in graduation rates between racial and athletic groups might also be attributable to precollege preparation.

Data reported by the American Institutes for Research (AIR) (1989) would seem to corroborate such a view. For students in college during 1987-88, the AIR found that for Black football and basketball players, the mean SAT score was 740 and the mean ACT was 14, whereas for non-Black football and basketball players the mean SAT was 890 and the mean ACT was 19. The report also showed that measures for Black athletes were skewed toward the lowest quartile, with approximately 45% of Black football and basketball players scoring below 700 on the SAT and 45% scoring below 15 on the ACT. By contrast, 6% of Blacks fell in the highest quartile on SATs (1060-1600), and only 8% were represented in the highest quartile on ACTs (24-36). It was also found that 61% of Black football and basketball players fell in the lowest quartile on high school GPA (B– or below) whereas only 8% fell in the highest quartile (A or A–). Such data are consistent with differences in graduation rates observed between athletic groups that vary by race.

### The NCAA, Proposition 48, and Graduation Rates of Athletes

Evidently, a conclusion that can be drawn from these data is that if improvement in graduation rates is a goal, everything else being equal, institutions should increase admissions criteria. The NCAA took such an approach in 1986 by implementing Proposition 48, a rule that requires freshman scholarship athletes to have a minimum high school GPA of 2.0 in 11 core courses and a minimum total SAT of 700 or an ACT of 15. Students satisfying only one of these criteria (i.e., partial qualifier) may be awarded athletic scholarships but are not permitted to practice or compete during their first year. Students who do not satisfy either of the criteria cannot be given athletic scholarship aid.

The effect of Proposition 48 can be examined by contrasting graduation rates between the prior cumulative average and the 1986 cohorts because the latter group was the first college class accepted under the new standards. The comparative improvements within and across races and sports (as seen in Figures 2.1 and 2.2) are directly related to higher SATs (874 vs. 957) and GPAs (2.85 vs. 3.11). Although the graduation rates for Black athletes still fall short of those for Whites, Black athletes who entered college in 1986 graduated at a rate 6% greater (41%) than the average for Black athletes who began college during the previous 3 years (35%). Also, the difference between White and Black athletes in 1986 was 16% compared to the classes of the previous 4 years, when the difference between Whites and Blacks was 20%. Supplementary analysis on the freshman class of 1984-85 also showed that if individuals who did not meet Proposition 48 standards (had they been in effect then) were removed from the 1984-85 cohort group data, differences in graduation rates between pre-and post-Proposition 48 classes would be eliminated. Consequently, it appears that increasing academic standards for freshman scholarship athletes is associated with increased graduation rates. Presumably, this can also account for the absence of pre-and post-Proposition 48 effects in the elite schools because their admissions standards have been, and remain, significantly higher than the criteria established by the NCAA.

More dramatic increases in graduation rates are anticipated when data for the freshman class of 1990 are analyzed because Proposition 42 should have an effect on this group. Whereas Proposition 48 allows students to be partial qualifiers, Proposition 42 will eliminate this provision. Students who do not meet a minimum standard on the SATs or ACTs *and* earn a high school GPA of at least 2.0 will not be eligible for an athletic scholarship under Proposition 42. The NCAA has authorized even more stringent minimums to go into effect in 1995. To qualify for athletic aid, freshman athletes with an SAT of 700 or an ACT of 17 will need a GPA of at least 2.5. Athletes with a 2.0 GPA will be required to have at least 900 on SATs or 21 on ACTs.

Although many have applauded the NCAA's efforts to address the issue of graduation rate, the NCAA's approach of elevating admission standards has been criticized by the Black Coaches' Association (BCA) ("Black Coaches Announce," 1990; Farrell, 1993). The BCA has argued that Proposition 48 is racially biased because Blacks tend to do more poorly on standardized tests than do Whites. John Chaney, basketball coach at Temple, maintained that "opportunities will be taken away from youngsters, and many more Black youngsters in particular" (Blum, 1993, p. A42) if standardized test criteria are used in an absolute way to identify students who are eligible or ineligible for athletic scholarships.

Data for the overall population of college students ("The Nation: Students," 1993) corroborate this by showing Whites to have a 197-point advantage on the SAT (938 vs. 741) and a 4.3-point edge on the ACT (21.3 vs. 17.0). Paralleling these racial differences, the AIR (1989) appears to corroborate this observation for athletes. Anticipating the effects of Proposition 42, the AIR also concludes that had Proposition 42 been in effect for students entering college in 1987, 45% of the Black football and basketball players would have failed to meet the SAT standard of 700, and 54% would have been below 15 on the ACT. In addition, 48% of Black football and basketball players entered college with a GPA under 2.1, making it likely that many athletes would also be eliminated by the GPA standard. George Reveling, basketball coach at the University of Southern California, added that it is "peculiar that we see the pool of Black athletes shrinking, whereas much of the funding contributions have come from the work of African Americans" (Farrell, 1993, p. 41).

### Two Interpretations of the Same Data

The net effects of Proposition 48 have tended to prevent less well prepared high school athletes from getting athletic scholarships or competing as freshmen. Notwithstanding this, the BCA has argued that in 1987, 65% of all Proposition 48 casualties were Black and that 91% of the casualties who were recruited to play basketball were Black. The BCA went on to report that during 1988-89, 600 individuals failed to qualify for athletic scholarships because of Proposition 48, and 90% (i.e., 540) were Black ("Black Coaches Announce," 1990). The AIR report further suggests that, under Proposition 42, an even higher percentage of Black athletes will become ineligible for athletic aid. The attempt by the NCAA to improve graduation rates by increasing standards for athletic scholarship eligibility appears to have had its intended effect, but in so doing it has alienated many Blacks in the athletic community who see the NCAA's policies as racially biased.

Another argument presented by this faction is that although the NCAA (1993) data analysis concludes that there are no differences in predicting graduation rates between Whites and Blacks using a combination of high school GPA and standardized tests, the resulting equation still accounts for only between 11% and 15% of the variance. This means that many other factors can determine whether an individual will graduate (e.g., individual motivation, support from coaches for academics, selected major, availability of academic tutors and counselors, campus climate, financial resources). Pascarella and Smart (1991) seem to corroborate this with a finding that participation in athletics for Blacks and Whites is associated with increased motivation for completing a degree. Furthermore, Walter, Smith, Hoey, and Wilhelm (1987) reveal that for a sample of 700 football players matriculating at the University of Michigan between 1974 and 1983, 86% of a hypothetical Proposition 42 group from that sample graduated from college. A study by Seller (1992) attempted to predict college GPA from a battery of predictors for 409 basketball players and 917 football players at Division I schools. He found that for Whites, 15% of the variance in GPA could be attributed to high school GPA, socioeconomic status, and SAT/ACT. For Blacks, only 4% of college GPA could be predicted, and only high school GPA and mother's occupation were significant factors.

The BCA also pointed out that although the graduation rate of Black athletes may be considered low by White standards, it actually surpasses that of the average Black across Division I schools. Taken together, such data are interpreted by this group to mean that participating in athletics actually serves to increase the probability that a Black student will graduate from college. Setting admission standards, and especially using standardized tests that (in the BCA's view) are racially biased, prevents potentially viable students from being eligible for athletic scholarships and is counterproductive.

On the other hand, some critics have argued that the criteria set by the NCAA are too low and that many students who are underprepared to do college work will still be allowed to matriculate and participate in athletics. Such critics point to the fact that the mean SAT for all students is 902 and the mean ACT is 20.6 ("The Nation: Students," 1993). Thus, requiring athletic scholarship recruits to get 700 on the SAT or 15 on the ACT, in addition to a high school GPA of 2.0, is not really setting a standard that is very meaningful. Critics have argued that for athletes entering college during 1984 and 1985, a high school GPA of 2.0 placed a student in the 1.5% percentile, meaning that 98.5% of students had a higher GPA (NCAA, 1991). Also, the NCAA predicted that a GPA of 2.0 was associated with an expected 5-year graduation rate of about 20%. Similarly, an SAT of 700 or an ACT of 15 placed a student at about the 30th percentile and was associated with an expected graduation rate of approximately 25%. Such predicted graduation rates are lower than rates observed prior to the implementation of Proposition 48.

In contrast to those who claim that standardized test criteria are racially biased against Blacks, proponents of higher standards have argued that graduation rates are predicted equally well from these measures for Blacks and Whites. Consequently, they have proposed that the use of such criteria need not be eliminated and that, instead, students need to do a better job of developing the skills and abilities that underlie what standardized tests purport to assess. Seemingly, such a position is consistent with the pleas made by Ashe (1977) and Edwards (1986) for Blacks to pay more attention to academic development and not to be taken in by the invidious social system that causes Black children to hone athletic skills at the expense of academic competencies (Lederman, 1992). This position calls for an even more stringent standard for becoming eligible for athletic aid.

Seemingly, both factions have valid arguments. Participation in athletics is associated with higher graduation rates, especially for Blacks. Also, graduation rates improve as admissions criteria increase. Despite arguments from both sides opposing Proposition 48, this legislation provides a reasonable compromise. Setting a national standard for awarding athletic grants attempts to screen out individuals who have little potential for academic survival. On the other hand, individuals from disadvantaged backgrounds, who may test poorly on SATs and ACTs, can still gain access to higher education by way of the partial qualifier route. The year in which a Proposition 48 student sits out provides an opportunity to acclimate to college life and remedy academic deficiencies without the burden of being overwhelmed by athletic involvement. If individuals succeed in the first year, they then become eligible to participate in the second year. Thereafter, the student is treated the same as any other student-athlete. If the individual fails to demonstrate academic prowess during the probationary year, athletic aid is withdrawn. Consequently, Proposition 48 acknowledges that test scores may be misleading and provides the opportunity for an individual to demonstrate academic viability. Although many Proposition 48 partial qualifiers have failed to progress into their second year, stories behind the success of individuals such as Anfernee Hardaway and Rumeal Robinson (Wiley, 1991) illustrate that test scores can be fallible in predicting academic success and that the BCA's contentions are credible.

Although Proposition 48 may have erred on the side of awarding athletic aid too often to individuals who fail academically, Proposition 42 appears to decrease this possibility by (a) increasing standards for granting athletic aid and (b) eliminating the partial-qualifier option. In essence, it eliminates more marginally prepared students. Consequently, it is understandable why coaches such as Chaney rebel against this legislation. As conveyed by Smith (1994), Chaney views his own success as resulting from educational opportunities that became available only because of his athletic prowess, and had Proposition 42 been in existence then—as it is now—an individual like Chaney would have been precluded from higher education despite his capacity to overcome deficits that may not have been his fault.

Seemingly, the key element that might help to resolve the Proposition 42 debate is to reinstitute the notion of probationary status. Athletic recruits who do not meet grant-in-aid standards could be allowed to demonstrate academic competence as partial qualifiers were allowed to do under Proposition 48. Coaches would commit scholarships to such individuals and become invested in their success as students. Upon demonstrating academic competence after a probationary year, students would be permitted to participate in athletics. If they elected to graduate over a 5-year period, they could still have the same 4 years of eligibility given to typical student-athletes. Such an option would conceivably build on, rather than attenuate, those factors operating within athletic programs that have resulted in graduation rate advantages to athletes found in this review.

Although debate will no doubt continue, especially as we learn more about the effects of Proposition 42, it is probably true that the entire athletic community from elementary schools through the college level now understands that the time when an individual could simply meander his or her way through school because of athletic prowess is at an end. Furthermore, the debate over graduation rates of athletes has helped to focus attention on the even more pressing issue of college graduation rates for Blacks.

## NOTES

1. A total of 296 schools are in Division I, and 245 responded to the *Chronicle of Higher Education's* survey.

2. During 1992-93, 49% of the football players and 64% of the basketball players in Division I were Black.

3. One estimate is that 60 hours a week may be devoted to athletics (Underwood, 1980).

4. McMillen and Coggins (1992) argue that graduation rate does not capture the ingenuity of athletic departments to channel athletes into "gimme" courses that lead to meaningless degrees.

5. Rankings were computed by combining information about students selectively, faculty resources, financial resources, graduation rate, and alumni satisfaction with ratings given by 1,726 college presidents, deans, and admissions directors on an institution's academic reputation.

6. Graduation percentages from individual schools were reported with associated frequencies: (a) 1-5, (b) 6-10, (c) 11-15, (d) 16-20, and (e) greater than 20. To obtain weighted means, the median for each category was used to multiply graduation percentage. For category (e), a frequency of 20 was used.

7. This percentage was obtained by using data from the subset of schools that report data for athletes.

## REFERENCES

American Institute for Research. (1989). *The experiences of Black intercollegiate athletes at NCAA Division I institutions* (Report No. 3). Palo Alto, CA: Center for the Study of Athletics.

America's best colleges. (1993). *U.S. News & World Report.*

Ashe, A. (1977, February 6). An open letter to Black parents: Send your children to the libraries. *New York Times,* sec., 5, p. 2.

Benson, M. T. (1993). *1993 NCAA Division I graduation rates report.* Overland Park, KS: NCAA.

Black coaches announce position regarding Proposition 48/Rule 42. (1990, January 18). *Black Issues in Higher Education,* p. 30.

Blum, D. (1993, July 7). Graduation rate of scholarship athletes rose after Proposition 48 was adopted, NCAA reports. *Chronicle of Higher Education,* pp. A42-A44.

Chalk, O. (1976). *Black college sport.* New York: Dodd, Mead.

Cross, T. L. (1993, Autumn). Why the *Journal of Blacks in Higher Education. Journal of Blacks in Higher Education,* pp. 4-5.

Edwards, H. (1986). The collegiate athletic arms race. In R. E. Lapchick (Ed.), *Fractured focus.* Lexington, MA: Lexington Books.

Edwards, H. (1988, August). The single-minded pursuit of sports fame and fortune is approaching an institutionalized triple tragedy in Black society. *Ebony,* pp. 138-140.

Eitzen, D. S., & Sage, G. H. (1986). *Sociology of North American sport.* Dubuque, IA: William C. Brown.

Farrell, C. S. (1993, November 4). Black coaches' boycott gains momentum and supporters. *Black Issues in Higher Education,* pp. 40-41.

Grundman, A. H. (1986). The image of intercollegiate sports and the civil rights movement: A historian's view. In R. E. Lapchick (Ed.), *Fractured focus.* Lexington, MA: Lexington Books.

Lederman, D. (1990, April 25). Panel examining Blacks and sports discusses possibility of boycotting colleges that fail to educate Black athletes. *Chronicle of Higher Education,* p. A36.

Lederman, D. (1992, June 17). Blacks make up large proportion of scholarship athletes, yet their overall enrollment lags at Division I colleges. *Chronicle of Higher Education,* pp. A1, A30-A34.

Lipsyte, R. (1992, March 27). Blacks on the court: Why not on campus? *New York Times,* p. B12 (N).

McMillen, T., & Coggins, P. (1992). *Out of bounds: How the American sports establishment is being driven by greed and hypocrisy—and what needs to be done about it.* New York: Simon & Schuster.

The nation: Students. (1993, August 25). *Chronicle of Higher Education* (almanac issue).

National Collegiate Athletic Association. (1991). *NCAA research report* (Report 91-02). Overland Park, KS: NCAA.

National Collegiate Athletic Association. (1993). *NCAA research report* (Report 92-02). Overland Park, KS: NCAA.

Pascarella, E. T., & Smart, J. C. (1991). Athletic participation for African American and Caucasian men: Some further evidence. *Journal of College Student Development, 32,* 123-130.

Reed, W. F. (1991, August 12). Culture shock in Dixieland. *Sports Illustrated,* pp. 53-55.

Savage, H. J., Bentley, J. T., McGovern, J. T., & Smiley, D. F. (1929). *American college athletics* (Bulletin no. 23). New York: Carnegie Foundation for the Advancement of Teaching.

Seller, R. M. (1992). Racial differences in the predictors for academic achievement of student-athletes in Division I revenue producing sports. *Sociology of Sport Journal, 9,* 48-59.

Smith, G. (1994, February 28). The whittler. *Sports Illustrated,* pp. 72-81.

Underwood, J. (1980, May 19). Student athletes: The sham and the shame. *Sports Illustrated,* pp. 36-73.

Walter, T., Smith, D. E. P., Hoey, G., & Wilhelm, R. (1987). Predicting the academic success of college athletes. *Research Quarterly for Exercise and Sport, 58,* 273-279.

Wiley, R. (1991, August 12). A daunting proposition. *Sports Illustrated,* pp. 27-45.

# 3

# Cultural Diversity on Campus
## A Look at Intercollegiate Football Coaches

Dean F. Anderson

University administrators, like administrators in many other institutions in American society, are attempting to increase the cultural diversity at all levels of the organization. Many university presidents have implemented programs aimed at expanding cultural diversity among faculty and staff. Other programs are initiated in an attempt to improve the cultural diversity among students. *The Chronicle of Higher Education* recently reported that blacks comprised only 6% of the full time undergraduate students at NCAA Division I institutions (Lederman, 1992). This figure remains about one half of the proportion of blacks in the total United States population.

Among these educational institutions, the area that probably is the most visible and receives the greatest amount of media coverage is intercollegiate athletics. Interestingly, although blacks are underrepresented as undergraduates at these institutions, they compose nearly a quarter of all scholarship athletes and nearly 43% of the football players (Lederman, 1992). Because of this overrepresentation of blacks as athletes in intercollegiate sports, it may seem reasonable to argue and indeed, many have, that here is a place in higher education where equal opportunity does exist. However, a more critical analysis would argue that this view of intercollegiate sports as a meritocracy based on skill and achievement actually obscures relations of dominance and subordination structured along lines of race (Birrell, 1989).

Little is known about the racial composition of intercollegiate athletic departments. Certainly, two of the most visible and prestigious university positions are the positions of athletic director and head football coach. The status sequence for these prestigious and powerful positions is embedded in the formal and informal structure of the organization. Within any occupation, perceived opportunity for advancement and growth can be very important in influencing work behavior, including aspiration level and, certainly, job-seeking behavior (Kanter, 1977). Thus, there is a need to examine career option viability or position access within athletic departments. One way to accomplish this is to study the social characteristics of individuals who presently occupy the position (Harlan, 1989). This investigation examined the racial and sports career characteristics of persons holding the positions of athletic director, head football coach, and assistant football coach at NCAA Division I-A institutions.

## METHOD

An examination of *The 1990-91 National Directory of College Athletics (Men's Edition)* resulted in the identification of 105 institutions that competed in football at the NCAA Division I-A level. After the completion of the 1990 intercollegiate football season in January 1991, these 105 NCAA Division I-A institutions were requested by mail to supply the researcher with a copy of their 1990 football media guides. These guides generally contain detailed biographical information concerning individuals working in the football program. Information was received from 88 of the institutions contacted (84%). Responding institutions included at least 75% of the members of each conference and of the major independent institutions participating at this level of college football.

Data were compiled for each athletic director, head football coach, and full-time assistant football coach. Strength coaches and recruiting coordinators were not included in the sample. These data included only information for athletic departments where men's and women's programs were combined or, when separate departments existed, for the men's department because it has historically controlled football. All athletic directors in this sample were male.

## RESULTS AND DISCUSSION

Results examining the race of person occupying each of the five positions during the 1990 season are presented in Table 3.1. The variable race was dichotomized into the two racial categories of whites and blacks because no other American ethnic minority group represented more than 1% of the total number of coaches and athletic directors in the sample. Thus, the data for blacks could sometimes include a small proportion of other minorities. Data show a significant relationship between race and position. Only three athletic directors (3.7%) and three head football coaches (3.5%) were identified as being black. At these two visible and prestigious university positions, blacks

**TABLE 3.1** Differences in Position, by Race

|  | Race | | |
|---|---|---|---|
| Position | White (%) (n = 779) | Black (%) (n = 143) | Total (N = 922) |
| Director | 96.3 | 3.7 | 81 |
| Head Coach | 96.5 | 3.5 | 86 |
| Offensive coordinator | 92.8 | 7.2 | 83 |
| Defensive coordinator | 93.1 | 6.9 | 87 |
| Assistant coach | 78.6 | 21.4 | 585 |

NOTE: Chi square = 42.99, $p < .000$; Cramer's V = .22, $p < .000$.

were almost completely absent. Similarly, only about 7% of the coordinator positions were held by blacks. Among assistant coaches, this increased to 21%. This is clearly less than the proportion of all scholarship athletes (25%) and football players (47%) who are black. These data suggest that organizational relations of dominance and subordination in intercollegiate football are structured along racial lines and may be grounded in the idea of "inherent" physicality (see Birrell, 1989).

Because becoming an assistant coach is often a prerequisite to becoming a coordinator and becoming a coordinator is a prerequisite to become a head coach and becoming a head football coach is frequently a prerequisite to becoming an athletic director, race may function indirectly to keep blacks from entering the pool from which head coaches and athletic directors have traditionally been selected. Only 13% of the athletic directors were found to have had no coaching experience, whereas 58% were found to have served as football coaches.

Racial discrimination may also occur as a result of the relationship between race and centrality of position played in college football. Previous research exploring career advancement and upward mobility into leadership positions in the sports milieu has found that centrality of the specific position one played while an athlete has been an important factor (Fabianic, 1984; Grusky, 1963; Leonard, Ostrosky, & Huchendorf, 1990; Loy, Curtis, & Sage, 1978; Massengale & Farrington, 1977). Much of this research in the sports milieu has used Grusky's (1963) model, which argues that structured behavior between position occupants is a function of spatial location (central and noncentral), nature of task (dependent and independent), and frequency of interaction (high and low). Combining Grusky's three criteria results in positions with potential for high interaction (central) and positions with potential for low interaction (noncentral). This research has clearly documented that playing a central

**TABLE 3.2** Differences in Position Played, by Present Position[a]

| Position Played | Present Position | | | | | |
|---|---|---|---|---|---|---|
| | Athletic Director | Head Coach | Offensive Coordinator | Defensive Coordinator | Assistant Coach | Total |
| Quarterback | 25.7 | 44.9 | 36.1 | 11.1 | 14.2 | 19.9 |
| Offensive line | 28.6 | 21.7 | 32.8 | 5.6 | 26.4 | 24.9 |
| Wide receiver/ running back | 20.0 | 8.7 | 14.8 | 7.4 | 18.2 | 16.0 |
| Linebacker | 8.6 | 11.6 | 8.2 | 25.9 | 16.7 | 15.7 |
| Defensive line | 5.7 | 4.3 | 1.6 | 16.7 | 9.4 | 8.6 |
| Defensive back | 11.4 | 8.7 | 6.6 | 33.3 | 15.1 | 14.9 |
| Total | 100.0 | 100.0 | 100.0 | 100.0 | 100.0 | 100.0 |
| | ($n = 35$) | ($n = 69$) | ($n = 61$) | ($n = 54$) | ($n = 424$) | ($n = 643$) |

NOTE: Chi square = 91.24, $p < .000$; Cramer's V = .19, $p < .000$.
a. Shown in percentages.

position has been associated with the likelihood of being selected for a leadership position in sports.

A related area of sociology of sports research has also found that centrality of position played was frequently related to race of the athlete (Braddock, 1981; Dougherty, 1976; Eitzen & Furst, 1989; Loy & McElvogue, 1970; Madison & Landers, 1976). With these research findings in mind, centrality of playing position of coaches along with the relationship between position played and race of coach were examined.

Results examining the relationship between present position and the football position played in college were significant (Table 3.2). Among athletic directors with college football playing experience, playing quarterback or offensive line were the most frequent positions identified, accounting for 55% of the positions played. Interestingly, wide receiver and running back were also frequently identified as positions played (20%) among athletic directors. The defensive positions were the least frequent positions played.

Among head coaches and offensive coordinators, quarterback was the most frequent position identified, 45% and 36% respectively. That was followed by the offensive line position, 22% and 33% respectively. In contrast to athletic directors, the wide receiver and running back positions were less frequent among occupants of these coaching positions. Once again, defensive positions were low in frequency. As may be expected, defensive positions were most frequently identified among defensive coordinators (77%). For the remaining assistant coaches, the positions played seemed to be more evenly distributed. This distribution of present coaching position with having played a central or peripheral position while a college athlete is very similar to what

**TABLE 3.3**  Differences for Assistant Coaches in Position Played, by Race[a]

| Position Played | White Coaches | Black Coaches | Total |
|---|---|---|---|
| Quarterback | 16.3 | 7.6 | 14.2 |
| Offensive line | 31.7 | 10.5 | 26.4 |
| Wide receiver/running back | 14.1 | 30.5 | 18.2 |
| Linebacker | 15.7 | 20.0 | 16.7 |
| Defensive line | 9.4 | 9.5 | 9.4 |
| Defensive back | 12.9 | 21.6 | 15.1 |
| Total | 100.0 | 100.0 | 100.0 |
|  | ($n = 319$) | ($n = 105$) | ($N = 24$) |

NOTE: Chi square = 34.45, $p < .000$; Cramer's V = .29, $p < .000$.
a. Shown in percentages.

Massengale and Farrington (1977) found for college football coaches in 1975. These results show little change over 15 years and seem to clearly indicate that within Division I-A college football, the probability of becoming an athletic director, head football coach, or a coordinator is related to the centrality of the position one played while in college.

Because few blacks were found at the positions of athletic director, head coach, or coordinator, an examination of position played while in college by race of coach was performed using only assistant coaches, of whom 21% were black (Table 3.3). Results show a significant relationship between position played and race. These data show that white assistant coaches were more than twice as likely to have played quarterback or an offensive line position than black assistant coaches, 48% compared to 18%. A reversed pattern was found for the player positions of wide receiver, running back, and defensive back where 52% of the black assistant coaches and only 27% of the white assistant coaches had played. For these assistant coaches, centrality of playing position was associated with race of the coach. Once again, these data suggest that race functions at least indirectly to keep blacks from entering the pool from which head coaches and offensive coordinators are traditionally selected.

Finally, data concerning centrality of the position coached, by race of assistant coach, was examined (Table 3.4).

These results were significant and clearly show that black assistant coaches were more likely to be found coaching the peripheral or noncentral playing positions of wide receiver and running back (48%) than white assistant coaches. In contrast, black assistant coaches were less likely to be coaching the central positions of quarterback and offensive line (11%) than white assistant coaches (36%). Among assistant coaches, position coached was also associated with race.

**TABLE 3.4**  Differences for Assistant Coaches in Position Coached, by Race[a]

| Position Coached | White Coaches | Black Coaches | Total |
|---|---|---|---|
| Quarterback | 9.6 | 3.3 | 8.2 |
| Offensive line | 26.6 | 8.1 | 23.5 |
| Wide receiver/running back | 16.7 | 48.0 | 22.6 |
| Linebacker | 19.6 | 13.0 | 18.2 |
| Defensive line | 15.0 | 19.5 | 15.9 |
| Defensive back | 12.5 | 8.1 | 11.6 |
| Total | 100.0 | 100.0 | 100.0 |
|  | ($n = 448$) | ($n = 123$) | ($N = 571$) |

NOTE: Chi square = 64.52, $p < .000$; Cramer's V = .34, $p < .000$.
a. Shown in percentages.

## CONCLUSION

This examination of the characteristics of individuals who occupied positions in the formal hierarchy of intercollegiate football at NCAA Division I-A institutions indicates that racial discrimination functions so that blacks are underrepresented among these visible and prestigious positions. This racial discrimination may be both intentional and unintentional, operating indirectly through social processes of organizational decision making that results in institutionalized racial discrimination. Clearly, athletic departments still perpetuate racial discrimination through the structural patterns of position relationships even when university policies forbid it and university presidents are committed to eliminating it within the institution. Access to the playing field has been gained. At the same time, vertical movement of blacks in intercollegiate football up the career ladder from the subordinate position of student-athlete to a position of dominance remains constricted. This suggests that relations of dominance and subordination in intercollegiate football may be structured along racial lines with a focus on inherent physicality as the key to the construction of dominant images of whites and blacks. Because institutional discrimination is not simply recognized or identified by intentions, these results point out the presence of institutionalized discrimination and some of its possible effects on career advancement, upward mobility, and career aspirations among American ethnic minorities within NCAA Division I-A athletic departments.

## REFERENCES

Birrell, S. (1989). Racial relations theories and sport: Suggestions for a more critical analysis. *Sociology of Sport Journal, 6,* 212-227.

Braddock, J. H. (1981). Race and leadership in professional sports: A study of institutional discrimination in the National Football League. *Arena Review, 5,* 16-25.

Dougherty, J. (1976). Race and sport: A follow up study. *Sport Sociology Bulletin, 5,* 1-12.

Eitzen, D. S., & Furst, D. (1989). Racial bias in women's collegiate volleyball. *Journal of Sport & Social Issues, 13,* 46-51.

Fabianic, D. (1984). Minority managers in professional baseball. *Sociology of Sport Journal, 1,* 167-171.

Grusky, O. (1963). The effects of formal structure on managerial recruitment: A study of baseball organization. *Sociometry, 26,* 345-353.

Harlan, A. (1989). Opportunities and attitudes toward job advancement in a manufacturing firm. *Social Forces, 61,* 766-788.

Kanter, R. (1977). *Men and women of the corporation.* New York: Basic Books.

Lederman, D. (1992, June 17). Blacks make up large proportion of scholarship athletes, yet their overall enrollment lags at Division I colleges. *Chronicle of Higher Education,* pp. A34-A35.

Leonard, W., Ostrosky, T., & Huchendorf, S. (1990). Centrality of position and managerial recruitment: The case of Major League Baseball. *Sociology of Sport Journal, 7,* 294-301.

Loy, J., Curtis, J. E., & Sage, G. (1978). Relative centrality of playing position and leadership recruitment in team sports. *Exercise and Sports Science Review, 6,* 257-284.

Loy, J. W., & McElvogue, J. F. (1970). Racial segregation in American sport. *International Review of Sport Sociology, 5,* 5-24.

Madison, D. R., & Landers, D. (1976). Racial discrimination in football: A test of the "stacking" of playing position hypothesis. In D. Landers (Ed.), *Social problems in athletics* (pp. 151-156). Urbana: University of Illinois Press.

Massengale, J., & Farrington, F. (1977). The influence of playing position centrality on the careers of college football coaches. *Review of Sports & Leisure, 2,* 107-115.

*The 1990-1991 national directory of college athletics (men's edition).* (1990). Amarillo, TX: Ray Franks Publishing.

# 4

## A Step in the Right Direction
### The Presidents Meet the Black Coaches

Richard E. Lapchick

I have wondered for years what it would take for those of us working in college sports to get out of the gate on the issue of racism in sports. The interest by the White House and the offer by the Justice Department to mediate between the National Collegiate Athletic Association (NCAA), its Presidents Commission, and the Black Coaches Association (BCA) may have brought us to the gate. It came in the aftermath of a threatened boycott of games by basketball coaches when they felt frustrated by the NCAA's tardy response to a series of issues.

To the casual observer, the issue was that the coaches were fighting for the restoration of a 14th scholarship in men's basketball. Such a resolution was soundly defeated at the 1994 NCAA Convention. That singular defeat, which was magnified by the media and a few coaches, was simply the flash point. It represented for them years of belief that the control of the game has been taken out of the hands of coaches and that they no longer had a meaningful voice in the game to which they had dedicated their careers. That belief crosses racial lines in the National Association of Basketball Coaches (NABC) and the BCA. Some college and university presidents, on the other hand, feel the real issue for coaches is that they want control of the game and not just a voice in running it.

But the black coaches have a host of other issues that go beyond presidents not listening to them or the number of scholarships available. Their issues cut across professional lines and affect any area of society where access by people of color or women is a question. This one happens to be sports:

- Of the 1,218 head coaching positions in Division I sports in which African American males compete (basketball, football, track and field, and baseball), 4.4% are held by African Americans.

A version of this chapter originally appeared in *The Sporting News*, January 31, 1994. Reprinted by permission.

- According to the most recent BCA survey, there are fewer than 200 African American coaches among the 5,000 assistant coaching positions in these sports, less than 4%.
- There are far more white males than African American females coaching women's basketball.
- There are six African American athletic directors in Division I, or 2%.
- There is not a single African American in a top-level position in the NCAA headquarters; new NCAA executive director Ced Dempsey promised to change this as a priority of his administration.[1]
- African American student-athletes graduate at slightly more than half the rate of white athletes. (However, it must be noted that they graduate at a higher rate than African American students in general.)
- Unlike other racial groups, African American student athletes make up a significant 6.1% of African American students on campus. That is three times higher than for whites (1.9%), six times higher than for Hispanics (1%), and 15 times higher than for Asians (.4%). It clearly raises the question of whether colleges use African American athletes for their brawn more than their brains.

The coaches argue that if we limit their access to young people through sports by increasing certain admission standards or by reducing the number of scholarships available, then we are hurling more youth into the abyss.

They say that new academic standards, due to go into effect in 1995, will dramatically decrease access for African American students.

Congresswomen Cardis Collins (D-Illinois) charged that research backing the changes was tainted. According to Representative Collins and the BCA, a core of the researchers, led by Jack McCardle, was hired to help shape the NCAA legislation that brought about the new regulations. That group was tied to an extremist philosophy known as Beyondism, which espouses genetic engineering or selective breeding. McCardle has denied the allegations of being associated with the group.

The standards were shaky enough to begin with by requiring both a 2.5 grade point average and a 700 on the Scholastic Aptitude Test (SAT) score.

Many educators agree that the SAT—a standardized test—is not a good predictor of college success for students who come from a lower socioeconomic background. Admissions officers say that a high school student with a 2.5 grade point average and good letters of recommendation would perform well in college and that sliding the scale down to a 650 SAT would have been appropriate and not limit access.

Between the background of the researchers and the potential effect of the standards, the NCAA convention passed Resolution 174, calling for complete review of the new initial eligibility standards, with a special emphasis on the effect of those standards on access to educational opportunities for minorities. That was progress.

The NCAA Council, with the support of the presidents, has commissioned a study of the effect of scholarship reductions in all sports on minority student athletes. That could lead to progress.

The Strategic Planning Committee of the Presidents Commission has made the theme of the 1996 convention "student athlete welfare, access and equity." That could lead to progress.

But the remaining problems are not new, and we have made little progress in addressing them. However, sport doesn't own the problems as much as it reflects what happens in society.

Until recently, the issue of race was hardly ever discussed within the NCAA or on individual campuses in athletic departments. John Thompson's personal boycott after the NCAA passed Proposition 48 in 1989 showed what black coaches had to do to make a point and have it stick. Before John, we seemed to think we could ignore or get away from one of the most tumultuous issues of our time. As Roberto Duran said in defeat, "No mas." As the BCA said with its threatened boycott, "Now."

The word *boycott* is not a welcome one in the world of sports. The thought of government interventions is even less welcome. So the NCAA got a double hit from the BCA.

It is ironic that all this is happening now. I know and respect many of the BCA's leaders. Their issues are ones I have fought for throughout my adult life. I have been with founder Rudy Washington on many occasions. John Thompson and George Raveling are two of the coaches I admire most. I recognize that if you are a person of color or a woman, you cannot simply put your issues on the table and expect meaningful results. History, both in and out of sports, has shown us that a dramatic push must occur to obtain real movement. From the BCA's point of view, a boycott was natural and necessary.

But I have also been part of the "reform movement" in college sports and have felt closely aligned with the presidents. Joe Crowley, president of the University of Nevada and the president of the NCAA, is one of my favorite people in college sports. He is as open as anyone I know on racial issues. He and Ced Dempsey tried to showcase a meeting with the Reverend Jesse Jackson and his top aide, Charles Farrell, during the NCAA convention. Agreeing to meet was one of Dempsey's first acts after being named to succeed Dick Schultz. Unfortunately, Jackson was ill and had to miss the meeting, but the symbolism was there.

The NCAA decided in San Antonio to conduct pilot diversity training programs in 1994. Southeastern Conference schools and more than 15 other athletic departments have already undergone training programs in 1994. The symbolism was there.

Five presidents (11%) on the 44-member NCAA Presidents Commission are African American. That is a significantly higher percentage than for presidents of universities in general and is far more than symbolism.

The right players on both sides are there along with the symbolism. Yet lines were drawn and meaningful discussions were not taking place. The presidents are there and should be in control. Many of us have fought for that for a long time. Yet mistrust lives on. The coaches need to be heard.

Boycotts. Government intervention. Dr. King's birthday. Dreams and dream makers. It all seems so familiar for those of us who were raised in and around the civil rights movement. But this is sports, and the same tools that affected the passage of the Voting Rights Act 30 years ago may now give coaches a voice if not a vote.

Crowley, Dempsey, and Judith Albino, the new chair of the NCAA Presidents Commission, sent a letter to the BCA and the NABC on January 14th. In a candid assertion of necessary movement, the letter said this:

> In recent months, sensitivity and understanding within the NCAA about the issues of access and equity have been heightened considerably. Without arguing how or why lines of communication became closed, they are opening now—between administrators and coaches among the diverse constituencies of the NCAA. . . . All of us at times have tired of talking, but when so little talking has been done for so long, it is a vital and valuable first step toward real change. We are ready to take the next step with you.[2]

If Mandela and DeKlerk, Arafat, and Rabin can come to profound agreements, then Raveling, Dempsey, and Thompson can do the same. On the international stage, each started as a hero to his constituency and a villain to his opposition. In each instance, the process of sitting at the table with the prospect of an open discussion leading to change that will better the lot of all constituencies brought them together. For them, 1994 holds out immense hope.

The role of the Justice Department and the interest by the White House could have the same result for these sports superpowers. We might actually get past the gate. It's time.

## NOTES

1. Dempsey fulfilled his promise a few months after his appointment.

2. The letter appeared in several newspapers. I had access to it by virtue of my position as broker between the NCAA and the BCA.

# 5

## The 1994 Racial Report Card[1]

Richard E. Lapchick

In recent years, a few high-profile incidents exposed the underlying prejudices that prevent many minorities from being considered for front office positions. While the public's attention was focused on the Marge Schott case, groups such as the Rainbow Commission for Fairness in Athletics and the Coalition for Equality in Sports insisted that the overwhelming majority of minorities performing on the field was grossly disproportionate to the lack of minority representation in team management. These groups were formed to use public pressure to ensure that steps be taken to reduce barriers for minority advancement. In part as a result of their efforts, 1994 was a year of notable progress.

Three of the four expansion teams in the National Football League (NFL) and the National Basketball Association (NBA) are owned in part by blacks. Deron Cherry (Jacksonville Jaguars) and Charlotte businessman William Simms (Carolina Panthers) became the only current black owners in the NFL. Isiah Thomas (Toronto Raptors) and Earvin "Magic" Johnson, who purchased nearly 10% of the Los Angeles Lakers, became new owners in the NBA.

Although many of the personnel positions on the expansion teams have not yet been filled, three teams named blacks to fill the role of general manager—Michael Huyghue, vice president for the Jacksonville Jaguars; Isiah Thomas, vice president in charge of basketball operations for the Toronto Raptors; and Stu Jackson, general manager and vice president of basketball operations for the NBA Vancouver expansion franchise.

In addition to the personnel decisions on expansion teams, M. L. Carr (Boston Celtics) was named vice president and chief of basketball operations; John Lucas (Philadelphia 76ers) was named vice president, general manager, and head coach; Bill McKinney (Detroit Pistons) was promoted to vice president of basketball operations; John Wooten (Philadelphia Eagles) was promoted to vice president of player personnel/operations; and Bob Watson

(Houston Astros) was named general manager. M. L. Carr, formerly the director of community relations; John Wooten, formerly a talent scout; and Bob Watson, formerly the assistant general manager, were promoted from within their own organizations. Bill McKinney had previously been a general manager and was recently named vice president.

The tremendous success of black coaches continues to break the stereotype that blacks lack the intellectual capabilities required to manage and coach at the highest levels. In 1987, Al Campanis, then vice president of the Los Angeles Dodgers, expressed a belief that blacks lacked some of the necessities to be field managers and general managers. The public nature of Mr. Campanis's remarks sparked a flurry of national media attention on the issue of minority hiring practices in professional sports. Since those remarks were made, a significant number of blacks have been hired as head coaches and general managers. The result has been a dismantling of false perceptions regarding the ability of blacks to manage and coach at the highest levels.

During the 1993-94 sports year, blacks were named as Coach of the Year in college basketball (Nolan Richardson—Arkansas Razorbacks), the NBA (Lenny Wilkens—Atlanta Hawks), and the National League of Major League Baseball (Dusty Baker—San Francisco Giants). In addition, Cito Gaston became the first black manager to win consecutive World Series championships, and Nolan Richardson became the second black coach to lead a team to a national championship in men's college basketball.

Additionally, Major League Baseball's Equal Opportunity Committee published a comprehensive report outlining the initiatives that owners have taken to improve the inclusion of minorities and women throughout baseball. Just prior to the release of this report in June, the National League named Leonard Coleman Jr., who is black, as its president. He replaced Bill White as the highest-ranking person of color in any of the three sports.

One of the most significant developments over the past year is baseball's commitment to contract with more minority and female vendors. The Equal Opportunity Committee reported that every team in the league is committed to doubling the dollar amount of contracts with minority and female vendors within the next year.

In the area of top management, the percentage of minorities employed remains very low. This year's numerous changes in ownership in the three leagues has produced an indication of future gains in top management positions for minorities. Another sign of increased opportunities for minorities is the action taken by new leadership in baseball. Two of the six members on baseball's Equal Opportunity Committee are new owners, Drayton McLane (Houston Astros) and Peter Magowan (San Francisco Giants). Currently, Houston has the league's only black general manager, and San Francisco is one of four teams with a black manager.

A new ownership group in Boston promoted M. L. Carr to be in charge of basketball operations for the Celtics. As of this writing, there are 14 head coaches or managers who are black or Latino in the three leagues. With two head coaching vacancies remaining in the NBA, last year's record high number of 15 minority coaches throughout the three leagues will likely be intact by the end of the summer.

However, top management positions (chairman of the board, chief executive officer [CEO], president, vice president, and general manager) continue to show minimal representation by minorities. NBA teams have 16 people of color (10%) working in high-level management positions; Major League Baseball (represented in tables in this chapter as MLB) has 10 (4%); and the NFL has six (5%).

Administrative positions (areas of business operations, community relations, finance, game operations, marketing, promotions, publications, public relations, and various other areas) continue to be predominantly held by whites. Sixteen percent of these positions are held by minorities in both the NBA and Major League Baseball, and 12% are held by minorities in the NFL.

There were no significant changes in minority representation on the field. Blacks now make up 79% of the players in the NBA, 65% of the players in the NFL, and 18% of the players in Major League Baseball. Latinos also compose 18% of the players in Major League Baseball.

## THE COMMISSIONERS AND LEAGUE OFFICES

There has been little change in the racial composition of the commissioner's office in the three leagues within the past year. Commissioners David Stern of the NBA and Paul Tagliabue of the NFL have taken the lead within their respective leagues to expand minority hiring as well as extend the role of their respective leagues in the community. Major League Baseball continues to be presided over by Bud Selig, owner of the Milwaukee Brewers. He has also encouraged outreach by major league teams within their own communities. In addition, the Executive Committee has been actively supporting initiatives by the Equal Opportunity Commission, cochaired by Jerry Reinsdorf and Bill Bartholomay, to double the dollar value of businesses to minority and female vendors.

Major League Baseball has taken a step toward improving minority representation by publishing its most comprehensive report outlining the initiatives of owners designed to afford minorities equal opportunity in hiring. There were significant areas of improvement in the central offices of Major League Baseball. Of executives and department heads, 23% were minorities in 1993-94. That is the highest percentage ever in baseball. The number of blacks employed in Major League Baseball's central offices has nearly doubled since 1989. Similarly, the number of employed Latinos has doubled from 6 to 12 since 1989. It should be noted that part of the improvement in minority representation is due to the expansion of the central offices over the past 5 years.

Furthermore, over the past 5 years, Major League Baseball central offices have seen a dramatic increase in the number of women employed (see Table 5.1). In 1989, there were only 48 female employees. Today there are 111—over half of the total staff. Major League Baseball reports that teams are currently using 501 minority-owned vending businesses and 1,228 female-owned vending businesses. This represents what may be sport's biggest area of improvement on the minority issue.

Gene Washington, who is black, was recently named director of football development in the NFL league office. In addition, two female attorneys were appointed—Jodi Balsam as attorney in the office of the league counsel and Belinda Lerner as staff labor attorney. Despite these hirings, the league office underwent a reduction in the percentage of minorities employed in management. Of the employees working in management, 18% are minorities as opposed to 23% in 1993 (see Table 5.2).

Of the three league offices, the NBA is leading the way in minority representation. John Rose, who is black, was promoted in January of 1994 to senior vice president over player relations and administration. He is one of three senior vice presidents in the league office. In addition, there are three vice presidents in the league office who are black. Nearly 23% of all management positions are held by minorities (see Table 5.3).

In addition, 47% of management positions in the NBA league office are held by women—including three vice presidents and 15 attorneys. This is by far the highest percentage of women working in any league front office.


## OWNERSHIP

Isiah Thomas and Earvin Johnson joined Edward and Bettiann Gardner, who are limited partners in the Chicago Bulls franchise, and Julio Iglesias and Amancio Suarez, who are part-owners of the Miami Heat, as the only other limited partners in the NBA who are minorities. This marks the first time that players who are black were given the opportunity to participate in ownership after retirement. Isiah Thomas purchased part of the Toronto Raptors in addition to being named the team's vice president in charge of basketball operations. Earvin Johnson, who purchased nearly 10% of the Los Angeles Lakers, is the only new minority limited partner whose access to ownership did not transpire with an expansion team. (See Table 5.4 for a breakdown of team ownership in 1994.)

**TABLE 5.1** Major League Baseball Employment Data, Central Offices: 1989 to 1994

| | 1989 | | 1990 | | 1991 | | 1992 | | 1993-94 | |
|---|---|---|---|---|---|---|---|---|---|---|
| | *Percentage* | n | *Percentage* | n | *Percentage* | n | *Percentage* | n | *Percentage* | n |
| Total employees | — | 93 | — | 116 | — | 133 | — | 141 | — | 198 |
| Black | 18 | 17 | 14 | 16 | 16 | 22 | 15 | 22 | 16 | 31 |
| Hispanic | 6 | 6 | 7 | 9 | 8 | 11 | 8 | 11 | 6 | 12 |
| Total (black and Hispanic) | 24 | 23 | 21 | 25 | 24 | 33 | 23 | 33 | 22 | 43 |
| Women | 51 | 48 | 55 | 64 | 54 | 73 | 58 | 83 | 56 | 111 |
| | | | | | | | | | | |
| Executives and department heads | | | | | | | | | | |
| Asian | | | 0 of 9 | | 0 of 11 | | 0 of 12 | | 0 of 21 | |
| Black | | | 0 of 9 | | 2 of 11 (18%) | | 2 of 12 (17%) | | 4 of 21 (19%) | |
| Hispanic | | | 0 of 9 | | 0 of 11 | | 0 of 12 | | 1 of 21 (4%) | |
| Women | | | 1 of 9 (11%) | | 1 of 11 (9%) | | 1 of 12 (8%) | | 2 of 21 (10%) | |

SOURCE: The data were provided by Major League Baseball's Equal Opportunity Committee.

50

**TABLE 5.2**  National Football League Employment Data

|  | 1993 | | 1994 | |
|---|---|---|---|---|
|  | *Percentage* | *Ratio* | *Percentage* | *Ratio* |
| Office management |  |  |  |  |
| White | 77 | 46 of 60 | 82 | 60 of 73 |
| Black | 18 | 11 of 60 | 15 | 11 of 73 |
| Latino | 3 | 2 of 60 | < 2 | 1 of 73 |
| Asian | 2 | 1 of 60 | < 2 | 1 of 73 |
| Women | 22 | 13 of 60 | 22 | 16 of 73 |
| Office support staff |  |  |  |  |
| White | 84 | 32 of 38 | 81 | 42 of 52 |
| Black | 10 | 4 of 38 | 11 | 6 of 52 |
| Latino | 3 | 1 of 38 | 6 | 3 of 52 |
| Asian | 3 | 1 of 38 | 2 | 1 of 52 |
| Women | 66 | 25 of 38 | 67 | 35 of 52 |

SOURCE: Provided by the National Football League office.

**TABLE 5.3**  National Basketball Association: Total Employees in the League Office[a]

|  | Professional | | Support | |
|---|---|---|---|---|
|  | *Percentage* | *Ratio* | *Percentage* | *Ratio* |
| White | 77 | 239 of 309 | 63 | 125 of 198 |
| Black | 20 | 62 of 309 | 25 | 50 of 198 |
| Latino | 2 | 6 of 309 | 8 | 16 of 198 |
| Asian | < 1 | 2 of 309 | 4 | 7 of 198 |
| Women | 47 | 145 of 309 | 59 | 117 of 198 |

SOURCE: Provided by the NBA league office.
NOTE: The NBA league data includes the league office, NBA properties, and NBA entertainment.
a. As of June 1994.

In the NFL, Deron Cherry with the Jacksonville Jaguars and William Simms with the Carolina Panthers became the only owners who are black. Both are part of multimember ownership groups. They join Dr. Norman Francis, a former part-owner of the New Orleans Saints, as the only three black owners in the history of the NFL.

Minoru Arakawa, as a partner in the investment group that purchased the Seattle Mariners, became a limited partner in ownership on July 1, 1992. The majority owner, Hiroshi Yamauchi, resides in Japan and is the only majority owner of a pro sports team who lives outside the United States or Canada.

The Equal Opportunity Committee for Major League Baseball reports that there are currently 6 minority owners-limited partners and 31 female owners-

**TABLE 5.4** Team Ownership for 1994

|  | NBA (%) | NFL (%) | MLB (%) |
|---|---|---|---|
| Majority owners (primary owner) | | | |
| White | 100 | 100 | 96 |
| Japanese | 0 | 0 | 4 |
| Women | 0 | 3 | 4 |
| Total owners (includes majority and limited partners) | | | |
| White | 94 | 96 | 97 |
| Black | 4 | 4 | 1 |
| Latino | 2 | 0 | 0 |
| Asian | 0 | 0 | 1 |
| Japanese | 0 | 0 | 1 |
| Women | 7 | 12 | 9 |

limited partners. Considering that there are 28 teams in Major League Baseball, these numbers are significant. Unfortunately, the committee is unable to identify the total number of owners-limited partners in the league. Thus, comparisons that provide perspective cannot be made.

Pam Shriver, who is part of the 24-member group that purchased the Baltimore Orioles, is one of the few female owners in professional sports who attained limited-partner status through a purchase in 1993-94. She is neither a relative of the majority owner nor the member of a family-owned team.

Meanwhile, women have ownership interest in excess of 5% of seven NBA teams; in all cases, the woman is a relative of the majority owner or a member of the family who owns the team. Marge Schott (Cincinnati Reds) and Georgia Frontiere (Los Angeles Rams—as of 1995, the St. Louis Rams) are the only female majority owners-senior partners in the three leagues. The NBA has no female majority owners or senior partners.

It should be noted that few teams in any of the three leagues are owned entirely by one person. Predominantly, franchises are owned by groups of investors, ranging in number from 2 to 25. Typically, teams owned by a group of investors designate one individual who functions as the CEO of the organization. Although the CEO is identified as "the owner," he or she is not necessarily a majority owner or senior partner.

## TOP MANAGEMENT

Currently, no minorities act as chairman of the board, president, or CEO of any team in any league. Three women occupy these positions in professional sports (see Table 5.5): Marge Schott and Georgia Frontiere preside over

**TABLE 5.5**  Team Chairmen of the Board, Presidents, CEOs for 1994

|         | NBA (%) | NFL (%) | MLB (%) |
|---------|---------|---------|---------|
| White   | 100     | 100     | 100     |
| Women   | 4       | 3       | 4       |

**TABLE 5.6**  Team Vice Presidents for 1994

|                | NBA        |     | NFL        |     | MLB        |     |
|----------------|------------|-----|------------|-----|------------|-----|
|                | Percentage | n   | Percentage | n   | Percentage | n   |
| White          | 87         | 97  | 93         | 56  | 94         | 111 |
| Black          | 12         | 13  | 7          | 4   | 2          | 3   |
| Latino         | —          | 0   | —          | 0   | 2          | 2   |
| Asian American | 1          | 1   | —          | 0   | 2          | 2   |
| Women          | 3          | 4   | 6          | 4   | 1          | 1   |

their respective teams. Susan O'Malley, although not an owner, is the president of the Washington Bullets. In May of 1991, she became the first woman to be hired as the president of an NBA franchise. She is described as the club's top business executive.

Although no minorities function as chairmen of the board, presidents, or CEOs, there continues to be an increase in the number of vice presidents who are minorities (see Table 5.6). In the past year, Stu Jackson (Vancouver expansion team), Bill McKinney (Detroit Pistons), Earvin Johnson (Los Angeles Lakers), John Lucas (Philadelphia 76ers), Isiah Thomas (Toronto Raptors), M. L. Carr (Boston Celtics), Michael Huyghue (Jacksonville Jaguars), John Wooten (Philadelphia Eagles), and Jorge Costa and John Yee (San Francisco Giants) became team vice presidents. Presently, 12% of the vice presidents in the NBA are minorities whereas 7% and 6% of vice presidents in the NFL and Major League Baseball, respectively, are minorities.

Currently, more minorities are principally in charge of day-to-day team operations than at any other time in the history of sports. In the past year, Bob Watson of the Houston Astros became the first black general manager in Major League Baseball. Stu Jackson was named general manager and vice president of basketball operations for the Vancouver expansion team. John Lucas of the Philadelphia 76ers was named vice president in charge of basketball operations, general manager, and head coach. Isiah Thomas purchased part-ownership in the Toronto Raptors and was named team vice president in charge of basketball operations. M. L. Carr of the Boston Celtics

**TABLE 5.7** Principal in Charge of Day-to-Day Team Operations for 1994[a]

|         | NBA | | NFL | | MLB | |
|---------|------------|---|------------|---|------------|---|
|         | Percentage | n | Percentage | n | Percentage | n |
| White   | 69 | 20 | 86 | 25 | 96 | 27 |
| Black   | 31 | 9  | 10 | 3  | 4  | 1  |
| Latino  | —  | 0  | < 4 | 1  | 0  | 0  |

NOTE: Figures include the Toronto Raptors, the Vancouver expansion team, and the Jacksonville Jaguars.
a. General manager, director of player personnel, and so on.

was promoted to chief of basketball operations. Bill McKinney of the Detroit Pistons was promoted to vice president in charge of basketball operations. Finally, Michael Huyghue was hired by the Jacksonville Jaguars to oversee football operations as the club's vice president, and John Wooten was promoted to vice president of player personnel and operations by the Philadelphia Eagles. These additions result in 14 blacks or Latinos functioning as the principal in charge of day-to-day operations of a team in the three leagues (see Table 5.7).

## COACHING POSITIONS

There has been a decrease in the number of minority coaches since 1992-93 when a significant number of minorities were named as head coaches or managers (see Table 5.8). Despite the naming of Butch Beard (New Jersey Nets) as a first-time head coach in the NBA, no gains were made because Quinn Buckner (Dallas Mavericks) and Fred Carter (Philadelphia 76ers) were fired at the end of the season. Wes Unseld also resigned as head coach of the Washington Bullets. Neither Major League Baseball nor the NFL saw any of its teams name a new head coach or manager who was a minority even though there were eight vacancies filled between the two leagues since June of 1993.

As Table 5.9 indicates, 23 assistant coaches (32%) in the NBA are black—the highest percentage of the three leagues. The NFL has 75 assistant coaches (22%) who are minorities—indicating an 8% improvement over the past two seasons. Of the 51 offensive and defensive coordinators listed, 6 (12%) are black. This is notable because these positions are considered pipelines to head coaching posts.

After the 1993-94 season ended, the Arizona Cardinals (David Atkins), Los Angeles Rams (Chick Harris), and New York Jets (Ray Sherman) hired offensive coordinators who are black. With Sherman Lewis of Green Bay,

**TABLE 5.8**  Head Coaches and Managers

|  | NBA[a] | | | NFL | | | MLB | | |
|---|---|---|---|---|---|---|---|---|---|
|  | Season | Percentage | n | Season | Percentage | n | Season | Percentage | n |
| White | 1988-89 | 80 | 20 | 1988 | 100 | 28 | 1989 | 96 | 27 |
| Black |  | 20 | 5 |  | — | 0 |  | 4 | 1 |
| White | 1989-90 | 78 | 21 | 1989 | 96 | 27 | 1990 | 96 | 27 |
| Black |  | 22 | 6 |  | 4 | 1 |  | 4 | 1 |
| White | 1990-91 | 78 | 21 | 1990 | 96 | 27 | 1991 | 93 | 26 |
| Black |  | 22 | 6 |  | 4 | 1 |  | 7 | 2 |
| White | 1991-92 | 93 | 25 | 1991 | 93 | 26 | 1992 | 89 | 25 |
| Black |  | 7 | 2 |  | 7 | 2 |  | 7 | 2 |
| Latino |  | — | 0 |  | — | 0 |  | 4 | 1 |
| White | 1992-93 | 74 | 20 | 1992 | 89 | 25 | 1993 | 79 | 22 |
| Black |  | 26 | 7 |  | 7 | 2 |  | 14 | 4 |
| Latino |  | — | 0 |  | 4 | 1 |  | 7 | 2 |
| White | 1993-94 | 81 | 22 | 1993 | 89 | 25 | 1994 | 82 | 23 |
| Black |  | 19 | 5 |  | 7 | 2 |  | 14 | 4 |
| Latino |  | — | 0 |  | 4 | 1 |  | 4 | 1 |

a. Figures for the NBA reflect the hiring of John Lucas in Philadelphia, P. J. Carlesimo in Portland, Butch Beard in New Jersey, Bob Hill in San Antonio, and Bill Fitch for the Los Angeles Clippers.

**TABLE 5.9**  NBA and NFL Assistant Coaches and MLB Coaches

|  | NBA | | | NFL | | | MLB[a] | | |
|---|---|---|---|---|---|---|---|---|---|
|  | Season | Percentage | n | Season | Percentage | n | Season | Percentage | n |
| White | 1989-90 | 78 | 51 | 1988 | 80 | 197 | 1990 | — | — |
| Black |  | 22 | 14 |  | 20 | 50 |  | — | — |
| White | 1990-91 | 79 | 46 | 1990 | 81 | 208 | 1991 | — | — |
| Black |  | 21 | 12 |  | 19 | 50 |  | — | — |
| White | 1991-92 | 67 | 51 | 1991 | 84 | 289 | 1992 | — | — |
| Black |  | 33 | 25 |  | 16 | 54 |  | — | — |
| White | 1992-93 | 73 | 49 | 1992 | 80 | 264 | 1993 | 80 | 133 |
| Black |  | 27 | 18 |  | 20 | 65 |  | 13 | 22 |
| Latino |  | — | 0 |  | — | 0 |  | 6 | 10 |
| Other |  | — | 0 |  | — | 0 |  | 1 | 2 |
| White | 1993-94 | 68 | 48 | 1993 | 76 | 217 | 1994 | 78 | 126 |
| Black |  | 32 | 23 |  | 23 | 65 |  | 14 | 22 |
| Latino |  | — | 0 |  | < 1 | 2 |  | 8 | 13 |
| Other |  | — | 0 |  | — | 0 |  | < 1 | 1 |

a. MLB statistics for 1990, 1991, and 1992 were unavailable.

**TABLE 5.10** Total Number of Coaches[a]

|  | NBA | | | NFL | | | MLB[b] | | |
|---|---|---|---|---|---|---|---|---|---|
|  | Season | Percentage | n | Season | Percentage | n | Season | Percentage | n |
| White | 1989-90 | 78 | 72 | 1989 | 84 | 274 | 1990 | — | — |
| Black |  | 22 | 20 |  | 16 | 51 |  | — | — |
| White | 1990-91 | 78 | 67 | 1990 | 85 | 285 | 1991 | — | — |
| Black |  | 22 | 18 |  | 15 | 51 |  | — | — |
| White | 1991-92 | 80 | 76 | 1991 | 85 | 315 | 1992 | — | — |
| Black |  | 20 | 19 |  | 15 | 56 |  | — | — |
| White | 1992-93 | 73 | 69 | 1992 | 81 | 289 | 1993 | 80 | 155 |
| Black |  | 27 | 25 |  | 19 | 67 |  | 13 | 26 |
| Latino |  | — | 0 |  | < 1 | 1 |  | 6 | 12 |
| Other |  | — | 0 |  | — | 0 |  | 1 | 2 |
| White | 1993-94 | 72 | 71 | 1993 | 78 | 284 | 1994 | 78 | 149 |
| Black |  | 28 | 27 |  | 21 | 77 |  | 14 | 26 |
| Latino |  | — | 0 |  | 1 | 3 |  | 7 | 14 |
| Other |  | — | 0 |  | — | 0 |  | < 1 | 1 |

a. Head coaches, managers, and assistants.
b. MLB statistics for 1990, 1991, and 1992 were unavailable.

there are now four offensive coordinators who are black. The Washington Redskins replaced Emmitt Thomas as defensive coordinator leaving only two defensive coordinators who are black—Ray Rhodes in San Francisco and Tony Dungy in Minnesota.

There was a slight increase in the number of coaches who are minorities in Major League Baseball. Fourteen percent are black and 8% Latino (see Table 5.10).

## MEDICAL STAFF

Of the 173 physicians who work for the teams in the three leagues, 166 (96%) are white (see Table 5.11). It should be noted that in almost all cases, team physicians also have private practices. Since last year, the following physicians who are minorities were hired: Dallas Mavericks appointed T. O. Souryal, who is Indian, as senior physician. Dr. J. R. Zamarano, who is Latino, acts as a consulting physician to both the Dallas Mavericks and Dallas Cowboys.

Each team maintains one doctor as a senior physician or primary doctor. Most teams list a number of other physicians in their media guides, but for

**TABLE 5.11**  Team Physicians

|        | NBA | | NFL | | MLB | |
|--------|-----------|---|-----------|---|-----------|---|
|        | *Percentage* | n | *Percentage* | n | *Percentage* | n |
| **1993** | | | | | | |
| White  | 98 | 66 | 98 | 66 | 94 | 32 |
| Black  | 2  | 1  | 2  | 1  | 3  | 1  |
| Latino | —  | 0  | —  | 0  | 3  | 1  |
| **1994** | | | | | | |
| White  | 95 | 59 | 97 | 71 | 95 | 36 |
| Black  | 2  | 1  | 1  | 1  | 2  | 1  |
| Latino | 2  | 1  | 1  | 1  | 2  | 1  |
| Other  | 2  | 1  | —  | 0  | —  | 0  |

the most part, these doctors are used as consultants and are not employed by the teams.

Dr. Clarence Shields Jr. of the Rams remains the only senior club physician who is black. There are no black senior physicians in the NBA or in Major League Baseball. Other black doctors listed on the medical staff for a professional team are Dr. Norman Elliot, associate physician for the Atlanta Braves, and Dr. Joe Clift, internist for the Golden State Warriors. Robert Flores, who is Latino, is a consulting physician for the Oakland Athletics. He and Dr. Zamarano (Dallas Cowboys and Mavericks) are the only two Latino physicians working for a team in any of the three leagues.

At the league level, the NFL office employs Dr. Lawrence Brown, who is black, as the NFL adviser for drugs of abuse. The NBA retains Dr. Lloyd Bachus, who is black, as the medical director of its aftercare program. Although more blacks and Asian Americans are receiving professional degrees in medicine, they have not been able to secure positions as members of medical staffs in professional sports.

Professional sports teams continue to lag behind the national average of minorities who are employed as physicians. According to the U.S. Bureau of the Census (1992, p. 392), 3.2% of the physicians in the United States are black, 4.4% are Latino, and 20.7% are female. In the three leagues combined, 4% of the physicians are minorities and none are women.

As Table 5.12 indicates, there also continues to be great disparity among races in the position of head trainer. Although the Washington Bullets hired Kevin Johnson, who is black, as their head trainer, only 5 (6%) of the 78 trainers in the three leagues are minorities. In the past year, there was no change in the number of minority trainers.

**TABLE 5.12**  Team Head Trainers

|                    | NBA | | NFL | | MLB | |
|--------------------|------------|----|------------|----|------------|----|
|                    | Percentage | n  | Percentage | n  | Percentage | n  |
| 1993               |            |    |            |    |            |    |
| White              | 92         | 25 | 92         | 25 | 100        | 23 |
| Black              | 4          | 1  | 4          | 1  | —          | 0  |
| Other              | 4          | 1  | 4          | 1  | —          | 0  |
| 1994               |            |    |            |    |            |    |
| White              | 89         | 24 | 92         | 26 | 100        | 23 |
| Black              | 7          | 2  | 4          | 1  | —          | 0  |
| Asian American     | 4          | 1  | —          | 0  | —          | 0  |
| Pacific Islander   | —          | 0  | 4          | 1  | —          | 0  |

## ADMINISTRATION: FRONT OFFICE

Individual teams in the NBA and NFL verified our data regarding administrative positions. We relied on the report published by the Equal Opportunity Committee of Major League Baseball (Alexander & Associates, 1994) after the committee suggested that the individual teams would not respond. Jerry Reinsdorf provided additional information. The manner in which the committee classified employees is significantly different from the detailed breakdown that we produce for the NBA and NFL. Thus, it is not possible to directly compare Major League Baseball statistics to statistics for the other leagues. For example, the report by the Equal Opportunity Committee classifies all team employees as either "front office employees" or "on-field staff." This type of broad classification fails to distinguish between executives and receptionists.

Tables 5.13 and 5.14 were provided by Major League Baseball's Equal Opportunity Committee.

Our definition of *administration* includes but is not limited to professionals who work in business operations, community relations, finance, game operations, marketing, promotions, publications, public relations, and various other positions. Of administrative posts in the NBA, 16% were held by minorities, and in the NFL 12%, are held by minorities (see Table 5.15).

The position of public relations director is key because this person is responsible for disseminating information to the press. In this capacity, the director of public relations has the ability to influence the way the media portrays the players and, in turn, affects fan attraction. In the three leagues, only five public relations directors are black—three in the NFL and two in the NBA. Don Lowery (New England Patriots) and Rob Boulware (Pittsburgh

**TABLE 5.13**  Major League Baseball Front Office Employees

| | 1989 | | 1990 | | 1991 | | 1992 | | 1993-94 | |
|---|---|---|---|---|---|---|---|---|---|---|
| | n | Percentage | n | Percentage | n | Percentage | n | Percentage | n | Percentage |
| Total employees | 1,854 | — | 2,032 | — | 2,216 | — | 2,281 | — | 2,357 | — |
| Asian | 22 | 2 | 23 | 1 | 34 | 2 | 41 | 2 | 37 | 2 |
| Black | 163 | 9 | 182 | 9 | 196 | 9 | 212 | 9 | 223 | 9 |
| Hispanic | 88 | 5 | 100 | 5 | 122 | 6 | 127 | 6 | 150 | 6 |
| Total minority employees | 273 | 15 | 305 | 15 | 352 | 16 | 380 | 17 | 410 | 17 |
| Women | 700 | 38 | 778 | 38 | 850 | 38 | 907 | 40 | 894 | 38 |

**TABLE 5.14**  Major League Baseball On-Field Staff[a]

| | 1989 | | 1990 | | 1991 | | 1992 | | 1993-94 | |
|---|---|---|---|---|---|---|---|---|---|---|
| | n | Percentage | n | Percentage | n | Percentage | n | Percentage | n | Percentage |
| Total employees | 1,588 | — | 1,673 | — | 1,608 | — | 1,817 | — | 1,924 | — |
| Asian | 4 | 3 | 7 | 1 | 9 | 5 | 9 | 5 | 9 | 5 |
| Black | 102 | 6 | 100 | 6 | 106 | 7 | 128 | 7 | 146 | 7 |
| Hispanic | 207 | 13 | 217 | 13 | 189 | 12 | 227 | 12 | 276 | 14 |
| Total minority employees | 313 | 20 | 324 | 19 | 304 | 19 | 364 | 20 | 431 | 22 |
| Major league managers | | | | | | | | | | |
| Asian | 0 | | 0 | | 0 | | 0 | | 0 | |
| Black | 2 | | 2 | | 2 | | 3 | | 4 | |
| Hispanic | 1 | | 1 | | 0 | | 2 | | 1 | |

a.  Includes managers, trainers, scouts, coaches, and instructors.

**TABLE 5.15** NBA and NFL Administration

|          | NBA |  |  | NFL |  |  |
|----------|--------|------------|-----------|--------|------------|------------|
|          | Season | Percentage | Ratio | Season | Percentage | Ratio |
| White    | 1992-93 | 86 | 554 of 644 | 1992 | 90 | 426 of 475 |
| Black    |        | 11 | 68 of 644 |      | 6 | 31 of 475 |
| Latino   |        | 2 | 14 of 644 |      | 3 | 15 of 475 |
| Asian    |        | 1 | 7 of 644 |      | 1 | 3 of 475 |
| Other    |        | < 1 | 1 of 644 |      | — | — |
| White    | 1993-94 | 84 | 701 of 833 | 1993 | 88 | 544 of 615 |
| Black    |        | 13 | 106 of 833 |      | 9 | 58 of 615 |
| Latino   |        | 2 | 118 of 833 |      | 1 | 9 of 615 |
| Asian    |        |    |           |      |   |           |
|   American |  | < 1 | 5 of 833 |    | < 1 | 3 of 615 |
| Other    |        | < 1 | 3 of 833 |      | < 1 | 1 of 615 |

Steelers) were hired during the current off-season, joining Rodney Knox (San Francisco 49ers), Arthur Triche (Atlanta Hawks), and Travis Stanley (Sacramento Kings). The Center for the Study of Sport in Society is not aware of any people of color who are currently employed as a public relations director for a Major League Baseball team. Three NBA teams have women who work as public relations director: Julie Marvel of the Golden State Warriors, Julie Fie of the Phoenix Suns, and Cheri White of the Seattle Sonics.

The administrative position most frequently held by minorities is that of community relations director, who oversees efforts in geographic areas that often consist of a large minority population. Minorities represent 50% of the total number of community relations directors in the NBA and 31% in the NFL (see Table 5.16).

Only two persons of color are in charge of finances in the three leagues. The highest-ranking financial officer on a team is usually referred to as a controller, vice president for finance, chief financial officer, or treasurer. Only the Atlanta Falcons and the Washington Bullets have a person of color with one of these titles. Four NBA teams have women who hold the position of controller: Cynthia Wilsky of the Atlanta Hawks, Amy Fowler of the Los Angeles Clippers, Charlene Hodges of the Portland Trail Blazers, and Pinky Bacsinilia of the Washington Bullets.

Charles Grantham, executive director of the NBA Players Association, said, "While the statistics presented in the *Racial Report Card* are invaluable, I strongly disagree that any league deserves an 'A.' To me, an 'A' reflects excellence in the area of minority hiring and promotional practices, ownership, and participation in worldwide licensing opportunities" (personal interview, July 1994).

**TABLE 5.16** NBA and NFL Key Professional Position

| | NBA | | | | NFL | | | |
|---|---|---|---|---|---|---|---|---|
| | *White* | *Black* | *Latino* | *Asian* | *White* | *Black* | *Latino* | *Asian* |
| **1993** | | | | | | | | |
| Public relations director | 92 | 8 | 0 | 0 | 96 | 4 | 0 | 0 |
| Community relations director | 41 | 59 | 0 | 0 | 69 | 25 | 6 | 0 |
| Chief financial officer | 95 | 0 | 0 | 5 | 96 | 4 | 0 | 0 |
| **1994** | | | | | | | | |
| Public relations director | 92 | 8 | 0 | 0 | 89 | 11 | 0 | 0 |
| Community relations director | 50 | 46 | 4 | 0 | 69 | 25 | 6 | 0 |
| Chief financial officer | 96 | 0 | 0 | 4 | 96 | 4 | 0 | 0 |

**TABLE 5.17**  NBA and NFL Support Staff Personnel

|                  | NBA (%) | NFL (%) |
|------------------|:-------:|:-------:|
| 1992-93          |         |         |
| White            | 78      | 89      |
| Black            | 14      | 5       |
| Latino           | 5       | 3       |
| Other            | 3       | 3       |
| Women            | 71      | 78      |
| 1993-94          |         |         |
| White            | 79      | 89      |
| Black            | 12      | 5       |
| Latino           | 7       | 4       |
| Asian American   | 2       | 1       |
| Other            | 0       | < 1     |

## SUPPORT STAFF

We have attempted to distinguish secretaries, receptionists, staff assistants, and aides from professional staff. Our intention was to accurately portray the racial composition of personnel in different levels of employment. By combining support staff and top executives under the umbrella of "front office staff," it is not possible to distinguish between secretaries and department heads. For this reason, we have identified the categories of *top management* (chairman of the board, CEO, president, vice president, and general manager), *administration* (professionals working in the front office) and *support staff* (administrative assistant, receptionist, secretary, staff assistant).

According to team media guides, the percentage of support staff who are minorities in the NFL remained consistent with last year (11%). Of the support staff employees, 5% are black and 4% are Latino (see Table 5.17).

Both the NBA and Major League Baseball employ minorities in 21% of the support staff positions on their respective teams. For the NBA, this represents a 1% decrease from last year, whereas for Major League Baseball, it represents a 1% increase.

## MINORITIES PLAYING PROFESSIONAL SPORTS

Professional sport is a rare sector of the economy where minorities play a major role. This is especially true in the NBA and the NFL. This past year remained consistent with the trend of increasing numbers of blacks playing professional basketball and Latinos playing professional baseball.

**TABLE 5.18**  Racial Composition of Players

|  | NBA | | NFL | | MLB | |
|---|---|---|---|---|---|---|
|  | Season | Percentage | Season | Percentage | Season | Percentage |
| White | 1989-90 | 25 | 1989 | 40 | 1990 | 70 |
| Black |  | 75 |  | 60 |  | 17 |
| Latino |  | 0 |  | 0 |  | 13 |
| White | 1990-91 | 28 | 1990 | 39 | 1991 | 68 |
| Black |  | 72 |  | 61 |  | 18 |
| Latino |  | 0 |  | 0 |  | 14 |
| White | 1991-92 | 25 | 1991 | 36 | 1992 | 68 |
| Black |  | 75 |  | 62 |  | 17 |
| Latino |  | 0 |  | 2 |  | 14 |
| White | 1992-93 | 23 | 1992 | 30 | 1993 | 67 |
| Black |  | 77 |  | 68 |  | 16 |
| Latino |  | 0 |  | < 1 |  | 16 |
| Other[a] |  | 0 |  | 1 |  | < 1 |

a. Twenty-two Pacific Islanders played in the NFL during the 1992 season.

As Table 5.18 indicates, blacks represent 79% of the players in the NBA, replicating the 2% increase that took place in 1993. Meanwhile, there was a 3% decrease, from 68% to 65%, in the number of blacks playing football. This represents the first decline in the percentage of black players in the NFL since we have been tracking this data.

The number of blacks playing Major League Baseball increased for only the second time in a decade, whereas the number of Latinos continued to rise. In 1994, nearly 200 players (18%) are of Latino descent. This is the highest representation in the history of the league. The number of Latinos playing professional baseball is equal to the number of blacks who are playing. Combined, they constitute 36% of the players.

## STACKING[2] IN PROFESSIONAL SPORTS

When Charlie Ward of the Florida State Seminoles was not chosen in the 1994 NFL draft, it marked the first time in the history of the NFL that the Heisman Trophy winner went unselected. He had guided his team to a national championship, produced very good passing statistics, and demonstrated tremendous leadership skills on the nation's most prolific offense for the previous 4 years. The reasons cited for not drafting him ranged from inadequate arm strength to lack of height. In addition, many NFL personnel, including John Wooten and Dennis Green, publicly stated that teams were not sure he

**TABLE 5.19**  Stacking in the NFL

|  | White Players | | | | Black Players | | | |
|---|---|---|---|---|---|---|---|---|
|  | 1983 | 1991 | 1992 | 1993 | 1983 | 1991 | 1992 | 1993 |
| Offense |  |  |  |  |  |  |  |  |
| Quarterback | 99 | 92 | 94 | 93 | 1 | 8 | 6 | 7 |
| Running back | 12 | 8 | 7 | 8 | 88 | 90 | 92 | 92 |
| Wide receiver | 23 | 10 | 11 | 10 | 77 | 89 | 88 | 90 |
| Center | 97 | 89 | 76 | 79 | 3 | 10 | 19 | 18 |
| Guard | 77 | 67 | 62 | 64 | 2 | 31 | 35 | 32 |
| Tight end | 52 | 49 | 39 | 39 | 48 | 51 | 59 | 60 |
| Tackle | 68 | 60 | 50 | 51 | 32 | 31 | 46 | 47 |
| Kicker | 98 | 88 | 83 | 94 | 2 | 0 | 7 | 0 |
| Defense |  |  |  |  |  |  |  |  |
| Cornerback | 8 | 4 | 2 | 1 | 92 | 96 | 98 | 99 |
| Safety | 43 | 20 | 12 | 18 | 57 | 80 | 88 | 80 |
| Linebacker | 53 | 29 | 28 | 27 | 47 | 68 | 71 | 72 |
| Defensive end | 31 | 28 | 26 | 27 | 69 | 70 | 73 | 71 |
| Defensive tackle | 47 | 44 | 30 | 30 | 53 | 54 | 67 | 63 |
| Nose tackle | n.a.[a] | 42 | 35 | 42 | n.a. | 49 | 60 | 58 |
| Punter | 0 | 92 | 85 | 91 | 0 | 3 | 10 | 3 |

NOTE: Of all players in NFL, 65% are Black, 34% are white, 1% are of other ethnic backgrounds (Pacific Islander, Latino, and Asian American).
a. Not available.

would sign an NFL contract, in part due to his NBA capabilities. Therefore, teams did not want to jeopardize wasting a draft pick.

Despite the growing number of college quarterbacks who are black, only 7 of the 96 quarterbacks who played in the NFL last year were black. Of those 7, only Randall Cunningham, Warren Moon, and Andre Ware were starters. Furthermore, only 4 of the league's 68 backup quarterbacks are black.

The position of quarterback is not the only position in the NFL dominated by a particular race. Sociologists have demonstrated that words such as *intelligence, leadership, emotional control, decision making,* and *technique* are associated with positions such as quarterback and center. Furthermore, they have demonstrated the association of descriptive words such as *speed, quick reaction,* and *athleticism* with positions such as wide receiver, running back, cornerback, and safety.

It is worth examining the positions held by blacks and whites. Of the running backs, 92% are black, as are 90% of the receivers, 80% of the safeties, and 168 of the 169 cornerbacks. Meanwhile, whites make up 79% of the centers, 64% of the offensive guards, and 93% of the kickers and punters (see Table 5.19).

Major League Baseball has a similar disproportionate representation of white players in "thinking positions" and black players in "speed positions."

Out of 505 pitchers on major league rosters, only 34 are black. Furthermore, of the 90 catchers in the league, only 3 are black. Meanwhile, blacks, who compose just 18% of the overall players in the league, make up over 50% of the outfielders (see Table 5.20).

Jerry Reinsdorf, cochairman of baseball's Equal Opportunity Committee and the owner of the Chicago White Sox, said, "There is no stacking in Major League Baseball. All the owners are trying to get the best player they can get" (personal interview, July 1994).

The NBA is the only league where a traditional thinking position is now filled overwhelmingly by players who are black. During the 1993-94 season, five starting point guards are white: John Stockton, Mark Price, Bobby Hurley, Vinny Del Negro, and Scott Skiles. The percentage of point guards who are white (18%) is consistent with the overall percentage of guards in the NBA who are white (15%) (see Table 5.21).

Although officials from all three leagues continue to insist that there are no racial implications to the absence of blacks in positions such as quarterback, pitcher, and catcher, the thinking positions continue to be dominated by white players and the speed positions by black players (see Tables 5.19 and 5.20).

## CONCLUSION

Attention to the issue of employment opportunities for blacks and minorities in professional sports is at an all-time high. After a significant increase in the number of black coaches during the 1992-93 season, there were some notable advances for minorities in the area of top management during the 1993-94 season.

Although the overall number of blacks in senior positions of team management is still quite low in comparison to the number of blacks performing on the field, the inroads made in the past 2 years will greatly enhance future opportunities for other black players who wish to go into management after retirement.

Women, on the other hand, have few opportunities in the management levels of team front offices. Rarely is a female found in an executive position on any of the teams in the three leagues. On the other hand, the commissioner's offices in all three leagues have recently hired a significant number of female executives.

Obviously, there is need for improvement in the sports industry in the hiring of qualified women and minorities. With so much attention on hiring former players, it is easy to forget that there are many positions for skilled professionals on each team. Few are filled by minorities or women. The sports

**TABLE 5.20** Major League Baseball Positional Breakdown

| | White Players (%) | | | | Black Players (%) | | | | Latino Players (%) | | | |
|---|---|---|---|---|---|---|---|---|---|---|---|---|
| | 1983 | 1992 | 1993 | 1994 | 1983 | 1992 | 1993 | 1994 | 1983 | 1992 | 1993 | 1994 |
| Pitcher | 86 | 84 | 82 | 78 | 7 | 5 | 5 | 7 | 7 | 11 | 12 | 15 |
| Catcher | 93 | 87 | 87 | 86 | 0 | 1 | 1 | 3 | 7 | 12 | 12 | 11 |
| First base | 55 | 57 | 69 | 63 | 38 | 28 | 19 | 29 | 7 | 15 | 11 | 8 |
| Second base | 65 | 60 | 58 | 47 | 21 | 21 | 13 | 21 | 14 | 19 | 26 | 32 |
| Third base | 82 | 76 | 75 | 71 | 5 | 12 | 12 | 13 | 13 | 12 | 12 | 16 |
| Shortstop | 73 | 52 | 42 | 50 | 11 | 14 | 8 | 8 | 9 | 34 | 50 | 42 |
| Outfielder | 45 | 36 | 33 | 31 | 46 | 49 | 50 | 51 | 9 | 15 | 17 | 18 |

SOURCE: Compiled by Northeastern University's Center for the Study of Sport in Society. Based on 1983, 1992, 1993, and 1994 opening-day rosters as reported in the *New York Times*, *USA Today*, and team media guides.

**TABLE 5.21**  NBA Positional Breakdown

|           | White Players (%) | Black Players (%) |
|-----------|-------------------|-------------------|
| 1992-93   |                   |                   |
| Guard     | 17                | 83                |
| Forward   | 20                | 80                |
| Center    | 45                | 55                |
| Total     | 23                | 77                |
| 1993-94   |                   |                   |
| Guard     | 15                | 85                |
| Forward   | 18                | 82                |
| Center    | 42                | 58                |
| Total     | 21                | 79                |

industry continues to have little diversity in positions such as physician, attorney or team counsel, accountant, financial officer, and vendor. Again, the advancement of blacks into key influential positions will likely improve opportunities for other blacks to be hired in professional positions previously dominated by whites.

One major area of significant gain is baseball's use of minority and female vendors. Currently, all offices and clubs are using minority and female vendors or contractors. The league is committed to doubling the dollar amount of contracts with minority firms within the next year. In addition, the teams have been asked to attain the same goal with regard to female-owned firms.

Our goal in issuing the *Racial Report Card* is to keep professional sports responding to the fact that professional sports, which represent America's most integrated workplace for players, are not too much better than society in terms of who is hired for front office and decision-making positions. White males continue to control the management on most teams in spite of enlightened leadership in the league offices of the NBA and the NFL and on Major League Baseball's Executive Committee.

# APPENDIX A
## Glossary

### Terms Regarding Race

For the purpose of this report, *race* will be defined as a group of people united or classified together on the basis of common history, nationality, or geographic distribution—humanity made distinct by genetically transmitted physical characteristics.

Under race, the following categories will be included as defined by the Council on Interracial Books for Children (see DeRosa & King, 1987).

**Black:** People of African descent. For the purpose of this report, black athletes of African, Haitian, or any other nation will be identified as blacks. Although some would prefer to use the term *African American,* the authors recognize that citizens of Africa, Haiti, and other lands are not African Americans in the traditional sense.

**Asian American:** Refers to people of Asian descent living in the United States, including people of Chinese, Japanese, Korean, Indian, Vietnamese, and Cambodian heritage.

**Pacific Islander:** Refers to people from the islands of the Pacific, such as the Philippines, Tahiti, Indonesia, Samoa, and Tonga. Native Hawaiian Islanders are Pacific Islanders as well as U.S. citizens.

**Latinos:** Refers to people from North and Central America (such as Mexico, Guatemala, Nicaragua, El Salvador), South America (such as Argentina, Brazil, Uruguay), and the Spanish-speaking Caribbean (such as Puerto Rico, Dominican Republic, Cuba). The term also includes Chicanos (Mexican Americans). The term *Latino* refers to a shared cultural heritage (black, Native American, and Spanish), a history of colonization by Spain, and a common language (Spanish).

**Native Americans:** Refers to the descendants of the original people who inhabited North, South, and Central America prior to their conquest by Europeans.

**Whites:** Refers to people of European descent, including the English, Irish, Italian, German, Greek, Dutch, Polish, etc.

### Terms Regarding Employment Categories

**Administration:** The professional personnel who direct the affairs of business operations, community relations, finance, game operations, marketing, promotions, publications, and public relations.

**Coaching staff:** The positions of head coach or manager, assistant coach, and instructor.

**Front office:** A very general term applied to all employees who do not manage, coach, instruct, or scout the players. For the purpose of this report, the term *front office* is applied to those professional employees working in administration (business operations, community relations, finance, game operations, marketing, promotions, publications, public relations, and various other areas). It does not include those employees working in top management, coaching, or as medical or support staff.

**Majority partner:** An individual who owns more than half of the team or franchise.

**Medical staff:** The positions of physician, head trainer, assistant trainer, and dentist.

**Minority owner or limited partner:** An individual who owns less than half of the team or franchise.

**Owner:** Individuals who act as majority partner or limited partner.

**Principal in charge of team operations:** The person responsible for the day-to-day operations of the team, including player personnel matters, selecting draft picks, signing free agents, and hiring (and firing) the coaching staff. These duties may fall under any one of the following job titles— general manager, director of player personnel, vice president in charge of team operations, director of team operations.

**Support staff:** The personnel who assist professional personnel through the positions of administrative assistant, receptionist, secretary, and staff assistant.

**Top management:** The positions of chairman of the board, chief executive officer, president, vice president, and the principal person in charge of team operations (i.e., general manager).

## APPENDIX B

**Methodology**

Data were collected by a research team at the Center for the Study of Sport in Society. After acquiring media guides for the individual teams in each of the three leagues, a preliminary report was composed that listed the name, job title, and race of every employee identified in the team media guides.

The preliminary reports were sent to the respective teams in the NBA and the NFL for confirmation. Teams in both leagues were asked to edit our preliminary findings for errors, and they were invited to add personnel changes made after the publication of the media guide. Major League Baseball denied our request to send preliminary data to individual teams for confirmation. Instead, Jerry Reinsdorf, cochairman of the Equal Opportunity Committee, provided corrections and additional information. In addition to the individual team data that were collected, the commissioner's office in all three leagues provided data on league personnel.

A final draft report was then sent to each league office for feedback, verification, discrepancies, and comments. All three leagues responded with edits and those changes were incorporated into the text.

In addition, data were gathered from *USA Today's Baseball Weekly, USA Today, New York Times, Boston Globe,* and *Hispanics in the Major Leagues* as well as from various reporters from around the country.

### NOTES

1. See Appendix A for definitions of terms regarding race and employment categories. See Appendix B for a description of the method of data collection for the "1994 Racial Report Card."

2. "Stacking" is the over- or underrepresentation of certain racial or ethnic groups at certain positions in team sports.

### REFERENCES

Alexander & Associates, Inc. (1994). *Major League Baseball: Report of the Equal Opportunity Committee.* (Available from Major League Baseball, Commissioner's Office, 350 Park Avenue, New York, NY 10022)

DeRosa, P., & King, J. (1987). *Guidelines for selecting bias-free textbooks and storybooks.* Cambridge, MA: Multicultural Project for Community Education.

U.S. Bureau of the Census. (1992). *Statistical abstract of the United States: 1992* (112th ed.). Washington, DC: Government Printing Office.

# 6

## There Is Gold at the End of This Rainbow
### Jesse Jackson Steps Up to the Plate

Richard E. Lapchick

Just as a snowstorm in Washington chilled the city and brought it to a standstill, the Reverend Jesse Jackson stoked the heat for the 300-plus activists and sports personalities at a meeting of the Rainbow Commission for Fairness in Athletics. Jackson promised a plan to combat racism in sports, to address the overall pain of racism in our society.

Although his audience was moved to form the first organization with roots in the 40 cities with pro franchises, many sports fans across America wondered what the fuss was about. Many white men envy the status of black pro athletes whose fame and fortune are beyond their reach. That 75% of the players in the National Basketball Association (NBA) and 65% of the players in the National Football League (NFL) are African American and 17% of Major League Baseball players are African American and 14% are Hispanic shows that pro sports can't be racist. If that is all you see, it's easy to proclaim progress against racism in sports.

However, Marge Schott brought us back to reality with her stereotypical statements about African Americans and Jewish people. Sports took another look at itself and found that our sports hierarchy, an overwhelmingly white domain, has, with notable exceptions, kept its door shut to people of color. Although these exceptions make sports better than society, it is not by much.

In a nation where so many live in despair, the hundreds of black millionaires in sports create an illusion of fairness. But an objective examination shows that in society as a whole, there is a widening gap between African Americans and other minorities and whites. There are two times as many African Americans (12.6%) unemployed as whites (6%). Salaries for African Americans with college degrees are 75% of whites with college degrees. There are three times as many poor African Americans as poor whites. The

A version of this chapter originally appeared in *The Sporting News,* March 15, 1993. Reprinted by permission.

income gap between whites and African Americans has increased over the past 20 years. A higher percentage of African Americans lived in poverty in 1990 than in 1970. Simply by being born black, one is sentenced to live 7 fewer years than if one is born white.

Racism denies most African Americans and other minorities access to "the good life." Sports becomes the cruel illusion for too many African Americans who see the stars and the money. Of African American high school athletes, 51% believe they can reach the promised land of the NBA, the NFL, or Major League Baseball. In reality, only 1 in 10,000 will. Pursuing the dream, 25% leave high school functionally illiterate.

Of black college athletes who play football and basketball, 44% believe they will make it to the pros. Only 3% will. African American football and basketball players graduate at half the rate of white football and basketball players.

*The facts are indisputable.*

There is a huge difference in comparing African American athletes from high school to college. In high school, when compared with African American nonathletes, they have a higher grade point average, are more involved in extracurricular activities that are not sports related, aspire to be community leaders, and feel good about themselves. In college, they are culturally isolated, have a lower grade point average, rarely participate in extracurricular activities, and have virtually no involvement in the community.

What happens to reverse the profile? Most leave high schools where there are many African American students, faculty, and coaches. In the community, there are African American role models who are not athletes. There is a support network. Then they reach college where 6% of the students at predominantly white schools are African American. Less than 2% of the faculty are African American.

There is an expectation that athletic departments would have a better racial mix, but of the 1,218 coaches in sports that African American males compete in most—football, basketball, baseball, and track and field—only 52 are African American. Most of them coach basketball. There were no African American coaches in Division I-A football in 1992. There were three in 1993. Of 5,000 assistant coaches, fewer than 200 are African American. Mike Garrett recently became the sixth African American athletic director.

*The facts are indisputable.*

It takes a heroic effort for African Americans or Hispanics to graduate. Jackson promises that the Rainbow Commission won't forget the colleges.

Unfortunately, the media help white America maintain stereotypes of African Americans. The stereotype frequently presents athletes as criminals. These images are more common as more African Americans play sports. Only 14% of freshman graduate in 4 years. If an athlete doesn't graduate in 4 years, we call him a "dumb jock." Eighty-six athletes were reportedly charged with sexual assault in 1992, but 200,000 rapes were reported, and a million took place. Still, some media suggest that athletes are "more inclined" to commit acts of sexual violence than are nonathletes. There were 120 drug cases involving athletes, yet there are 2 million coke addicts. Can we really conclude anything about athletes and drugs? Of the 542,968 thefts in 1992, athletes committed 92. Should we look at athletes as potential thieves? We read so much about University of Washington football players carrying guns, yet 37% of Massachusetts high school students say they carry weapons to school. It doesn't say the athletes made good choices; it says being an athlete does not predispose one to being bad. But that is not the way the media always report it.

The problem of using the media as the filter on race in sports is difficult when you consider there are two African American sports editors on 1,600 daily newspapers, none in the 40 pro cities. There are six African American columnists, and 38 of 780 beat writers are African American; 90% of 1,600 dailies have no African Americans in sports. In 1991, of 60 CBS, NBC, and ABC producers and directors, 1 was African American; at ESPN, 4 of 38 producers and directors were African American; and of play-by-play announcers on the three networks, two were African American (Jackson, 1993).

Even for professional athletes, the sports world shuts the door at the end of their careers. In 1993, 11 of the 83 head coaches or managers are minorities; 91 of 373 assistant coaches in the NBA and NFL are African American. Of front office management and support staff in Major League Baseball, 9% are African American. That statistic has been consistent for 4 years.[1]

During the 1992 season, there was a smaller percentage of African American pitchers (5%) than there was in 1983 (7%). Of catchers, 1% are African American. During the 1992 season, 92% of quarterbacks were white. Sport calls these the thinking positions. Meanwhile, in professional football, African Americans made up 90% of the running backs, 89% of the wide receivers, 96% of the cornerbacks, and 94% of the defensive backs. Sport calls those reactive speed positions. Just as in corporate America, whites attribute brain power to whites and physical power to African Americans.[2]

*The facts are indisputable.*

But circumstances have changed, and the consciousness of society has been transformed. Despair has put communities on edge and on notice. After

Rodney King, what more was needed to prove how deeply racism permeates our society?

I am one of the many who credit Jackson for the courage and wisdom to create the Rainbow Commission. The indisputable facts cry out for it.

NBA Commissioner David Stern and NFL Commissioner Paul Tagliabue have made ending racism a high-profile issue for their leagues. Although there is a great deal that still can be done in the NBA and NFL, baseball has shown its failure to respond to racism. Marge Schott does not own this problem. Baseball owns it. Ultimately, society owns it. Yet the spotlight is on baseball, and the Rainbow Commission has let the owners know that they have until April 5—Opening Day—to put forth an acceptable plan or face action in their 28 cities.

I also give credit to Charlie Grantham, the executive director of the NBA Players Association, for forming the Coalition for Equality in Sports—a coalition to the players' associations in the NBA, NFL, and Major League Baseball with the NAACP, the Urban League, and the Southern Christian Leadership Conference to encourage players to speak out against racism in sports.

The pressure on baseball—and all sports—is the key. The most important fact is that most organizations rarely will open up because it is the right thing to do. Most will only change as a result of sustained pressure. The formation of the Rainbow Commission and the Coalition for Equality in Sports represents a two-pronged pressure point that could be an undeniable force in sports. If it is, then society will be better off for it.

## NOTES

1. See Chapter 5, "The 1994 Racial Report Card."
2. See Chapter 5, "The 1994 Racial Report Card."

## REFERENCE

Jackson, D. (1993, September 2). Muted voices in the newsroom. *Boston Globe*, p. 15.

# 7

## The Use of Native American Names and Mascots in Sports

Richard E. Lapchick

I can imagine Ted Turner the first time people confronted him about owning a team called the Braves that rallied around the Tomahawk Chop.

If I were Ted I would have thought, "Excuse me, but don't you know my credentials as a progressive figure in the world of sports? I brought the Soviets and Americans together for the Goodwill Games. Hank Aaron, baseball's most outspoken inside critic on racial issues, is a high-ranking executive for these same Braves. Communications is my field. CNN informs you. How can I be called racist?"

I could understand if that were his response. I was there. I played freshman basketball for the St. John's Redmen. My father coached the Redmen, and he was affectionately called "the Big Indian." He worked there 20 years and never had reason to question the nickname or the wooden Indian mascot.

That all changed late one evening in 1969 at Mama Leone's Restaurant, near the old Madison Square Garden. Whenever we were there to eat after a game, people would come up to my father to greet him, ask for an autograph, or sit down with him. This night started no differently until an older man who appeared to be in his late 60s, like my father, asked if he could join us.

As he sat down, he told my father how much he admired him as a coach and as someone who helped to integrate basketball. We smiled until he added that these things made it particularly embarrassing that my father coached a team called the Redmen and was called the Big Indian. This man was an Indian.

That was the first time that we had ever thought about what the Redmen meant. It began to conjure up memories of headlines: "Redmen on the Warpath," "Redmen Scalp Violets [NYU]," or "Redmen Scalp Braves

A version of this chapter originally appeared in *The Sporting News*, April 7, 1993. Reprinted by permission.

[Bradley]." The Braves even "hung the Redmen" once. Something was wrong with the picture.

Here was the man who helped integrate basketball being thought of as racially offensive. I was a fledgling civil rights activist in graduate school. Suddenly I understood when friends asked why I would associate myself with the Redmen. It came up for another 25 years until St. John's, like other universities that came to understand, rid itself of the Indian symbols and name.

Too many haven't. Forty-six colleges and universities and five professional teams use Native American names and symbols. Would we think of calling teams names such the "Chicago Caucasians," the "Buffalo Blacks," or the "San Diego Jews?" Could you imagine people mocking African Americans in black face at a game. Yet go to a game where there is a team with an Indian name and you will see fans with war paint on their faces. Is this not the equivalent to black face?

Although the thought of changing tradition is often painful, the sting of racism is always painful to its victims.

There are some who say that names are meant positively, that to be called a "Brave" is a compliment. Invariably, they are whites who think they know the attitudes of the people in question. There are even Native Americans who don't challenge that view.

Michael Haney is not one of them. Haney, whose mother is Lakota and father is Seminole, is a leader of the National Coalition on Racism in Sports and the Media. People say Haney does not represent the thoughts of all Native Americans. But there is no question Haney represents enough who call the names and symbols offensive that we need to listen.

I hope Turner will hear the chants outside Atlanta stadium and reopen the issue.

Urban America is falling apart, and we need to do all we can to heal it and become one people. We must recognize that anti-Semitism is not just the problem of Jews, that sexism is not just the problem of women, that racism is not just the problem of people of color. I hope we are more sensitive to words used to describe them.

The fact that history has ignored the incredible pain we have inflicted on Native Americans does not now give us the right to ignore their largely muted call. Turner has the power to make Haney and his people heard. Turner needs to bring us together with America's first people. We don't need him to bring us the news. He needs to make the news.

# 8

## Seated at the Table of Brotherhood
### Sports Transforms LaGrange, Georgia

Richard E. Lapchick

I knew I was doing a favor for some very good friends by driving to the airport at 4:45 a.m. to fly to LaGrange, Georgia, for a "civic luncheon." Driving back from the airport that night, I realized the favor had been done for me.

Logan Airport had been closed most of the day before with a snowstorm that pushed Boston past its snowfall record. I hadn't counted on the 20 minutes it took to scrape the ice off the car, and I barely made the 6:15 flight. Skimming along the icy roads, I felt I should be going to the office to catch up. But I wanted to do this for Ron Davis and Bobby Rearden.

The luncheon was to commemorate the "I Train in LaGrange" athletic facility, which grew out of discussions nearly a decade ago between Davis, Rearden, and Andy Young. If Atlanta were awarded the 1996 Olympic Games, these three men would commit to the establishment of a unique training facility. It would be for athletes from developing nations, especially Africans, to train somewhere in the United States.

Davis, a track star from Harlem, knows how sports dreams are made. Yet he knew the sting of racism after he sympathized with John Carlos and Tommie Smith's medals-stand protest at the Mexico City Games in 1968. Davis coached track in various African nations for the next two decades. But bringing some of those athletes to train in America and being able to come home for good would be special. He wanted to be near his elderly mother and father.

Rearden is a successful Georgia native and a man committed to improving life in the state. He helped bring the Olympic Games to Atlanta. LaGrange, population 26,000, is about 65 miles south of Atlanta. About 60% of the residents are white; the rest are black.

LaGrange was not known as a safe stopping point for civil rights workers in the 1960s. Some of the black leaders at the luncheon told me that they would not have gone to LaGrange during most of their lifetimes.

---

A version of this chapter originally appeared in *The Sporting News*, March 21, 1994. Reprinted by permission.

Young, former mayor of Atlanta, ambassador to the United Nations, and lieutenant of Martin Luther King, Jr., was the speaker. But before he got up, I realized I was in the middle of a social transformation. So did he.

Every community near an Olympics wants a part of the global happening. LaGrange is no exception. It is too far from Atlanta to be an official venue, so it accepted this seemingly strange piece to welcome mainly African athletes. This is a community where not long ago it was not easy for blacks and whites to appear together in social situations.

Two years and 50 athletes from 12 countries later, the day had come to show America what was happening. It was something.

I sat next to Young at the head table, gazing out in wonder at what we saw. There were about 800 people at the luncheon. There were Olympic athletes who collectively had won 18 medals. There were five athletes from the 1968 team, including Bob Beamon, who demolished the world record in the long jump in Mexico City. No one mentioned the symbolism as it gently settled on the audience. These were the athletic troops who were with the risk takers who stood up for what was right 25 years ago. I can only imagine the attitudes of whites in LaGrange toward them in 1968. Now the whites in the audience joined fellow black residents in a tumultuous standing ovation.

By day's end it was the people of LaGrange who were the celebrities. More than 100 local school children marched to Olympic music while carrying the flags of nations from every corner of the globe. A high school choir belted out the national anthem. The locals didn't need this luncheon to know what had happened in this town. It was for the outsiders from Boston and even Atlanta.

It is a time when our children are growing up with hate implanted in their hearts. It is a time when the global community seems more fractured than ever as seemingly peaceful nations become former neighbors' killing fields. But in LaGrange, residents have opened their community and their homes to people of other nations.

Young quoted an old religious saying about the spirit of God settling in to transform a people. He said he felt it there in LaGrange. I have frequently talked with audiences about the only three totally integrated events I had ever attended where I knew that people wanted, even needed, to be together. The first was when Nelson Mandela spoke on the banks of the Charles River in Boston; the second was Arthur Ashe's funeral; the third was Reggie Lewis' funeral. After the luncheon, I told Bobby and Ron that I would be adding a fourth.

As people were filtering out, Dr. Madvah Naik said, "God bless you, Ron. I have been in LaGrange for 22 years, and I never thought I would see this day. It is a new community where love can flourish. Thank you."

# PART II

# Gender in Sport

## Introduction

In 1972, Congress passed Section 901 of Title IX of the Education Amendments Act. It stipulated that "no person in the United States shall, on the basis of sex, be excluded from participation in, be denied the benefits of, or be subjected to discrimination under any education program or activity receiving Federal financial assistance" (Bartlett, 1993, p. 222). It took nearly 20 years for college sports to seriously address this attempt to establish parity between the sexes through legislation. Overall, it has not met expectations, yet it has served as a vehicle for women in athletics to pursue equal standing and oppose institutionalized sexism. It has taken litigation and the threat of further court battles to finally get the athletic community to confront the long-existing disparity between men's and women's college athletics. In 1993-94, 105,190 of the 295,174 National Collegiate Athletic Association (NCAA) student-athletes were women. That broke 100,000 for the first time but left women with only 36% of the total more than two decades after the passage of Title IX (Acosta & Carpenter, 1992).

Since the passage of Title IX, application of its tenets has been resisted most adamantly by those who argue it will "ruin college football." Traditionally, NCAA institutions have dedicated substantial proportions of athletic department budgets to football programs, including a disproportionate number of scholarships. Proponents for maintaining this imbalance suggest that it is warranted due to the superior amount of money generated by football. Just as this book was going to press, the American Football Coaches Association called for new congressional hearings on Title IX to eliminate its application to football or to remove the law's proportionality standard. These efforts were met head-on by advocates for gender equity.

Clearly, the way in which men and women's college athletics are distinguished goes far beyond budgets and scholarships. Perhaps one of the more dramatic examples of the different treatment extended to male and female college athletes is seen annually during the NCAA basketball tournaments held in March. Although the women's games present superbly skilled athletes and drama equivalent to the men's games, the women's tournament is scarcely available on national television. Whereas we must wait for the women on television at the Women's Final Four, the men's first-round games are broadcast nationwide. Networks often attribute this to the belief that Americans are far more inclined to watch competitive men's sports than women's games.

This presumption also contributes to a reluctance to form professional women's leagues. Although the best male college basketball players have professional opportunities awaiting them in the National Basketball Association, Europe, and the Continental Basketball Association, women who play college basketball are often competing for the last time at such a high level of organized competition. Basketball, as well as virtually all women's team sports, affords few opportunities as a paid profession. Rather, female athletes remain confined to American professional sports careers in individual competition such as tennis, golf, and figure skating. To play basketball, they must go overseas.

Despite failed attempts to incorporate women into leagues to participate in traditionally men's sports, high school athletics has witnessed a handful of instances where girls have gained membership on boy's teams. Furthermore, there have even been examples of girls successfully participating in male sports that have historically been considered "inappropriate" for women. Between 1993 and 1995, national media attention focused on high school girls who competed on various Texas high school football teams. In 1994, Angel Vandegriff from Norristown, Pennsylvania, became the nation's first girl to record victories against boys in wrestling—including two pins.

These rare cases forecast a challenge awaiting athletic administrators in the coming years. In addition to challenging society's norms, the participation by girls in traditionally male sports has caused some to question the propriety of girls and boys competing against each other in physically aggressive sports.

Some scholars have suggested that male athletes associate their views of masculinity with their participation in extensive physical competition that often includes accepted physical aggression. Likewise, defining manhood through participation in violent contact sports facilitates inferior images of women. The correlation between participation in exclusively male sports that reward violence and the formation of demeaning attitudes toward women has been identified by some as a contributor to off-the-field incidents of violence against women. The increasing scrutiny of male athletes who are allegedly involved in violent acts against women has led researchers to examine the contribution of aggressive sports to the violent treatment of women.

This section addresses many of these issues from different standpoints. Donna Lopiano offers a personal account of her experiences with male bias as both an athlete and an athletic administrator. Lopiano is the director of the Women's Sports Foundation, the cutting edge organization for increased sports opportunities for women. She has testified before Congress, contributed to sexual harassment policies for college administrators, and helped popularize women's sport as athletic director at the University of Texas at Austin.

While sharing her childhood aspirations to become a member of the New York Yankees, she chronicles the inherent obstacles that often discourage many women from reaching their full potential as athletes. Her chapter assesses the current status of women's athletics and draws on her experience to identify ways to improve opportunities for women in the future.

The "Gender Equity in Athletics Title IX Educational Fact Sheet" answers many questions about gender equity, especially as they relate to the controversy with football coaches.

Jackson Katz presents a provocative essay on the way in which the sports culture facilitates male supremacy. He focuses on the use of violence, military metaphors, sexist language, male hostility toward women's sports, and the power of male coaches as father figures. Katz is among the pioneering figures in the movement to make men aware of the destructive nature of gender violence. One of America's most sought-after speakers on this subject, he helped develop the first program in the country that attempts to get male athletes involved in stopping gender violence against women. The program, known as Mentors in Violence Prevention (MVP), is based at the Center for the Study of Sport in Society. MVP trains male athletes on college campuses to be leaders in this movement. In the process, MVP looks closely at the concept of masculinity, especially as it exists in the sports culture. The material for Katz's article is largely based on his own personal experiences, which include playing football.

Byron Hurt joined Katz in the MVP program after being Northeastern University's star quarterback. Hurt quickly emerged as a leading voice on black masculinity, both within the MVP program and in the community. He is currently producing a widely anticipated documentary film on black masculinity and has written extensively on the subject. Hurt's contribution to this book looks at his special area as it relates to the sports culture.

An article by the *Boston Globe*'s Alison Bass looks at the effect of MVP in light of recent research that suggests athletes are reported for sexual assault on college campuses more than other male students. Bass considers the views of numerous scholars on the subject of athletes and violence against women and assesses programs designed to use athletes as peer educators.

Richard Lapchick focuses on Houston Oilers' lineman David Williams who caused a controversy in 1993 when he missed a National League Football (NFL) game to be present when his wife gave birth to their first child. "David Williams and Family Choices," describes why the actions of Williams, although seemingly normal to many, were relatively unheard of for NFL players.

Debra Blum of the *Chronicle of Higher Education* contributes a stark look at the general failure by the NCAA to achieve gender equity in college sports programs. Looking at the disproportionate number of male athletes, male sports teams, and scholarships allotted to male student-athletes, Blum discusses the recent increase in Title IX lawsuits filed as well as the increased involvement of the Women's Sports Foundation to bring public attention to the resistance to fully comply with the law.

Finally, Richard Lapchick's "Eliminating the Battle of the Sexes in College Sport" examines how the struggle for gender equity is often manipulated by opponents into other political issues. He explains how some insinuate that advances for women will hurt African American student-athletes, thus dividing women and people of color when they could be a powerful united force. He also outlines how attempts to justify delays in affording equal opportunity along financial grounds are unfounded.

## REFERENCES

Acosta, R. V., & Carpenter, L. J. (1992). *Women in intercollegiate sport: A longitudinal study—15-year update, 1977-1992*. (Available from the authors, Brooklyn College, Brooklyn, NY 11210)

Bartlett, K. T. (Ed.). (1993). *Gender and law: Theory, doctrine, commentary*. Boston: Little, Brown.

# 9

# Growing Up With Gender Discrimination in Sports

Donna Lopiano

I never really wanted to be the executive director of the Women's Sports Foundation or the director of Women's Athletics at the University of Texas at Austin or a coach or teacher. From the age of 5, I dreamed of the day that I would pitch for the New York Yankees. And I didn't just dream. I practiced and prepared myself for that career. Every day after school, I would throw 500 pitches against the side of my parents' garage. By the time I was 10, I had developed a rising fast ball and an impressive curve that would drop off the table, and I was hard at work on a Bob Turley drop. There was no doubt that I was more than prepared to take the first step in the rites of passage to becoming a major league ball player—Little League.

I can remember the Saturday morning when I and a bunch of the "guys" on my street went to tryouts. We were nervous, but I knew that I was good. I remember my intensity—the serious way I threw the ball and swung the bat. I remember how good it felt trying to make my glove "pop" every time I caught the ball. I was drafted number one and was not surprised. I was bigger, faster, more coordinated, and simply better than all of the boys.

Imagine my excitement when we were assigned to teams and lined up for uniforms! My team colors were navy blue and white—Yankees colors! And we were getting real hats, wool baseball caps for which you had to know your head size—not those caps with plastic backs. Everyone knows how important uniforms are to little kids. Well, I was literally trembling with excitement. The moment ranked high as one of the best feelings of my life.

I was standing there, punching my hand into my glove, grinning, when a very tall father came to stand beside me. He held a rule book that was opened to page 14. On the right-hand side of the page were four words that would change my life forever: "No girls are allowed." For the first time in my life, I was told that I couldn't play with my friends. I was devastated. More disappointed rather than angry. I cried for 3 months and couldn't even bring myself to go to the park after school to watch my friends play the game I was supposed to be playing.

I didn't really get angry about this terrible occurrence until I was much older. You see, I had secretly rationalized that even if I were allowed to play baseball, I was too small to make it in the major leagues. I rationalized being satisfied with my status as an internationally recognized softball player. That is until Ron Guidry enjoyed his years of stardom as an all-star pitcher with the New York Yankees. Ron Guidry—5 feet, 10 inches tall and 170 pounds soaking wet. I have exceeded both of those parameters for most of my life. It was hard to take.

My second surge of anger came when I saw the film *A League of Their Own* and discovered the All-American Girls Professional Baseball League. My second rationalization was revealed. I had convinced myself that it was OK not to have played for the Yankees because, after all, no women had ever played baseball. It would be different if some women had had a chance to play. And they had.

My anger is not the volatile kind. It's the kind that stews under the surface for a long time. And its not really about not being able to play for the New York Yankees. It is all about someone's telling me that I could not pursue my dream, my most passionate belief about how good I could be and what I wanted to do in life. I am angry about the prospect of any child being told that he or she cannot chase a dream—cannot even try. I do what I do today because I do not want any little girl to feel the way I felt or to go through life wondering if she could have realized her dream.

Despite this early devastating experience with gender discrimination, I was more fortunate than most girls. At least I wasn't programmed by my parents to limit my dreams to gender-appropriate roles. I grew up with parents who did not know the meaning of sex role stereotypes. Not because they were not taught these stereotypes but because their aspirations for their children in terms of educational opportunity and success superseded any notion of traditional male or female roles.

The children of Italian immigrants, both of my parents experienced the subtle and not-so-subtle pains of ethnic and socioeconomic-level discrimination. The Great Depression prevented both of them from finishing high school and taught them what it was like to be without money and food. They had to go to work to support themselves and to help support their families. They viewed with envy those who had the resources to go to college. They viewed with envy those who could labor with their minds rather than their bodies. They both became obsessed with the importance and power of education rather than money.

Their view of a good life was not material wealth. It was clear that education was the way to gain the respect of your peers. Being a good person and being respected by your peers was the wealth they pursued.

Their lack of educational opportunity created a sensitivity about the importance of education. Their number one goal in life was to acquire the financial resources necessary to guarantee that their children had every educational opportunity. My father communicated this concern about the importance and necessity of education. My younger brother and sister and I heard about it every day: "You can have everything you want, as long as you go to college and get a good education." This obsession with education overshadowed any need to conform to a sex role stereotype.

Whereas my father's enduring influence was a focus on learning, my mother brought an equal gift to the table—a confident, "you can do anything" attitude. During World War II, my mother was part of the first wave of women employees taking the place of men in factories, earning good wages, and proving themselves the equals of men. My mom had "attitude"—the confidence of someone who knew she was good at what she did and could be self-sufficient rather than dependent on any other person. Although she probably didn't think about it at the time, she entered marriage and family life as a choice rather than as a preordained expectation or necessity. She transferred that confidence and independence to me simply by her example. I saw, heard, and felt her attitude every moment I was with her. To my mom, no task was too hard or goal too high that it couldn't be attempted and conquered. It was OK for me to aspire to be whatever I wanted to be. It was no accident that my first career aspiration was to be the first woman on the moon.

Both of my parents learned from working hard and watching others. After the war, they started a family with my mom staying home to take care of me. My dad worked from early morning to late at night as a waiter and kitchen help for low wages. He and my mom figured it out right away that if they both worked at their own business there would be a bigger payoff than working for someone else. So they started a restaurant.

They understood from experience that financial success meant freedom from all sorts of discrimination. They saw that in a capitalist society, financial success resulted in the people's respect for your achievement even if you didn't have an education. Achieving educational degrees in a capitalist society resulted in that same respect. Being educated increased one's prospects of financial success.

This understanding of the relationship between achievement, financial success, education, and respect was the root of their work ethic. When you were respected for your achievements, people didn't notice your ethnicity as much as they did when you had no visible demonstration of achievement.

To my parents, their children's educational success depended on reading books. My mother read to me all the time. We also did crossword and other word puzzles. So my life was filled with the adventure and joy of books. The oldest of three children born 5 years apart, I possessed both the junior and senior editions of the *Encyclopedia Britannica* by the time I was 7. I had hundreds of books and was a regular library worm. I can remember reading three and four books a day and loving every minute of it.

Reading was education. Good grades were education. All of these things were expected and rewarded: dollars for As, compliments for finishing books, applause for education. I learned to love learning because it was so rewarding. My educational achievements made my parents happy, so I wanted to do well in school.

All achievements made my parents happy—even sports achievements. My dad and mom loved sports. My mom played basketball in seventh and eighth grades, and she reflects on how good she was simply because she was tall. I grew up proud of being tall and of the advantages of size. My dad took me to Yankee games. I grew up on a street with 15 boys and only one other girl. Sports were an integral part of my life.

Although I could not pursue my dream of playing major league baseball, I was luckier than most girls. My parents found a softball team on which I could play. And it wasn't just any team. That team, the Raybestos Brakettes, was the most famous and well-supported women's softball team in the United States. At the age of 16, I played in the first world softball championships in Australia and completed a trip around the world. I saw Hawaii, New Zealand, Australia, Manila, Hong Kong, Taiwan, India, Tehran, Italy, France, Holland, Germany, and London. Few girls or women had such an opportunity. Because the college I attended was close to the town where I played softball, I was able to play with that team from 1963 through 1973, during both my high school and college years.

I decided to be a physical educator and coach and eventually an administrator because I loved sports. I wanted to stay close to what I loved to do, and I certainly loved teaching sports and physical education and, finally, administering those same sports programs. I never seriously considered another profession because of this passion for sports.

I went to a state teachers college to pursue my new dream of being a college coach well before college athletic scholarships for women were offered—a good decade before. As a national-caliber athlete in basketball and softball and a pretty decent field hockey and volleyball player, all of my national tournament competition occurred outside of school sports. My corporate-sponsored softball team played open amateur softball, and we stayed together to play open amateur basketball and volleyball, too. My finest hockey experiences came as a member of U.S. Field Hockey Association club hockey teams.

I was able to take advantage of these unusual opportunities for women of my era because my parents were successful businesspeople. I had my own car. I could afford to buy my own sports equipment and travel to practices that were often far away from my school. I was a member of the "advantaged" class. My parents were right. If you had the money, you could access your dreams. But I was also fortunate enough to be involved with one of the few teams in the country that received extraordinary financial support from a large corporation. With all the teams I played on outside amateur sports, from the ages of 16 through 26, I never played on the same team with an African American woman, although I did play against a few.

Until the age of 26, sports was my life. School came easy. I did school because I had to. I did sports during every waking moment because I loved to. What I learned in school was what I was told to learn. None of it was meaningful in the sense that I could identify with an experience that I had in reality. I did my student teaching as an undergraduate physical education major in the mid-1960s—well before I read my first feminist book, well before I intellectually understood the meaning of sex role stereotyping. I can remember conducting a softball game between my fifth and sixth graders and not giving it a thought that the girls wanted to be cheerleaders. I let them. I did not ask whether any of them had dreams of being softball players. I acted the same as all who came before me. I didn't question or push the envelope.

Apart from playing for the Brakettes, gender discrimination in sports lurked around every corner of my life. I wasn't allowed to play for my high school softball team unless I gave up playing for my outside softball team. Every job I held in educational sports, as a coach or administrator, paid me less than my male counterparts received. I knew, since entering the field in the early 1970s, that the chances of my ever getting to be the boss were slim to none. At Brooklyn College from 1970 to 1975, as an assistant professor of physical education, I started my career in athletic administration by volunteering for assistant athletic director duties. Eventually, I received release time for the assignment. I did this job in addition to coaching three teams and teaching two undergraduate and one graduate theory courses.

I was fortunate in that I became a "boss," an athletic director, during a curious one-time window of opportunity for female administrators that occurred during the mid-1970s. The regulations promulgating Title IX, a federal law prohibiting gender discrimination in educational programs, including athletics, had just been issued. High schools and colleges across the country were faced with the requirement of offering varsity sports opportunities for girls and women. Many university athletics programs were headed by football coaches who doubled as athletic directors. They didn't want to have anything to do with women's sports. They didn't value sports opportunities for women, and they didn't want to be saddled with the responsibility for developing or paying for them. They simply didn't need the extra work or burden of financial responsibility. At big-time football schools where the football coach-athletic director received whatever he wanted, this meant that the women's athletics programs were established as separately administered entities from men's programs and another athletic director was hired to run them. The University of Texas at Austin was one such program.

Only 29 years old, the university hired me on the strength of my educational credentials (an earned Ph.D. in athletic administration), experience as an assistant athletic director (which few women had), and athletic achievements, despite severe reservations that I was a very aggressive "Yankee." I remember going to my first football game and having an alumnus and major donor stand up and put his hands on my shoulders, saying, "Howdy, you must be Donna Lopinino [sic], our new director of ladies athletics!" Texans really didn't have much practice with Italian names. I responded that I was this person. He smiled and said, "My friend Lorene tells me that you are going to be a very reasonable woman." Lorene was Dr. Lorene Rogers, then president of the University of Texas.

Less than 3 weeks after being hired, I managed to get into a political maelstrom—although I wasn't aware that my job was endangered until almost 6 years after the fact. It was a great lesson in naïveté and having the right people step forward to protect you. It was also a great lesson in the power of knowledge.

It was a difficult time for women's sports, despite the existence of Title IX. Darrell Royal, the football coach-athletic director at the University of Texas was president of the American Football Coaches Association. He had just returned from Washington, D.C., where he met with another football crony who lived on Pennsylvania Avenue, then president of the United States, Gerald Ford. The headlines across the country read "Title IX and Women's Sports to Be the Death of College Football." Fear was rampant that the money required to develop women's sports programs would be taken away from football. John Tower, Senator from the state of Texas, had recently offered to Title IX the Tower Amendment that would exempt football and men's basketball from being included in the regulations. The effect of the Tower Amendment, were it to pass, would be to gut Title IX in that close to 80% of all athletic funds were being expended on these two sports.

One morning I received a call from an attorney in Washington, D.C., who was putting together a panel of experts in women's sports to testify before the Senate subcommittee conducting hearings on the Tower Amendment. This lawyer was trying to get ammunition to prove that exempting men's football and basketball and their budgets from Title IX calculations would relegate female athletes to half of the participation opportunities of men and perpetuate a system in which women athletes were given next to nothing to exist whereas male athletes were treated like kings. She was frantic because no college or university would give her their budgets for men's and women's sports. She informed me of her plight, and I told her not to worry. I knew Darrell Royal; he had just given me some great football tickets, and I was sure that he would give me a copy of his budget if I asked. I told her that I would call her back.

I trekked across campus to Darrell's plush offices (my office was in the old women's gym built in the 1930s) and asked if I could have a copy of his budget. He said, "Sure, just ask my secretary," and it was a cinch. I went back to my office and called the attorney to assure her that I would send both Darrell's and my budgets. Darrell's budget was a multimillion dollar affair that was 30 pages thick. My budget was 1 page. I believe the total budget was $70,000, of which $20,000 was my salary and $10,000 was our total expenditures on athletic scholarships. The D.C. attorney was speechless. There was a moment of silence before she asked, "How about coming to Washington to testify before Congress on how your women's budget compares to your men's budget?" I responded, "I would be honored." All I could think of was calling my mom and dad to let them know and thinking how proud they would be that their 29-year-old daughter would be testifying before Congress!

I did go to testify and I didn't lose my job. Fortunately, Dr. Rogers (president of the University of Texas) called me the morning I was to leave and told me to do two things that, as I found out later, enabled her to defend my actions. First, she said, you must make a courtesy visit to John Tower to explain to him that you are testifying as an expert in athletic administration and are not representing the views of the University of Texas at Austin. Second, she said, in your written and oral testimony, be sure to make the same disclaimer that you are an expert rather than representing the university. I did both things, and she was therefore able to defend my actions on the basis of free speech and the fact that I held a university lecturer appointment. University professors were always testifying before Congress as experts in various subjects, she was able to say.

Close call. As I look back on the experience, I recognize how important my education was. I had the Ph.D. I was qualified for a university faculty appointment and for my contract agreement as director of women's athletics. Being a faculty member afforded me considerable protection and was due to the respect in which my degree, my education, was held. On that occasion, the power of my education allowed me to do something that many others, older, wiser, and more politically adept, would have never attempted to do. Thank God for the ingredient of naïveté too.

Finally, what I learned in theory was "kicking in" because these concepts were finally becoming applicable to my experiences in reality. I had learned in the classroom that power was usually derived from three sources: knowledge, position, and authority. Knowledge is simple. You know more than anyone else about what you are trying to do. Position is simple too. Am I the boss or in a position to dictate or effect change because it is my area of responsibility? Authority is a little more subtle but not really. Do I have the power of money or influence? A good example is a football booster who gives $4 million to a university. Would the president listen to what he has to say about women's sports? I didn't need to be a rocket scientist to realize that the key to changing the world of sports and treating women equally would always be a matter of knowing more than those who didn't want women to be treated fairly. Getting into a decent position of power, even if it wasn't the top position, and getting the respect and support of people who are in positions of power and who have money and influence was the next important step.

My 17 years at the University of Texas as director of women's athletics allowed me to practice in this campus-level world of power. My current position as executive director of the Women's Sports Foundation lets me use those skills in a much larger and more powerful context.

On the college campus, the authority power group is relatively small—influential alumni, major donors, former trustees (current trustees carry influence by virtue of their current positions); those in positions of power at the level of vice president, president, and trustees are also few in number. In the national arena in which I am now playing, the big players are more numerous and both easier and harder to touch—easier in that I am not as easily blocked from influencing them with knowledge. Nationally, people get to be successful people because they are master students, eager to learn, and listeners, as opposed to local parochial power brokers who use their positions to prevent distribution of knowledge—sheer muscle to prevent getting to anyone's brain. Looking back at my campus days, getting to the right people was a task in and of itself. At the national level, powerful people are easier to get to but harder to deliver knowledge to because they have to deal with so much information that one needs the right time, place, and message as well as the right person to deliver it. So campus access to power is an issue of physical accessibility. National access to power is an issue of method of delivery, a much more subtle game—the difference between checkers and chess.

The higher you go in power structures, the more important it is to see the big picture. You need to see where you are going and be able to anticipate all the problems you will encounter along the way to get there. You also need to deal on multiple fronts with ever changing parameters. One of the most valuable exercises I ever experienced in my professional life was being involved in the development of "Twenty Challenges for the Next Twenty Years," a Women's Sports Foundation blueprint on how those committed to gender equity must act to give to those following in our footsteps and to ensure that no girl or woman will face unfair barriers to sports participation.

The twenty challenges are based on four simple hopes: (a) that our society will accomplish a basic cultural change toward full acceptance, support, and encouragement of girls and women who participate in sports and fitness so that there is no longer a contradiction between being a woman and being an athlete; (b) that we will value men's and women's sports and sports participants equally; (c) that all benefits and opportunities in sports and fitness will be equally available to men and women; and (d) that women will have learned how to use sports and fitness to enhance their health and well-being and that the contributions of participation in sports and fitness activities to their health will be better understood and recognized by all women. To translate these hopes into reality, all of us must work on a number of challenges.

*1. Role Model Responsibilities.* We must give direction to girls following in our footsteps by accepting our responsibilities as role models, conducting girls' sports clinics, and speaking to girls about the importance of sports participation and how much fun they can have playing sports. Young athletes will imitate us whether we want them to or not. We must know that our words and behaviors will be repeated by those who admire our achievements. Girls in particular are in need of female athletes, coaches, and athletics career role models because the print and electronic media do not regularly transmit these images. We must do more to encourage their participation in sports and sports-related careers.

*2. Parental Education, Support, and Example.* We must encourage all parents to introduce their daughters to sports and fitness participation at an early age, to understand the importance of participation by example, and to support the efforts of all girls and women in sports. All parents must be educated about the benefits of sports participation for girls and those factors that encourage girls to start and continue their sports participation. Parents must also know that their children will mimic *their* sports and fitness participation.

*3. Media Coverage and Images.* We must work to increase media coverage of women's sports, encourage more balanced coverage of men's and women's sports, and discourage sexist images and descriptions of female sports participants and the use of unrealistically thin ideal female images for promotional purposes. When girls do not see images of women achieving in sports, they do not envision themselves as sportswomen or believe that society values their sports participation. It is inappropriate for women athletes to be portrayed as sex objects in athletics settings or to be described in a manner that devalues their skill or participation vis-à-vis their male counterparts. Unrealistically thin women in advertisements create unfair pressures on females to be thin. Eating disorders are a serious problem in the general female population and especially in sports where there is an aesthetic value attached to thinness.

*4. Support the Sports Programs of Youth-Serving Agencies.* We must work to ensure that community-based, youth-serving agencies receive adequate financial support and make a special effort to increase girls' participation in their sports programs. Many children do not have the financial means to participate in sports or play in settings where sports participation is possible. If our children are not provided with the opportunity to play on sports teams or participate in similarly positive youth group activities, they will be more susceptible to involvement in gangs and other negative pursuits.

*5. Early Encouragement.* We must encourage others to give books about female sports heroes and sports equipment and apparel to girls at an early age and take boys and girls to watch women's sports contests. Children form values at an early age. Girls must know that sports participation is valued, especially when girl athlete images are omitted from traditional media (i.e., girl sports heroes in books, on television, and in newspapers). When girls see that only boys receive sports gifts and sports heroes are always men, they assume that sports participation is not as acceptable for girls as it is for boys and that there are no female sports heroes.

*6. Girls Playing With Boys.* We must encourage boys and girls to play with and against each other in fairly matched contests and competitive formats to encourage respect for each other's abilities. Although boys and girls should have separate and equal opportunities to participate in sports at the highest skill levels because there are real physical differences between genders, there must also be opportunities for males and females to play with each other.

*7. Homophobia.* We must oppose the use of homophobia to discourage girls from participating in sports. The negative use of the lesbian female athlete stereotype discourages girls from participating in sports and is offensive to both heterosexual and homosexual female athletes.

*8. Salary Discrimination.* We must support the principle of equal pay for equal work in the context of purses for professional sports events as well as salaries in sports-related careers and work to encourage corporate support of female athletes and women's sports. Women athletes and women in sports-related careers are still underpaid in comparison with their male counterparts.

*9. Professional Team Sports Opportunities.* We must encourage the establishment of professional sports opportunities for women in the United States. There are limited opportunities for talented female athletes in team and individual sports to continue playing at the elite level without traveling to Europe to participate on professional teams or to compete in individual sports. Professional athletes represent the dreams of young people who love sport. There must be women in these dreams.

*10. Amateur Sports Act.* We must encourage the U.S. Olympic Committee (USOC) and our national sports governing bodies to achieve gender diversity and equity in governance and participation opportunities. Few of our country's national sports governing bodies are currently in compliance with the 1978 Amateur Sports Act. This law requires nondiscriminatory sports opportunities for girls and women at the grassroots and elite level as athletes, coaches, officials, and administrators. The act also prohibits discrimination in the conduct of programs and contains a specific charge to meet the needs of women and physically challenged athletes through support and financial assistance and adequate representation on USOC and national sports governing body governance structures.

*11. Title IX.* We must work to ensure that schools and colleges provide female athletes with equal sports participation opportunities, equal educational opportunities funded by athletic scholarships, and the same benefits as male athletes. Few if any schools and colleges are currently in compliance with Title IX of the 1972 Education Amendments Act, which requires that women be provided equal opportunities to participate and receive the benefits of athletic participation in secondary and postsecondary educational institutions that receive federal funds.

*12. Concerns of Women Athletes of Diverse Races.* We must support the issues and concerns of women athletes of diverse races. Sports and sports-related career participation by women of color is significantly lower than for women in general.

*13. Concerns of Disabled Women Athletes.* We must support the issues and concerns of disabled women athletes. Sports and sports-related career participation by physically challenged women is significantly lower than for women in general.

*14. Employment Discrimination.* We must encourage women interested in sports to pursue sports-related careers and employers to hire more women in these positions. Women in sports-related careers experience employment and salary discrimination at every level and are significantly underrepresented in all sports-related careers. These women represent the future career dreams of many women who love sport.

*15. Right to Participate in All Sports.* We must support the rights of girls and women to participate in every sport, including those in which women have not traditionally participated (i.e., football, wrestling, and so on) and those that discriminate on the basis of age. There is evidence of the interest of mature women to stay involved in sports. All sports should consider the establishment of competitive divisions by age.

*16. Gender Testing.* We must oppose gender testing in sports if it is not done for both genders and if tests are invalid or inappropriate with regard to assessment of physical advantage. Society cannot impose a double standard on girls participating in sports by asking them to prove they are female whereas males go unquestioned. We must not continue to impose this unfair burden on female athletes, especially when gender testing is invalid and the results of gender tests inappropriate.

*17. Embrace a Healthy Model of Sport.* We must embrace and promote a sports model based on positive values in which all athletes and officials are treated with respect, achieving one's best effort is placed above the value of winning, athletes do not attempt to physically harm one another, and all players, spectators, and sports leaders demonstrate the highest standards of sportsmanship and ethical conduct. A significant decline in sportsmanlike conduct at all levels of sports and the valuing of winning over all other benefits of sports participation are well documented.

*18. Promote Research.* We must promote systematic research on the relationships between athletic and fitness activity and the prevention of physical and mental illness among women. Less than 3% of all research is done on women. Even less is done on the effects of exercise on the health of women despite clear indications from limited research that benefits are significant.

*19. Sexual Harassment and Unethical Relationships.* We must empower female athletes to be intolerant of sexual harassment and unethical relationships between sports leaders (i.e., coaches, administrators, and so on) and athletes over whom they have authority. Athletes, coaches, and other athletics leaders receive little or no training in the area of ethical conduct. Typically, inappropriate relationships between coaches and athletes are seldom reported and, when discovered, perpetrators go unpunished. Given the close relationship between athletes and coaches and the athlete's dependence on the coach for technical knowledge and emotional support, athletes are often confused about inappropriate relationships and too accepting of physical and emotional abuse.

*20. Nonuse of Performance Enhancing Substances.* We must oppose taking any illegal or banned substance that alters the normal functioning of the mind or body for the purpose of enhancing athletic performance. Taking such substances is a decision to cheat, endangers one's health, and encourages others to cheat.

I've grown up with gender discrimination in sports and have chosen to stay in an organization, the Women's Sports Foundation, that keeps me in the middle of trying to get rid of that discrimination. These 20 challenges will undoubtedly keep me busy. What has always kept me from being overwhelmed with the magnitude of the task of eliminating unfairness to girls and women who want to play sports is the realization that big change is really an accumulation of a lot of very small individual acts over time. I keep going back to the answers my mother used to give to my seemingly incessant questions and statements: "Mom, it's not fair." "Mom, could you do this?" "Mom, why can't I be an altar boy?" "Mom, why can't I play for the New York Yankees?" She would always throw the responsibility back on me while at the same time offering her assistance. "What can we do?" "How about you doing it." "If its not fair, what could you do about it?"

# 10

## Gender Equity in Athletics Title IX Education Fact Sheet

National Collegiate Athletic Association

**Access to educational sports programs, mandated by Title IX of the 1972 Education Amendments Act, is a critical women's health issue.**

Of all people with osteoporosis (brittle bones), 80% are female, and one of every two women over the age of 60 has osteoporosis. These are women who never had the chance to play sports and were never encouraged to play or be physically fit.

The combination of calcium plus weight-bearing exercise is crucial in the prevention of osteoporosis, a $15 billion per year health problem.

### Facts

- Eighty percent of all people with osteoporosis are female.
- Three of four women aged 35 to 74 fall below the recommended daily intake for calcium.
- Calcium intake is down because women are concerned about the fat content of traditional forms of calcium, such as milk and other dairy products. For the past 30 years, milk consumption has been dropping, and intake of diet soft drinks (with no nutrient value) has been increasing. The number one reason that women are drinking less milk is concern about fat content.
- Half of all Americans don't realize that skim and 1% milk have the same nutrients as whole milk but with little or no fat.

Girls who participate in as little as 2 hours of exercise per week significantly reduce their risk of breast cancer, a disease that will affect one of every eight women.

Reprinted by permission of the Women's Sports Foundation, Eisenhower Park, East Meadow, NY 11554.

Fact

- Participation in 4 hours of exercise a week, the minimum practice time of most girls' sports teams, reduces the risk of breast cancer by 40% to 60%.

Girls and women who participate in sports have higher levels of confidence, stronger self-images, and lower levels of depression. Sports is an investment in the psychological health of women. Legislators and the general public must press the OCR in the Department of Education to fully enforce Title IX. Schools and colleges are simply ignoring the law.

Facts

- Girls and women receive only 35% of all athletic participation opportunities and a third of all athletic scholarship moneys. Male college athletes are still getting $179 million dollars per year more than female college athletes.
- Parents are having to go to court to have their daughters treated fairly. Over 30 Title IX cases have been brought to court in the past 3 years, with the plaintiffs prevailing in every case. Yet the OCR has never asked the Justice Department to assist its efforts in gaining Title IX compliance at the high school or college level. Twenty years after the adoption of Title IX, few if any high schools or colleges are offering equal opportunity athletics programs.
- Most universities aren't close to being in compliance with Title IX according to 1992 facts documented by the National Collegiate Athletic Association (NCAA):

| Division I-A | Female (%) | Male (%) |
|---|---|---|
| Participation | 29 | 71 |
| Athletic scholarships | 28 | 72 |
| Operating budget | 20 | 80 |
| Recruiting budget | 16 | 84 |

**Because participation in sports provides significant benefits, it is important to oppose current efforts to (a) amend Title IX to eliminate application to football, (b) remove the proportionality standard, or (c) provide unnecessary protection for men's nonrevenue producing sports?**

We should not treat our daughters differently than we do our sons or maintain that the well-being of our daughters is not as important as that of our sons who play football. Football doesn't need any protection. It's a myth that football makes all the money to fund other sports. Football brings in more money than other sports, but it spends more than it makes.

Facts

No one is advocating that football be eliminated. The number of players on a football team can be maintained and football expenses reduced as long as all schools follow the same rules and expenditure limits. For example, even if football scholarships were reduced from the current maximum of 85 to 50, 50 full scholarships could be spread among 85 players, and moneys saved would permit institutions to add two or three women's teams.

- Some maintain that "football makes money and should get more support." There cannot be an economic justification for gender discrimination. We can't say that I can't afford to treat my daughter as fairly as I treat my son. We have to share.
- College football doesn't make money. It's a myth. Approximately 65 schools of 1,200 in the country have football teams that pay for themselves. Even in Division I-A, the big-time NCAA college football schools, 35% of those schools are running average annual deficits in football alone of $1.1 million a year.
- Everyone's tax dollars support athletics. All those people contributing to booster clubs for football are getting a tax break—a tax deductible contribution. We have to pay more taxes because of those tax deductions.
- At most schools, spending for football accounts for 40% to 50% of all operating dollars. If football is excluded from Title IX coverage, it will receive license to continue to spend more than it brings in, further exacerbating inequities in women's sports and resulting in more men's teams in other sports being dropped.

There is no validity to the contention that because women don't play football, football should be excluded from Title IX coverage. Title IX doesn't require that men and women have the same sports. Title IX recognizes that men and women have different sports interests. That's why Title IX requires "equal participation opportunities" and not the same sports. If 100 men want to play football, that's fine. The school can choose to have 100 women compete in field hockey, volleyball, and synchronized swimming.

Facts

- Few men play field hockey in this country, participate in synchronized swimming, or play as much volleyball as women. Should we eliminate those sports from Title IX?
- Approximately 500 high school girls are playing on boys' varsity high school football teams this year. Women have never been given the opportunity until recently to play football. Maybe there will be women's football.

The purpose of laws prohibiting discrimination is to bring the disadvantaged population up to the level of the advantaged population, not to make male athletes suffer as have female athletes who weren't given a chance to play. Boys' sports should not be cut in an effort to comply with Title IX.

## Facts

- Title IX requires nongender discriminatory sharing of limited financial resources, and there is great flexibility in what an institution can do to comply with the law. The problem is not that there isn't enough money; it's how we are choosing to spend our money. Schools should not be cutting men's nonrevenue producing teams, such swimming, wrestling, and gymnastics, when they are spending money on putting football teams in hotels the night before home football games. College presidents are afraid to tell football coaches to reduce spending, so they cut men's teams in other sports and blame gender equity. This is not right.
- Title IX's requirement that an institution should accommodate female students as well as it accommodates male students, the so-called proportionality standard, is only fair. Girls deserve the same opportunity to play sports as boys. Requiring girls to prove that they are interested in sports in order to receive the opportunity to play is a double standard. No one asks boys whether they are interested in playing.
- Research clearly indicates that boys and girls and their parents believe that sport is equally important for boys and girls. Girls simply aren't being given the same encouragement or opportunities to play. High school participation numbers reflect the same discrimination as college programs. Boys receive twice the opportunities to play as do girls.
- There will never be enough participation opportunities at the high school or college level to meet the interests of boys or girls. These opportunities are limited by what schools can afford. For example, there are approximately 200,000 men and 100,000 women participating on college varsity teams in the NCAA. These opportunities will never fully accommodate the needs of over 5 million boys and girls participating in high school athletics. The fairest way to parcel out limited resources and participation opportunities is to have athletic opportunities match up to general student enrollment.

## Institutions can comply with Title IX without cutting men's sports or damaging football.

## Facts

- The problem is that few school leaders practice fiscal discipline. Men are not losing participation opportunities because of women's athletics. According to the NCAA, participation slots for women increased between 1989 and 1993 by 10,000. But participation slots for men also increased by 10,000 during that same time period, giving them 65% of all participation opportunities in college athletics.

- Conferences, leagues, and the NCAA have not been willing to legislate expenditure limitations, lower scholarship limits, even require fewer games if that's what it takes to make sure that men participating in nonrevenue-producing sports as well as women get the chance to play.
- Sports at the college level is an educational enterprise, not a professional one. If football or any other sport wants to operate in the same way a pro sport does, then proponents of that approach must go into business outside of our educational system, and the sport should not receive the benefits of nonprofit status, such as tax deductions for boosters. All taxpayers support high school and college sports. Taxpayers have daughters and sons who deserve to be treated equally.

## Congress never intended to exclude football from Title IX, and that was not the purpose of the Javits Amendment.

### Facts

- On four different occasions, Congress has refused to exclude football or other revenue-producing sports from Title IX.
- The Javits Amendment stated that legitimate non-gender-related differences in sports could be taken into account—for example, the differing costs of equipment or event management expenditures. The amendment does not protect football because it has a higher number of participants.

## Encouraging exercise and the prevention of health problems is less expensive than treating disease.

It is important to support (a) public and women's health education efforts, (b) any legislation that would require daily physical fitness classes for all elementary and middle schools students in the United States, and (c) any bill or program supporting health research on women?

### Facts

- Only one state currently has a daily physical education requirement for grades K through 12 (Illinois). Budget cutbacks often hit physical education first.
- One of every four American children is obese (weight exceeds 20% over recommended weight for age). Obesity increases health problems and costs as the child gets older. Levels of obesity among children and adolescents have risen an average of about 45% between 1960 and the early 1980s.
- High school girls who play sports are less likely to be involved in an unwanted pregnancy, less likely to be involved with drugs, and more likely to graduate from high school.

# 11

## Masculinity and Sports Culture

Jackson Katz

When I was in sixth grade, the fastest girl in my class publicly challenged me to a race. I was the fastest boy. This confrontation would be our school's small contribution to the sports world's version of the "battle between the sexes," which peaked a year later in 1973 when women's tennis champion Billie Jean King beat the aging men's star, Bobby Riggs, in an enormously hyped showdown in the Houston Astrodome.

Before I won that race, I went through two grueling days of self-doubt and anxiety about the possibility that I might lose to a girl. It wouldn't simply have been embarrassing. It would have been devastating to my masculine identity. Being beaten in a physical contest by a girl, in my early adolescence, would have seriously damaged my emerging self-confidence. And my friends wouldn't have let me forget it.

Over the past generation, many other men have faced similar sports-related challenges to their masculine identities. This was, perhaps, an inevitable by-product of the revolution in women's sports. Sadly, the effects of these challenges on men have sometimes gone beyond damaged egos. Consider this recent case. According to press reports, in the fall of 1994, a 250-pound American arm wrestling champ lost a match to a woman in a bar in Tijuana, Mexico. He had never before lost. According to several patrons of the bar, the champ was a physically intimidating and rude man, and nobody "messed" with him.

Then, one night in September, a petite waitress challenged the champ to a match. Everyone thought it was funny. No one thought she could win, but she was serious. Whoever lost the match had to buy a round of beers for everyone. The woman won in less than 20 seconds.

Humiliated, the champ paid for the round of beers and had his picture taken shaking the waitress's hand. Then, as his friends mocked him for losing to a girl, he walked out, kicking a couple of chairs. His friends thought he had only gone out to drink a beer. But he never returned.

The big man had gone to his trailer, consumed two six-packs, and blown his head off with a 45. The bar owner said that everyone who knew him knows why he killed himself: He was too macho to bear the shame of losing to a "weak" woman.

Admittedly, this story is an extreme illustration of the power of sports in shaping male gender identity. But boys' and men's fear of losing to girls and women in athletic competition, and our sense of shame and inadequacy when we do, is too common to be dismissed as the mere insecurities of specific individuals. Rather, it is indicative of the importance of sports in our culture (and others) in defining, across class and race, what it means to be a man.

In recent years, a growing body of research and writing has explored some of the ways the sports culture helps to construct various masculinities. Since the early 1970s, feminist activists and theorists in sport sociology have been examining how women's lives are shaped by sports. They have focused specifically on how increased participation by women in competitive athletics has changed and will continue to change women's lives and influence cultural definitions of femininity.

Inspired by this work, a number of male (and some female) thinkers have focused on how the sports culture produces and reproduces both individual male identities and masculine hierarchies of power. Sociologists Don Sabo and Michael Messner have pioneered some of the important work in this field. But much remains to be done, both academically and in the world of sports-related social activism. The rest of this essay surveys a few key areas where the sports culture plays an important role in the construction of masculinities.

## COACHES AND MALE SOCIALIZATION

Sports contributes to cultural constructions of masculinity and reinforces male-dominant social and economic hierarchies in numerous ways. Consider, for example, the role played by organized sports in the socialization of young males. Some of this socialization is positive. Young boys learn important lessons from sports about perseverance, working hard to achieve goals, and the value of collaboration and teamwork. Unfortunately, they also learn powerful lessons about male superiority.

It is well-known that some coaches use female terms as put-downs to "motivate" young male athletes. When a coach says to his male players "Come on, ladies, let's move it," or "The way you guys are playing, you should be wearing skirts," he is powerfully reinforcing the ideology of male supremacy. The message is clear: Because being called a female is a slur, to be a woman is to be degraded. Even after nearly three decades of the modern women's movement, young boys in Little League or Pop Warner football are still routinely exposed to this sort of sexism. At an early age, they learn to equate femaleness with the undesirable qualities of weakness, fragility, and being a loser.

But they're not just learning these things about women. They're also learning to be ashamed of their own vulnerabilities. They're learning that to be "real men," they must negate and deny any feelings or traits that have been deemed to be "female." One of the roots of men's violence against women is not so much hatred of women, per se, as it is men's hatred of those parts of ourselves that have been characterized as "womanly." How can men respect in women what we've been taught (by coaches and others) to be ashamed of in ourselves?

Coaches are important teachers and male role models in the lives of young boys. Many young male athletes spend more time with their coaches than with their own fathers. Coaches and players sometimes develop a bond that can last many years after the player has moved on. Coaches often act as surrogate fathers, modeling a version of manhood to the young males who look to them for guidance and structure. This can be a positive experience when coaches are talented, progressive men. Some have children of their own and understand how to respectfully teach and mentor boys and young men.

However, many coaches are not good role models for young boys and adolescents. Some are young men themselves and cannot handle the responsibility of teaching and disciplining younger males. Some aren't mature enough or are otherwise incapable of providing a nonsexist model of masculine behavior. Few communities in this country rigorously screen male coaches for an enlightened consciousness about gender. Coaches are rarely required to have the ability or sensitivity to guide young males through complex shifts in gender roles catalyzed by the women's movement over the last 30 years.

Furthermore, the continuing popularity of the Lombardian ethic ("Winning isn't everything; it's the only thing") often creates pressure on coaches at all levels to win at the expense of other more socially responsible goals. Although a coach may be arrogant, abrasive, and distant—even psychologically or physically abusive—as long as he produces winning teams, he will likely be rewarded with popularity in the community, better contracts, and promotions. The message to his players is clear: Winning games is more important to being a well-respected and successful man than possessing less traditionally masculine qualities, such as empathy and gentleness.

## FOOTBALL AND THE CONSTRUCTION
## OF MILITARIZED MASCULINITY

Democratic societies require a certain measure of cooperation from the citizenry in order to pursue militaristic policies, especially to go to war.

Sending young men to war requires indoctrinating enough of them (and their families) into a militarized version of masculinity. The sports culture, and especially football, helps to shape this militarized masculinity.

Some coaches and athletic administrators have a military or police background. This is especially true of the older generation of coaches who predated the end of the military draft. My own high school football coach was an ex-Marine with the classic buzz-cut hair. He used to tell us we were boys playing a man's game and constantly used war metaphor in his coaching. During one season, after a key player was ruled ineligible, our coach said "When you're trying to take the hill, you're gonna lose some men on the way up."

Football games routinely include uniformed military personnel or color guards as part of the pre- or postgame ritual. During the 1991 Persian Gulf War, more than half the U.S. population was treated to a militaristic spectacle at halftime of the Super Bowl. Armed services advertisements appear disproportionately on televised sporting events and in male-oriented sports magazines. Sports announcers frequently employ military metaphors to describe events in a game or to lavish praise on exceptional players (e.g., "He's the type of guy you want to go into battle with").

In high school and college, football functions as a rite of passage into manhood analogous in some ways to military service (although it requires much less commitment and involves far less mortal risk). It also functions as a proving ground for further masculine achievement.

For example, after football season in my senior year of high school, a classmate who had already signed up for the Marines paid me a high compliment. We weren't friends. We came from very different ethnic and family circumstances. He was a tough kid from a socially marginalized clique. I was more of a mainstream jock. He was in the vocational and I was in the college preparatory program. One day as I walked past him in the school parking lot, he called me over. "You should really consider joining the Marines," he said. "You have what it takes." I was flattered. Although I had no intention of joining the Marines, I had proven to this hard guy, on the well-manicured grass of a small-town high school football field, that I had the necessary qualities to be one of the "few good men" who are the first to kill and be killed in armed conflict.

## SPORTS AND THE OLD BOY NETWORK

Over the past generation, feminists have been trying to dismantle some of the formal and informal impediments to women's equality in the business world. The symbiotic relationship between the sports world and the business world is one of the key informal barriers to gender equality in business.

Sport is big business in the United States. College and professional sports and their related industries make up a multibillion dollar enterprise. Many nonsports corporations have a financial interest in or do business with sports teams. In the male-dominated business world, sport plays an important role in facilitating and solidifying business and professional relationships.

The golf course is considered by many to be an ideal site for business meetings. Many corporations entertain clients and reward loyal employees in plush luxury boxes at major stadiums. There are thousands of sports bars, boosters clubs, and other fraternal organizations that organize around sporting events. In groups of men, knowledge about sports often has a tangible social and business currency. It provides an area of common interest, a topic for friendly discussion, and perhaps more important, a litmus test for membership in the "old boy network" of the business fraternity.

In this arena, women and men who have no experience with or interest in male sports are at a distinct disadvantage.


## SPORTS AND VIOLENT MASCULINITY

The sports and violence connection has deep historical roots. In fact, the term *arena* derives from the Roman custom of spreading *harena,* or sand, in the den of lions to soak up the blood of the victims. According to lexicographer Dr. Wilfred Funk, the term *harena* came to be applied to the amphitheater itself, which was usually sanded. Later, the word entered our language minus the initial *h* as arena.

In the modern era, in sports such as football, ice hockey, and lacrosse, the ability and willingness to hit opponents hard is virtually required of most positions. Basketball play, too, has become increasingly physical. Knocking out your opponent is the ultimate victory in boxing. Athletes who succeed at these sports (and some others) tend to be highly admired by their peers. In fact, studies have shown that being an athlete is still the foremost criterion for male popularity when judged by both male and female adolescents.

What this means, of course, is that some of the most respected adolescent and adult males are viewed in demonstrably aggressive and violent activities. These males help to provide a masculine standard against which all males judge themselves. Also, because violence is equated with masculinity, it is impossible, in the context of these sports, to be too violent. That would be like saying someone is "too masculine." On the other hand, if a male is not sufficiently aggressive, his masculinity is likely to be called into question.

It would be simplistic to suggest that playing or watching violent sports *causes* boys and men to be violent, either against each other or against women. But it would be equally naive to deny any connection between an institution as influential as the sports culture, which often glorifies violent masculinity, and the pandemic of violence committed by boys and men in the homes and streets of our country.

# 12

## The Image of the Black Male

Byron Hurt

The image of the Black male dominating American mainstream popular culture has, in essence, become a monolithic art form. Time and time again we see and hear strong Black males blatantly wearing their masculinity on their sleeves, displaying it as openly as they display their talent and skill. Many athletes and rap artists talk disparagingly about the hostile environment that has shaped their hardened consciousness. They boast how, with strength and courage, they survive the hard-core elements of their neighborhood. They tell compelling stories of growing up young, Black, and male in the "hood"—a place where masculinity is affirmed by acting tough as nails and staring death in the face. In most cases, courses in rational thinking and conflict resolution are not offered on the street. Lessons in fighting and the art of wearing a psychological "hard hat" are.

It's no wonder that you see a culture of young, gifted Black men displaying an impenetrable gaze, hard enough to make even death turn away and flee. The intimidating stare, the in-your-face dunk, and the Black male bravado of the 1990s has replaced the love and compassion, brotherhood and unity of the 1970s. For many Black men, it is a demonstration of power and control. Athletic arenas provide a major forum for Black males to claim their masculinity through the power of expression. In sports, the Black male can openly say, "Hear me; see me; this is who I am," in a way that is denied in almost any other profession or trade. In rap music, the hypermasculine machismo is the rapper's way of reclaiming the power that is lost the moment he finds out that being Black and male is different from anything else in America.

As a 25-year-old Black male and resident of Roxbury, Massachusetts, I see the images portrayed in the rap videos and athletic arenas carried out on the streets of Boston and the playgrounds in my home state of New York. I see Black males walking down the street wearing a hardness on their faces and masculinity on their chests. I see young men on the basketball court taunting opponents in a fashion that is exclusive to Black male culture.

Sometimes, when the situation calls for it, I do the same. It doesn't matter that I graduated from college and profess to "know better" than to participate in the game of acting tough and playing hard. I am a product of the same socialization process that makes it unacceptable for many men to let down their guard and back down from meaningless confrontation and senseless violence. The fear of being labeled "soft" or "weak" is too great. For Black men, a history of oppression and rejection has left us vulnerable and power-less. Living in a society that scoffs at male vulnerability makes it especially difficult for Black males to remove our psychological hard hat. Hence, the hypermasculine, rap-in-your-face dance-in the-end-zone phenomenon has become an essential element of the Black male persona. Fortunately for me, I have learned much about my own masculinity and what it means to be a man. I have dropped my facade of being ultratough and hypermasculine. I see its effect manifesting itself through masculine violence in the street and on the playing field. The recurring theme of life in the hood is getting old to me now, especially after surviving the saturation of an entire genre of blaxploited gangster movies—the Boy'z in the Hood era, if you will.

Many Black men in my generation, including myself, can relate to the films and rap songs that speak to the core of our reality. The words spoken about our environment in Black popular culture today are real and glaring. Disheart-ening as they may be and as glamorized as they have become, the feelings are real. Rap music in particular has become a voice to vent those feelings, and as a result, it has come under tremendous fire. Athletics has become the profession of choice for young Black males and consequently, the institution of sport is increasingly becoming vilified. In many aspects, it should. But I think critics of rap music are missing the warning signs being held by my generation of Black men. A cry for help is emanating from the mouth of an entire gender-specific culture.

In recent months, several rap songs, speaking of the days of yore, have raced to the top of the music charts. "Back in the Day," by newcomer Ahmad, and "Can It All Be Simple" by new rap group Wu-Tang Clan, along with Black popular culture's recent preoccupation with the lifestyle of the 1970s are two examples. Currently, they dominate the culture. Apparently, there were fewer drugs and less violence in the culture during the 1970s. The emergence of the Black middle class and the gains of the civil rights move-ment in the 1960s increased the possibility of opportunities for African Americans and gave our parents hope for the future. Spike Lee's, "Crooklyn" and Matty Rich's, "The Inkwell" both attempt to reunite today's popular culture with wholesome family values of the past. Could this be a time when the roughest and the toughest are desperately seeking refuge in the innocence of their past?

I believe we are pondering our childhood for a reason. Are Black males wearing psychological hard hats to camouflage the gut-wrenching turmoil and inner pain caused by the inner-city environment? If you listen closely enough, you'll notice that a new category of music has emerged. Let's call it "inner-city blues" music. The "harder than hard" mentality is an escape from our fragile, "softer than soft" emotions. Indeed, the acknowledgment of such sensitivities could be damning evidence against a hard-core rapper or a hard-core society, exposing all of the real feelings locked deep inside. Let's remember, these are all emotions God gave us to feel. But somewhere along the line, someone told us that showing those feelings wasn't cool.

I am concerned. I know there is more to my generation than the rough and tough image that has been glamorized and embraced by our culture. I know that there is more depth and breadth to our generation than Tupac Shakur or Snoop Doggy Dogg, two rap artists who remain celebrated in the face of criminal charges.

I love rap music. I am a part of the hip-hop generation. I love sports. I am a former college quarterback. But I am concerned about the facade being portrayed by rappers and athletes who are enthralled with proving their masculinity. False bravado, instant gratification, negative attitudes, and deviant behavior, for the most part, have replaced lost youth, lost innocence, and lost lives. Those attitudes are penetrating many of our young impressionable boys, sending the wrong message of what it means to be a man. Lyrics that condone the mistreatment of Black women infiltrate the minds of millions of young Black boys, contributing to negative attitudes and violence against women.

We are losing a generation—a generation that is misguided and confused, a generation of Black men struggling to make a way for ourselves, but we can't see the forest through the trees. Today's Black male rap musicians are the voices screaming for help. I know America hears our songs and enjoys our athletic prowess, but is anyone listening to our cries?

# 13

# How Jocks View Women

Alison Bass

After two college football players were charged with the brutal gang rape of a 31-year-old woman, a university official recalls, one of the young men commented: "What's the big deal? She's only a prostitute."

When he heard that comment, Dana Skinner, associate athletic director for the University of Massachusetts at Lowell, began to think there might be something wrong with the way his athletes viewed women. That's when he decided to introduce his football, basketball and hockey teams to a novel program designed to prevent sexual violence.

"I realized these players would probably think that any woman wouldn't be deserving of respect," said Skinner, a former basketball player and coach. Male athletes tend to see themselves as superior to women, "and there's a culture out there that encourages this."

Anecdotal evidence appears to support Skinner's observation. Every few weeks, there is a news story linking athletes with some form of sexual aggression: The West Point football players disciplined for groping female cadets is one example, as were the convictions for rape that sent the two UMass—Lowell football players to prison last year.

There is also a growing body of research that suggests a connection between sexual violence and male "cultures" that put women down to build men up. The latest study, released last month [November 1994][1] by researchers at UMass—Amherst and Northeastern University, found that varsity athletes at top-ranked National Collegiate Athletic Association (NCAA) Division I schools were significantly more likely to commit on-campus sexual assaults than other male students.

This chapter originally appeared as "How Jocks View Women: Old Issue Gets New Scrutiny," by Alison Bass, in the *Boston Globe,* December 5, 1994, pp. 39-42. Reprinted courtesy of the *Boston Globe.*

Specialists who study sexual violence are quick to note that only a small percentage of athletes are ever involved in sexual assaults, and not all agree that there is enough evidence to conclude that athletes are more likely to be involved than non-athletes. In the most recent study, only 15 student-athletes were reported for rape, attempted rape and unwanted intimate touching out of 107 perpetrators reported to the judicial affairs offices or campus police at 30 Division I schools.

Researchers stress that sexual violence has many causes. For example, a 1993 study that found a disproportionate number of athletes involved in sexual aggression revealed at the same time that several other factors are stronger indicators of who will engage in unwanted sexual contact or rape.

"There are more powerful predictors—alcohol use, nicotine use and personal feelings of hostility toward women," said Mary Koss, professor of family and community medicine at the University of Arizona at Tucson and author of that study.

Excessive drinking has long been linked with sexually aggressive behavior, possibly in part because it loosens inhibitions. Hostile attitudes toward women, sometimes shaped by abuse and domestic violence during childhood, also play a role. And smoking, though not itself a cause, can be a marker for other traits that Koss believes are linked to sexual violence. Students who smoke today often come from lower socioeconomic classes and tend to be risk takers.

Although athletic involvement is not the most potent predictor of sexual violence, Koss and others say the correlation is too strong to ignore. In the UMass study, student-athletes made up 3.3 percent of the male population but accounted for 19 percent of assaults reported to judicial affairs offices. (The researchers also analyzed sexual assaults reported to campus police but found that far fewer incidents were reported through this channel.) The percentage of athletes involved in reported assaults was slightly higher than average, a difference too small to be statistically significant.

In light of these findings, some specialists are calling for athletic officials, particularly those coaching the contact sports of football, basketball and hockey, to change the way they foster competitive spirit among their athletes.

"I think there's enough evidence out there to say, 'OK, we've got a problem. How do we fix it?'" said Todd Crossett, a professor of sports management at UMass—Amherst and lead author of the latest study.

Mary DeRosa couldn't agree more. Her teenage daughter was one of nine girls who were allegedly sexually assaulted or harassed by Gerard Thorpe, a star football player at Millis High School. Thorpe was arrested and charged in November 1993 with three rapes, intimidation of witnesses and various episodes in which he was said to have grabbed or fondled girls, sometimes in school hallways. Even though Thorpe was not allowed to attend classes, he was permitted by school officials to continue playing football and basketball for Millis High.

Thorpe, who is scheduled to go on trial for the sexual assaults this month in Dedham Superior Court, had previously been convicted of assault and battery with a beer bottle, court records show.

Mary DeRosa faults the culture of organized sports for encouraging Thorpe to be violent. She is even angrier with a culture that she says rallies around the accused athlete, rather than his victims.

"The school and the community were on the boy's side." DeRosa said in a telephone interview. "Everyone blamed the girls for this."

Because that happens often, women who are raped by well-known athletes are less likely to report the crime to police, says Veronica Reed Ryback, director of the rape crisis intervention program at Beth Israel Hospital. (Overall, the National Crime Victims' Research and Treatment Center in South Carolina recently estimated that 84 percent of all rapes go unreported.)

"It has been my experience that women feel more intimidated by high-status athletes precisely because they are seen as heroes on campus or in society at large," Ryback said. "These women are afraid of the publicity and the high-profile nature of the courtroom situation."

Their high profile, however, can also work against athletes says Kathryn Reith, a spokeswomen for the NCAA, because high-profile athletes are more likely than others to attract media attention when they get into trouble. As a result, the public may be left with an exaggerated impression of how often athletes are involved in sexual violence.

Some researchers agree that there is insufficient evidence to say that athletes are any more likely to rape than other men engaged in group activities.

"To me, sexual violence is clearly a problem of masculinity in our society," said Richard Lapchick, director of the Center for the Study of Sport in Society at Northeastern University. "I think that any time men get together as a collective group, . . . they would be just as likely to be involved as athletes in sexual assaults."

Several researchers say evidence is building that sexual violence can be fostered by organized sports and other male cultures whose core values are built around aggression and competition. Two published studies have documented a higher incidence of gang rape on campus by students on organized sports teams and in fraternities.

Sports sociologists Michael Messner and Donald Sabo say nothing inherent in sports makes athletes especially likely to rape. Rather, it is the way that competitive sports are organized to promote aggressiveness and male bonding.

"Central to this group dynamic is the denigration of anything feminine. And integrally related to this misogyny is homophobia," Sabo and Messner write in their new book, *Rethinking Masculinity*.

Byron Hurt, a 24-year-old former star quarterback at Northeastern who now co-directs a campus program aimed at preventing sexual violence, agrees. "One of the biggest insults you can give a young boy growing up is to say he throws like a girl," Hurt said. "That sort of putting down happens often for young boys, and that's where the whole notion of masculinity develops their negative attitudes toward women."

Calling a player who fumbles the ball "a skirt," or worse, is one of the ways young athletes define themselves as a distinct group, researchers say. In the process, they learn to treat females as dehumanized objects, rather than human beings with feelings of their own.

"Dating becomes a sport in itself and 'scoring,' or having sex with little or no emotional involvement, is a masculine achievement," write Sabo, a professor of social science at D'Youville College in Buffalo, and Messner, an associate professor of sociology at the University of Southern California in Los Angeles.

These attitudes are reinforced by the practice of segregating male college athletes—giving them their own dorms and having them eat at "training tables." Reith notes that the NCAA recently pushed through federal legislation making it illegal, as of August 1996, to house and feed student-athletes in separate facilities.

"This may have an effect on lessening the sort of sports culture Don Sabo and Michael Messner seem to be finding," said Reith, the NCAA spokeswoman. "I also think our member institutions should look at instituting programs on sexual responsibility and making them mandatory for student-athletes."

## NOTE

1. This study was recently published as "Male Student-Athletes Reported for Sexual Assault: A Survey of Campus Police Departments and Judicial Affairs Offices," by Todd W. Crossett, Jeffrey R. Benedict, and Mark A. McDonald, in the *Journal of Sport & Social Issues,* Vol. 19, No. 2, May 1995, pp. 126-140.

# 14

## David Williams and Family Choices

Richard E. Lapchick

Owners of teams talk the talk. "We are a family. We take care of each other."

Some teams are run that way. Apparently the Houston Oilers don't fall into that category. In case you missed the story, David Williams is the Oilers' $2 million-a-year offensive tackle who chose to miss a 1993 game against the New England Patriots in Foxboro, Massachusetts, so he could be with his wife, Debi, when they had their first child. Williams said, "I love football. But I have more in my life, and my family comes first."

The Oilers fined him $111,111—the equivalent of one week's pay—for missing the game. Williams, although surprised by both the team's reaction and the enormous public attention, did not challenge the fine but asked the Oilers to donate the money to a charity.

His offensive line coach said that missing the game was like missing action in World War II. Somehow it is difficult for me to equate World War II with the Patriots-Oilers game. But we do talk about games as war, teams as armies in combat, and coaches as generals.

Although many players were quietly sympathetic, others threw jabs at Williams by saying they and their wives planned pregnancies so they had their children in the off-season. That makes sense until you account for couples who become pregnant either by chance or because they are among the 1% to 2% of couples for whom birth control devices don't work. Or they may be among the 7% who have fertility problems and work incessantly to get pregnant at any time.

Family values. We heard about them over and over again during the Bush-Clinton campaign. Of course, it was a loaded and coded term for each camp. But underlining the debate was the fact that the family structure in America is in disrepair. The economy is bad, people are out of work. Men,

A version of this chapter originally appeared in *The Sporting News,* November 18, 1993. Reprinted by permission.

long identified with their work, feel they are having their masculinity challenged on many fronts.

Here is a man who stood up for his own family and, unconsciously, may have stood up for all men who want to say to the boss, "I love my work, but there will be times when I have to stay home to take care of my wife or my children."

Many men identify with football players. Maybe the Oilers' decision and the subsequent uproar will wake men up to see that being there with their wives at births is not only right but is also possibly the most wondrous experience one can ever have. Sport captures people's imaginations. Tragedies, triumphs, and controversies in sport have frequently been a wake-up call for the rest of us.

Think about it. How many stories did we read or hear about on TV concerning the 8 million gambling addicts in America? Pete Rose put those stories on page 1 and on the nightly news.

We called cocaine a "recreational drug" and virtually ignored America's 2 million addicts until Len Bias's death taught us it was lethal.

Stories about Ben Johnson forced us to learn more about steroids. We found that many of the steroids consumed in America are used by nonathletes under the age of 16 who feel the need to beef up their frail images of themselves.

Polite society thought that the AIDS plague was the property of gays and drug users. Then Magic Johnson and Arthur Ashe made it mainstream. If a million teen pregnancies a year from heterosexual contact didn't scare kids into using condoms, maybe our afflicted sports heroes gave them pause.

My own doctor told me that since Reggie Lewis's death, more of his male patients are watching their hearts and trying to reduce stress in their lives.

Obviously, none of these athletes chose to make a stand to teach us these things. David Williams wasn't consciously taking a stand when he went to the hospital instead of Foxboro. David Williams may be to real family values what Pete Rose has been to gambling awareness, what Len Bias and Ben Johnson were to drug awareness, what Magic Johnson and Arthur Ashe were to AIDS awareness, and what Reggie Lewis was to heart disease and stress.

The greatest difference, of course, is that the other examples were rooted in tragedy. The birth of Scott Williams is a daily celebration for David and Debi Williams.

# 15

## Slow Progress on Equity

Debra E. Blum

All the talk about achieving gender equity in college sports programs has led to little action.

More than 2 years after a survey by the National Collegiate Athletic Association (NCAA) showed that male athletes received the lion's share of sports opportunities and scholarships, a survey by the *Chronicle of Higher Education* found that little has changed.

The NCAA's survey of Division I colleges revealed that in the 1990-91 academic year, male athletes had outnumbered female athletes by about two to one, and institutions gave roughly twice as much athletic scholarship money to men as to women.

The *Chronicle*'s survey of those same institutions' performance in 1993-94 found slight increases in the proportion of athletes who are women and in female athletes' share of athletics scholarships. But sports opportunities and grant money for women continue to lag far behind those for men, even though women made up more than half of the colleges' undergraduates.

### WHAT CONSTITUTES PROGRESS?

For some coaches, athletes, fans, and college-sports officials, the small gains represent significant progress. They fear that more rapid shifts would undercut support for historically strong athletic programs for men.

But for many, including women's-rights advocates who have been fighting for years for more and better athletics opportunities for women, the slow progress is insufficient.

This chapter originally appeared as "Slow Progress on Equity," by Debra E. Blum, in the *Chronicle of Higher Education,* October 26, 1994. Reprinted by permission.

The NCAA's survey was the first to examine the relative treatment of men and women's college-sports programs on a national level.

That survey, based on responses from 253 of the 298 Division I colleges in 1990-91, found that while women accounted for 50.3 percent of the students at those institutions, they made up 30.9 percent of the varsity athletes. It also found that the average Division I college had spent 30.4 percent of its scholarship money, 17.2 percent of its recruiting dollars, and 22.6 percent of its total sports budget on women.

Since the NCAA reported the data only in the aggregate, the *Chronicle* subsequently collected the survey information on an institution-by-institution basis (*Chronicle of Higher Education,* April 8, 1992).

The *Chronicle*'s new survey was intended to follow up on the progress of the colleges that provided information for 1990-91.

Of the 301 Division I colleges in 1993-94, 257 participated in this year's survey.

Last academic year, according to the survey, women made up 50.8 percent of the undergraduates and 33.6 percent of the varsity athletes at the average Division I college. Female athletes, the survey found, received 35.7 percent of the money spent on athletic scholarships.

Here are a few of the survey's other findings:

- Among the 181 Division I colleges that provided the information to the *Chronicle* in both 1990-91 and 1993-94, all but 22 gave proportionately more scholarship money to their female athletes last year than they had given four years before. All but 61 showed an improvement in the proportion of women among their varsity athletes.
- At 162 Division I institutions in 1993-94, the proportion of the scholarship money that female athletes received was the same as the proportion of female athletes in the varsity program, or greater.
- Last year, women received less than one-quarter of the athletic scholarship money at 23 Division I colleges. Women made up the majority of the student bodies at all but seven of those institutions.
- Women received the smallest proportion of scholarship dollars at Mississippi Valley State and Alcorn State University, which gave, respectively, 18.2 and 18.5 percent of their grant money to female athletes. The University of Southern Mississippi reported the lowest participation rate for female athletes: 19.4 percent. Also below the 21 percent mark were Alcorn State, Mississippi Valley State, and the University of Southwestern Louisiana.

Interpreting the findings and comparing the survey results from the different years must be done with caution.

In various years, for example, institutions may have counted the number of athletes differently. The squad size in one year could have included "walk-ons," while in the other year it might have included only scholarship athletes. Some colleges may have counted twice the athletes who participated in two sports; others may not have done so.

Adding up athletic scholarships is fraught with similar problems. Whether an institution counted athletes who were sitting out a year of competition but still receiving grant money, or included the financial assistance it gave out for summer school, for example, could have affected the results.

## DISPUTE OVER SIGNIFICANCE

In addition, even if unqualified comparisons of the surveys' results could be made, college officials dispute how significant the numbers are in the first place. They say it is useless to examine the figures without examining the entire sports program at each college. Indeed, some respondents sent their *Chronicle* survey forms back with letters or notes attached explaining their institution's plans for adding women's teams or for changing the way scholarships were awarded.

Geoffrey Bannister, the president of Butler University, wrote in a letter declining to participate in the survey that changes were under way in Butlers' sports program.

"At this point in time," he wrote, "publication of data on the current situation in 'snap shot' fashion cannot give proper account to the history and intentions of the institution in this important area and may unintentionally confuse our external constituencies."

Despite the possible flaws, comparing the surveys' results offers a rough approximation of how the situation for female athletes at colleges that play in the NCAA's top division has—or has not—changed over the last four years.

## STUDIES AND LAWSUITS

The time between the two surveys has been a busy one for gender equity in college sports.

After the NCAA released its study in early 1992, the association created a special panel to help individual institutions and the NCAA decide what they could do to further equity for women. Last year the new head of the U.S. Education Department's Office for Civil Rights announced efforts to beef up the agency's enforcement of Title IX of the Education Amendments [Act] of 1972, the law that bars sex discrimination by institutions that receive federal aid. And more and more female athletes and their coaches have filed lawsuits, claiming Title IX violations in their institutions' sports programs.

Given all the activity, Christine Grant, the head of women's athletics at the University of Iowa, finds the results of the *Chronicle*'s survey especially disheartening.

"There's been legal action, and a great many promises, committees, and panels, and yet the national picture is still as it is," she says. "Any progress has got to be welcomed, but I think the rate of change is totally insufficient, and my observation is that women have been too patient for too long."

Other college officials put a more positive spin on the survey's findings. They point to the many institutions where the proportion of scholarship money women received was greater than their representation among the varsity athletes. That, they say, signals a commitment to providing resources to women's sports.

Other officials say that athletics opportunities for women are probably improving at a faster rate than the survey results demonstrate. They say, for example, that while the proportion of female athletes at the average Division I institution had increased by only 2.7 percentage points from 1990-91 to 1993-94, it probably didn't take four years for that change to occur.

"The collection of data in 1990-91 was not the starting gun," says James J. Whalen, president of Ithaca College, who headed the NCAA's gender-equity panel. "I think many people will say that the improvements have been over a shorter period of time, that change has happened over the last 18 months. It will be very interesting to see the change after this year, because I think we're seeing the addition of more teams and the outcome of other changes that institutions have been planning."

## "THERE WILL BE NO EXCUSES"

Donna Lopiano, executive director of the Women's Sports Foundation, likens the past several years to the several years following the passage of Title IX, when colleges were debating what course to take in light of the new law. She says that such things as the NCAA's survey in 1992 and recent court decisions in favor of female athletes have renewed colleges' interest in assuring equity for women in sport. But, she says, it takes time.

"Think of what it takes to add even one sport," Ms. Lopiano says. "We're talking about higher education institutions that don't do anything without committees, studies, and more committees. A more significant progress ruler would be to do the same survey four years from now. By then, there will be no excuses."

The problem with measuring progress in any year, however, is not only that it's difficult to make comparisons but also that not everyone agrees on what ought to be measured. What the definition of gender equity is, exactly, and what Title IX specifically requires of college-sports programs remain hot questions.

One measure of Title IX compliance—but a controversial one—is "proportionality." Proportionality is achieved when the percentage of men and women on athletics teams mirrors the rates of men and women in the institution's undergraduate student body.

## THE SAFEST WAY

The Education Department's civil-rights office says that in the absence of proportionality, sports programs may prove their compliance with Title IX either by showing a history of continually expanding athletics opportunities for the underrepresented sex, or by satisfying the "interests and abilities" of that sex.

Proportionality does not require fixed quotas. But without hard and fast rules to test the other criteria, the courts and many institutions have decided that keeping the percentages of female students and female athletes in the same range is the safest way of complying with Title IX.

"I think we'd all feel better if we were at the magical comparable number," says Wally Groff, athletic director at Texas A&M University.

If Mr. Groff is right, many of his colleagues may be uneasy.

According to the *Chronicle*'s survey of Division I colleges, only 16 institutions had achieved proportionality in 1993-94. At those colleges, the proportion of female athletes was greater than, or not more than 5 percentage points below, the proportion of women in the undergraduate student body.

But, as officials at Western Carolina University will attest, the numbers don't always tell the whole story.

Western Carolina got a clean bill of health from the civil-rights office several years ago even though the proportion of women in the student body was more than double the proportion of female athletes. After a Title IX compliance review in 1992, the agency said that the institution's sports program "equally effectively accommodates the interests and abilities" of women.

In a "letter of finding," the agency noted that the university is located in a rural area, where the small number of high schools have too few sports offerings to be considered sufficient "feeder" programs for college athletics. The letter also pointed out that no female students at Western Carolina had expressed an interest in sports beyond what the institution offered.

Since the office's review, the university has added a women's golf team. Last year, women at the university made up almost 49 percent of the student body and just under 26 percent of the athletes.

"We are confident that we have met all the mandates of Title IX, but the question of gender equity may still remain," says Larry Travis, Western Carolina's athletic director. "Hopefully, in years to come we'll be able to do more for women as interests in sports on our campus grows."

# 16

# Eliminating the Battle of the Sexes in College Sports

Richard E. Lapchick

W omen's opportunities for participation in sports will continue to be an issue in college sports. It is long overdue, 21 years having elapsed since the passage of Title IX, the federal legislation that banned any discrimination against women—including in sports.

Women and girls have made some astronomical gains in those 21 years. At the high school level, there are nearly 2 million girls participating in athletics compared with fewer than 300,000 in 1972. In 1992, more than 96,000 women participated in college sports compared with 74,000 in 1982. At the college level, there are slightly more than an average of seven sports offered to women. In 1978, the year Title IX went into effect, there were fewer than six.

Most of the remaining news isn't so good. College sports didn't, or was unwilling to, go all the way in implementing the law. Otherwise, we could now have parity. We could say, "Amen."

By waiting, college sports is reacting to a series of court decisions that have favored gender equity. And by waiting, the only way to respond for most colleges is to cut men's sports to either create more opportunities for women or reduce the number of opportunities for men.

It has become a sports version of the battle of the sexes. Men who rarely talked about racial equity are saying the cuts in men's sports are going to hurt African Americans most because football is the primary target of those cuts, and 43% of football scholarships go to African Americans. Women versus men; African Americans versus women. Here we go again, pitting ourselves against one another.

A version of this chapter originally appeared in *The Sporting News*, January 3, 1994. Reprinted by permission.

Some of the remaining disparities indicate why this issue is so compelling. Over 90% of women's programs were directed by females in 1972. Currently, that number is a dismal 17%. The percentage of women coaching women's teams has declined from more than 90% in 1972 to 48% in 1992. Men's athletics still outspends women's athletics 2 to 1 in scholarship, 3 to 1 in expenses, and 4 to 1 in recruiting. Finally, the average number of men's sports per school offered today is nearly nine compared with seven for women.

I frequently speak to athletic directors. They all say the issue is a monster. Many say they believe in gender equity but don't see how they can pay for it without totally dividing their departments and devastating men's sports. A few simply don't believe women's sports should be treated as seriously as men's sports.

Either way, nearly all athletic directors say dealing with the issue is ruining the fun of college sports. I sympathize with them. Change invariably decreases the fun—at first. There was a feeling that "the public," that is traditional white male sports fans, wouldn't have cared to watch African Americans play sports or, later, that they wouldn't watch African Americans coaching sports. Instead, it has created an entirely new fan base, while keeping the white male fan.

We have already had the opportunity to see women's sports with a marketer's vision. It is no accident that Donna Lopiano is the director of the Women's Sports Foundation and one of the most persistent voices for gender equity in America. When she was in charge of women's sports at the University of Texas, the women's basketball team set NCAA attendance records— soaring from 23,000 in 1980-81 to more than 135,000 in 1988-89. She knew how to market a product at that level with a brilliance similar to that of the National Basketball Association's David Stern.

By marketing women's sports, we can create yet another fan base of women who might enjoy the games enough that they begin to support men's sports as well. Let male fans see topflight women's sports and they might become fans of what are new sports to them.

We are talking about how to finance a basic social right for women, when in fact, we now finance men's sports, very few of which make money. Clearly, college sports has higher purposes than just making money. We've got to stop defining it as women versus men or women versus blacks and men.

It is an opportunity, an investment in our future. Although it will cost money in the short run, in 3 to 5 years, I believe women's sports, well marketed and well packaged will bring money into the athletic departments so we can restore the cuts.

# PART III

# Athletic Uses and Abuses

## Introduction

The year 1994 presented the nation with two equally insightful yet disturbing reminders of the current dilemma facing many young black teenagers growing up in America. The film documentary *Hoop Dreams* and the book *The Last Shot: City Streets, Basketball Dreams* both chronicle the lives of youths in Chicago and New York who aspire to become professional basketball players. Having virtually no academic preparation for college and little experience outside of basketball, these young men invest their hopes in a game that can sometimes be a cruel business. These accounts epitomize what is wrong with a system that so heavily favors the institutions and not the young men who pass through them as basketball players.

The Center for the Study of Sport in Society was heavily involved with *Hoop Dreams*. At the request of the producers, the Center designed a curriculum to accompany the release of the film. The curriculum was piloted in the Boston area and has since been disseminated to different parts of the country.

Even as these two works were causing renewed public discussion on the education of high school and college athletes, two New England newspapers disclosed sensitive and highly controversial information relating to the academic standing of the players on the University of Massachusetts' men's basketball team. Preseason polls had the UMass team ranked among the nation's top three. By midseason, the Minutemen reigned briefly as the number one team in the country. Meanwhile, journalists questioned the legitimacy of the institution's academic standards required for the players on the team. The disclosure of poor grade point averages of individual team members raised ethical issues over privacy and the appropriateness of publicly disseminating the personal records of student-athletes.

John Calipari, the head coach, defended his institution's academic record regarding athletes by citing the admirable graduation rate of previous scholarship basketball players. These circumstances are an indication of why annual National Collegiate Athletic Association (NCAA) meetings have become dominated by discussion over Proposition 48 and Proposition 16 standards.

Many college presidents continue to advocate raising the required Scholastic Aptitude Test (SAT) scores, high school grade point averages, and core class requirements for incoming freshman student-athletes. On the other hand, some college coaches insist that raising the minimum required SAT score would unfairly affect minority student-athletes. Most coaches agree about raising core requirements and grade point averages.

As mentioned in earlier chapters, the appeal of competitive sport continues to grow rapidly. Sport is an integral part of our culture. Children aspire to be professional athletes more than any other occupation (Louis Harris & Associates, 1990, p. 15). Elementary children are aggressively courted by coaches from top high school teams as well as by the nation's leading colleges. Televised games and exposure to athletes are at an all-time high. For example, the new NCAA television contract with CBS is worth $1.7 billion dollars. Money accompanying exposure can ultimately combine to present a tremendous potential for exploitation of individual athletes as well as harming the games' integrity. A significant number of student-athletes complete their 4 years of eligibility and leave school without a degree.

Extreme arguments, such as abolishing the notion of "student-athlete" and merely paying college athletes, have continued to surface as a remedy for the seemingly conflicting combination of *student* and *athlete.* Clearly, the system has flaws and provides opportunities for abuse, but the suggestion to pay players is not an answer to ensuring academic integrity and would ultimately reduce educational opportunities for thousands of youths.

This section begins by providing a historical perspective of NCAA legislation intended to deal with academic standards for student-athletes. Stanton Wheeler, a Yale Law School Professor, discusses the status of intercollegiate athletics and its role in higher education. Focusing specifically on revenue-producing sports, he connects the numerous scandals in the early 1980s to the reduction in academic standards, increase in television revenues, the elimination of freshman sports, and the 1-year grants-in-aid for athletes.

Raymond Yasser's essay describes the legal ramifications of athletic scholarships. He projects the effect that the NCAA's proposed reduction in sports scholarships will have on the black community. He ends by offering a proposal that would reserve previous sport scholarships for the active recruitment of promising black students who are interested in pursuing law, medicine, engineering, and other professional fields.

The issue of academic standards has been one of the most volatile issues in high school and college sport. With so many saying that the term *student-athlete* is an oxymoron, Lapchick writes that the real oxymoron is the term *dumb jock*. The article "Academic Standards for Athletes: A Debate in Black and White" examines the various issues in the debate on academic standards and how the component on standardized tests has served to further polarize the racial issue.

The compelling accounts of Fred Buttler and Paul Moore—two former student-athletes who are African American—demonstrate both the negative as well as the positive potential for young men who are recruited to play college sports. Both players were functionally illiterate when they began to receive recruiting letters from colleges. Moore's coach, who happened to be a psychologist, took a special interest in Moore, had him tested and discovered a learning impairment. Moore enrolled in courses for the learning disabled, which ultimately helped him raise his reading level to that of an 11th grader before he graduated from high school with a 2.3 grade point average and 700-plus SAT score. He accepted a football scholarship to Florida State and graduated as his eligibility was completed.

On the other hand, Buttler entered and exited college as a functional illiterate. Having been allowed to slide through classes under the presumption that he would one day be a wealthy professional athlete, Buttler found no professional offers after using up his 4 years of college eligibility. He became a factory worker, was temporarily incarcerated, and ultimately slipped into obscurity. Stories like these have led some to advocate compelling universities to ensure an education to athletes through the scholarship agreement.

*Chicago Tribune* writers Ed Sherman and Barry Temkin present an article from their award-winning five-part series on the conflict between academics and sports in Chicago area schools. A growing phenomena in many of our nation's cities is for junior high school age boys to be recruited to attend powerhouse high schools with tremendous sports programs. Nowhere has this trend become more controversial than in Chicago. In particular, they look at the strain that demanding sport schedules put on academic studies.

This section includes another award-winning article that shows how an overemphasis on winning can cause athletes to lose perspective and engage in self-destructive behavior. The *Austin American-Statesman* studied eating disorders among student-athletes at the University of Texas in the late 1980s.

Despite the growing emphasis on winning, often at the expense of learning, a Lou Harris survey indicated that many high school athletes are receiving positive growth in other areas of their personal lives through sports participation. A synopsis of the Harris study, while portraying the unrealistic aspirations of high school athletes who believe they will become professional athletes, suggests a promising trend among students who recognize that sports can serve as a deterrent to drug use and alcohol consumption while promoting school success and involvement in the community and improving race relations.

This section closes with "A New Beginning for a New Century: Intercollegiate Athletics in the United States." This report summarizes the work of the Knight Commission, a blue-ribbon group of college presidents, public figures, corporate leaders, and leaders in college sport. It gives a formula for rectifying the historic abuses, emphasizing the need for presidential control.

## REFERENCE

Louis Harris & Associates, Inc. (1990, October). *High school students: Attitudes on human rights, community activity and steps that might be taken to ease racial, ethnic and religious prejudice.* (Available from the Center for the Study of Sport in Society, 360 Huntington Ave., 161 CP, Boston, MA 02115)

# 17

## Knowns and Unknowns in Intercollegiate Athletics
### A Report to the Presidents Commission

Stanton Wheeler

### EXECUTIVE SUMMARY

The Agenda for Reform of the Presidents Commission of the National Collegiate Athletic Association (NCAA) cites the need for sound information to guide a national dialogue on the role of intercollegiate athletics in American higher education. What makes this need all the more urgent is that, to date, much of the discussion and debate about athletic policy has proceeded through argument by anecdote, with each side's position illustrated by occasional examples but rarely by concrete evidence. Within this context, the Amateur Athletic Foundation of Los Angeles has attempted to review efforts to conduct systematic studies of intercollegiate athletics and to identify beliefs, knowns, and unknowns in the field. We commissioned 10 working papers summarizing the knowns and unknowns in the areas of competence of each of the authors. The papers were then discussed at a meeting that included the authors, the senior staff of the Amateur Athletic Foundation of Los Angeles, and a small number of invited guest commentators.

There are indeed some "knowns" about intercollegiate athletics, a principal one being that athletes in the revenue-producing sports of Division I football and men's basketball score much lower on the average than do nonathletes on a number of measures of academic attainment and are generally more poorly prepared than other students for academic life. But the central conclusion resulting from this inquiry is that existing knowledge regarding the conduct and effects of intercollegiate athletics is fragmentary. The subject of intercollegiate athletics is characterized by piecemeal studies, often conducted with samples of unknown representativeness and usually without the kind of access to institutional records that would provide accurate, high-quality data.

We realize that calls for further study and inquiry may seem futile or unnecessary to those who think they know the answers, but we are convinced that there are such significant areas of ignorance that the Presidents Commission should lend its authority to the launching of a comprehensive study of intercollegiate athletics. The study would require the careful selection of a representative sample of colleges and universities reflecting the various NCAA divisions and subdivisions. At each institution, the study would contain five separate inquiries.

1. *Financing of athletic programs.* This study would examine detailed financial data from the different institutions, along with a close examination within each institution of how money is handled for athletic programs and how both surpluses and deficits are allocated.

2. *Governance and administration.* This study would examine in detail the governance and management of intercollegiate sports programs on each campus: the role of athletic directors and their staffs, coaches, faculty athletic representatives, the admissions office, the development office, the board of trustees, the president, and the alumni and booster organizations. A core part of the study would address how the athletic department relates to the rest of the university.

3. *Life after intercollegiate athletics.* This would be a retrospective study in which student-athletes admitted to the sample colleges and universities in 1981 would be interviewed 7 years later. The central questions would be these: Where are they now? What are they doing? What role did intercollegiate athletics have in the process?

4. *Academic and social experiences of student-athletes.* This study would be based on interviews with and records of a sample of freshman and upperclassmen at the colleges and universities to learn how student-athletes compare with other students not only in the classroom but in relationship to all aspects of college life and in their efforts to prepare themselves for life after college.

5. *Academic support systems.* The goal of this study would be to document in detail the kinds of academic support and counseling programs available to student-athletes and to discern whether the academic counseling that student-athletes receive is helping them to improve as students or serving only to enable them to meet the formal requirements of eligibility for athletic performance.

Other studies would also be beneficial to the Presidents Commission and to national dialogue of the nature described in the Agenda for Reform. These studies would address the distinctive features and problems of historically black colleges and their athletic program, the precollege experience of the student-athlete, the state of women's athletic programs, the career lines and the pressures on coaches, the question of student representation and involvement in deliberations affecting them, and the question whether changes in the structure of NCAA deliberations are needed to improve the quality of its decision making. Some of the studies might be incorporated as part of the more general inquiry; others might be undertaken independently.

The success of such a comprehensive effort will depend heavily on the commitment of university presidents to the enterprise. The techniques for designing surveys, interviews, questionnaires, and other instruments for extracting data, as well as the tools of analysis are well developed and well understood. The central problem is gaining access to adequate data in the first place. Cooperation will be forthcoming if the presidents require it.

There may be many areas where the Presidents Commission can move ahead with proposed legislation without waiting for the results of these inquiries. But that does not mean the inquiries should be put aside. These inquiries should be thought of as core, baseline studies that will provide an anchoring point for future inquiries as well as a basis for action in 1989.

Implementation of such a set of inquiries will itself require careful thought and planning. The Presidents Commission will be helped by the fact that many of the needed talents are available on the faculties. A small advisory oversight group could work directly with those conducting the studies as well as with the Presidents Commission. The NCAA should be represented on such a body, and the studies should be designed to mesh, insofar as possible with ongoing NCAA efforts. A number of other organizations in higher education should also be prepared to lend their expertise.

Funding for such a comprehensive effort should come in part from the NCAA itself, but the conduct of intercollegiate athletics and its effects on higher education and on the public make it a problem of truly national scope. It warrants attention and help in financing by the nation's leading philanthropic institutions. Big-time intercollegiate sports has long been a part of the American way of life, but its excesses are now threatening the integrity of higher education. Solutions to such an important problem should be based on systematic knowledge rather than anecdotal evidence.


## BACKGROUND

Scandals and irregularities in intercollegiate athletics are hardly a new phenomenon. The NCAA was born near the turn of the century in an effort to regulate football, and the Carnegie Commission of 1929 noted with despair the corrupting influence of commercialized intercollegiate sports and called on university officials to take constructive action. Events of the past 15 to 20 years once again bring intercollegiate sports into the limelight, this time with the added factor of potential television revenues at a level vastly beyond the financial benefits available in the earlier eras.

The intercollegiate athletic scene began changing fairly dramatically in the major revenue-producing sports of football and men's basketball during the decade of the 1970s. During that period academic standards were made less stringent (i.e., the 1.6 "predictor" rule was dropped in favor of the 2.0 high school grade point average [GPA]), when freshmen became eligible for varsity competition, when athletes received 1-year grants-in-aid with the possibility that they might not be renewed, and when the monetary payoff from TV for having very successful, big-time programs became a force producing ever greater pressures—pressures to expand the number of coaches, the number of athletic grants-in-aid, the playing schedules and practice periods, and perhaps especially the pressure to recruit athletic talent without serious regard for the athlete's interest in or readiness for higher education. Pressures on the would-be professional athlete were great also, as college athletic programs provide virtually the only training ground for a professional career in football and basketball.

The 1980s has been a period when many of the unfortunate effects of these pressures have surfaced. Widely publicized illegalities, irregularities, or both at universities as diverse as Maryland, Georgia, Minnesota, Southern Methodist, Tulane, and Southern California brought embarrassment to some and anger to others.

The NCAA is the reigning regulatory body for the vast majority of intercollegiate athletics, and its enforcement activities have responded to the increased pressures. The enforcement staff expanded during the 1970s, and enforcement activities have taken place at a far higher rate in the 1970 to 1985 period than in the prior 15 years.[1]

Although the NCAA is the creature of its member colleges and universities, until recently the direct leadership of those institutions showed relatively little interest in the NCAA regulatory process. But with the formation of the Presidents Commission in 1984, questions of the appropriate balance between athletes and academics rose to the forefront of attention at the NCAA meetings. The Presidents Commission successfully pressed for legislation establishing minimum academic qualifications for participation in intercollegiate sports (Bylaws 5-1-[j]), and increased penalties for NCAA rules violations (the so-called death penalty). More broadly, they called for a fresh assessment, at the level of basic principles rather than narrow and particular rules, of the proper role of intercollegiate athletics in higher education. Should the universities of our nation accept the fact that big-time intercollegiate athletics has become a quintessentially American institution, unparalleled in the university world of other nations, and accept the fact that it is in the business of mass commercial entertainment? Should they separate, and separately regulate, the sports of football and men's intercollegiate basketball, because these two so command public interest and provide both the major financial benefits and the major costs and problems? Or should they make efforts to de-emphasize these programs, reduce their scale and intensity, and make them more compatible with the educational mission of the university?

These are the questions that concern the Presidents Commission and that will lie at the center of the discussion in the months ahead. To a degree, these are questions of values that can only be answered by argument and persuasion. But matters of fact may also serve a crucial function. What became apparent to many on the Presidents Commission was that the discussion of these critical issues was fueled largely by the trading of anecdotes—for example, one person's horror story of an athletic program gone wrong is declared an extreme and unusual case, countered with another person's story of an athlete of humble origins who goes on to great academic as well as athletic success and who represents a triumph for the current system of big-time intercollegiate athletic success and who represents a triumph for the current system of big-time intercollegiate athletics.

It was in this context that the Amateur Athletic Foundation of Los Angeles asked the Presidents Commission if it would be useful for them if we would review existing studies of intercollegiate athletics to try to establish the knowns and unknowns in the field and then make recommendations for further specific and concrete inquiries that would help all parties to the discussion obtain a fuller understanding of the way the system is currently working and of the effects it is having on the athletes and the universities that are its main participants. The commission requested such a review.

To respond to the request of the Presidents Commission, we asked 10 persons, each of whom was familiar with one or another issue in intercollege athletics and had done research on the subject, to prepare rough working papers summarizing the knowns and unknowns in the areas of competence.[2] The papers were then discussed at a meeting that included the authors, the Amateur Athletic Foundation senior staff, and a small number of invited guest commentators.[3] In this document, we restrict ourselves to the major conclusions and put forth our main recommendations.[4]

## KNOWNS AND UNKNOWNS

### The Academic and Social Experience of Student-Athletes

Studies at a variety of universities have shown consistently that athletes in revenue-producing sports (Division I football and men's basketball programs) score lower on average than do other athletes and nonathletes on a number of measures of academic achievement, including college admission tests, high school GPAs, and rank in their high school graduating classes. In college, athletes in big-time sports programs have lower college GPAs and graduate less often than do athletes in nonrevenue sports. Although athletes as a whole probably graduate at about the same rate as do nonathletes in the general student body, there is considerable evidence that big-time college athletes do less well in this regard. What these and other findings suggest is that college athletes in big-time programs are often more poorly prepared than other students to cope with the rigors of academic life. And what is true of athletes in general is even more true of recruited black athletes.

Evidence relating to the student-athlete's life in college is less substantial than information relating to grades and test scores. There is suggestive evidence that male athletes in Division I revenue-producing programs are far more likely than athletes at the Division II and III levels to report that they feel pressure to be athletes first and students second, and they are more likely to feel that their coaches make demands that prevent them from being top students. Research also points to a number of coping strategies used by athletes who are struggling in the classroom to remain eligible.

Much, however, is not known. Solid descriptions of the athlete's relationship to other students and to campus life are not available, although many have expressed concern that eating and living arrangements along with practice and game schedules combine to make athletes a segregated class on many campuses. And we can find no studies that compare athletes with what some regard as a natural comparison: other student specialists, such as those immersed in the performing arts, student government, the student newspaper, or those who need to work while in school, who therefore have time pressures arguably similar to student-athletes.

## Life After Intercollegiate Athletics

Although there are occasional suggestive studies—a survey of former football and male basketball players from five Big 10 schools, a follow-up study of former Notre Dame football players—we were unable to find any systematic and general documentation of the experiences of student-athletes after the end of college. It is widely believed that concentration of students' energy in a single activity such as athletics deeply affects not only their experience in college but their later lives and careers as well. Certainly, through anecdotal evidence, we know of many successful people who played intercollegiate athletics, as well as of those who leave college without the personal development necessary for a productive life. But we have no research that examines systematically the postcollege experiences of student-athletes from different backgrounds and races, different schools, playing in different divisions, and in different sports. We lack the data to answer three central questions: Where are they now? What are they doing? What role did intercollegiate athletics have in the process?

## Academic Support Systems

We know that attention is being given by many schools to assisting student-athletes with their academic activities through counseling programs. Where athletic departments have undertaken to provide assistance, the amount and quality vary widely. NCAA Division I schools generally have larger budgets and larger support programs than do smaller institutions. There is much debate, however, over whether such support programs should be operated by athletic departments or by student services divisions. There is also concern over the prescriptive nature of many programs, where decisions about courses and majors are made for the athlete by others.

Given the recruitment of many athletes with marginal academic records, it is crucial to know whether in practice academic support programs are more concerned with improving or maximizing student performance or with simply keeping athletes eligible for athletic competition. Yet little has been done to answer this basic question or, more generally, to discern which kinds of counseling and support systems seem to work best.

## Governance and Administration

There are many, besides presidents, who contribute to the operation of intercollegiate athletics: athletic directors and their staffs, coaches, faculty athletic representatives, the admissions office, the development office, the board of trustees, and alumni and booster organizations. However, our knowledge of the governance and administration of intercollegiate athletics is sketchy at best. Although problems in men's athletics have been with us from the first years of intercollegiate sports, most treatises on university administration skip the subject of intercollegiate athletics as if it did not exist. There has been little or no study of the role of faculty members or trustees. The same is true of admissions and development offices. Beliefs abound: Until recently, university presidents have not been overly concerned with intercollegiate athletics; athletic directors have always been more wary of control by others than themselves as booster groups are often made up of the political and economic elite within the greater university family and are therefore quite powerful.

Whether these beliefs are true or not, on many governance issues our ignorance is nearly complete. We know that many presidents spend a lot of time on athletics, but we do not have a clear understanding of the range of governance and oversight mechanisms that are now in place. Do those with few abuses of NCAA rules have a different structure of governance that those with many? Are there legitimate reasons for treating the administration of athletics differently than we do any other department or program? These and other related questions require a much more detailed and thorough examination of governance than it has received.

### Financing of Athletic Programs

Relative to other areas, the financing of athletic programs is fairly well documented. We know that the rise of intercollegiate sports as mass commercial entertainment has brought millions of dollars to some colleges and universities, especially from television contracts for football and men's basketball. Yet some programs are becoming more expensive to operate. And despite TV revenues, we know that the vast majority of university intercollegiate athletic programs, including football and men's basketball, operate at a deficit. But the true nature of athletic department finances is difficult to judge because information on all expenditures is very difficult to obtain, even from public institutions. NCAA-sponsored studies are based on approximately half of all NCAA institutions, and published reports to date do not distinguish between the major subdivisions of the Division I schools. In addition, the available reports, by focusing primarily on operating expenses rather than the more comprehensive expenditures (which would include outlays for property, plant, equipment, and debt service payments) may well underestimate both the number of institutions operating at a deficit and the dollar magnitude of the deficits. In short, more detailed expense and revenue information is needed to make informed judgments about the handling of money for athletic programs.

The concerns giving rise to the Presidents Commission grew largely out of irregularities in the NCAA's Division I-A and I-AA programs, and it is a concern for those programs and athletes that lies at the core of the above review of knowns and unknowns. We realize football and men's basketball are not the only sports where problems are raised. On occasion, baseball, hockey, women's basketball and volleyball, and track and field for both men and women will be subject to some of the same pressures associated with football and men's basketball.

But although focusing on Division I, we felt that for a variety of reasons any review and any further study should cover intercollegiate athletic programs for both women and men in all sports and at all levels of competition. A main reason is that the major programs can be better understood when seen in comparison with the others. Also, there may be particularly creative ways of organizing athletics at the other levels that could be adopted at Division I. Another major reason is that the systems are interdependent: The treatment of programs in the revenue-producing sports has consequences for all the other programs. Finally, the main *structural* change in intercollegiate athletics during the 1970s and 1980s has been the development of women's athletic programs and their governance by the NCAA. Concerns of equity and equality require that those programs, too, be reviewed. In any event, as we examined the range of issues confronting intercollegiate sports, we came up with a number of topics about which further inquiry seems warranted.

*Women's Athletic Programs.* The situation of women athletes is different from that of their male counterparts. Although there has been an expansion of women's programs, their revenue sources are different, and they present different problems. Studies to date suggest that, unlike their male counterparts, women athletes differ little from nonathletes on their campuses. Although this may change with the emergence of large-scale programs in sports such as women's basketball, the differentials in preparedness for college that exist for male athletes in revenue-producing sports are not currently posing the same level of problem for women's programs.

Coaching for women poses a different issue. Fifteen or 20 years ago, women coaches predominated in women's intercollegiate programs. Despite the overall growth of women's programs, the percentage of women coaches has declined, and there are serious questions about how to recruit women coaches and how to develop female role models for female athletes. With respect to leadership, although there are a number of schools with separate directors of athletics for women, the vast majority of women's programs are part of a more general athletic administration. And in the crucial area of grants-in-aid, the question of an equitable distribution for women's programs is paramount. The distinctive problems of women's athletic programs need to be examined.

*The Situation of Black Athletes.* The experience of many blacks in intercollegiate athletics is certainly different from that of whites. Although black athletes play an important role in many athletic programs and may be a majority on some athletic teams, blacks are often only a tiny minority of the general student body. Furthermore, there are very few black coaches and even fewer black head coaches. These realities create unique challenges to black youngsters, especially those involved in the highly public world of NCAA Division I men's basketball and football.

Many black male athletes entering college are only marginally prepared to do college work but are lured by the proposition of a free college education, while still developing the possibility of a professional career in sports. The drive toward a career in professional sports is reinforced by the continuous media image of black male athletic heroes, making acceptance of a scholarship offer likely even if the student has limited interests in higher education.

Because, generally, the number of black athletes attending predominately white universities is small, the danger of alienation from actual and perceived racism and social isolation from faculty and general student body is great. This encourages "clustering" by blacks in academic majors and often leads to disengagement from academics.

In several areas of the nation, the integration of blacks into university athletic teams is relatively recent. Considering the important contributions that black male athletes make to intercollegiate sports today, it is crucial to know more about their situation. What is the environment like for them at predominately white institutions?

Even less is known of black women athletes. How do their experiences differ by background, size of school, and the school's racial mix? And what is the effect of so few black coaches, either male or female?

The historically black colleges and their athletic programs pose a different set of problems. Athletes in their programs are more typical of other students on their campuses, but historically black colleges do not have the same potential for revenue generation as other colleges and universities, and this poses special problems for them. They may also expect to be differentially affected by the establishing of minimum test scores for freshman eligibility. Indeed, NCAA policies adopted across all institutions may have differential effects on these distinctive schools, and it will be important to know about and consider those effects when considering NCAA legislation.

*Coaches.* Given the intensity of big-time college sports programs, athletes may spend more time with coaches than with any other person on the campus. We know from anecdotal accounts that many of these experiences are highly rewarding. But the growth of coaching as a full-time occupation and the jump in salary to six-figure levels is a recent phenomenon, and coaches today may be under extreme pressures. We need to understand better how those pressures are dealt with by coaches and why some seem better than others at encouraging the student's academic development while still producing competitive teams. We also need to know what messages regarding the balance between athletics and academics are given to coaching staffs by their institutions. Coaches are the critical link between the student and the athletic program. Thoughtful policy making requires a full understanding of the situation of the coach in relation to the college community.

*Recruiting the High School Athlete.* We know that recruiting violations constitute a large share of the NCAA's enforcement activities and that many schools have elaborate and expensive recruiting systems. We also know that high school athletes learn much about their choice of colleges and universities from coaches during the recruitment process. But there is only a dim under-standing of what messages are in fact conveyed and whether current regula-tions restricting contacts between student and a school may actually work against the student's ability to make a fully informed choice.

It is too early to discern conclusively the effects on high school students of the "no pass, no play" legislation in some states or the effects of the recently enacted Bylaw 5-1-(j). This is a matter that deserves careful study. But indications are that if student-athletes understand early enough what the expectations are, so that they can take appropriate preparatory courses, the vast majority can bring their academic performance up to the required levels.

*The NCAA as a Deliberative Body.* The NCAA began as a small regulatory effort. Its decision-making procedures have changed over the years as the NCAA has grown to represent hundreds of member schools. Does the NCAA model fit today? This question was not at the center of our deliberations, but it emerged frequently as a by-product of our discussion of other issues. Do the economic and social consequences of NCAA decision making require more opportunity for informed discussion and debate prior to action?

*Student Participation in Decision Making.* An important purpose of the NCAA, articulated in its constitution, is "to initiate, stimulate and improve intercollegiate athletic programs for student-athletes." It is the student-athlete whose performance draws the attendance, gate receipts, and television reve-nues. It is also the student-athlete who most directly experiences the conflict between academics and athletics and whose life is altered by every NCAA decision regarding basics such as season length, practice times, travel time for away games, let alone grant-in-aid support. But the NCAA is a member-ship body of institutions, not individuals, and those who have primary voice are presidents, athletic directors, and faculty athletic representatives. There are some mechanisms for getting student input into the decision-making process, but it seems only fair to ask whether the methods by which student-athletes can register their concerns are adequate or should be enlarged.

## PROPOSED STUDIES

No single study can answer all the questions raised in this brief review. The Presidents Commission cannot do everything, especially in a limited time frame. But a number of the most important issues can be addressed through one comprehensive inquiry with several related parts, and that is what we propose.

The key to the success of such an inquiry is in the very careful selection of a representative sample of institutions. The sample needs to reflect each of the major divisions and subdivisions of the NCAA, although it might over-sample the Division I programs so that they could be examined in more detail. The sample would need to include traditional powerhouse schools in the revenue-producing sports, as well as some of those recently on the rise. And it would, of course, reflect the differences between public and private institutions, large and small; regional differences; and differences between schools with reputations for clean, trouble-free programs and those with a history of abuses.

With a carefully selected sample as the core, the study would proceed with five related inquiries at each college or university. Two of the studies would focus on the institution as a whole:

1. *Financing of athletic programs.* This study would examine detailed financial data from the different institutions, along with a close examination within each institution of how money is handled for athletic programs and how both surpluses and deficits are allocated.

2. *Governance and administration.* This study would examine in detail the governance and management of intercollegiate sports programs on each campus: the role of athletic directors and their staffs, coaches, faculty athletic representatives, the admissions office, the development office, the board of trustees, the president, and the alumni and booster organizations. A core part of the study would address how the athletic department relates to the rest of the university.

The three remaining studies would focus on the experience of individual student-athletes. Ideally, these would be longitudinal studies, where the same student-athletes are interviewed and reinterviewed as they move through the system. The problem, of course, is that such studies would take several years to complete. In view of the time problem, we propose three inquires that could be carried out over a 1-year period, once the design and pretesting were completed.[5]

3. *Life after intercollegiate athletics.* This would be a retrospective study in which student-athletes admitted to the sample colleges and universities in 1981 would be interviewed 7 years later. The central questions would be these: Where are they now? What are they doing? What role did intercollegiate athletics have in the process?

4. *Academic and social experiences of student-athletes.* This study would be based on interviews with and records of a sample of freshmen and upperclassmen at the colleges and universities to learn how student-athletes compare with other students not only in the classroom but also in relationship to all aspects of campus life and in their efforts to prepare themselves for life after college.

5. *Academic support systems.* The goal of this study would be to document in detail the kinds of academic support and counseling programs available to student-

athletes and to discern whether the academic counseling that student-athletes receive is helping them to improve as students or serving only enable them to meet the formal requirements of eligibility for athletic performance.

These studies would be undertaken with students and programs at the same universities and colleges as the institutional studies. When the components are put together, one should be able to establish patterns, if they exist, between the way programs are governed and financed on the one hand, and the way they are experienced by student-athletes on the other. That is the great strength of a comprehensive study as opposed to a series of piecemeal, independent inquiries.

Some of the special problems we noted could be examined within this framework. For example, with appropriate sampling of individuals in the various programs, it should be possible to examine the distinctive problems of black athletes and of women athletes. It might also be possible to make a special inquiry among coaches at some of the sampled schools, as well of their recruiting efforts. But studies of modes of student participation in governance, or of possible changes in NCAA decision processes, would probably require separate inquiries.

This comprehensive inquiry should go a long way toward answering some of the persistent questions facing the Presidents Commission. Are the abuses of athletics—admitting unprepared students, giving them little academic help, isolating them with other athletes, and using their athletic talents without developing the academic and personal skills—rare, or do they occur with great frequency? When they occur, are they spread in a random fashion across big-time sports schools, or are they concentrated in particular types of programs? Do they occur only under certain types of governance procedures? Do the students themselves feel helped and aided by the programs, or do they feel exploited? What types of students, in what types of programs, seem to profit most? These are only a few of the questions such an inquiry should help answer.


## IMPLEMENTATION


The success of such a comprehensive effort will depend very heavily on the commitment of university presidents to the enterprise. The techniques for designing surveys, interviews, questionnaires, and other instruments for extracting data, as well as the tools of analysis, are well developed and well understood. The central problem is gaining access to adequate data in the first place. Cooperation will be forthcoming if the presidents require it.

There may be many areas where the Presidents Commission can move ahead with proposed legislation without waiting for the results of these inquiries. But that does not mean the inquiries should be put aside. These inquiries should be thought of as core, baseline studies that will provide an anchoring point for future inquiries as well as a basis for action in 1989.

Implementation of such a set of inquiries will itself require careful thought and planning. The Presidents Commission will be helped by the fact that many of the needed talents are available on their faculties. Those faculties contain not only professors who have specialized in higher education but also those who are intimately familiar with the problems of sampling design, survey design, and data analysis. A small advisory oversight group could work directly with those conducting the studies as well as with the Presidents Commission.

The NCAA should be represented as a body, and the studies should be designed to mesh, insofar as possible, with ongoing NCAA efforts. The NCAA has detailed familiarity with many of the problems these studies would address, and they have been conducting related studies of their own. It will ease the burden such studies place on university officials if any new data collection efforts can be coordinated with those already underway through NCAA sponsorship. The proposed studies, however, do range far beyond the inquiries usually undertaken through NCAA initiative, and it is appropriate that the primary oversight group, although having NCAA representation, be composed primarily of university-based faculty who have the specialized knowledge and skills such studies require.

Other organizations beside the NCAA can be of great help. For example, the National Association of College and University Business Offices is a great resource for those studying aspects of higher education. And the Association of Governing Boards knows a great deal about governance and the way higher education operates. These are only two examples of the need to draw on a wide range of individuals and organizations.

The cooperation of universities and colleges in this process will be made easier if it is recognized that this comprehensive inquiry is not aimed at naming or blaming any particular situation or program. That is the function of an elaborate NCAA enforcement mechanism, and this inquiry should never be confused with it. The institutions as well as their individual participants should be kept anonymous, for the aim is to learn, not to bring sanction against programs.

There is no reason to believe that the scandals that have afflicted some institutions occur in the majority of programs. Indeed, common sense tells us that most of the programs, especially in smaller colleges, suffer few of the abuses that make the headlines when they are reported. But the apparently increasing frequency of abuse, the substantial deficits run up by many programs and pressures to produce not merely competitive but winning programs have combined to bring the spotlight on questions of institutional integrity. No study will solve the problem of institutional integrity. But a comprehensive inquiry may inform us in much more depth and detail about the nature and extent of the problem and may also lead to possible solutions. The Presidents Commission may well be able to act immediately with regard to many of the issues it faces. But it should also take the leadership in helping us promote a factual basis for understanding exactly how pervasive the problems are and what might be done about them.

## NOTES

1. NCAA public disciplinary actions occurred at the rate of 6.9 per year for the period from 1955 to 1969. That figure jumps to 11.3 per year for the period 1970 to 1984. That the irregularities are largely in the revenue-producing sports is clear: Of the 145 disciplinary actions where specific sports are mentioned, 47.6% are in basketball and 44.8% are in football. All other sports combined make up the other 7.6%.

2. The 10 persons and their topic areas are listed in appendix.

3. See appendix.

4. Those who prepared papers and the commentators have each responded to earlier drafts of material and have had opportunity to comment in detail, but they have not necessarily seen the final draft and no formal action has been taken by the group as a whole. Also, it should be noted that this document in no way represents an official policy statement of the Amateur Athletic Foundation Board of directors, who have not reviewed the document.

5. We would hope that the studies could become the first stage in a longitudinal inquiry to be completed in future years.

# APPENDIX

| Name and Affiliation | Field |
| --- | --- |
| Dr. Susan Birrell<br>Department of Physical Education<br>  and Sports Studies<br>E-102 Field House<br>University of Iowa<br>Iowa City, IA 52242 | Women in intercollegiate sports, campus life for female athletes, organization of women's athletics |
| Dr. Steven Danish<br>Chair, Department of Psychology<br>Virginia Commonwealth University<br>810 W. Franklin Street<br>Richmond, VA 23220 | Effects of intense concentration on athletics and later careers of student-athletes, motivational and related issues |
| Dr. E. Stanley Eitzen<br>Department of Sociology<br>Colorado State University<br>Fort Collins, CO 80523 | Differential preparation for and experience in college athletics; effect of race, sport and gender on GPA, SAT, major courses, and graduation rates |
| Dr. Stephen Figler<br>Physical Education Department<br>Cal State University, Sacramento<br>6000 J Street<br>Sacramento, CA 95819 | How academic counseling works for student-athletes in different kinds of programs, big time and small time |
| Dr. James Frey<br>Department of Sociology<br>University of Nevada/Las Vegas<br>Las Vegas, NV 89154 | Effects of governance structure types; division of authority among trustees, administrators, athletic directors, and so on; role of NCAA on athletic experience |
| Richard E. Lapchick<br>Director<br>Center for the Study of Sport in Society<br>Northeastern University<br>360 Huntington Avenue, 161 CP<br>Boston, MA 02115 | Effects of intercollegiate athletics on high school students; recruiting, problems of adjustment to university life for new recruits; the experiences of the black athlete |

Dr. Arthur Padilla
Associate Vice President for Academics
University of North Carolina
910 Raleigh Road
Chapel Hill, NC 27514

Financing intercollegiate athletics; making
or losing money; special problems of
predominately black institutions

Dr. Allen Sack
Department of Sociology
University of New Haven
300 Orange Avenue
West Haven, CT 06516

Differences in the experience of college
life for athletes versus nonathletes; among
athletes, differences between those in
major revenue-producing programs and
others

George Sage
Department of Athletics
University of North Colorado
Butler Hancock Hall, Room 223
Greeley, CO 80639

Knowns and unknowns in coach-athlete
relationship, effects of coaches' career
interests on relationship, coaching culture
among intercollegiate coaches

Raymond Winbush
Director
Johnson Black Cultural Center
Vanderbilt University
P.O. Box 1666, Station B
Nashville, TN 37233

Fate of black athlete relative to white
athlete in intercollegiate programs,
predictors of relative educational success
of black athletes vs. white, the differential
effects on blacks of being in Division I,
II, and III programs

## DISCUSSANTS

Dr. Merrily Baker
Director, Women's Athletics
University of Minnesota
250 Bierman Building
516 15th Avenue, S.E.
Minneapolis, MN 55455

Professor John C. Weistart
School of Law
Duke University
Towerview Road
Durham, NC 27706

Dr. Margy Gatz
Faulty Athletic Representative
Director, Clinical Studies
University of Southern California
Seeley G. Mudd Building
University Park
Los Angeles, CA 90089

Mr. Jefferey H. Orleans
Executive Director
Council of Ivy Group Presidents
70 Washington Road, Room 22
Princeton, NJ 08540

Mr. Ray Gillian
Assistant to Chancellor Slaughter
University of Maryland
Main Administration Building
College Park, MD 20742

Mr. Pat Hayashi
Assistant to Chancellor Heyman
University of California, Berkeley
200 California Hall
Berkeley, CA 94720

## AMATEUR ATHLETIC FOUNDATION STAFF

Stanton Wheeler
President

Anita DeFrantz
Vice President for Sports Programs

Conrad Freund
Vice President for Finance
  and Administration

Steve Montiel
Vice President for Sports Programs

Richard B. Perelman
Consultant

Judith Pinero
Vice President for Sports Programs

# 18

# Athletic Scholarship Disarmament

Raymond Yasser

In the world of big-time intercollegiate sports, the highly recruited athlete receives an athletic scholarship. To be sure, in the vast majority of cases, the award has nothing whatsoever to do with "scholarship," and everything to do with athletic ability. Indeed, the term *athletic scholarship* is an oxymoron.

Many recipients of athletic scholarships are marginal students at the university they attend. The receipt of free tuition, fees, room and board, and books is an award for athletic prowess, given with the understanding that the recipient will make a good faith effort to "play ball." The modern scholarship is a 1-year deal, renewable at the discretion of the university. Typically, athletes who are able to compete on the playing field and remain eligible by staying above the school's academic floor will have their scholarships renewed for an additional year. Real progress toward a degree is not ordinarily a condition precedent to the renewal of the award.

The National Collegiate Athletic Association (NCAA) dictates to individual member schools the maximum number of athletic scholarships permitted for each sport in the various divisions. Year to year, the numbers vary as the partisan interests of particular divisions and sports jostle for position at the annual convention. For example, the most recent and lively source of controversy has had to do with the limits on football scholarships in the most competitive division. Alarmed by recent cost reduction moves, big-time coaches are lobbying to have the overall grant limit set at 90 grants-in-aid. The current rule will reduce the overall total to 85 beginning in the fall of 1994. Apparently, the concern of coaches is that they cannot administer effective programs with "only" 85 scholarships. The lament of coaches in other sports is similar; coaches invariably lobby for more scholarships. And the NCAA steps in to resolve it all, setting the limits, which in reality operate as floors among the collegiate powerhouses.

One of the most startling facts about all this is that individual schools have felt the need for the NCAA to limit them in this way. It's as though the schools are saying, "stop me before I give still another athletic scholarship to a marginally qualified athlete."

I think it's time for the Presidents Commission of the NCAA to get it together to issue a national mandate for what I have dubbed "athletic scholarship disarmament." I would start with an across-the-board cut of 50% in the number of athletic scholarships available for men. This disarmament mandate must be accompanied by a commitment by each university to allocate the 50% saved to academic scholarships for disadvantaged, academically motivated applicants. What this means is that we would have a cost-free reallocation of scholarship resources. The new recipients of the old athletic scholarships would simply be composed of students rather than athletes. The lament of the coaches notwithstanding, the existing scholarship limits are unconscionably high. Consider the salubrious effects of athletic scholarship disarmament.

## THE MESSAGE TO THE COMMUNITY

This type of cut will send an important message to the national community about the proper role of athletics in the life of a university. It will also send an important message to people in disadvantaged communities.

The prevalent message in disadvantaged communities today is that athletic prowess provides the most readily available ticket to the university. Athletic achievement is more highly valued than academic achievement. Universities must take responsibility for communicating this flawed message. They must also take responsible action to communicate a new and more sensible message. The most readily available ticket to the university must be provided to those people in the community who have shown a commitment to academic excellence. Clearly, scholarship reallocation in the form of athletic scholarship disarmament sends the most sensible message.

## THE EFFECT ON COMPETITION
## AND MARKETABILITY

Powerful athletic interests will, of course, blanch at the mere mention of such a proposal. But athletic scholarship disarmament does not mean the destruction of highly competitive and marketable intercollegiate athletics. In fact, such a move will, I believe, reinvigorate intercollegiate competition because more schools will be able to compete at the highest levels. Athletic talent will be spread about more broadly. Traditional collegiate powerhouses will not be able to "warehouse" athletic talent. New fans, many of whom are now turned off by the hypocrisy of intercollegiate athletics, will be drawn to a more pure intercollegiate system. Old fans are unlikely to turn away from intercollegiate sports just because more of the athletes are now really students, too.

The powerful and well-entrenched athletic interests will claim that this kind of "radical" step will destroy intercollegiate competition. But think about this claim. Why is it that Oklahoma, for example, cannot field a highly competitive football team with only 45 athletic scholarships? Or that Duke could not field a highly competitive basketball team with only 6 athletic scholarships? Remember too that the disarmament is across-the-board. It is possible that the overall performance level would drop, but isn't it clear that the drop, if there is one, would be imperceptible to the fan? Moreover, the fan would see fewer entrenched sports powers and more broad-based competition for national prominence. The better argument is that this radical step—what I have called massive athletic scholarship disarmament—will prevent big-time intercollegiate sports from destroying itself.

## THE EFFECT ON CAMPUS DIVERSITY

It is extremely important that this disarmament not be viewed by the black community as an attempt to "whiten" intercollegiate sports. Rather, it must be both implemented and viewed as a profound national commitment to increase the number of black lawyers, doctors, engineers, and other professionals. This, after all, is what the disarmament program is all about. That is why the disarmament plan must be accompanied by detailed and verifiable plans to allocate those scholarship resources that are no longer going to be spent on athletic scholarships to academic scholarships for disadvantaged minority applicants, with special emphasis on recruitment and retention of black students. It is most unlikely that these kinds of programs will be viewed unfavorably if a legal challenge is mounted.

If this agenda is honestly pursued, the number of black and minority students on each campus will be increased because scholarships previously given to white athletes will now be awarded to academically promising disadvantaged students. In fact, the disarmament plan should serve to increase the number of black and minority students on the campus.

The number of black students on campus will increase as a result of the disarmament plan, but another very important change will also take place. Where before disarmament a disproportionate number of black students were athletes, disarmament will significantly reduce this disproportion. It will also decrease the perceptions that lead to the damaging stereotypes, which in turn contribute to our racial problems. And as a very practical matter, it simply makes more sense for a *university* to recruit and enroll academically talented black students than it does to recruit and enroll athletically talented, but often academically marginal, black athletes.

# 19

## Academic Standards for Athletes
### A Debate in Black and White

Richard E. Lapchick

The issue of higher academic standards for athletes has, unfortunately, widened the already huge chasm between the races. Because standardized achievement tests have been a major part of all three attempts at higher standards, the emotional debate will only get more intense.

For decades, athletes have been viewed as "dumb jocks." That sign of contempt is even more frequently attached to black athletes. Athletes aren't expected to be as smart as other students. Jokes are often made about athletes' intelligence. Even athletes joke among themselves about poor grades, frequently in an attempt to mask the pain.

Media exposure of low graduation rates was followed by a public outcry and threats of intervention by the Congress. Old sports names such as Senator Bill Bradley and congressman Tom McMillen and nonsports names such as members of Congress John Conyers, Ed Townes, and Cardiss Collins were regulars on our sports pages. It all led to a movement for higher academic standards by the colleges and, increasingly, by high schools.

The advent of the reform movement was helped along by embarrassed and enlightened college presidents. In 1983, the National Collegiate Athletic Association (NCAA) passed Proposition 48. Developed under the leadership of the Presidents Commission, Proposition 48 was designed to create new eligibility standards for incoming freshmen.

Under Proposition 48, an incoming college freshman, to be eligible to play a sport in the freshman year at any NCAA Division I program, had to (a) maintain a C high school average in 11 core curriculum courses and (b) score above a 700 on the combined verbal and math sections of the Scholastic Aptitude Test (SAT) or a 15 on the American College Test (ACT). The new standards referred only to the athlete's academic record in high school.

The core curriculum and grade point standards won widespread approval. However, the requirement for minimum scores on standardized tests angered black educators and civil rights leaders. Many educators agreed that standardized achievement tests are culturally and racially biased. Black leaders charged that Proposition 48 would limit black athletes' opportunities to obtain college athletic scholarships.

The NCAA conducted an analysis prior to implementation that seemed to bear out that fear. The study looked at entering freshmen in 1981. It showed that 86% of black players in men's basketball and 75% of black players in men's football at the nation's largest schools would have been ineligible as freshmen. At the same time, 33% of white players in men's basketball and 50% of white players in men's football would have been ineligible.

Nevertheless, when implemented in the fall of 1986, Proposition 48 actually sidelined far fewer athletes. According to NCAA figures, only 10.3% of football players and 11.4% of basketball players overall had to sit out in 1989-90. Although the earlier NCAA study predicted that more than 80% of black athletes would have been ineligible, 16% were actually ineligible in 1989-90. In previous years, the results were even better.

Although Proposition 48 continued to have a disproportionately heavier impact on blacks (approximately 65% of all Proposition 48 admissions between 1986-87 and 1989-90), the percentage of all black athletes who failed to meet Proposition 48 requirements is about one fifth the number predicted in the NCAA study. The predictions of academic disaster proved wrong; student-athletes, black and white alike, have convincingly met the new standards.

Although reluctant at first, I now support Proposition 48. However, I still agree with the concern of educators and civil rights leaders who believe that scores on standardized tests are not effective measures of the academic potential of all students.

Apparently, the presidents were not satisfied and helped pass Proposition 42 at the 1989 NCAA convention. This reignited the fiery debate about Proposition 48. The new proposition, combined with the standards established by Proposition 48, would have meant that someone who did not qualify could not receive an athletic scholarship in the first year. Under the original Proposition 48, the athlete could have received the scholarship but could not have played in the first year.

Considering that the large number of so-called Prop 48 students were black, the new rule reopened the issue with an intensity never experienced before in college sports. John Thompson walked off the court in Georgetown's first game after the NCAA convention to protest Proposition 42. Thompson's enormous stature, coupled with the drama his walkout created, forced academic and athletic officials to air the debate publicly. Many coaches maintained that Proposition 42 would deny student-athletes the chance to get an education if they could not receive a scholarship. They would not have the chance to prove themselves academically. Temple basketball coach John

Chaney called it "racist." Proponents such as Arthur Ashe said Proposition 42 would put increased pressure on high school players to study harder.

I was strongly opposed to Proposition 42. The smaller than predicted number of Proposition 48 ineligible students cited above indicates that the threat of loss of eligibility was already effectively putting pressure on high school student-athletes. Furthermore, of those who failed to meet the standards in 1986-87 and 1987-88, 79% were in good academic standing in 1988-89. That was on par with their fellow students who had originally met the Proposition 48 standards. Academic advisers said that they were able to pay more attention to the Proposition 48 students because they were identified as being "at risk."

But the heaviest weight against Proposition 42 came when that NCAA study mentioned earlier was analyzed. Of the 69% of all black male athletes who would not have met Proposition 48 standards, 54% graduated. This stood in dramatic contrast to the 31% of all black male athletes in that class who graduated. In other words, the black students who came in at risk graduated at a much higher rate than did regular student-athletes. Many were given that extra emphasis on academics in their first year.

Delegates at the 1990 NCAA Convention effectively eliminated the problems with Proposition 42 by allowing Proposition 48 ineligible students to receive institutional aid based on need. This resolution came as a compromise from the Presidents Commission.

As the 1990s wore on, the reform movement sometimes sputtered, only to be shocked back into high gear. The publication of graduation rates was an impetus for the Presidents Commission to plant themselves in a position to control college sports once and for all.

Still, the legacy of the early days has left so much to do. Race and gender were still major question marks as the NCAA delegates deliberated in San Diego in January 1995. The lines were drawn between the presidents and the black coaches over a new set of initial eligibility standards. The presidents backed Proposition 16, which requires either a higher high school grade point average (GPA) or higher standardized test scores than those required by Proposition 48 to be eligible in the freshman year. If a student had a 700 SAT score, Proposition 16 mandated a 2.5 (C+) GPA in 13 core courses. If a student had a 2.0 GPA, he or she would need a 900 on the SAT tests.

Proposition 16 was originally passed in 1994. When black college basketball coaches threatened to walk out en masse 5 days later, federal mediation was set in motion to try to reach a compromise. Discussions between the presidents, the NCAA, and the Black Coaches Association took place throughout 1994.

The coaches said their opposition was based on wanting more opportunities for potential African American student-athletes. They favored making all freshmen ineligible so that freshmen would have a year to acclimate themselves to the new academic and social realities of college life.

I was right in the middle on this one. I work closely with many of the presidents and also with the coaches associations. There is just too much evidence that such tests are culturally biased against those who come from lower socioeconomic backgrounds. Thus, I can support moving toward a 2.5 or C+ GPA but doing so without the use of standardized tests.

I have long favored a policy in which all freshmen student-athletes in the revenue sports would be ineligible to participate in competition. They would be allowed to practice with their teammates. This would allow them the opportunity to adjust to college life without the demands of their sport to impede their progress. If the student-athletes make good academic progress toward graduation, they could earn a fourth year of eligibility. Such legislation would eliminate the need for Proposition 48 and be fair to everyone.

Sport had the opportunity to do something about the racially charged climate in America. To go ahead with the legislation that is perceived by many to be tinged with a racial intent (I personally do not believe it is) without compromise leaves the leadership open to damaging criticism. What will African American students and student-athletes back on campus think? How will leaders in the African American community appraise the decision? The local repercussions are simply not yet predictable.

National leaders, both in the Congressional Black Caucus and in the civil rights community, are ready to wrestle with the NCAA over this issue. The Reverend Jesse Jackson was in San Diego to weigh in on a number of issues regarding race and sports, including his opposition to Proposition 16.

Sustaining the tenets of Proposition 16, the NCAA membership chose to delay implementation by 1 year until August 1996 while voting down freshmen ineligibility. Neither side was left totally happy, but it momentarily forestalled a potentially bitter fight with racial overtones.

Many felt that the coaches were hypocritical about wanting to provide "opportunity" for African American children. I have no doubt that some were. But when the likes of John Thompson and George Raveling talk about saving lives, I believe in them. There is a reason that you can go into any black community in America and see Georgetown jackets and caps on so many residents. John Thompson has worked hard and earned their respect as a man even more than as a successful coach.

Others felt the presidents were hypocritical about saying they care about all African American students, not just about those who play for their teams. I have no doubt that some were. But some of the most outspoken presidents calling for increased standards have among the best records regarding hiring black coaches, faculty, and staff.

Overall, I have long believed that such efforts on both sides at the college level are attempts to address the problem in the wrong place. Approximately 99 of every 100 high school student-athletes won't play Division I college sports. Proposition 16 will *never* affect them. However, if the 99 who won't play in college played under increased standards at the high school level, then everyone would have at least some chance to get the opportunity that the presidents open up for students of color who are not athletes.

Requiring higher academic standards for high school athletes has been a distant goal in most parts of the nation. When Proposition 48 was first passed in 1983, less than 100 of the 16,000 school districts in the United States had a minimum C average for participation in extracurricular activities. Texas became the first state to adopt a "no-pass, no-play" policy. Texas is now just one of a growing number of states where at least a C average is required. The others are California, Hawaii, Mississippi, New Mexico, and West Virginia. Hundreds of local districts have acted where states have not.

By 1995, the results of the no-pass, no-play policy were evident: (a) Grades improve with increased academic standards; (b) those who participate in extracurricular activities do much better academically than those who do not; (c) coaches rally to assist their players academically if standards are put in place. The predictions of academic disaster for athletes who were asked to do more proved false. The players produced and improved their performance just like they do on the field or court. It should not have surprised us as much as it did. The fable of the dumb jock is slowly being buried.

Such high schools standards clearly create more opportunities outside of sports for the intellectual development of a new generation of African American leaders empowered to meet the challenges of the 21st century. As it stands now, the only urban children with a chance are those who are either supremely talented athletes or who somehow have emerged as the academic crème de la crème, unscathed by the problems that plague their schools and communities.

College presidents and coaches could have an enormous effect if they lobbied in their institutions' own communities for higher academic standards at the high school level. Only then will we be fully able to address higher education's greatest embarrassment: As low as the graduation rate is for Africa American student-athletes, it is higher than the rate for African American students as a whole.

That is a problem that presidents, faculty, and coaches can work on together. But we can no longer wait until African Americans arrive on our campuses like immigrants arriving on our shores. They have been here and their parents have been here. It is time to recognize that these are the children of our forefathers, and they are fully entitled to the American dream that now seems so elusive to so many.

# 20

## Two Ways to Go
### Only One Is a Winner[1]

Richard E. Lapchick

It is easy to understand why young boys have stars in their eyes. Average salaries in pro basketball and baseball are now exceeding $1 million a year, and those in football and hockey are increasing at their own record paces. Boys see the players' beautiful wives. They see them endorsing products.

When an athlete appears gifted in his sport, individuals, frequently unconsciously, begin to take away responsibilities for things off the court. Some teachers may want to help student-athletes stay eligible by giving them better grades. Guidance counselors may recommend a less demanding course. Coaches may only talk about winning championships.

It is not easy for student-athletes to stay on course academically and to demand the best of themselves on and off the court. *Hoop Dreams,* the highly acclaimed movie released in 1994, follows the lives of two Chicago basketball players. It clearly shows the pressures of an increasingly complex world on Arthur Agee and William Gates, the two real-life characters of the movie. Witnessing drugs, teenage pregnancy, gang violence, and economic struggles can serve to make the good life of pro sports seem even more attractive. To many, it seems like the only life possible.

The Lou Harris survey on high school athletics, highlighted in Chapter 23, shows that a growing number of athletes are taking back the responsibility for their own lives. The educational curriculum designed by the Center for the Study of Sport in Society for *Hoop Dreams* will, we hope, develop this sense of empowerment even further.

The lives of Fred Buttler and Paul Moore show how poorly and how well, respectively, the system can serve the student-athlete. Learning about the tragedy surrounding Buttler's life made me feel compelled to get involved in the issue of academics and athletics full-time. The story of Paul Moore inspired me to realize the unlimited possibilities for human growth.

## FRED BUTTLER

Fred Buttler is but one tragic example of a man who didn't make it in the pros and paid the price for not being properly educated. Buttler's classic case reveals how the educational system can abuse athletes, especially black athletes.

Even as a third-grade student at Warren Lane Elementary in Inglewood, California, people said the 8-year-old Fred possessed enormous physical promise. They watched as he beat older children in every sport he took up, telling him he would someday play in the NFL. However, his mother saw his struggles in the classroom and asked that he be held back in the third grade to improve his reading skills. She was incredulous when school officials promoted him to Monroe Junior High School after the sixth grade. She was told not to be so concerned, that he was progressing at a normal pace.

An instant football sensation at Monroe, he still could not read. Fred and four other black athletes were called the "Hersheys" by the nearly all-white student body. Mrs. Buttler sat in disbelief as she and Fred were told he was "just too bright to be in the eighth grade" and was leapfrogging the eighth grade into Morningside High. Mrs. Buttler complained to the Monroe administration that it was not fair to send an illiterate to high school. She was patronizingly told, "It's the best for Fred."

Fred accumulated a 3-year C+ average at Morningside while never opening a book. There was no need to do so; all the teachers made "special arrangements" for the star football player. At times, he handed in blank exams; they were returned with all the right answers. At other times, he was given oral exams. Most of the time, he didn't have to take any exams. There was no point—he could not read them.

Fred Buttler said later that the teachers always made him feel good and gave him confidence that he would make the pros: "No matter how much trouble I had understanding things in class, I always figured I would make a good living playing ball for the pros. . . . Football was going to make me famous. And I knew I wasn't just dreaming because everyone told me I was good." He graduated from Morningside with a second-grade reading level— about the same level he had when his mother requested that he be left back in the third grade 9 years before. None of the big Division I-A schools would touch Fred and advised him to go to junior college. Despite the fact that he couldn't read the playbook, he received a football scholarship from El Camino Junior College.

Cal Mersola is now a professor of physical education and contemporary health. He was a quarterback and receivers coach and adviser at El Camino when Fred went there. Mersola stated frankly that "you didn't have to read or write to be in junior college. Fred survived by taking 12 units of vocational courses and physical education classes. He took a few academic classes, but I don't know how he got through them. Fred could barely write his own name. He couldn't write his address." Fred helped lead El Camino to two outstanding seasons as a cornerback. He assumed that after 2 more years of college he would end up with a pro football contract. Mersola suggests that while Fred was good, "no one thought he was good enough to make the pros." But no one told Fred. The big schools still would not go after him.

Cal State—LA recruiters were told by Mersola that Fred couldn't read or write. He told them "there was no way Buttler could graduate, that he wouldn't even graduate from El Camino." Cal State still wanted him. Fred decided to attend Cal State—LA. Mersola told me that he spent many hours filling out Fred's complicated admissions and grant-in-aid forms.

Fred was promised remedial reading help at Cal State, but he never received it. "I think some of the coaches were probably happy I couldn't read," he recalled, "because that meant I wouldn't waste time on schoolwork since that way I could concentrate on playing for them." The dream continued during his first year and a half at Cal State.

Buttler maintained a C+ average as a physical education major and played well. But the great interest and the support from the faculty seemed to expire as his eligibility ran out at the end of the fall semester. Fred flunked out of Cal State within months.

Dr. Al Marino spent a great deal of time with Buttler. Marino was associate chair of the Physical Education Department and associate athletic director at Cal State—LA. He remembered with considerable anguish: "Fred Buttler had no business in higher education. He knew he could not read or write. He can't be totally absolved of blame. . . . At some point he must have taken inventory of his own skills. Fred Buttler was not stupid. He made the decision to apply to college; he had to understand that he would have to be a student, that he would have to read and write."

However, Fred Buttler had been told since elementary school that going to school was simply his ticket to the pros. There were never any programs to develop his academic skills, even when his mother demanded them.

However, Buttler was hardly Marino's target. "There were many guilty people, but the largest culprit was the system and the program into which he was admitted. . . . Cal State—LA deemed him acceptable. After that it's an educator's job to educate him—essentially to educate an illiterate. It was like he was going into battle without any weapons. Fred Buttler did not have the skills to survive at a university."

Blame is usually affixed to the coach or athletic department. Marino was direct in his comments: "If you're looking for guilt, you must look to the department chair who is responsible for all of the students enrolled in physical education classes. Academic integrity at that time was not of the highest order. The athletic director, in this case, was not at fault."

In the end, Fred Buttler had no degree, no offers to play pro football, and no skills to use for gainful employment. And he still could not read. That was 1976. He became a factory worker and lived with his mother.

The death of his father brought more suffering into Fred's life. Fred was jailed when a gun went off at home, killing his father. He was not allowed to attend the funeral. However, he was soon released after the charges were dropped when the police determined that it had been an accidental shooting. Fred was not able to visit his father's grave, because he could neither read a map nor the street signs to find it.

If Buttler had demanded a quality education in return for his outstanding athletic contributions, perhaps his story might have had a happier ending. However, that would have been asking a great deal from a process that started in elementary school. At the age of 9 or 10, kids shouldn't have to make such decisions. And, in this case, Fred's mother had tried to intervene on his behalf. But the educational system was in full gear, stripping this young man of his future.

Neither Fred Buttler nor his mother could be located a decade after the Cal State—LA experience. No one at Warren Lane Elementary, Monroe Junior High, or Morningside High could provide any information about Fred. Mersola and Marino did not know where he was. It was as if he never stepped foot on the face of the Earth. Dr. Marino is no longer at Cal State—LA. The "hypocrisy of athletics in higher education" influenced his decision to leave the academy. He now works for a securities firm.

Buttler is only one poignant example of someone who didn't make it in the pros and paid the price for failing to receive an adequate education.

Tom "Satch" Sanders is a former Boston Celtic great, the first great defensive forward in the National Basketball Association (NBA). Now vice president for Player Programs with the NBA, Sanders sounded an ominous warning: "I remember when a high draft pick was cut from the Celtics one year, and he sat in front of his locker with his head down crying out 'What am I going to do now?' The young man did not have a college degree, and without basketball felt completely lost. I was to see this scene repeated many times during my career as a player and coach. Those of us who made it can count dozens of others who weren't prepared for the big fall. They are the tragedies. Buttler's story is not unique."

Some gain comfort from thinking Buttler's situation *is* a unique instance. Kevin Ross played basketball for Creighton University, an outstanding Jesuit school. Kevin was neither prepared to enter Creighton nor able to succeed there. When his 4 years of college eligibility ran out, he attended Marva

Collins's Westside Preparatory School in Chicago, beginning in the fifth grade.

Then Dexter Manley, the great Washington Redskins star, testified in the Senate that he went through 4 years at Oklahoma State as an illiterate and had to learn to read and write on his own while playing pro ball. Many believe that the tremendous lack of self-confidence that this produced had to have contributed to Manley's cocaine problem.

Nonetheless, everyone wants to think of Buttler or Ross or Manley as the ones who fell through the cracks. But if 25% to 30% of high school football players are reportedly functionally illiterate, then there are thousands of Fred Buttlers, Kevin Rosses, and Dexter Manleys out there waiting to happen. That price is a great one for so many of our young student-athletes who somewhere in their careers become simply athletes.


## PAUL MOORE: A LIFE WITH HOPE

By finally beginning to ask more of our student-athletes academically, we have dodged the ultimate disaster. Athletes have produced wherever we have asked more of them academically. The problem is that we ask too infrequently. Most involved in education finally realize that we cannot afford to allow student-athletes to be used to try to build athletic powers when they do not receive a real opportunity to complete an education that prepares them for life.

The inspiring story of Paul Moore and his teammates is the antidote for all the bad news stories. It opens our eyes to the way things should be conducted.

In Dade County, Florida, Clint Albury took over as coach of Killian High School early in the 1980s. When he realized his team's grade point average was a frightening 1.3, he instituted a mandatory study hall. His players were eligible according to state eligibility standards. Nonetheless, Albury brought in honor students to tutor his athletes. In a specialized study hall, they taught math and English 3 days a week, science and history the other 2.

The team's seniors graduated with a grade point average that had been raised to 2.45. No one failed a course. All had met Proposition 48 standards. At the end of the season, 23 of the 27 senior players signed scholarship offers with colleges and universities. That was believed to be the highest number of signed players in Dade County history—and testimony to Albury.

Perhaps a bigger testimony was the fact that of the 57 seniors who played for Albury while he was coach, 40 had either graduated or were on track to graduate from college in the 1990-91 year. But the most startling case was that of Paul Moore. He was the type of player who many would say could never be eligible under a no-pass, no-play policy with a minimum C average requirement. He would, according to the argument, be victimized by society's good intentions. Moore was reading on a first- or second-grade level 3 years ago.

Albury, who is black and a psychologist, made no assumptions about Moore's intelligence. He had Moore tested and discovered a learning disability. Then Coach Albury got him into a program for learning disabled students. He graduated with an 11th-grade reading level, earned a 2.3 grade point average in core courses, and exceeded 700 on the Scholastic Aptitude Test (SAT). Redshirted as a freshman, he was playing regularly in his junior year in 1990 for highly ranked Florida State. He had a 2.6 grade point average and graduated on time. In his senior year, Moore scored Florida State's winning touchdown against Miami. Albury's own no-pass, no-play rule proved effective. He had faith that his players could do the academic work.

In an ideal sense, educators say there is much to learn from sports. It teaches the virtues of self-discipline, hard work, group problem solving, competitive spirit, and pride in accomplishment. It provides many lessons about limits and capabilities, about dealing with failure and adversity, about teamwork and cooperation. These are all lessons that can be translated into being a good student, member of the community, or corporate citizen. But the athletes must understand that these skills are transferable into other areas of their lives.

The overall message to the players has to be that the school will provide special attention to its student-athletes to ensure their academic preparation. However, in exchange for this, it will be expected that student-athletes will fulfill the same academic requirements as all students.

Then we won't have to wonder what will happen when the cheering stops. We will have athletes whose full human potential has been developed to prepare them for life after sports.

## NOTE

1. Quotations in this chapter come from interviews conducted by the author in June of 1987.

# 21

## Student-Athletes
### So Much Work, So Little Time

Ed Sherman
Barry Temkin

$B$illy Greenwald slipped into his seat in the lecture hall. Around him, there was the usual muffled noise of students filing in for the 10 a.m. American society course.

The lecture focused on immigrants in the workforce. The senior running back on Northwestern's football team spent most of the time in class with his head down, taking notes. That's more than some of his classmates.

Off in a back corner, an extremely tall student was draped over two chairs, catching up on his sleep. His size, along with the fact that he was wearing a Northwestern warm-up suit, suggested—later confirmed—he was a basketball player.

Greenwald, though, stuck with the lecture, as he did for four years as a full-time student and a full-time athlete who finished his eligibility this fall.

After taking a full load of classes on that fall morning, Greenwald grabbed a quick lunch before heading to Northwestern's practice facility. There, he lifted weights for an hour, was involved in meetings for another hour and then practiced for $2\frac{1}{2}$ hours. Of the hitting and intensity during practice, Greenwald said, "It's like a game."

He left practice at 6:15, ate dinner and then went to study. At least, he tried to.

"You feel like laying down and taking a nap," he said. "Sometimes I do."

It's a grind that allows no time for excess. As for having a social life during the season, Greenwald said, "If I did, I'd die."

It's the life of a student-athlete. It's not the life of a normal student.

Like most athletes on college campuses, Greenwald wondered what it would be like if he were one of them—a normal student.

"I think about it," he said. "Who knows what would happen?"

Greenwald thought some more. Then a few minutes later, without being prodded, he allowed, "My biggest regret is that I haven't been able to study as much as I'd like. I can't put in as much effort as I'd like. I just don't have the time."

The life of a student-athlete is perpetual motion. It's one long no-huddle offense. Days start early and end late, if they end at all.

"You could use 28 hours," said Purdue running back Corey Rogers.

Existing as a student-athlete means making compromises. Often, academics comes out on the short end.

According to a *Tribune* study, athletes live in a constant state of exhaustion during the season, making studying difficult. "You take for granted that you're always going to be tired," said former Wisconsin linebacker Gary Casper.

Athletes miss excessive class time because of travel requirements. Former Illinois basketball star Bruce Douglas estimated he missed a month's worth of classes during the season. In addition, besides the mandatory time they spend on their sport, athletes put in countless hours either on their own, or from the sometimes spoken and unspoken prodding of coaches.

"It's a bear," said former Wisconsin basketball coach Steve Yoder. "I know it is by the preparation we have to do for a game. The players try to read a chapter, get a report done and then do everything we give them. It's a lot of pressure."

Even the most academically inclined find themselves having to take easier major programs to compensate for the time-demands of their sports. Those who aren't as academically motivated usually seek shortcuts to try to get by in the classroom.

And sadly, the rigors of being both a student and an athlete takes the enjoyment out of both endeavors. The common phrase used: "It's a job."

"People look at us and see our scholarships and say we should feel fortunate," said Illinois offensive tackle Mike Suarez. "But they don't understand. Football is a job in itself." The lines often get blurred.

"I tell people my playbook is another textbook," said former Northwestern tailback Bobby Jackson. Ron Brown, director of academic support services for athletes at Pittsburgh, viewed the situation with regret. "The one thing you hear most from the athlete is that it's no fun anymore," Brown said. "We've taken the fun out of sport."

NCAA reformers thought they had addressed the problem in passing legislation at the 1991 convention. Known as "the 20-hour rule," the regulation prohibited athletes from being required to put in more than 20 hours a week on their sport on a mandatory basis. It was hailed as a major reform because student-athletes would be able to spend more time as students than athletes.

If that were only the case.

According to most coaches and players, the "20-hour rule" has had little or no impact in reducing the demands on a student-athlete.

"Personally I don't think the 20-hour rule made a difference," Brown said. "One of the hopes we were banking on was they would take greater advantage of the college experience. From what I've seen, I don't think students are spending any more time on academics."

Few violations, mostly minor, have been reported.

When football coach Earle Bruce was let go at Colorado State, it was disclosed his players weren't being given a mandatory day off, as required by the legislation.

"I like the rule, because it restrains those coaches who might abuse it," said Illinois football coach Lou Tepper. "In the Big 10, four or five coaches would go beyond that number if permitted."

Yet, technically, all the coaches go beyond the limit, Tepper included. "The 20-hour rule" has a lot of stretch in it.

"There a lot of shades of gray," said Purdue football coach Jim Colletto. "It's not as idealistic as everyone would like it to be."

For instance, playing a game counts only three hours in the overall total. That hardly includes travel time, pregame preparation, warm-ups and post-game meetings. Most college football games themselves go way beyond three hours.

The Northwestern baseball team had a week last April where it played eight games, including three double-headers; the NCAA counts a double-header as one game. To say the players spent less than 20 hours on their sport that week would take some creative accounting.

Robert Copeland, an associate dean at Illinois, once pegged the time allotment for an Illinois football player at 65 hours per week. While that's excessive, most athletes estimate they spend at least 35 to 40 hours a week on their sport when everything from travel time to taping is included.

For some, that includes the off-season, too. Football has 15 days of spring practice, which cuts into the players' studying time. The commitments, though, go beyond the mandatory practice time.

During the football off-season, the NCAA allows eight hours for mandatory conditioning programs.

"Eight hours? Ha, ha, ha," the Illinois's Suarez said. "That won't work. Our volunteer time goes beyond eight hours."

Suarez, a junior, trains at least six days a week, instead of the four required by Tepper. It's part of the athletic mentality that the better-prepared player is the best player.

"I have no choice because I need to be getting stronger," Suarez said. He said the coaches don't tell him he has to spend that much time in the gym, "but they don't discourage it." He labeled the arrangement "voluntary-mandatory."

"I don't ask our players to put in more than eight hours," Tepper said. "I don't have any problem with players putting in the extra time if they can fit it into their schedule. If there is a great percentage of players working beyond eight hours, I'd say that's a great advantage to us."

During the football season, coaches can't lock players up in rooms and make them watch film for hours as they did in the past. The players, however, still watch film on their own time.

But there's a price to the players, and it comes in the form of physical and mental fatigue.

Athletes hardly are the only people on campus who put in large amounts of time in extracurricular activities. Many others work long hours at jobs to help meet expenses.

There's a difference, however.

"The emotional and physical fatigue: It's not like working at Macy's," said Allen Sack, a Notre Dame football player in the 1960s who has done extensive research on athletics and academics as a professor at the University of New Haven.

"None of my students is expected to risk his body every day. Most people never deal with that kind of exhaustion, with the exception of the military."

The toll is considerable. Studying isn't high on the most-desired list once practice ends.

"The last thing you want to do is crack a book," said former Illinois lineman John Janata. "You sit there with an ice pack on your shoulder, another one on your knee. The ice is dripping all over your book, it's not the best way to approach your studies."

## GOING THROUGH THE MOTIONS

The pressure of playing their sports adds to the strain. Miss an important free throw and the sick feeling goes to class with you the next day. Try being a quarterback at Notre Dame and having to prepare for the upcoming game with Florida State. Suddenly, English Lit doesn't seem as important.

"The hardest part is you're supposed to go to the classroom, and that's supposed to be the only thing on your mind." said former Notre Dame quarterback Rick Mirer. "Then you go to the field, and that's supposed to be the only thing on your mind. It's hard to separate the two."

Many athletes aren't able to. Often, academics gets cast out of mind, especially during a pressure time like the NCAA basketball tournament.

Illinois' Douglas remembered attending classes where he was there in body only.

"During the basketball season, in a month, I'd be lucky to be in class for a week," said Douglas, who completed his eligibility in 1986. "Then you're so tired when you get back from a road trip. It's tough. You lose a game, you're upset. Then you come back home, and boom, you're out of energy. You basically go through the motions."

Going through the motions requires adjustments. For most students, college means long hours in the library and the occasional all-nighter.

Yet athletes, some of whom are marginal students, don't have that luxury. So they look for shortcuts.

"The balance was difficult," said Sack. "Candidly, I took courses that allowed you to survive as an athlete and a student. A student-athlete has no business playing college sports and taking 15 hours."

Some athletes reluctantly use alternatives as a last resort. T. J. Rayford, a Northwestern basketball player, started out majoring in engineering. But he couldn't handle the workload and continue to play basketball. So he switched majors to psychological services.

"I couldn't do what I wanted to do," Rayford said. "I'm satisfied now, [but back then] I felt kind of cheated. It's not like I can't do the work. But if I go through it now, I won't get the grades because of the time demands."

Marvin Cobb, a former academic adviser at Southern Cal, said athletes used to choose majors simply because they offered classes in the morning, allowing the afternoon to be free for their sport. "If the professors didn't teach in the morning," he said, "the athlete would go on to something else."

In some cases, the athletic priorities run even deeper. Copeland remembered the case of an Illinois football player who was in academic trouble during the 1980s. It turned out he consistently was skipping his 1 o'clock class. The reason? His position coach scheduled a meeting for that time.

"How many times are athletes late for practice? Late for a game?" asked De Paul academic adviser Shirley Becker. "Very rarely. They have their priorities."


## FEELING THE SQUEEZE

The frustration of trying to do both sometimes boils over. On a cold February day, Purdue's Rogers was on his way to the football team's mandatory workout.

Rogers was taking 18 hours that semester and spring practice was coming up, where he would feel the squeeze even more. He was upset.

"I'm tired of school," he said. "I'm tired of football. What makes me mad is the work. Go to classes, go the library. The work piles up. Put an hour in at the study table. Lift weights. Go to practice. Eat. Maybe I'll have five minutes left to call my mom."

Does it feel like a job?

"Oh yes," said Rogers. "It's hard being young and having to do all that stuff."

Then he added the student-athlete's credo: "I'm tired of it, but I've got to do it."

The student-athlete has no other choice.

Sunday in perspective: No cures, just bandages to cover the academic hypocrisy prevalent in major college sports.

# 22

## Spotting, Treating Troubled Athletes Can Be Difficult

Shelly Sanford
Suzanne Halliburton

### FORMER UT SWIMMERS ACKNOWLEDGE TEAM HAD OBSESSION WITH WEIGHT

A majority of former University of Texas women swimmers interviewed by the *Austin American-Statesman* over the past six months agreed that almost everyone on the team was obsessed with her weight, but they differed in assessing how many of their teammates had eating disorders.

The *American-Statesman* contacted 18 athletes who swam for former Coach Richard Quick from 1983 to 1988. Quick led UT to five NCAA titles in six years before leaving for Stanford last September. Of the 18:

Two refused to comment.

Three said they were diagnosed as bulimic, a disorder characterized by cycles of eating binges followed by artificial methods of purging the food, such as inducing vomiting, taking laxatives and taking diuretics. For four consecutive years, the UT swim team had at least two athletes practicing bulimia regularly.

Two—Tiffany Cohen and Kim Rhodenbaugh—have retired from the sport. Cohen spent nine weeks at St. David's Hospital for treatment of bulimia late last year, and Rhodenbaugh went through six months of outpatient treatment, ending in January, at the Austin Eating Disorders Clinic. "There were more people who had a problem," said Cohen, estimating there might have been 10 to 12 during her three years at UT. "Their problem wasn't as bad as mine, as full-fledged like mine was. But they were there."

Ten said they used some unhealthy means of losing weight, ranging from fasting to laxatives to eating non-nutritious food.

Eleven said they were aware a number of their teammates were obsessed with weight.

Twelve said weight goals set by . . . Quick led to weight obsessions.

---

Terrianne McGuirk Kingsbury, an All-American in the butterfly, had problems getting down to Quick's goal of 125 pounds her freshman year.

Kingsbury, now a nurse in Fort Washington, Pa., said no one knew she used laxatives, so no one sent her to counseling. Instead, she broke the dangerous habit when she entered UT's nursing program her junior year and realized how damaging it was to her body.

"When you do these things, you don't want someone to help you. Losing weight is the only thing you want," she said. "And you are not thinking, 'This is so bad for me.' I never told anybody, and I don't think anybody ever knew. It's just so hard. I just recall it being so hard to lose weight."

Tori Trees, a tall, lanky backstroker, said she lived on Captain Crunch cereal while training for the Olympics in the summer of 1984.

"They should put me on the Captain Crunch box," she said. "I weigh about the same as when I quit. I lost a lot of muscle in different areas. I still think about it [weight]. Not having to get up in the morning and swim relieves so much pressure. I can sleep at night. I like to do other things. I would say I'm not as stressed as when I swam."

Many thought Kara McGrath, the team's captain in 1987, had an eating disorder her freshman year. McGrath said looking back now, she probably was borderline anorexic (a disorder characterized by self-starvation; some anorexics starve themselves to death). She lost 15 pounds by eating very little nutritious food to prepare for the 1984 Olympic Trials. She didn't make the Olympic team and gradually gained the weight back the next two years.

"I think part of it was that I thought that was the way to success as far as swimming," said McGrath, now an assistant coach at the University of Michigan. "I think that I was kind of naive because I thought those people on top were just naturally [thin]."

Many swimmers said they knew about each other's obsession with weight, because that was always what they talked about in the locker rooms and dormitories. Most suspected the others were losing weight improperly.

"Food was the thing that was on everybody's mind all the time," said Susan Johnson, a 1988 Olympian and two-time All-American. "It was on my mind from the minute I woke up. The only time I didn't think about it was when I was in the water swimming.

"Some people would not eat the day before weighing in, and some people would throw up, take laxatives—do anything to weigh in lighter that day."

Tracey McFarlane, who won a silver medal in the 1988 Olympics, didn't think many teammates had eating disorders. But she said weight was on her mind constantly her freshman and sophomore years at Texas. She said the most drastic measure she took was to fast one weekend before weighing in so she would be at the goal set by Quick.

"I was obsessed with it," McFarlane said, "because someone was always drilling it in my head, saying, 'You have to be this weight, this weight.' "

Trees, looking back on her years at UT, said she realized how the sheer stress of making weight caused so many problems.

"With the stress, there is no telling what you will do," she said. "You can look back on your mistakes, but I don't know if you can change them. It is hard on their bodies. We swam so much—five to seven miles per day—and just eating salads and taking diuretics wasn't going to cut it."

Many swimmers said mandatory weigh-ins should be abolished. A number of swimmers blamed Quick's stringent adherence to weight goals for their obsessions, yet some of them also defended him. Quick would meet individually with swimmers at the start of each season and tell them how many pounds he thought they should weigh to swim the most effectively.

Debbie Risen, an All-American backstroker and graduate assistant under Quick, believes weight goals are necessary. The swimmers weren't disciplined enough to lose the weight themselves, she said. However, Risen also said she did not like weighing in and that goals did cause problems.

"It happens because of the way the coaches are, but I can almost feel 100 percent that they don't do it on purpose," Risen said.


## SECRECY SHROUDS EATING
## DISORDERS, BUT THERE IS HELP

Four-time All-American Kara McGrath listened to the painful confession of a University of Michigan swimmer who forces herself to throw up so she can stay skinny.

McGrath, an assistant coach at Michigan, was a borderline anorexic during her freshman year at the University of Texas, so she could draw on her own experience to comfort the swimmer.

"This girl came to me because she had a problem. She was not thin, and I never suspected it. The girl really didn't want anybody to know," McGrath said. "She swam for a team in Germantown, Pennsylvania, so she was around a lot of elite swimmers, and she said that is where she learned about bulimia. I'm anxious to get back with her and see what has happened."

The frustrating part for McGrath is that all she can do is share her experience. She cannot force the swimmer to stop throwing up or seek professional help. She cannot even be sure that the swimmer who came to her is the only one with a problem, because most people with eating disorders keep them secret.

What to do about female athletes with eating disorders is becoming an issue at universities with highly competitive programs. Problems such as anorexia (starvation) and bulimia (eating binges followed by vomiting or using laxatives and diuretics to purge the food) are on the rise, especially among athletes in swimming and track, where weight goals are enforced.

Officials in the UT women's athletic department confirmed they have directed 12 current athletes to off-campus treatment programs for eating disorders. A survey a few years ago indicated 10 percent of UT's female athletes had at least one eating disorder and another 20 to 30 percent showed signs of having a disorder.

Donna Lopiano, UT's women's athletics director, recognized that there was a problem about a year and a half ago. She called in 40 experts, including all of the women's coaches, to discuss what to do. The group, which also included doctors, trainers and nutritionists, is called "The Performance Team." It publishes a newsletter that is sent to universities around the nation.

In May, the women's athletic department held a breakfast fund-raiser that brought in $3,000 to help with the eating disorders problem. Performance Team director Randa Ryan, an exercise physiologist at UT, said the money would be used to publish more newsletters on how to deal with eating disorders.

Ryan said an athlete has several options if she believes she has an eating disorder. UT has an eating disorders program available to all students, and Ryan said many athletes may go there for help and not inform the athletic department.

"There could be kids getting help that we don't know anything about, and we encourage that," Ryan said. "If an athlete is uncomfortable talking to a coach, or talking to me, they are educated to [go to] other sources to get help. The health center is one; there are many private authorities and self-help groups. There are several layers of help going on."

If an athlete goes to Ryan, she makes an evaluation and determines where to go for assistance. If outside counseling is necessary, the athlete usually is directed to St. David's Hospital.

After conferring with the hospital's counselors, the athlete has the option of obtaining outside counseling or entering the St. David's Eating Disorders Clinic. The average inpatient stay at St. David's is six to eight weeks and costs roughly $4,000 per week. Darla Hailey, a counselor at St. David's, said family insurance generally covers the cost.

Although a new NCAA rule allows universities to pay for outpatient treatment of eating disorders, it does not allow them to spend money for hospitalization. Lopiano said no UT athletic department money has been spent for treatment of athletes with eating disorders.

Ryan also feels the frustration of her limitations. She can't force an athlete to get treatment; all she can do is make suggestions. And because those who have eating disorders are so secretive, many of the problems go undetected. An athlete can finish her eligibility without telling anyone about her disorder.

"The diseases are ones of secrecy and denial, and the only classic identification is going to be a severe anorexic whom you can see," Ryan said. "As the general public becomes more educated and we become more clear as to how we are going to identify those individuals, then the population becomes more defined."

In addition to the Performance Team and St. David's programs, UT encourages athletes to see an outside nutritionist if they are having trouble losing weight or want to learn about proper nutrition.

Records obtained by the *Austin American-Statesman* through the Texas Open Records Act showed that UT has paid $2,122 of a total bill of $14,500 for at least 15 athletes to see private nutritionists Sandra Richards and Laurie McDonald.

Richards said she counsels the athletes on an individual basis but would like to have a group class on nutrition and stress management in the future.

"I am the how person," Richards said. "They say they need to lose weight and improve performance, and I am the person who tells them how to do it. A lot of them are in a time squeeze, and they don't have much money.

"If they are on a healthier diet, sooner or later their weight will stabilize."

Helen Spear, a counselor for UT's eating disorders program, said she tries to change the athlete's focus.

"I wouldn't have them weigh in," Spear said. "I try to get them to focus less on their weight and maybe more on what they are trying to achieve in their sport."

Former UT swimmers agree that eliminating mandatory weight goals would help. Most of the swimmers interviewed by the *American-Statesman* said former UT Coach Richard Quick stressed being thin so much that they would do anything to get their weight down and please him.

"There is no doubt that there are some people who struggled with their weight goals," Quick said, "and that they had trouble getting there—very similar to the frustration they feel when they set a time goal and can't get there.

"The way we tried to address the problem at Texas was that if anybody had an eating disorder we tried to get them professional assistance. But that didn't involve the coach."

Quick, who won five NCAA championships in his six years at UT, left last September to coach at Stanford.

Mark Schubert, who replaced Quick, also sets weight goals. Two current swimmers who also swam for Quick said they would feel more comfortable approaching Schubert if they thought they had a problem. However, Susan Johnson, who is on the roster for next season, said Schubert yelled at her about her weight in front of several male swimmers during preparation for the 1988 Olympics.

Schubert did not return the *American-Statesman's* telephone calls. McGrath, who swam for Quick for four years, said she wishes she had known in her freshman year that other people had similar problems. She lost 15 pounds in one season and, like the swimmer who approached her at Michigan, thought she was alone.

1984 Olympian Kim Rhodenbaugh, 23, went through six months of outpatient treatment for bulimia at the Austin Eating Disorders Clinic. She said she would like to find a way to reach athletes who have eating disorders and help them build their self-esteem, an underlying problem that contributes to the disorders.

"It has changed my life," Rhodenbaugh said. "I believe I can set out to conquer anything. I have conquered something that was my enemy for years."

# 23

## Athletes Learn the Lesson
### The Lou Harris Survey

Richard E. Lapchick

We may have turned the corner on the issue of academics and athletics. It has been argued for decades that playing big-time sports in high school and college may lead to the exploitation of athletes. Low graduation rates, low scores on standardized tests, and a presumed overemphasis on sports at the expense of education, seemed to uphold the argument. The publicity regarding racism in sports in the aftermath of Marge Schott and Al Campanis (see Chapter 1) dampened the hope of those who believed that playing in sports helped ease racial tensions.

According to a recent national survey by Lou Harris (1993), many African American high school student-athletes, although still carrying the unrealistic belief that they can be the newest rising stars, now clearly understand that playing sports is a vehicle that can deliver educational, social, and life skill benefits that will help them be productive members of society. They don't have to *play* for the Bulls: They can be a team doctor or attorney.

However, the Harris study found that African American student-athletes continue to have unrealistic aspirations of playing in college and in the pros: 51% believe they can make the pros (vs. 18% of white student-athletes).

The results of the Harris survey give us hope that such fantasies may not lead to shock and emotional letdown.

If you are a 14-year-old African American, you recognize that the color of your skin may, in all likelihood, limit the range of your life's choices. You have less chance to finish high school, go to college, and be employed than if you were white. You have, by far, fewer chances of making it big in corporate America or as a top administrator or professor in college. Just turn on the TV and you will see that.

In communities driven by despair, athletes in the Centers for the Study of Sport in Society's outreach program realized that they can't afford to snuff

---

A version of this chapter originally appeared in *The Sporting News*, December 6, 1993. Reprinted by permission.

out hope. So, while not throwing sand on the fires of desire, athletes have been telling youth to keep hope alive but to balance it and prepare for the future through school.

Harris reports that outreach athletes have had a substantial and a sustained effect, especially among African American student-athletes. Harris found that 76% of African American student-athletes favor a minimum C average for eligibility in sports. Currently, 44 states do not require a C average. Student-athletes are asking for more.

As dropout rates in urban communities soar, 57% of African American student-athletes said playing sports helped "a great deal" in staying in school. Fifty percent said playing sports helped them "a great deal" to become better students.

Apparently, even athletes who believe they will make the pros aren't ignoring academic preparation. It is the first evidence that we are reaching these young people. With the understanding that one needs academic and athletic goals, playing in sports has clear benefits to African American students who may have dug a collective grave for all those who have exploited them in the past.

Among the social benefits of competing, sports seems to help African American student-athletes to avoid the drugs and alcohol that dominate the lives of many teens: 65% said playing in sports had helped "a great deal" in avoiding drugs; 60% believed playing in sports had the same effect in avoiding alcohol.

Harris pointed out another major benefit, "It was critical to see that at a time when racial and ethnic tensions boil over in school into serious conflicts almost every day, the survey showed that team sports create friendships that cut across racial lines; 76 percent of all white and African American student-athletes reported that they became friends with someone from another racial or ethnic group through playing sports."

We don't get together as equals in many places in America. In our racially charged society, this may prove to be the ultimate benefit of sports, fulfilling the dream of Jackie Robinson.

In my early experiences, the world of sports was littered with broken promises and unfulfilled dreams. This is the best news I have yet seen that sports is beginning to deliver on these promises it has made for all these years.

## REFERENCE

Louis Harris & Associates, Inc. (1993). *Racism and violence in American high schools: Project TEAMWORK responds.* (Available from the Center for the Study of Sport in Society, 360 Huntington Ave., 161 CP, Boston, MA 02115)

# 24

# A New Beginning for a New Century
Intercollegiate Athletics in the United States

Knight Foundation Commission on Intercollegiate Athletics

"As our nation approaches a new century," the Knight Foundation Commission observed in 1991, "the demand for reform of intercollegiate athletics has escalated dramatically." Today, that escalating demand is being matched by accelerating reform. College and university presidents, along with the leaders and members of the National Collegiate Athletic Association (NCAA), have taken advantage of a swelling chorus for reform to make a new beginning in college sports. Although barely implemented today, the full effects of recent reforms will be visible as the 21st century dawns.

The distance college sports have traveled in three short years can be measured by developments in public opinion. In 1989, pollster Louis Harris asked if big-time intercollegiate athletics were out of control. Across the United States, heads nodded in agreement: 78 percent of Americans thought that the situation was out of hand. In 1993, 52 percent of the public continued to agree. This significant 26-point decline represents how far college sports have come. The fact that about half of all Americans remain troubled represents the distance yet to go. Nevertheless, a new air of confidence is measurable and can be seen in other findings of the Harris survey: In 1989, nearly two-thirds of Americans believed state or national legislation was needed to control college sports; less than half feel that way today. Earlier negative views of the NCAA have turned into positive marks for its efforts to control excesses in college sports.

What accounts for the impressive turnaround in perceptions? The improvement is no accident, but a response to the highly visible pace of reform in recent years. Since 1989, college and university presidents, the members of the NCAA and athletics leaders have addressed a single goal with singular concentration: restoring integrity to the games played in the university's

Reprinted by permission of The Knight Foundation Commission on Intercollegiate Athletics, 1043 Morehead Street, Suite 100, Charlotte, NC, 28204.

name. They have created a structure of reform that can reshape the conduct, management and accountability of college sports. The new Harris poll tells us the American people are paying attention.


## REFORMS OF RECENT YEARS

In 1991, this Commission proposed a new model for intercollegiate athletics, a kind of road map entitled "one-plus-three," in which the "one"—presidential control—would be directed toward the "three"—academic integrity, financial integrity and independent certification.

Such a model, this Commission believed, represented higher education's only real assurance that intercollegiate athletics could be grounded in the primacy of academic values. NCAA legislation in recent years has put this model in place.

These changes promise to reshape dramatically the environment for intercollegiate athletics. In 1989, the NCAA's Presidents Commission was tentative about how best to challenge the *status quo* in intercollegiate athletics. Established in 1984 as a compromise to a more ambitious effort to ensure presidential control of the NCAA, the Commission found itself five years later on the defensive. But by 1993, the Presidents Commission was in firm control of the Association's legislative agenda. Presidents Commission recommendations have dominated three successive NCAA conventions. With majorities of 3-1 or better, the Commission has pushed through preliminary cost reductions, new academic standards and an athletics certification program. Of even greater long-term significance, the 1993 legislation created an NCAA Joint Policy Board, made up of the Association's Administrative Committee and officers of the Presidents Commission, with authority to review the NCAA budget and legislative agenda and to evaluate and supervise the executive director. Presidential leadership is the hallmark of today's NCAA.

In 1989, student-athletes could compete in their first year of college if they had finished high school with a "C" average in 11 core academic subjects, along with combined Scholastic Aptitude Test scores of 700. This weak foundation, combined with lack of attention to academic progress, meant that, five years later, many student-athletes found themselves far short of a college degree. By 1995, eligibility to play in the freshman year will require a 2.5 high school grade point average ("C+" or "B-") in 13 high school academic units.[1] One year later the 13 units must include four years of English and one year each of algebra and geometry. Meanwhile, graduation rates for student-athletes are published annually and, effective this academic year, student-athletes must demonstrate continuous, satisfactory progress toward graduation: They are now required to meet annual benchmarks in both grades and coursework applicable to a specific degree. Academic integrity is being restored; student-athletes will now be students as well as athletes.

Three years ago, athletics finances were escalating beyond reason. Colleges and universities were in the midst of a kind of athletics arms race: Deficits mounted . . . the costs of grants-in-aid mushroomed . . . athletics budgets ballooned beyond institutional reach . . . and it was unclear who employed some "power" coaches, since their outside income often dwarfed university compensation. Today, the number of grants-in-aid for men in Divisions I and II of the NCAA has been reduced 10 percent; coaching staffs have been trimmed; athletics budgets are reviewed as part of a new certification process; cost containment is the subject of a major new study; and coaches must have annual written approval from their presidents for all athletically related outside income. Universities have made a start in restoring order to the financial side of the house of athletics.

Finally, in 1989, too many big-time athletics programs had succeeded in imposing on universities a great reversal of ends and means. They had, this Commission found, become self-justifying enterprises in which winning-at-all-costs had pushed aside the educational context of athletics competition. Beginning this Fall [1993], each NCAA Division I institution will have to participate in a certification program once every five years. This program requires each institution to examine four key areas—institutional mission, academic integrity, fiscal integrity and commitment to equity—and (the most important factor) permit an external jury of academic and sports peers to evaluate and verify its findings. The new program promises to align means and ends.

The certification process is the capstone of the reform movement and will remain one of the movement's genuine legacies. Because it involves the entire campus community in a detailed examination of athletics policy issues, certification embodies the standards and values befitting higher education. By calling for regular self-examination of every corner of big-time programs under the bright light of outside peer review, certification should curb abuse before it starts, instead of after the damage has been done.

Meanwhile, on campuses and in conferences across the country, athletics and academic leaders have drawn new energy from the reform movement. Often using the "one-plus-three" model as their lens, presidentially appointed task forces, trustees and athletics boards have examined again the goals and operations of their athletics programs.

## CHALLENGES AHEAD

This progress is encouraging, but the struggle for reform is far from won. Winning that struggle is what the "one-plus-three" model is all about. Academic and athletics officials now possess a new framework within which to tackle the many problems of college sports: abuses in recruiting, the bane of the college coach's life; the compulsion of boosters to meddle in athletics decision making; the search for television revenues and the influence of the entertainment industry on intercollegiate athletics; the relationships among high school, junior college, college and professional sports; the need to respect the dignity of the young men and women who represent the university on the playing field; the obligation to further strengthen academic standards so that the profile of student-athletes matches that of other full-time undergraduates in admissions, academic progress and graduation rates; and the imperative to meet the needs of minority student-athletes, particularly those from backgrounds of inner-city or rural poverty.

As this Commission's tenure draws to a close, two great issues, cost containment and gender equity, dominate athletics policy discussions. These are first-order questions, significant problems requiring the best thinking of the nation's university and athletics leaders. Part of their complexity lies in the fact they are intertwined: Costs should not be controlled at the price of rebuffing women's aspirations. Opportunities for women must be provided in the context of controlling outlays for athletics programs that already cost too much. The cost control and equity dilemmas have to be addressed together.

*The Cost Explosion.* Despite recent modest reductions in athletics expenses, the hard work of cost reduction lies ahead. Quite apart from athletics, American higher education entered the 1990s facing its bleakest financial prospects since World War II. All institutions, including most flagship public and private universities, are in the midst of harrowing financial reductions, often involving staff and faculty layoffs, enrollment ceilings and the elimination of academic departments. In this environment, athletics programs can expect no special immunity from the financial hardships facing the institutions they represent.

NCAA figures indicate that throughout the 1980s, athletics programs engaged in a financial arms race: Athletics costs grew twice as fast as academic salaries and three times faster than inflation. The urge to be nationally competitive, no matter the expense, assumed its own dynamic. Despite conventional wisdom, about 70 percent of Division I programs now lose money, many of them operating deeply in the red. It seems clear that athletics programs stand in need of the same kind of financial restructuring the larger academic community is already experiencing. On most campuses, athletics operating costs can be reduced substantially. But athletics programs will not disarm unilaterally. The active support of conferences and the NCAA is critical to effective cost control.

*Gender Equity.* Against the backdrop of the imperative for cost reduction, the unfinished agenda of equity for women also demands attention. Most campuses are struggling to meet the requirements of Title IX of the Education Amendments [Act] of 1972, even as case law defining those requirements is being made. In general, according to an NCAA study of gender equity study released in 1992, Title IX regulations call for accommodating the athletics interests of enrolled women, allocating financial assistance in proportion to the number of male and female participants and making other benefits equivalent. Slowly, often in the face of opposition, opportunity for women to participate in intercollegiate athletics has become a reality.

But the opportunity is not truly equal. On many campuses, fans would be outraged if revenue-generating teams were expected to make do with the resources available to women. Even leaving out of the equation the major revenue-generating sports, football and men's basketball, women's programs generally operate on smaller budgets than men's. No matter the cause, the situation carries with it the threat of continued legal and Congressional scrutiny into whether young women are denied the benefits of participation in college sports.

The equity issue transcends athletics politics because it goes to the heart of what higher education is all about. Colleges and universities advance their intellectual mission by placing a premium on fairness, equality, competition and recognition of merit. These values are as important in the department of athletics as they are in the office of the dean. Keeping faith with student-athletes means keeping faith with women as well as men. The goal to keep in mind is the imperative to create comparable opportunities for participants, whether men or women, while controlling costs.


## A PROMISE AND A CHOICE


If that goal is to be reached, the "one-plus-three" model advanced by this Commission will be put to a severe test. Tempted to believe the battle for reform has been won because the framework is in place, presidents may turn their attention to other demands. That must not be allowed to happen. Presidential neglect of these issues is a sure formula for giving ground on the progress already made.

This Commission believes the reforms enacted to date represent some of the most encouraging developments in intercollegiate athletics since the NCAA was established in 1906. But optimism about the reforms and their potential must be tempered with realism. Reform is not a destination but a never-ending process, a race without a finish. That is why the new NCAA certification program is so significant. By requiring presidents, trustees, faculty members, athletics administrators and coaches to examine the integrity of their sports programs every five years, certification keeps the process alive.

Maintaining the momentum for reform is important. The reforms of the last three years remain a promise yet to be kept: They will be implemented fully in 1995-96. This means that not a single student-athlete has yet entered and completed college under these changes. The first student-athletes to do so will graduate, at the earliest, in 1999. The certification program is ready to be launched, but it will not complete a full cycle of all Division I institutions before the 1998-99 school year. Making judgments today about the effects of these changes is premature; their real effects will appear at the end of the decade.

Moreover, no matter how deep-rooted reform is, it cannot transform human nature. Even with the new changes fully in place and working effectively, no one should be surprised when some institutions continue to be embarrassed by revelations about their athletics departments. People in college sports are like people everywhere: Most want to do the right thing; but some will try to skirt the rules, inevitably getting themselves, their associates and their institutions into trouble because, sooner or later, they will ignore the line dividing the acceptable from the unacceptable.

But realism should not give way to pessimism or cynicism. Cynics may dismiss the reform effort, but they do so at their own risk. Something fundamental has changed in college sports. It is perhaps best illustrated by support for the Presidents Commission reform agenda from coaches, athletics directors, conference leaders and faculty representatives. Because not everyone is ready for reform, this support is far from universal; nevertheless, it is impressive.

What has changed fundamentally is the following: The institutional indifference and presidential neglect that led to disturbing patterns of abuse throughout the 1980s have been replaced with a new structure insisting on institutional oversight and depending on presidential leadership backed up by trustee support. The leaders and members of the NCAA now have a framework for meaningful reform if they have the will, the courage and the perseverance to use it.

Along with that framework come new responsibilities. It was once possible for college sports administrators on the one hand, and university presidents and trustees, on the other, to evade responsibility for the difficulties of intercollegiate athletics. Each side could plausibly claim the other possessed the authority to act. That claim no longer holds water. The "one-plus-three" model places authority exactly where it belongs both in the councils of the NCAA and on individual campuses. Presidents today possess the power they need and, with the backing of their trustees, the responsibility to act.

The presidents of the nation's colleges and universities have reached a kind of Rubicon, a point of decision, with regard to their athletics programs. They face a choice about how to proceed, a choice between business as usual and making a new beginning.

Business as usual in college sports will undermine American higher education. It leads inexorably to regulation of intercollegiate athletics by the courts or Congress. That is a consequence no one wants, but many, unwittingly, may invite.

The second choice strengthens American higher education. The Harris poll convincingly demonstrates that the American people respect college sports when they are grounded in the larger mission of the university. As the United States approaches a new century, the new beginning represented by a strong "one-plus-three" model promises to restore higher education's moral claim to the high ground it should occupy.

These choices and their consequences are what is at stake in the athletics reform movement. The final words of the members of the Knight Foundation Commission on Intercollegiate Athletics to the leaders of the nation's colleges and universities are an echo from long ago. In 1929, the Carnegie Foundation for the Advancement of Teaching published a landmark study taking presidents to task for their failure to defend the integrity of higher education. There can be no doubt that presidents today have the opportunity to put that long-standing criticism to rest. A genuine assessment of the value of the current reform movement cannot be made by today's observers. The true test will be applied by historians of the future, because they will ask whether today's presidents employed their power wisely and chose well.

## NOTE

1. Under a proposal adopted at the 1992 NCAA convention, initial eligibility requires that by 1995, high school student-athletes present a 2.5 grade point average (out of a possible 4.0) in 13 core high school units, along with a combined SAT score of 700 (ACT [American College Test] score of 17) in order to compete in their first year of college enrollment. A sliding scale permits a higher aptitude test score to compensate for a lower grade point average, but no student-athlete can compete in the first year with SATs below 700 (ACT below 17), with a high school grade point average below 2.00, or with fewer than 13 of the core requirements.

# PART IV

# Stereotypes, Myths, and Realities About Athletes

## Introduction

At the close of the 1994-95 National Football League (NFL) season, San Francisco 49ers' cornerback, Deion Sanders, was named the NFL's Defensive Player of the Year. Analysts agreed that he helped the 49ers win the Super Bowl. While he was dazzling fans on the football field, he was also accused of assaulting a police officer, recorded a CD that trivialized the importance of education and portrayed wealth as a way to attract fawning women, and participated in a fistfight with a former teammate and friend during a nationally televised game.

In 1992, a Nike commercial attracted some unfavorable reviews for featuring Charles Barkley declaring that he was not a role model. Meanwhile, they were eager to take advantage of his great appeal to encourage the young to buy shoes. Much of the criticism came from those who insisted that athletes are duty bound to be positive examples as a result of their unsurpassed visibility. Barkley later clarified that his point was to suggest that parents should be kids' leading examples, not professional athletes.

Sanders and Barkley never chose the path of the role model. O. J. Simpson secured it as a player and as an entertainer. His precipitous fall after the brutal murder of his ex-wife and her friend further called the role model status of athletes into question. Although professional players have differing opinions on being automatically called "role models," there is a growing public debate over the notion that sports heroes are the best examples for our youth.

The growing skepticism is, in part, a product of the ever increasing scrutiny of the off-the-field lifestyles of athletes. The images of athletes participating in charity work for the poor, actively working with young people to reduce illiteracy, and speaking out against the perils of alcohol and drug use are overshadowed by the more than occasional reports of athletes charged in the commission of crimes, banished from competition for violating league drug policies, and fined, suspended, or both for violent altercations on the field.

Although Barkley's argument for the disassociation of athletes from role model status is shared by some people both in and out of the world of sports, the obvious drawing power of athletes warrants the use of athletes in the promotion of social programs. The Center for the Study of Sport in Society was among the first to use athletes to foster social change in the mid-1980s, and now many groups are using athletes as spokespersons.

Student-athletes working with the center and the National Consortium for Academics and Athletics made an enormous contribution in their communities. In 1993-94 alone, they worked with 588,497 young people. Among their activities, they participated in reading programs in more than 50 elementary and middle schools, monitored programs with juvenile offenders and drug users, and worked in homeless shelters, soup kitchens, and shelters for battered women. Furthermore, they worked with at-risk youth in more than 60 communities, established black athletes as role models for youth, and established programs to encourage terminally ill children in more than 75 hospitals. They worked with special Olympians and taught physical education classes in a system that had terminated them after budget cuts.

Just months after O. J. Simpson was charged with murdering his ex-wife, Florida's largest and oldest shelter for abused women arranged for six past and present members of the Miami Dolphins to speak at a symposium regarding their personal experience with abuse against women. The mere presence of NFL players talking about domestic abuse attracted national attention to the forum.

In addition to employing athletes as spokespersons, there continue to be notable instances in which athletes make admirable transitions from player to civic servant. The 1994 elections saw the state of Oklahoma send two former football players to Congress. Steve Largent, an NFL record-breaking receiver with the Seattle Seahawks, and J. C. Watts, a former standout with the Oklahoma Sooners, joined a host of other former athletes currently serving in the nation's capital. Watts is the first black Republican to be elected to the House of Representatives from the south since Reconstruction.

Perhaps the single largest change to affect sport in recent years is the new power structure that frequently sees players having more leverage than their coaches. Fueling the debate over athletes as role models is the unprecedented wealth afforded to young athletes who obtain multimillion dollar contracts right out of college. The practice has led to well-publicized feuds between coaches and players and led *Sports Illustrated* (Taylor, 1995) to suggest that "a form of insanity is spreading through the NBA like a virus. . . . its carriers, pouting prima donnas who commit the most outrageous acts of rebellion, include some of the league's younger stars" (p. 19). This growing disrespect for authority has again raised the question of whether today's younger athletes merely mirror the trends of society at-large or help establish patterns of behavior.

The fast track from high school to college to professional sports continues to keep attention on the legitimacy of athletes as students. The NCAA's annual publication of graduation rate statistics reveals that scholarship athletes, in general, graduate at a rate equivalent or superior to the rest of the student body. Yet the notion lingers that athletes are merely "dumb jocks" and that revenue-generating sports programs are little more than factories for the professional leagues.

Two recent New York City schoolboy phenoms emphatically highlight the argument. In 1994, high school Player of the Year, Felipe Lopez, chose to stay in New York City and attend St. John's University. He did so because he wanted to give New York's Hispanic population a role model to believe in. Although St. John's had a disappointing basketball season in the always tough Big East, Lopez averaged nearly 20 points per game while obtaining a 3.8 grade point average in his first semester.

In contrast, 1995's top New York City basketball star, Stephon Marbury, announced that he was attending Georgia Tech. He said that Felipe had the Big East and, therefore, he wanted the Atlantic Coast Conference for his stage. Marbury acknowledged that his selection of a college was based on basketball and which school would best enhance his opportunity for the pros. Tech coach Bobby Cremins had a great reputation for developing pro guards, including Kenny Anderson. Marbury is fortunate in that Georgia Tech has a fine academic reputation.

In this section, Lawrence Wenner offers a critical essay on the dangers associated with viewing athletes as role models. Focusing on the contrasting views of Charles Barkley, Vince Coleman, Reggie Lewis, and Martina Navratilova, Wenner examines how athletes view themselves with respect to the role model title.

Richard Lapchick's "Gender Violence and Lessons Learned From the Simpson Case" follows this. Lapchick calls the case America's wake-up call on gender violence. The piece also considers the dilemma that takes place when all athletes are automatically ordained as role models and the corollary that when an athlete has a serious problem it diminishes the potential of all others to be role models. Lapchick concludes that both propositions are equally false.

Lapchick's "Violence in Sports" was written during the 1994 NBA Finals. Coming on the heels of criticism over the perceived increased in violence during NBA games, Lapchick suggests potential sources for the increase of on-the-court fights and notes that the fights in the NBA actually succeeded years of brawls in baseball and hockey.

Gary Sailes investigates the stereotypes specifically associated with black student-athletes on college campuses. Sailes discusses beliefs about intelligence, academic integrity, and academic competitiveness. He also assesses the validity of perceptions related to intelligence, academic preparation, style of play, competitiveness, physical superiority, athletic ability, and mental temperament in African American athletes.

This section also includes an argument to involve college coaches in the development of NCAA legislation. After the dismissal of a few prominent coaches in 1993 and the disdainful treatment of Duke coach Mike Krzyzewski's comments at the 1993 NCAA Convention, Lapchick wrote, "The Rules of the Game Are Changing: College Coaches in the 1990s." This piece generally argues for allowing coaches to have a voice with college presidents and athletic directors in the quest to improve academic conditions for student-athletes. If coaches are part of the decision-making process, they will be more likely to support the changes.

Finally, this section concludes with an article by Lapchick calling on coaches and the companies that support them to become involved in the community.

## REFERENCE

Taylor, P. (1995, January 30). Bad actors. *Sports Illustrated,* pp. 18-23.

# 25

# Intersections as Dangerous Places
## Theories and Role Models in Sport Studies

Lawrence A. Wenner

This issue of the *Journal of Sport & Social Issues* has me thinking about intersections: intersections in the doing of sports studies, intersections in experiencing sports in everyday life. Intersections are inherently dangerous places. On the road, nasty collisions regularly happen at intersections. Different people heading different directions with different purposes all attempt to pass through. The intersection is not the ultimate destination for most. Intersections are necessary evils. It is a place one negotiates to get somewhere else. One does not normally head for the intersection to meet people. In fact, we regulate intersections so that we don't meet others in a crash. Stop signs, yield warnings, traffic lights, and protected turn lanes all tell us that when we enter an intersection we are not entering a natural place.

## INTERSECTIONS AND SPORTS ROLE MODELS

On a more personal level, I am trying to sort out the goings on at another dangerous intersection, one where I experience sport in my everyday life. This is the intersection of sports role models. Here we see that although some of the signs are marked, they aren't to be believed. Other signs are seemingly contradictory. Yet others, although the directional warnings have been clearly verbally announced out in the open, have not been posted by the authorities.

On one hand, Charles Barkley impresses on me, courtesy of a Nike ad campaign, that he isn't a role model. The sign is marked but not to be believed. Charles may say "don't do as I do" out of one side of his corporatized mouth, but out of the other comes "buy these shoes" and be like Charles, the meanest, toughest, fly-high guy to jam one in your face. Don't be like me, but buy so you can be like me. Polysemic? Sure, but the lesson is clear: Be expedient. Do what you need to do. Say what you need to say. It matters not if it's contradictory, only if its cool.

The recent heart attack and death of Boston Celtic star Reggie Lewis shows how unsuccessfully sports figures, sports teams, and the sports press deal with the role model issue. One can forgive Mr. Lewis for the situation, in over his head in an athletic socialization process that values the culture of risk more than the culture of life. Understandable in this context was the Boston Celtic nonresponse when confronting contradictory diagnoses of Mr. Lewis' condition. Needing longer shelf life for return on investment, they hoped the glass might be half full. But the press, too, hoped for good product, the archetypal sports role model story, the comeback against all odds. Little was seen in the press calling for the Celtics to expedite a third diagnosis. And the press did not seem to "round out" the story with alternative "success stories" of athletes who had fruitfully adapted after a shortened playing career. It is easy to second-guess here. But the role model lessons are clear: Sport matters more than life, and further, it is natural, normal, and desirable to believe so.

It was fortunate indeed that the saga of Vince Coleman of the New York Mets and his unfortunate firecracker escapades were played out in close proximity to the mourning of Reggie Lewis and the lauding of him for his community service activities. Perhaps sports and the sports press took the right course here, largely scolding and disowning Coleman. Still, the lessons of Coleman are less clear. Like Lewis, he was a product of a sport socialization system that strips mere mortality from athletes. Like Barkley, shouldn't he be given the chance to say, "I am not a role model"? This is a dangerous intersection. Different rules for different players.

Nowhere was this clearer than in the coverage of one role model who didn't die, didn't throw a firecracker, and didn't say, "I am not a role model." Late in July, Martina Navratilova was honored at a benefit for Gay Games IV, which will be held next June (1994) in New York. Although 15,000 athletes are expected at the Gay Games and the event is arguably the most important in fighting homophobia in sports, this kickoff event received coverage only by Bob Lipsyte in the *New York Times*. In San Francisco, a city with a large and open gay population, the event received small play in the back pages of the news section, but nowhere did it appear in the sports section. Perhaps, for now, gay sports are not sports, and Navratilova's story is not the story of an athlete's struggle against adversity. But it is a story of a role model, and it is about to enter the intersection. Although the rules of the intersection depend on who is the traffic cop, it remains that intersections are inherently dangerous places.

# 26

## Gender Violence and Lessons Learned From the Simpson Case

Richard E. Lapchick

$A$s is usually the case with a tragedy that becomes a spectacle, lessons to be learned from the nightmare of the O. J. Simpson story are being buried by the spectacle. Like many others, I don't want to believe that O. J. is a double murderer. But it has become harder and harder to argue with the evidence that has been presented. We have been so wrapped up in the personal fall of a star who appeared to be the perfect role model that we have not had much time to deal with the fact that Nicole Simpson was found with her throat cut and that Ronald Goldman was stabbed 22 times.

About the only thing good that can come out of this is if it serves as America's wake-up call on the issue of gender violence. It took the death of Len Bias to help us to stop calling cocaine a recreational drug. It took Pete Rose's problems to get the media to report on America's 8 million gambling addicts. AIDS was a disease of "other people" until Magic Johnson and Arthur Ashe made it a mainstream topic.

Domestic abuse is so hidden that few knew that Nicole had placed nine 9-1-1 calls to the police for protection from O. J. Not many knew about his pleading no contest in a domestic-violence case in 1989. The courts did not even make him fulfill his obligations after the sentencing. Men have not perceived domestic violence as a big problem.

It wasn't just O. J.'s celebrity that kept it quiet. As recently as 1991, only 17 states even kept data on reports of domestic-violence offenses. Many states lumped all aggravated assaults together, whether the perpetrator was unknown or the victim's husband.

A version of this chapter originally appeared in *The Sporting News,* July 4, 1994. Reprinted by permission.

Maybe, just maybe, things will be forced to change now because of all the attention on this case. If it had changed earlier, Nicole Simpson might still be alive.

Why should we have forced change long ago?

- In Los Angeles County alone, a women is killed by her significant other every 9 days.
- Nationally, four women are killed by their significant others every day.
- Three million incidents of gender violence against women are reported every year.

Medical expenses from domestic violence total at least $3 million annually. Businesses lose another $100 billion in sick leave, absenteeism, and nonproductivity. Of battered women who are employed, 20% end up losing their jobs, partially as a consequence of the fact that abusive husbands and boyfriends harass 74% of employed battered women at work. More than half of male abusers also beat their children.

Domestic violence is criminal behavior that should require not only counseling but severe consequences. I have heard many people who don't want to believe that O. J. is guilty say that he was too smart to leave behind such a trail of evidence. Others have said that he was too rich, that if he wanted Nicole killed he would have hired someone. What most don't understand is that acts of gender violence are not committed in rational moments by rational people. Generally, they are attempts by men to obtain or sustain power and control.

I have heard others say that O. J.'s being a former athlete contributed to a mentality that he could get away with abuse. This act of violence has nothing to do with O. J.'s being a former athlete. None of the others who murdered 1,400 wives and girlfriends last year were reported to be athletes. O. J.'s status as a former athlete made it page 1 news, but it did not cause Nicole Simpson's death.

I have heard countless people say that athletes should no longer be looked at as role models. They reel off names such as Mike Tyson, Wade Boggs, and Pete Rose. There are 3,200 pro athletes, more than 100,000 college athletes, and 2 million high school athletes. Please don't paint them all with the same brush. The problem isn't that athletes shouldn't be role models. It's that all athletes shouldn't be automatically designated as such. They need to be prepared to serve before serving.

Will this be our wake-up call? A former pro athlete I have known for 10 years called me last week. He told me that after watching the O. J. Simpson story break, he recognized for the first time that he was a batterer and asked if I could get him help.

# 27

# Violence in Sports

Richard E. Lapchick

As I watch the 1994 National Basketball Association (NBA) playoffs, all I seem to hear and read about is the escalation of violence among NBA players. The brawls have been stunning for the number of players involved.

I don't like watching it any more than the next observer, and I find myself walking away from the TV. But there is so much discussion about the game's being ruined and how the league has lost control of its players. I go to my office, and staff people are wringing their hands in disgust and discomfort.

People seem to accept as a fact that we are witnessing a phenomenon—as if we don't expect fights to happen in National Hockey League (NHL) games, as if we are surprised to read about dugouts emptying out after a batter takes a hard one to his body, as if it comes as news to us that football players are told to take out the opponent's quarterback. These things happen at any time in the season in Major League Baseball, the NHL, or the National Football League. In the NBA, the fights seem more concentrated in the playoffs. The tension is higher, everything is at stake in our winner-take-all, runners-up-are-losers society.

Why all the focus on the NBA? I can think of a few factors. First, during the playoffs, more people are watching games. Most have no perspective on whether the fights went on all season long. They didn't. Second, the players' muscles are more apparent—and perhaps, more threatening—in the NBA than in other sports. I have to wonder if a third reason is at play here: Does the intense fighting in the stretch fit the typical white stereotype of blacks being more prone to violence than whites? Everything is certainly (if not clearly) being viewed through a white prism.

A profile of writers indicates the potential for bias within the media. There are 1,600 daily newspapers in the United States. Only two have African

A version of this chapter originally appeared in *The Sporting News*, June 13, 1994. Reprinted by permission.

American sports editors, none in the 38 cities with pro teams. There are 7 columnists and only 38 of 780 beat writers who are African American. An incredible 90% of the 1,600 dailies had no African Americans in sports at all! Hitting closer to home, *The Sporting News* has one African American columnist and no African American editors. In television, decisions about what goes on the air are made by producers and directors. Our most recent data from 1992, showed that of 60 producers and directors at CBS, NBC, and ABC, one was African American. There were 4 of 38 at ESPN.

I do not want to overemphasize the importance of a racial undertone. On the other hand, I cannot emphasize enough that we live in the most violent society in the developed world. On the streets, we use our bodies and, all too frequently, our weapons to resolve disputes.

Can we really expect that this behavior would not penetrate the world of sports? When we read that an athlete was arrested for carrying a gun, how do we juxtapose this with the knowledge that 21% of high school students carry a weapon to school each day? Or that 2,000 high school students are assaulted on high school grounds each hour of every day.

The bottom line of the 1994 Children's Defense Fund's annual report: A child is killed by a gun every 2 hours in America; more children have died from guns in the last decade than American soldiers died in Vietnam in a similar period.

Do athletes who act violently or bizarrely have a negative effect on our children's values? If not, they certainly don't give children a boost.

It will be interesting to see how the NBA's sanctions against fighting work out. Fines are useless for players making more than $1 million each year. I think game suspensions will have a positive effect. Dennis Rodman's one-game suspension arguably cost the better Spurs team a chance to move to the next round. Rodman seems to be in his own orbit. Derek Harper, on the other hand, is a solid workman. His two-game suspension almost launched the Bulls to "four-peat."

The frequency of sanctions against fighting under Brian Burke, in his first season as NHL vice president, had a positive effect. An NHL rule that the first player to leave the bench will get a 10-game suspension has resulted in a 7-year absence of bench-clearing brawls.

Does the immediacy and certainty of heavy penalties in sports have any application in society? I was never what was called a "law and order" person in the 1960s and 1970s, but it does make me think.

# 28

## An Investigation of Campus Stereotypes
### The Myth of Black Athletic Superiority and the Dumb Jock Stereotype

Gary A. Sailes

Sport has become an extremely important part of American culture. The pervasiveness and importance of American sports have grown with increased media coverage (Leonard, 1988, p. 413). Consequently, however, the growth of American sports has contributed to the evolution of specific sports stereotypes and myths, most notably the "dumb jock" stereotype and the myth of athletic superiority among African American athletes in intercollegiate and professional sports.[1]

### SPORTS STEREOTYPES

**Dumb Jock Stereotype**

The historical origins of the dumb jock stereotype can be traced to 500 B.C., when Greek athletes were criticized for the inordinate amount of time they used in preparation for competition and for neglecting their intellectual development. Greek athletes were characterized by some philosophers of the period as useless and ignorant citizens with dull minds (Coakley, 1990, p. 46).

Recent media attention challenging the scholarship of college athletes, particularly in the revenue-producing sports of basketball and football, has tainted the academic credibility of college student-athletes. Reports of high school student-athletes not meeting National Collegiate Athletic Association (NCAA) minimum academic standards to establish college eligibility, accounts of college student-athletes failing their courses, and the particularly

This chapter originally appeared as "An Investigation of Campus Stereotypes: The Myth of the Black Athlete," by Gary A. Sailes, in the *Sociology of Sport Journal,* Vol. 10, pp. 88-97. Reprinted by permission of the author.

low graduation rates among major college basketball and football programs foster the belief that anti-intellectualism exists among college student-athletes. Concurrently, Hollywood movies (Org in *Revenge of the Nerds, 1 & II*), television situation comedies (Coach in *Cheers; Coach*), and television commercials (including some for athletic shoes) perpetuate and profit from the dumb jock image, facilitating its acceptance by the American public.

Beezley (1983) chronicled the development of the dumb jock stereotype traditionally associated with college football players. Although the dumb jock stereotype was prevalent in American sports culture, its origin and validity could not be confirmed. Similarly, Nixon (1982) found no evidence to support the stereotype of the dumb jock. McMartin and Klay (1983) had similar findings and also reported that positive and favorable attitudes were held about students who were also athletes. Lederman (1990, p. A29) reported that regardless of the low graduation rates of football and basketball players, the overall grade point averages and graduation rates for college student-athletes were slightly higher than for the ordinary college student. Although prevalent, the dumb jock stereotype appears to have no scientific basis.

### Racial Stereotyping

A 1988 investigative report by the *Philadelphia Inquirer* sought to answer the question, Are African Americans better athletes than whites? (Sokolove, 1988). Similarly, a 1989 NBC special program hosted by Tom Brokaw, entitled *The Black Athlete: Fact or Fiction,* focused on a related question: What accounts for the success of African American athletes in American sports? Davis (1990) argued that the need to analyze African American success in sports is a racist preoccupation emanating from fear generated within the white status quo. African Americans comprise 12% of the total population in the United States; however, a disproportionately higher number of African American athletes participate on college and professional teams in the three major revenue-producing sports (basketball, baseball, and football). Approximately 21% of professional baseball players, 73% of the players in the National Basketball Association, and 57% of the athletes in the National Football League are African American (Coakley, 1990, p. 208). The NCAA (1989) reported that virtually all the colleges participating in Division I basketball and football have integrated teams and nearly all of the records in the three major sports at the college and professional levels are held by African Americans.

Unsubstantiated race-oriented sports myths have evolved as people attempt to explain the success and overrepresentation of African American athletes in certain American sports (Leonard, 1988, pp. 239-240). Most myths attempting to rationalize the dominance of African Americans in specific sports generally have little scientific credibility. For example, there remains the popular belief that African American athletes are physically superior to white athletes, and that their superior body build is genetically determined, given them an advantage over their white counterparts. Many believe this advantage accounts for the success among African American athletes in specific sports (Coakley, 1990; Leonard, 1988; Sokolove, 1988). Although some physical differences are apparent between African Americans and whites as a whole, it remains to be demonstrated that anatomical and/or physiological differences between African American and white athletes contribute significantly to the dominance of either over the other in sports competition (Coakley, 1990; Davis, 1990; Eitzen & Sage, 1989; Leonard, 1988; McPherson, Curtis, & Loy, 1989; Sailes, 1987, 1991; Sokolove, 1988).

Stereotypes about African American inferiority also find adherents in many segments of American culture, including sports. Steele (1990) argues that one race-oriented component of white superiority and black inferiority is intelligence. Support for the physical superiority myth indirectly contributes to the belief that the African American athlete is mentally and intellectually inferior to the white athlete (Davis, 1990; Hoose, 1989; Sailes, 1991). Conceptions about the dumb jock stereotype are therefore related to racial stereotyping. This racist attitude leads to the discriminatory practice of channeling African Americans away from the central positions (i.e., leadership, decision making) in college and professional sports (Coakley, 1990; Eitzen & Sage, 1989; Leonard, 1988; Schneider & Eitzen, 1986). For example, Al Campanis, former Los Angeles Dodgers general manager, exposed racial stereotyping in sports when he made the assertion on national television that African Americans may not have the "necessities" to be managers in professional baseball (Hoose, 1989). Positional segregation (often referred to as *stacking*) is prevalent among college and professional baseball and football teams (Jones, Leonard, Schmitt, Smith, & Tolone, 1987; Schneider & Eitzen, 1986).

Lombardo (1978, p. 60) noted two distinct stereotypes that have emerged regarding African American males. Known as "the Brute" and "the Sambo" stereotypes, they were developed by whites to maintain their superior position in society and to denigrate African American males, keeping them subordinate. Whereas the Brute stereotype characterized the African American male as primitive, temperamental, overreactive, uncontrollable, violent, and sexually powerful, the more popular Sambo stereotype depicts him as benign, childish, immature, exuberant, uninhibited, lazy, comical, impulsive, fun loving, good humored, inferior, and lovable. Lombardo criticized the Harlem Globetrotters for their continued perpetuation of the Sambo stereotype in sports and for compromising the integrity of African Americans.

Many of the myths regarding African American athletes suffer from scientifically unacceptable assumptions and are not substantiated by research.

Moreover, the variables affecting the sports socialization and sports participation patterns of African American athletes in American sports emanate from
the social constraints placed upon them by the dominant culture and their
determination to overcome them (Coakley, 1990; Eitzen & Sage, 1989;
Leonard, 1988; McPherson et al., 1989; Sailes, 1987, 1991; Sokolove, 1988).
Although less serious, the dumb jock stereotype can have an effect on white
athletes, but it has a compounding effect on African American athletes.

## Conceptual Model

Most studies uncovering racial improprieties in sports assume that racist
attitudes that lead to acts of discrimination are the primary antecedents. Few,
if any, studies attempt to determine the extent to which actual cultural or racial
stereotyping endures in American sports. Further, assuming that racist attitudes lead to acts of discrimination in American sports, without scientific
evidence of cultural or racial stereotyping, creates gaps in the literature. This
study sought to determine the extent of racial and athletic stereotyping,
utilizing racial and gender differences as a foundation to investigate the
prevalence of white male hegemony among college students.

This investigation sought to determine the presence of and relationship
between intellectual stereotyping and racial stereotyping to provide some
validation for the assertion that stereotypical and racist attitudes prevail in
American sports. Beliefs about intelligence, academic integrity, and academic
competitiveness among male college student-athletes as well as assumptions
about intelligence, academic preparation, style of play, athletic competitiveness, physical superiority, athletic ability, and mental temperament among
African American athletes were investigated. It was hypothesized that intellectual stereotyping and racial stereotyping do exist, that there is a relationship
between the two, and that these beliefs vary by race and gender.

## Instrument

No studies were available that surveyed racially or intellectually oriented
beliefs about college student-athletes. Consequently, it became necessary to
develop a questionnaire to complete this investigation. Informal interviews
with college students, college student-athletes, and college and high school
coaches, as well as precedents in the related literature depicting the relationships between culture, race, and sports, were used as guides in the development of the instrument employed in this study.

The questionnaire was designed to reveal subjects' perceptions or beliefs
regarding specific stereotypical beliefs about college student-athletes and
African American athletes. The questionnaire contained 30 items and em-

ployed a 5-point Likert scale coded in the same direction ranging as follows: 5 = *strongly agree,* 4 = *agree,* 3 = *undecided,* 2 = *disagree,* 1 = *strongly disagree.* Sample questions included in the instrument were as follows: "Generally, athletes are not as smart as the average student." "Generally, blacks are better athletes than whites." "Black athletes are not as academically prepared to be in college as the average student."

The conceptual model, conceived by collapsing the 30 items in the instrument, produced several dependent variables. For athletes, they were intelligence, academic integrity, and academic competitiveness. For African American athletes, they were intelligence, academic preparation, athletic skill orientation (style), competitiveness, physical superiority, athletic ability, and mental temperament.

## METHOD

### Subjects

The questionnaire was administered to 869 undergraduate and graduate students enrolled in lecture hall classes who were randomly selected from the course registration booklet at Indiana University. The respondents were informed some questions might make them uncomfortable but were encouraged to respond to each item as sincerely and objectively as possible.

Subjects participating in the study were identified accordingly: African American students = 45, white students = 786, other = 38, males = 427, and females = 442. The author employed the *t* test to determine differences by race and gender.

### Results

When the *agree* and *strongly agree* categories were combined, examination of the data revealed that approximately 45% of the subjects felt that college student-athletes were not as smart as the average college student, almost 44% felt student-athletes took easy courses to stay academically eligible, and 37% felt student-athletes were not as academically competitive as the typical college student (see Table 28.1). Despite this finding, only 10% of the sample were willing to reveal that they felt college student-athletes were "dumb jocks."

Approximately 12% of the sample felt African American athletes were not as smart as white athletes, whereas approximately 25% felt African American athletes were not academically prepared to attend college. And 22% of the sample felt that African American athletes demonstrated a playing style

**TABLE 28.1** Evidence of the Dumb Jock Stereotype

| Dependent Variable | Agree (n%) | Undecided (n%) | Disagree (n%) |
|---|---|---|---|
| Intelligence | 45.5 | 2.5 | 51.9 |
| Academic integrity | 43.8 | 31.7 | 23.8 |
| Academic competitiveness | 37.0 | 24.3 | 37.6 |

**TABLE 28.2** Evidence of Athletic Racial Stereotypes

| Dependent Variable | Agree (n%) | Undecided (n%) | Disagree (n%) |
|---|---|---|---|
| Intelligence | 11.9 | 25.4 | 61.8 |
| Academic preparation | 25.4 | 29.1 | 44.5 |
| Style | 22.3 | 27.7 | 48.6 |
| Competitiveness | 9.3 | 26.2 | 63.4 |
| Physical superiority | 20.2 | 22.2 | 56.6 |
| Athletic ability | 33.1 | 19.0 | 46.8 |
| Mental temperament | 12.7 | 33.7 | 52.2 |

different from their white counterparts. Moreover, just over 20% of the sample felt that African American athletes were physically superior to the white athlete, and approximately 33% of the respondents indicated they felt African American athletes were more skilled and were better athletes than their white counterparts. Finally, 12.7% of the sample felt African American athletes were temperamental (see Table 28.2).

Statistically significant differences were revealed on several variables contained within the conceptual model in the comparisons by gender and race.

## Dumb Jock Stereotype

Significant differences were evident on two of the dependent variables: intelligence for race, and academic integrity for both gender and race. Specifically, whites ($M = 2.67$) felt more strongly than blacks ($M = 2.22$) that college student-athletes were not as intelligent as the typical student. Concurrently, males ($M = 3.29$) felt more strongly than females ($M = 3.15$) and whites ($M = 3.24$) felt more strongly than blacks ($M = 2.88$) that college student-athletes took easy courses to remain eligible to compete in varsity athletics (see Table 28.3).

## African American Athlete Stereotypes

Significant differences emerged on the dependent variables intelligence and academic preparation for both gender and race. Specifically, males ($M =$

**TABLE 28.3**  Evidence of the Dumb Jock Stereotype, by Race and Gender

| | Mean | | Mean | |
|---|---|---|---|---|
| Dependent Variable | Black (n = 45) | White (n = 786) | Male (n = 427) | Female (n = 442) |
| Intelligence | 2.22 | 2.67* | 2.68 | 2.61 |
| Academic integrity | 2.88 | 3.24* | 3.29 | 3.15* |
| Academic competitiveness | 2.66 | 2.98 | 2.98 | 2.95 |

*p = .05.

**TABLE 28.4**  Evidence of Racial Stereotyping, by Race and Gender

| | Mean | | Mean | |
|---|---|---|---|---|
| Dependent Variable | Black (n = 45) | White (n = 786) | Male (n = 427) | Female (n = 442) |
| Intelligence | 1.80 | 2.35* | 2.44 | 2.19* |
| Academic preparation | 2.24 | 2.72* | 3.29 | 3.15* |
| Style | 4.11 | 3.01* | 2.66 | 2.62 |
| Competitiveness | 2.93 | 2.26* | 2.15 | 2.45* |
| Physical superiority | 2.93 | 2.77 | 2.52 | 2.43 |
| Athletic ability | 2.93 | 2.75 | 2.78 | 2.77 |
| Mental temperament | 2.02 | 2.49* | 2.55 | 2.39* |

*p = .05.

2.44) and whites ($M = 2.35$) felt more strongly than females ($M = 2.19$) and blacks ($M = 1.80$), respectively, that white athletes were more intelligent than African American athletes. Additionally, on a specific question, males ($M = 2.74$) felt more strongly than females ($M = 2.58$) that white athletes received better grades than African American athletes. Also, males ($M = 3.29$) felt more strongly than females ($M = 3.15$) and whites ($M = 2.72$) felt more strongly than blacks ($M = 2.24$) that African American athletes were not as academically prepared to attend college.

Significant differences were found for the dependent variables competitiveness and temperament for both gender and race, and style for race. Females ($M = 2.45$) and African Americans ($M = 2.93$) felt more strongly than males ($M = 2.15$) and whites ($M = 2.26$), respectively, that African American athletes were athletically more competitive than white athletes. African Americans ($M = 4.11$) felt more strongly than whites ($M = 3.01$) that African American athletes had a different playing style than white athletes. Concurrently, whites ($M = 2.49$) and males ($M = 2.55$) felt more strongly than blacks ($M = 2.02$) or females ($M = 2.39$), that African American athletes were temperamental (see Table 28.4).

## DISCUSSION

This investigation generated substantial evidence disclosing the presence of the dumb jock stereotype in some of the groups examined. Indications of negative perceptions of the intellectual competence and academic integrity among college student-athletes were evident. Whites felt more strongly that the typical college student-athlete was not as smart or as academically competitive as the typical college student, whereas whites and males believed college student-athletes took easy courses to stay eligible to compete in college sports. These attitudes prevail despite the literature to the contrary (Lederman, 1990). This suggests some white and male college students may hold superior attitudes regarding their education and intelligence, may not be well informed about the overall academic success of college student-athletes, or may believe media and cultural depictions of athletes as intellectually inferior. It is interesting to note that attitudes implying the presence of the dumb jock stereotype were prevalent among the subjects, yet most were reluctant to disclose their beliefs in that particular stigma.

This investigation was able to validate the presence of racial stereotyping regarding African American athletes. The data revealed whites and males held stronger negative stereotypical beliefs than blacks and females about African American athletes. Generally, whites and males felt more strongly that the African American athlete was not as academically prepared to be in college as the average student, received lower grades than white athletes, and was not as intelligent as white athletes. These findings are analogous to the assumption that African American athletes are intellectually inferior to their white counterparts, which is questioned in the literature (Coakley, 1990; Davis, 1990; Hoose, 1989; Leonard, 1988; Sailes, 1987, 1991; Sokolove, 1988).

It is reasonable to assume the white subjects had minimal contact with African American athletes, which might account, to some extent, for the prevalence of their stereotypical attitudes. It is interesting to note that the same groups who believe college student-athletes were not as smart as the typical college student also felt African American athletes were less intelligent than their white counterparts. It appears evident that sports stereotyping carried over to racial stereotyping.

Males felt more strongly than females that African American athletes were temperamental. These findings support the existence of the "brute" stereotype (Lombardo, 1978) in sports, which characterizes the African American athlete as temperamental and overreactive. It is conceivable that current depictions of African American men both in the media and in college and professional sports contribute to the prevalence of the brute stereotype evident in this study.

It is interesting that women and African Americans did not hold as strongly negative views regarding sports stereotyping. Women and African Americans felt African American athletes were more competitive and had a different playing style. The literature supports these contentions offering sociocultural interpretations. Further, subsequent interaction among African Americans would contribute to the adoption of fairer and more realistic orientations about athletic participation and the elimination of negative stereotypes, particularly when sport is viewed much more seriously within the confines of African American culture (Sailes, 1987). The so-called old boy network, which is predominantly white and male, perpetuates and maintains the status quo for its own benefit, even to the extent of perpetuating negative stereotypes about other cultural and ethnic groups (Davis, 1990; Hoose, 1989; Steele, 1990). African Americans and women participating in this study appear to be somewhat exempt from that preoccupation.

## CONCLUSIONS

There appears to be more support for the dumb jock stereotype compared with athletic racial stereotyping. It is possible that the subjects were more reluctant to disclose their true feelings, which might have been recognized as racist responses. There is considerably less guilt associated with holding a dumb jock stereotype, which could explain its greater prevalence in this investigation, although even subjects in this sample were reluctant to state outright that athletes are dumb jocks. Although no specific test was made of the connection between dumb jock and racial stereotypes, it is apparent that if "jocks" are perceived as "dumb," and if black athletes are perceived to be neither as intelligent nor as academically prepared as white athletes, it would be logical to assume that there exists a compounding effect in the perceptions of the subjects.

This study was not without its limitations. The sample consisted of Indiana University (IU) students, and approximately 65% of IU students are from the state of Indiana. The scope of this study is obviously limited to those dimensions. It is possible the attitudes and perceptions of Indiana University students are not necessarily representative of other groups. However, the findings contained in this study have value in that they substantiate the presence and continued existence of racial and social stereotyping and validate the possibility of their existence elsewhere.

The exposure of racial and social stereotyping is quite possibly an indication of underlying social problems that prevail at IU. Coakley (1990) noted the social isolation and undercurrents of subtle racism experienced by African American athletes at predominantly white schools. Investigations such as this further illustrate the attitudinal problems permeating intercollegiate and professional sports, American colleges, and society as a whole and the need for continued education and change.

## NOTE

1. Throughout this chapter, the term *athletes* refers specifically to male athletes. The stereotypes under consideration are not nearly as well developed for female athletes, and this study focused specifically on male athletes.

## REFERENCES

Beezley, W. H. (1983). Images of the student athlete in college football. In S. Kereliuk (Ed.), *The university's role in the development of modern sport: Past, present, and future* (pp. 447-461, Proceedings of the FISU Conference-Universiade '83 in association with the Tenth HISPA Congress). Edmonton: University of Alberta.

Coakley, J. J. (1990). *Sport in society: Issues and controversies.* Boston: Times Mirror/Mosby.

Davis, L. R. (1990). The articulation of difference: White preoccupation with the question of racially linked genetic differences among athletes. *Sociology of Sport Journal, 7*(2), 179-187.

Eitzen, D. S., & Sage, G. H. (1989). *Sociology of North American sport.* Dubuque, IA: William C. Brown.

Hoose, P. (1989). *Necessities: Racial barriers in American sports.* New York: Random House.

Jones, B., Leonard, W. M., Schmitt, R. L., Smith, D. R., & Tolone, W. L. (1987, March). A log-linear analysis of stacking in college football. *Social Science Quarterly,* pp. 70-83.

Lederman, D. (1990, July 5). Athletes in Division I found graduating at higher rate than other students. *Chronicle of Higher Education,* p. A29.

Leonard, W. M., II. (1988). *A sociological perspective of sport.* New York: Macmillan.

Lombardo, B. (1978). The Harlem Globetrotters and the perception of the black stereotype. *The Physical Educator, 35*(2), 60-63.

McMartin, J., & Klay, J. (1983). Some perceptions of the student-athlete. *Perceptual and Motor Skills, 57*(3), 687-690.

McPherson, B. D., Curtis, J. E., & Loy, J. W. (1989). *The social significance of sport.* Champaign, IL: Human Kinetics.

National Collegiate Athletic Association. (1989). *The status of minority participation in intercollegiate sports.* Palo Alto, CA: American Institute of Research.

Nixon, H. L. (1982). The athlete as scholar in college: An exploratory test of four models. In A. O. Dunleavy, A. W. Miracle, & C. R. Rees (Eds.), *Studies in the sociology of sport* (pp. 239-256). Fort Worth: Texas Christian University Press.

Sailes, G. A. (1987). A socioeconomic explanation of black sports participation patterns. *Western Journal of Black Studies, 11*(4), 164-167.

Sailes, G. A. (1991). The myth of black sports supremacy. *Journal of Black Studies, 21*(4), 480-487.

Schneider, J., & Eitzen, S. (1986). Racial segregation by professional football positions, 1960-1985. *Sociology and Social Research, 70,* 250-262.

Sokolove, M. (1988, April 24). Are blacks better athletes than whites? *Inquirer: The Philadelphia Inquirer Magazine,* pp. 16-40.

Steele, S. (1990). *The content of our character.* New York: St. Martin's.

# 29

# The Rules of the Game Are Changing
## College Coaches in the 1990s

Richard E. Lapchick

Although many adult fans would love to have the fame and fortune of a Dean Smith or Mike Krzyzewski, most would have a difficult time adjusting to the constant rule changes that have redefined coaching in the 1990s.

Lou Campanelli was only the most highly publicized case during a year when several coaches have been fired for allegedly abusing their players. When head basketball coach Mike Newell was fired by Lamar on April 20, he joined Earle Bruce, Tom Miller, and Keith Ambrot as coaches who were fired in 1993 for being too abusive of their players.

Coaches were especially concerned and outspoken about Campanelli's case because he was fired in midseason, a virtually unprecedented move in college sports. Some outside of the coaching fraternity wanted to ignore Campanelli's firing as his team, the University of California, suddenly started winning big-time and ended the season with a great run in the National Collegiate Athletic Association (NCAA) tournament. Others wanted to forget it because Todd Bozeman, the new coach, was African American.

However, fellow coaches would not forget, and it was a big issue at the Convention of the National Association of Basketball Coaches in New Orleans. The rules of the game needed to be and are changing. However, according to many coaches, administrators have left them out of the loop.

In 1980, the number one, and perhaps only rule that mattered, was winning. That would help sell tickets and increase chances for TV coverage. Coaches who followed this rule stayed at their schools for long periods of time and earned good but hardly sensational salaries. No one pointed a finger at the coaches unless they lost.

Then scandals began to reveal that student-athletes were more athletes than students. Basketball players graduated at a rate of 27% according to a *USA*

A version of this chapter originally appeared in *The Sporting News,* May 10, 1993. Reprinted by permission.

*Today* survey in 1985. For African American student-athletes, the rate was estimated to be 20%. But such numbers were always controversial because schools did not have to report their rates.

By the mid-1980s, the media began to publicize cases of college student-athletes getting in trouble with the law. The roof really caved in when Len Bias died in his Maryland dorm of a cocaine overdose in 1986. The spotlight on the University of Maryland revealed that coach Lefty Driesel's players had a graduation rate of only 30%. Everyone pointed the finger at Lefty. It was the coach's fault.

With so much attention on Maryland and Driesel, we forgot to mention that hardly anyone in the nation, in or out of sports, recognized the lethal potential of cocaine or that their basketball graduation rate was actually higher than the national average! In reality, the scandal belonged to the nation and to college sports, not just Driesel and the University of Maryland.

So we rewrote the rules for coaches. You have to win, sell tickets, get the team on TV, make the NCAA tournament, graduate your student-athletes, and help them become socially ready for the real world. The new rules, which were desperately needed, were developed by university presidents who began to reclaim control of athletic departments. Except for the Knight Commission, coaches were not asked their opinions, resulting in a major rift between coaches and presidents. The rift became a chasm when the NCAA, at the direction of presidents, reduced the number of assistant coaches each school could have. Duke's Mike Krzyzewski, one of the sport's most highly respected coaches, was not well received at the 1993 NCAA Convention. His message was simple: Give coaches a voice so they are part of the changes we require of them.

Back to the latest rule change. Presidents, athletic directors, coaches, and commentators rarely if ever publicly discussed coaches who abusively yelled at players. Who was to define abuse?

So college players are now talking more openly about coaches who they feel are abusive. Long accepted coaching practices are now being routinely challenged by players and university administrators. And it is not only at schools with big-time sports programs, as administrators at Central Michigan and Iowa Wesleyan have discovered.

There is no question that physical and mental abuse must be halted. With the mirror held up, most coaches would agree. College coaches are now very well paid. Some are making 10 times what they could have earned in 1980 when the coach's job was simpler and clearly defined. With increased fame, income, and prestige, coaches have decreased job security as lifetime jobs rarely, if ever, now exist. Over the past 5 years, there has been nearly a 25% turnover rate *per year* for Division I basketball coaches.

Today, coaches are asked to be fully accountable for who they recruit to our campuses. They should also be accountable for and assist in helping student-athletes understand what they must do academically and socially after they arrive.

We are all compelled to adapt to an ever changing world. However, to be fair, we should include coaches when we change the rules. Coaches must be part of the discussion of changes for two reasons. First, it is only fair that they be part of the process that will directly affect their ability to do their jobs. Second, they are much more likely to buy into any change when they are part of formulating it.

Finally, when we are ready to make sweeping policy changes, we must give the coaches the necessary support required. Taking away an assistant coach at the same time we add responsibilities to the head coach doesn't make good sense. Ask the coaches!

# 30

## The Need for a New Code of
## Ethics Going Beyond the NCAA

Richard E. Lapchick

There has been much discussion of the issue of money in college sports in the aftermath of the resignation of Dick Schultz, who was the executive director of the NCAA from 1987 to May 1993. That discussion has focused on two specific subjects as if they were tied together. Some said that if the sanctions against the University of Virginia or the resignation of Schultz could take place over $50, interest-free loans to student-athletes, then how can we countenance coaches and schools making fortunes when some student-athletes must live in poverty on our campuses if they have no financial support from their families.

These are two separate issues. One speaks of rules that keep student-athletes who come to our campuses without resources poor. That poverty in the midst of plenty on the campus can induce the student-athlete to cheat to get money for ordinary expenses, such as going to a movie or buying a pizza.

The other issue is, Should coaches be paid such lucrative wages? Should their salaries exceed that of their presidents? Should they get fabulous packages for TV and radio shows, camps, and sneaker contracts?

First things first. I don't agree with those who say that all or even most student-athletes are exploited by our colleges. Yet the recently released Round 2 of published graduation rates by the National Collegiate Athletic Association (NCAA) shows that we still have a long way to go in the revenue sports of football and basketball. Surely, too many leave without a meaningful education or a chance for the pros. However, if an athlete gets an education and is able to live the life of a regular student, then the college has kept its part of the bargain. If the average cost for tuition, room, and board run to

A version of this chapter originally appeared in *The Sporting News,* June 14, 1993. Reprinted by permission.

$60,000 for 4 years, then that's a good return for an 18-year-old. The betrayal comes when the education is not there.

Many argue that to have the best chance to get an education, student-athletes need to be integrated into the social and cultural life on campus. Yet NCAA rules on what they can receive make this difficult to achieve. The NCAA does not allow them to get money above room, board, and tuition. The NCAA does not allow them to work during the school year. How can we expect student-athletes, arguably the most visible people on campus, to not be able to do what most other students can do?

So if their families cannot send them money, as is the case with a large number of student-athletes recruited from urban areas, then we are expecting them to eat just dorm food and live a quiet life in their rooms. It shouldn't work that way. We talk about the need to include them. Yet our rules seem to make this harder to achieve. We need to give them a modest stipend just to be fair. I'm not talking about a large amount of money, such as pay for play. What I'm talking about would be $100 to $200 per month to allow them to do the little things that are part of going to college.

That brings us to the second issue. Coaches can be the pivotal person in the lives of their players. When coaches motivate players to be the best they can be on the court or playing field, in the classroom, and socially on campus and in the community, then chances are very good that players will really be student-athletes.

If the coach does all that while winning for the school, then I don't have a problem with coaches making what the marketplace is offering. Much has been made about Duke's Mike Krzyzewski's million-dollar deal with Nike as if he should have said no!

Krzyzewski did not create the marketplace. He did not tip the scales of justice to create small pockets of affluence nearby to people who live without homes. Realistically, it is nearly impossible to justify that anyone is worth a million dollars a year for anything. Moreover, it is both absurd and horribly unfair that the average annual salary for high school teachers is less than Michael Jordan makes for an evening's work.

However, that is the distorted value system we have in America and in most every other country. It is why kids would rather hear from athletes than from teachers, lawyers, or doctors. It is the marketplace and the reality. We should be critical and wary of the system that created this distortion of values. Yet although we try to reorder those values and eliminate the distortions, we can also use those distortions for the public good.

Sneaker companies bestow great wealth on famous coaches for the use of their names. These companies need to develop a code of ethics for those they sign. In the very big time, the shoe contract pays more than the school's contract for the coach. Can you imagine if Reebok, Nike, and all their competitors announced that they would not sign any coaches without a graduation rate of 75%. Or if their coaches had to commit to 10 hours per week of working with kids in the off-season? Or if, in addition to their players having to wear the gear on the court, they were expected to tutor 13-year-olds on the verge of dropping out of school?

Can you imagine the college president or athletic director who tells recruits that part of the educational process at their school will be that each college student-athlete will be involved in a sports ethics corps serving the surrounding community in various ways? Or the athletic director who gives away game tickets to kids in the community with 100% attendance at school or steadily improving grades?

Suddenly, we would have turned the distorted values upside down. Coaches and their players would become symbols of hope for too many children who otherwise live in despair. I have visited schools where coaches and student-athletes were mandated to do these things. At first, some have balked. Then, given the taste of their personal power to do more than win games or run up stats, they want more. People are rarely given the opportunity to help others. A former Peace Corps volunteer said, "I didn't know I could make a difference. No one ever asked. President Kennedy asked."

The nation is asking. We are calling out to these people we call role models to use the platform society has given to them to help us change some of those values that may have placed them higher on the social order than they may really be entitled to be. Ironically, when they do so they will have earned the place that society gave them too readily.

Don't be cynical about it. Coaches and athletes have become successful because they are coachable themselves. The qualities that made them great in sports can do the same in society. It is up to society to ask them to help transform the values that that same society has helped to distort.

# PART V

# Media and Sport

## Introduction

Broadcast and print media are largely responsible for the images that people see and remember. The most vivid memories in 1994 involving athletes were news events that occurred away from the playing field. The new year was ushered in with the unforgettable site of Nancy Kerrigan writhing in pain after being clubbed across the knee by a hired assailant. As the plot unraveled, it linked Tanya Harding, Kerrigan's chief skating rival, to the attack and added a bizarre drama to the Winter Olympics. The skating feud between Kerrigan and Harding dominated the early days of the Olympic competition.

The Kerrigan-Harding incident was eclipsed by live coverage of O. J. Simpson being driven down a Los Angeles freeway while a fleet of L. A. Police cruisers followed and thousands of spectators lined the roadsides to watch. Before the year ended, every major network would carry live coverage of the case involving double murder charges leveled against one of America's most celebrated former professional athletes.

Coverage was accompanied by criticism of the media's handling of these news stories. Initial coverage of the Simpson case produced an abundance of attention to his football career and hero status. The fact that two families were suffering in anguish over the savage murder of their family members frequently seemed trivialized. Furthermore, caricatures of Simpson that appeared in some national publications raised criticisms of racial stereotyping— most notably an artist's alteration of O. J. that appeared on the cover of *TIME*

*Magazine* shortly after his arrest. Meanwhile, the Kerrigan-Harding incident was quickly manufactured into a soap opera story with headlines invoking military slogans to describe their competition on the ice. This act of violence vaulted skating to the most popular sport of the Winter Olympics and put female skaters on the covers of magazines around the world.

Few people stop to consider whose views are reflected in the events that are selected for news and the subsequent manner in which they are portrayed. The viewpoints conveyed through the press are largely the product of a homogeneous group of reporters and editors. For example, the announcement by Sugar Ray Leonard that he had both abused drugs and abused his wife quickly became a national story about a boxer who had a drug addiction. Left virtually unmentioned was the fact that a world champion fighter had been beating his wife. The writers and editors decided that it was less newsworthy. Likewise, O. J. Simpson's conviction for spousal abuse received little attention in 1989.

In addition to determining what issues qualify as news, the media decides which individuals will be reported on and how they will be described. Historically, blacks and women have been shut out as writers and editors. This is particularly prevalent in sports where there is such a significant percentage of black and female athletes. Although the number of black athletes continues to increase annually, black reporters, columnists, and editors have rarely been given opportunities to cover the games. Although women used the courts to solidify their right to access locker rooms in the 1970s, resistance to their presence continued to be a volatile issue as recently as 1990. This section discusses the effect that disproportionate representation by racial minorities and women in the media has on the perceptions formed by the general public.

Ron Thomas's original article describes the profound effect that the dominance of white males has had on the depiction of blacks in the media. Beginning with the entrance of Wendell Smith, the first black sportswriter to have a byline in a major daily newspaper, Thomas traces whatever "progress" has been made since then. He concludes that despite the notable increase in the number of black sports writers since Smith's day, there is a gross underrepresentation of blacks in the positions of columnist, editor, and producer. Furthermore, those who have obtained positions are frequently confronted with comments and insinuations that are laden with racial overtones. Thomas was formerly with the *San Francisco Chronicle* and *USA Today* and is now the codirector of the Sports Institute.

Mary Schmitt discusses the state of women in the sports media today. The president of the Association for Women in Sports Media, she is also a writer for the *St. Paul Pioneer Press.* Schmitt is uniquely qualified to assess the status of women who are working in the media. She outlines some of the significant progress made over the last 20 years, most notably the large increase in female reporters covering sports as well as the increase of female editors on major sports dailies. Furthermore, she describes the current battle taking place in newspaper boardrooms where women are currently facing tremendous resistance from their male supervisors.

Bethany Shifflett and Rhonda Revelle provide an example of how female athletes receive inferior coverage on the sports pages. In their article "Gender Equity in Sports Media Coverage: A Review of the NCAA News," they identify a practice that is prevalent in most sports sections.

Finally, Sandy Padwe examines the conflict of interest that sports reporters face when covering local teams. Padwe is a former senior editor for *Sports Illustrated* and is now a professor of journalism at Columbia University. Among other issues, he discusses how the promotion of a sport for the purpose of increasing newspaper circulation can present ethical dilemmas when reporting on an unfavorable act will likely result in negative attention to the team.

# 31

## Black Faces Still Rare in the Press Box

Ron Thomas

If Wendell Smith, the first black sportswriter to have a byline on a major white-owned daily newspaper, were alive today he would no doubt be thrilled about who he would see on the playing fields and other sporting venues.

More athletes and coaches look like him than he could ever have imagined: In pro basketball and football leagues 79% and 65% of the players are black, respectively; there are black quarterbacks and pro hockey players, black National Basketball Association (NBA) and National Football League (NFL) head coaches, and black Major League Baseball managers. The last two World Series were won by the Toronto Blue Jays, managed by Cito Gaston, who is black.

And if Smith, who died in 1972, were alive today, he would no doubt be appalled about who he would see in today's press boxes—almost no sports journalists who look like him.

In 1947, Smith, who was instrumental in Jackie Robinson's breaking baseball's color barrier, joined the *Chicago Herald-American* after an illustrious career at the *Pittsburgh Courier,* a black newspaper. For the next 25 years until his death, Smith covered professional boxing, basketball, and baseball in Chicago. Beginning in the late 1960s for the *Chicago Sun-Times,* he was one of the establishment media's first black sports columnists. He was also a television sportscaster.

Smith's knowledge, style, and guts made him a standard setter for all sports journalists to emulate. Not only did he crusade for Robinson, but he also paved the way for Kenny Washington's integration of pro football's modern era and campaigned for integrated housing for black baseball players during spring training in the South.

The Hearst chain recognized his talents in 1958 when he was awarded its top sportswriting award. Smith's colleagues fondly eulogized him in 1972 when he died at the age of 58. "Someone once called Smith a 'sportswriter with a built-in social conscience,' and that description seems so apt," *Sun-Times* reporter Lacy J. Banks (1972) wrote.

" 'Not only have sports people lost a friend,' said boxing champion Muhammad Ali. 'The world has lost a beautiful human being' " (Banks, 1972).

In 1994, Smith received the ultimate tribute—being inducted posthumously into the writer's wing of the Baseball Hall of Fame. One would think that he had paved the road for—and proven the stock of—future black sports journalists. So imagine the chagrin, and maybe the disgust, that Smith would feel if he knew how few of today's sports journalists are black.

In 1994, 47 years after Smith's breakthrough, only 1 black beat reporter covered a Major League Baseball team—Brad Turner of the *San Gabriel Valley Tribune* reported on the Los Angeles Dodgers—compared to 268 beat reporters listed in Major League Baseball's media guide. Just three other black reporters covered baseball on a national basis.

Only 7 full-time black sports columnists write for the nation's 1,600 daily newspapers, according to figures compiled by the Sports Task Force of the National Association of Black Journalists. Furthermore, there are only 300 black print sports journalists, including editors and copy editors. That's a significant increase since 1973 when I entered the profession as one of about 15 black sports reporters nationwide. Still, it constitutes only a small group to offer opinions and act as image makers on today's sports pages.

Although 65% of pro football players are black, only 11 of 251 (4.3%) NFL beat writers were black during the 1993 season. Not bad, however, compared to the racial balance of NFL teams' radio announcers. Counting 72 play-by-play announcers and color analysts, just 1, or 1.3%, was black—New York Jets play-by-play announcer Paul Olden.

Excluding traditionally black universities, it's doubtful that the percentages would be much better regarding the coverage of college football, where 42% of Division I players are black. For instance, a sampling of 19 prominent bowl games after the 1993 season revealed that of 57 announcing positions, only 7 were filled by black sportscasters. Basketball has the highest percentage of black players of any team sport in the United States: 77% of NBA players and 64% of Division I college players. But only 22 of 186 (11%) NBA beat writers and 12 of 115 announcers (10%) during the 1993-94 season were black, according to the league's media guide, and the numbers of black sportscasters announcing college basketball games is probably less than 5% when black universities are excluded.

*Sports Illustrated,* by far the nation's most prominent sports magazine, has a virtual absence of black editorial staffers. Of 102 editors, department heads, writers, reporters, and copy editors listed on its masthead in a September 1994 issue, only 5 were black. That included 4 of 53 writers-reporters, 1 of 11 copy editors, and no department heads or editors. Mark Mulvoy, *SI*'s managing editor, did not respond to several requests for an interview about his publication's hiring practices.

ESPN, the influential all-sports network, has 12 black announcers, according to director of communications Mike Soltys.[1] They include studio hosts, reporters, and game announcers for various sports, but Soltys, claiming confidentiality, would not reveal the total number of announcers ESPN employs.

Behind the scenes, where the ultimate power of the sports media reins, Smith would find even less integration within print and broadcast journalism. Among the nation's 1,600 daily newspapers, 6 have black sports editors. Only one, Garry Howard of the *Milwaukee Journal Sentinel,* works in a city with a professional sports team or a population exceeding 200,000.

And among sports broadcast producers and directors, who control the content of televised events, and radio talk show hosts, who can heavily sway public opinion, rest assured that a black face would be rare indeed. For instance, only one of ABC's 15 producer-directors is black, and just one of the Fox Network's 16 NFL producer-directors is black.

The sports media's hiring "traditions"—in the worst sense of the word— are doubly troubling because black athletes dominate the highest levels of America's major sports. By all logic, sports is the area of journalism where one would expect the greatest black representation, not near invisibility.

The "Golden Age of Black Sportswriters" lasted until about 1970, when followers of black athletes gathered most of their information from black-owned newspapers such as the *Chicago Defender, Pittsburgh Courier, Amsterdam News,* and *Baltimore Afro-American.* Those publications featured skillful, politically aware writers such as Smith, Sam Lacey, Joe Bostic, Billy Nunn, and A. S. (Doc) Young, all of whom chronicled the exploits of "colored" and "Negro" stars, and kept the heat on the white sports establishment by constantly pressuring for integration.

In an interview with *Chicago Tribune* baseball writer Jerome Holtzman, Smith recounted how he began pushing for baseball's integration after he became the *Pittsburgh Courier's* sports editor in 1938. As about 50 white National League managers and players passed through Pittsburgh, Smith would ask them if they "would welcome a Negro player as a teammate." The vote was 75% in favor, 25% opposed—a crucial revelation because owners had resisted integration by claiming white players wouldn't tolerate it.

Smith eventually arranged a tryout for three players (Robinson, Sam Jethroe, and Marvin Williams) with the Boston Red Sox. Nothing came of it, but afterward, Smith told Brooklyn Dodgers owner, Branch Rickey, about the tryout, which sparked Rickey's interest in Robinson. On October 23, 1945, Robinson signed a minor league contract with Brooklyn's farm team in

Montreal, and Smith became his biggest booster and spring training chaperone in harshly segregated Florida, where spring training was held.

In 1947, Robinson's ascension into the major leagues literally changed American sports forever, and the face of sports journalism began to change, too. Beginning in the late 1960s, fewer and fewer readers bought black newspapers, shifting their allegiance to larger, white-owned newspapers that were covering an increasing number of black sports heroes. With that shift, came the virtual disappearance of the black sportswriter—whom white editors almost never hired—and amid the rising popularity of televised sports, the black broadcaster is still barely present.

The problem perplexes *New York Times*' columnist Bill Rhoden,[2] who recited a litany of possible reasons that white editors and station managers are so reluctant to hire black sports journalists. "Maybe it's because sports has been such a delicious job that they want to keep it to themselves," he said. "It's been one of the choicest jobs in the newsroom, [second only to] being a foreign correspondent, and look how [few] black foreign correspondents there are. You travel, play golf on the road. It could be, 'We're keeping these jobs to ourselves.'

"Is it that it's entertainment? Is it that there's money floating around? Is it that sports means a lot in terms of manhood and nobility, and therefore whites have to cover it? And sports leads to a lot of social structures. Sports, in a large part, was significant in integrating colleges. Sports has a lot to do with defining the soul and guts of this country, so it may be that whites don't want blacks writing about it."

Because black sportswriters traditionally have been advocates for racial equality, Rhoden wonders if editors fear that they will form an alliance with black athletes. He can imagine editors worrying that "we could lose control. Will our readers go for that, in light of the fact that anything that becomes predominately black in our society becomes devalued?" Add all those comments together and one wonders if Rhoden believes that a conspiracy exists to keep blacks out of the sports media.

"I think it's a buddy network, an old-boy network," Rhoden said. "It doesn't even need to be a conspiracy; it's just understood." Consequently, ridiculous situations still exist such as Brad Turner's being 1994's only black Major League Baseball beat reporter. Hearing him recall some of the travails he endured during his rookie season on the beat, one is reminded of tales told by black athletes from the 1950s.

"In general, it's been good," Turner[3] said about his relationship with the five other reporters who travel with the Dodgers. But the bad times often have been annoying and, sometimes, downright insulting.

Turner, 35, had been mainly covering pro basketball for the *Bakersfield Sun* before joining the *Valley Tribune* in his eighth year as a sportswriter. After arriving in Vero Beach, Florida, for spring training, the other beat reporters were very helpful in showing him the logistics of training camp and explaining the intricacies of baseball contracts.

To his amusement, he also found that he had become the press corps' designated expert in black slang. For instance, Delino DeShields, a black player whom the Dodgers had acquired from Montreal during the off-season, had told some white reporters that he looked forward to playing in Los Angeles because he would get more "props" from the increased media coverage.

What does DeShields mean by props, white reporters asked Turner. "He'll get more respect when he gets to L.A.," Turner explained. But a few days later, when the reporters asked Turner a similar question, he told them, "I'm not going to be your ethnic translator."

Turner also found that his colleagues were surprised when he consistently scooped them after Darryl Strawberry, the team's black outfielder, turned up missing. They kept wondering how the rookie on the beat got those stories. Turner, who had a tight relationship with a close friend of the Strawberry family, humored them, saying, "Well, guys, I'm just doing my job. If you want to know what's happening tomorrow, just give me a call."

But some incidents couldn't be sloughed off, and most of those involved Terry Johnson, a reporter for the *South Bay Daily Breeze* who has covered the Dodgers for 15 years. In Johnson, Turner had a helpful colleague and an infuriating pest wrapped into one package.

When it came to covering the sport, Turner said Johnson couldn't have been more cooperative. For instance, on Turner's first day on the beat, a story broke about Strawberry's involvement in a tax evasion case, and Johnson made sure that Turner was filled in on all the facts.

"You have to help the young guys all you can," Johnson[4] said. "People did that when I first came up so it's only fair that I pass it on."

"He was amazing like that," Turner said. "Being new, I didn't know a lot about anything. But he would say, 'Don't worry. We'll show you around. We'll have breakfast together. We'll have lunch together. You'll find baseball writers are a lot closer than basketball writers.' And that was true. For that first month, he was great at that."

But Johnson's irritating teasing—"Everyone gets it from me," he said— slowly enraged Turner. One writer told Turner it was Johnson's way of having fun. "But he crosses racial boundaries, and I don't think that's funny," Turner replied.

In retrospect, neither does Johnson. "I feel very badly about this whole matter," he said a year after the incidents occurred. "I have always considered Brad to be a friend. I have known him for many years. I certainly picked on the wrong subject to tease him on. It was not the thing to do. I regret that very much, and I have told him that more than once."

Turner said that early in spring training, Johnson, who runs a mock "kangaroo court," fined Turner over a lighthearted matter, which didn't bother Turner at all. But a few days later, he barely tolerated Johnson's telling him, "You've been fined twice a day just for being black."

Johnson said Turner "kind of laughed about it and said, 'I guess you have to do that every day because that's not going to change,' " and Johnson considered his own remark just part of the "gallows humor" of the press box.

But Johnson said he later realized that "Brad was the only person on the beat who was nonwhite, and I certainly was not sensitive to that." Johnson attributed his insensitivity to the fact that he has "never been the one who is different."

Turner said Johnson made racial comments so often that Johnson even began to upset some white reporters. When Turner asked Johnson to stop the racial remarks, Turner said Johnson replied, "All right, bro." But soon after, their big blowup occurred in the Montreal press box. Turner said he was writing a story when Johnson walked up to him, handed him a form and said, "Here darkness, fill this out." Turner refused, and when Johnson asked why, Turner said, "Look at the way you approached me." Then Turner became enraged. "Hell no, I'm not going to do a goddam thing!" Turner recalled saying. "You better back up. . . . Look at this press box. I'm the only black here; I have to live with that. If I fly somewhere I might be the only black on the plane other than the floor mats. I don't have to put up with that."

Johnson said he immediately offered an apology, but Turner didn't speak to Johnson for 2 months. "To him, it was just another joke," Turner said. "But to me, it was racist."

Why did Johnson make the "darkness" remark? "I just used a line I read somewhere in a book," Johnson said. "I didn't think about it, and that's the problem. I didn't think."

"After that happened," Turner said, "he told somebody it was hurting him that I wasn't talking to him. He started going out of his way telling me things I had no way of knowing." For instance, when the Dodgers played in Houston, Johnson informed Turner that Dodgers catcher Mike Piazza had a history of hitting well in the Astrodome, something Turner, as a rookie reporter, would not have known.

Johnson said he "wasn't trying to buy forgiveness" but was just trying to help a colleague. Turner appreciated the gesture, but it couldn't erase the fact that Johnson had added to the burden Turner already felt as the league's lone black beat reporter. "I'd go to the hotel and I might be the only black there but the bus boy," Turner said. "You don't need [racial needling]."

On the other hand, black players and coaches were ecstatic about Turner's presence. "You see a shocked look on their face when they see a black reporter," he said. "One guy said, 'Good! We got a bro here! We need this here! Come talk to me!' "

And when Turner met Giants manager Dusty Baker for the first time, Baker was stunned to see him. "I can't remember, in all my [eight] years of playing for the Dodgers, seeing a black beat reporter," Baker told him. Then Baker just shook his head and said, "That's something."

It certainly is.

## WHY THE SPORTS MEDIA
## NEED BLACK JOURNALISTS

Since Jackie Robinson, sports generously has granted itself an undeserved exemption from racial scrutiny. The in-house myth has been that the playing field is color-blind and all coaches desire only the best players—regardless of race.

Many sports editors and station managers apparently have taken the same stance toward hiring black journalists. "What difference does it make," they seem to ask, "if a game is described by someone who is black or white?" Following are a few examples of why a racially balanced perspective makes a major impact on the quality of a sports article or broadcast.

Without a doubt, overpraising white athletes for their smarts and hustle and black athletes for their physical attributes—almost to the exclusion of each other—is the sports media's trait that most infuriates black journalists.

"There is no other spectrum of American culture in which black men are numerically put in such a so-called positive role," said *Boston Globe* news columnist Derrick Jackson[5], a former sportswriter. "If white people point to any black people as heroes, it would be black athletes. . . . Last time I looked, the collective salaries of black athletes is about $1.6 billion a year, and that's really underestimating. If they can't get parity in the language, what hope is there for average black folks who are not revered?

"It's very clear that white athletes walk onto the field with intelligence as a given. With black athletes, that line historically has been blurred with terms of quickness, speed, jumping ability. The black is praised from the toes up and the white athlete from the brain down."

That is why, in a 1982 *San Francisco Chronicle* article about racist images of the NBA, I wrote, "Contrary to popular lore, if you give a black toddler a toy basketball, he will not automatically waddle over to the nearest waste-basket, pirouette 180 degrees and stuff the ball behind his head into the garbage can—any more than a white toddler shown a basketball for the first time would immediately execute a heady, but slow, give-and-go for a back-door layup" (Thomas, 1982).

Jackson carefully researched the quality of comments made about white and black players by announcers during the 1987 and 1988 NFL playoffs and five college basketball games. Two university-affiliated researchers broke down the comments into four categories: brawn, brains, weakling, and dunce. The outcome was telling. In football, where 60% of the starters were black and 39% white, 65% of the comments about black players were about brawn, and 77% of the comments about white players were about brains.

In basketball, where 62% of the starters were black and 38% white, 77% of the comments about black players were about brawn, and 63% of the comments about white players were about brains.

Predictably, black players almost monopolized the dunce comments, "earning" 90% of them in pro football and 82% in college basketball. Meanwhile, white players received 86% of weakling comments, such as "He is not fast, but . . . ."

To demonstrate these findings, Jackson cited an NFL playoff game quarterbacked by Philadelphia's Randall Cunningham, who is black, and Chicago's Mike Tomczak, who is white. During the game, after play-by-play announcer Verne Lundquist noted Cunningham's running ability, commentator Terry Bradshaw chimed in with "This guy is an ATHLETE! He's NOT a quarterback, he's an ATHLETE! A guy who has the ability to RUN and break tackles." But while Tomczak was on the sidelines, Bradshaw said, "SMART . . . Notice no one's around him. He's got his HEAD in the game" (Jackson, 1989, p. A25).

But it was Cunningham who passed for 407 yards that day and has played in the Pro Bowl three times. Tomczak? He's bounced around the league like a Ping-Pong ball and now is with his fourth team.

To Paul Olden,[6] who announces pro football and Major League Baseball games, the white-black, brains versus brawn dichotomy defies all logic. What makes this stereotype so ludicrous is that because roughly 77% of NBA players are black, a great majority of black players' points are scored against slower, less agile black defenders. The same applies to NFL receivers versus cornerbacks, both positions filled almost exclusively by blacks.

"The assumption is just because he's black he is faster than anyone," Olden said. "There are a lot of slow black players too. Andre Dawson [the Major League Baseball player] can't run a lick. He's thin and he looks fast, but he can't run 90 feet in an hour."

James Brown,[7] a black sportscaster who does play-by-play on college basketball games for CBS and hosts the Fox Network's NFL show, said Jackson's research was the catalyst for two sensitivity seminars that CBS held for its announcers before National Collegiate Athletic Association (NCAA) men's basketball tournaments in recent years. He said that some white announcers got bored with the topic after the first session, but others were sincerely interested and concerned—especially basketball commentator Tom Heinsohn.

"He had been the target of a number of articles . . . and even though he didn't consider [what he said on the air] racist, he wanted to understand how he was being perceived," Brown said. "We had a two-hour or three-hour conversation."

Brown credited former CBS executive producer Ted Shaker with implementing the seminars, but Brown would like to take the concept one step further. He would like announcers to see actual tapes of their repeatedly using stereotypes, because many of them suffer from denial. "Let them hear it," Brown said. "Even though you have the conversation [about stereotyping], a lot of guys say 'I don't do that,' because it's unconscious." And if Brown has a good working relationship with a white announcer who uses a stereotype, "You better believe I point that out," he said.

There's another slice of the brains-brawn controversy that frustrates Brown. "When you happen to see a black athlete who speaks very well, he's described as articulate," Brown said. "Whereas you wouldn't hear that with white athletes because it's assumed."

Year by year, Jackson believes this brains-brawn discrepancy is lessening because black reporters and announcers have made white journalists aware of the stereotype. "I definitely hear more intelligent comments being given to African American athletes," Jackson said. And in a *Globe* column, he wrote that his most gratifying memory of the 1993 NCAA basketball tournament occurred when an announcer said a white player "exploded" through the lane to score. But Jackson cautioned that networks cannot relax because an enlightened white announcer probably will not pass on his awareness of stereotypes to younger colleagues.

For Kelly Carter,[8] who covers the Los Angeles Lakers for the *Orange County* (California) *Register,* her pet peeve is the "poor boy makes good" theme that so often is written about black athletes. "It's great for kids to know they can overcome the odds, but people think every black athlete in the world grew up poor," she said. In contrast, "It's so rare when you read about white players: 'What was it like growing up? What were Christmases like?' Her policy toward the rags-to-riches theme? "There's always another angle," she said.

That same stereotype arose when Carter worked for the *Pittsburgh Press.* One of the sports editors there became suspicious because University of Pittsburgh basketball star Charles Smith had a new car. The editor suspected that someone connected to the athletic department must have purchased the car illegally until Carter pointed out that "I had a brand-new car when I was 15. I know there's a lot of cheating in athletics, but some black parents do have the money to buy their kid a car."

Another version of the money angle bothers Brown. With black athletes, he believes there's a tendency to hone in on their material possessions. "Jones just signed a $4.2 million contract, then bought a $900,000 house and two $60,000 sports cars," would be a hypothetical example. But if an article was being written, for instance, about high-priced white quarterbacks, Brown said the buying power reference would be much more vague. "There may be some tangential mention that John Elway has done quite well acquiring car dealerships."

Sometimes a sports department can benefit from the mere presence of a black reporter because he or she establishes a special rapport with an African American athlete or coach. Merlisa Lawrence, who recently resigned from *Sports Illustrated,* remembers Temple's black basketball coach, John Chaney, complimenting her by saying, "You remind me of my mom." Sorry, there isn't a white person on Earth who could have evoked that feeling from Chaney.

Spencer Tillman,[9] an NFL running back who also is a Houston sportscaster, sees a different type of connection between black athletes and reporters during tense postgame situations. "I think white reporters have less tolerance with black players, lack of desire to do an interview," Tillman said. "I have seen many black athletes, particularly young ones, if they had a bad day they don't want to talk about it. White reporters will say, 'You have an obligation, you're a public figure and you have to talk about a bad day just like a good day.' Which probably increases animosity."

Given the same situation, Tillman said black reporters have an ability to empathize, thereby often changing the player's mind. "I think it's something unstated in a black face: 'You had a bad game. I know you're upset. Tell me what happened.' "

The need for more black copy editors was nevermore evident than in 1986, when *Newsday's* Leon Carter[10] (now assistant sports editor with the *New York Daily News*) felt insulted by the flippant use of the term *Dred Scott.*

The Dred Scott decision (named after a black slave seeking his freedom in 1857) capped one of the most important cases in U.S. Supreme Court history because the court ruled that no black person—free or slave—was a U.S. citizen and also stated that Congress could not prohibit slavery in U.S. territories.

The decision remains a sore point with black Americans. Yet during the 1986 baseball playoffs, *Newsday* printed the banner headline "Dred Scott" to express the New York Mets' dismay at having to face Houston's ace pitcher, Mike Scott, in a key game. Carter, who had not worked the day before, picked up the paper at his home "and immediately threw it down. It immediately made me angry."

The headline had appeared on a news side story, and that night Leon found out that it had been written by a white assistant managing editor. Leon approached him and asked if he knew why the headline was offensive. "Now

I do," said the editor, who had heard that Leon was upset. But the night before, "He needed a headline and he did not know who Dred Scott was," Leon said. "Had you had a black person on his level or some black on the copy desk, it might not have happened."

Leon's struggle had only begun, because a of couple days later "Dred Scott" showed up in three *Newsday* sports stories. "Now I was back on the warpath," he said. Leon then talked to sports editor Dick Sandler, who informed his staff that the phrase should be used only to refer to the court case. Then Leon put a copy of the case history in everyone's mailbox in the sports department, which wasn't appreciated by all.

"One white baseball writer balled it up because he thought I was taking it too far," Leon said. "He felt, 'We're not trying to put down black folks; we're just trying to use a catchy phrase.' "

To *Washington Post* columnist Mike Wilbon,[11] there is no more egregious wrong in sports journalism than the fact that there are so few black sports columnists in the nation.

Referring to the predominance of middle-aged, white male sports columnists, Wilbon asked, "Why should all the images be shaped by one group of people? Everybody has their own truth, and I want to hear more than one truth."

And a black columnist's sense of truth undoubtedly will be based on a broader range of experience than that of a white columnist. Like the late Arthur Ashe, Wilbon believes that "being black in America is having another job. You've observed much more in life than your little corner of the world. I can operate almost as comfortably in an all-white setting as in an all-black setting." Black civil rights leader W. E. B. DuBois called it being "double conscious."

It's a trait Wilbon says whites usually don't possess: "Their lack of awareness [of black people] is stunning," he said.

The effect that being black has on Wilbon's work was evident on August 3, 1993, when his column recounted the funeral of Boston Celtics star Reggie Lewis. He had died of heart failure at 27, and in addition to being an all-star performer, Lewis had endeared himself to Boston residents by providing free Christmas turkeys to the city's poor.

For every writer in attendance, Lewis' funeral was a sad event. But only a black person could have written Wilbon's column, because it summoned forth the despair he felt about having attended so many funerals of young black males under 50—whether or not they were famous athletes: "I filed past Reggie Lewis in that casket but I couldn't look. Couldn't. Coping with death is very personal and I can't look at any more young, talented black men in coffins. This is my issue. I couldn't go to Arthur Ashe's funeral. I didn't read much about Jerome Brown's death. If I could have gotten out of this assignment I would have. I've spent the better part of the past seven years—starting with the death of Len Bias—looking at black men, young ones, in caskets. If it isn't a gunshot wound, it's cocaine, or a car wreck, and if not that, then a contaminated blood transfusion, or idiots in the projects making an annual game of killing the class valedictorian, and if not that, it's the equivalent of walking the street having a heart attack, which is essentially what happened to Reggie Lewis. People of all ages and races die, I know that. But the numbers of black men dying young (many from killing each other) is slowly killing me" (Wilbon, 1993, p. C1; used by permission of the *Washington Post*).

## WHY SO FEW?

If black sports journalists' contributions are so valuable, why are there so few of them? It was rare for sports pages to address racial discrimination until Al Campanis revealed baseball's racist attitudes in 1987 when he stated, in a few moments of televised loose-lipped inebriation, that blacks didn't have the "necessities" to be managers and general managers. That statement ignited a firestorm of criticism against baseball as sports reporters attacked its hiring practices and biases with heretofore unseen fervor.

In coming years, as sports figures such as NFL commentator Jimmy (the Greek) Snyder and Cincinnati Reds owner Marge Schott unveiled their racial paranoia, more pressure was put on teams to integrate their coaching and front office staffs, and in some cases there has been noteworthy progress. Meanwhile, white sports editors and station managers have been creeping along in the shadows, hiring other whites in the comfort that virtually no one in the media will force them to stare into the mirror.

"It's ironic from our perspective," said Greg Aiello,[12] the NFL's director of communications, "because we get the spotlight turned on us and we feel we've made significant strides. But if someone turned the focus on the media, I don't think their record would compare very favorably to ours." That record includes a ratio of one black sports journalist for every five daily newspapers in America, a ratio that embarrasses Sandy Bailey, chairperson of the Associated Press Sports Editors' (APSE) Minorities and Women's Committee. In 1993, she was the first woman APSE president, and although she was personally involved in many efforts to develop minority sportswriters, she was appalled by many of her colleagues' reluctance to hire or promote black journalists.

Before Campanis, they could have pleaded ignorance about the value of integrating their staffs. But in 1988 and 1989, the Sports Task Force of the NABJ conducted several APSE seminars in which the whys and hows of minority hiring were explained, and the topic continues to be discussed today within the APSE.

In terms of increased hiring, the overall response has been a collective yawn. "How much more [awareness training] do we need?" asked Bailey,[13] a *Sports Illustrated* senior editor. "I don't know. It totally befuddles me."

Bailey noted that editors listen dutifully to seminars about the importance of having blacks and women on their staffs but then return to virtually all-white male work environments where managing editors exert little pressure to integrate the sports department.

"They've regarded [sports] as specialty groups and let them go their own way," Bailey said. "It's been good old boys run amok, hiring not their relatives but their friends, and most of their friends look like themselves.

"I think it's [lack of pressure]. Mostly, you don't turn your world upside down unless you have to, and as long as your product reflects the world that you know, you don't see the gross imbalance. And you can make your numbers look decent by hiring that high school writer or backup football writer or hiring that black person to run the agate [typing in box scores] desk. But you still don't have anyone [black] who decides what will go into that paper that day—other than whether they will send the corrected box score—and don't have anyone corporately speaking for your publication."

It galls Mike Wilbon that there are only 7 black full-time sports columnists among the nation's 1,600 daily newspapers. Why so few? Wilbon cites several possible reasons: the small number of black sportswriters with 15 to 20 years experience, the fear of an outcry from white readers, an "Al Campanis complex" among white sports editors who secretly feel black writers don't have the "necessities" to be columnists.

"I think sports editors are worse than NFL general managers and owners," he said. "It's the same people—[hiring] brothers, cousins, frat brothers. Why should they be different than the people who refuse to hire a black quarterback, a black coach? It's the same mentality . . . the same unwillingness to share power and the reins."

Bill Dwyre,[14] the *Los Angeles Times* sports editor since 1981, said he has never hired a black columnist because "there hasn't been an opportunity." Mike Downey and Jim Murray are his longtime columnists and Dwyre doesn't foresee them leaving.

But because Los Angeles has about 500,000 African American residents (and potential readers), has Dwyre ever thought of creating a columnist slot specifically for a black writer? "That's something we [he and *Times* editor Shelby Coffey III] talked about a great deal and is not too far around the corner. We talk and then the economy goes sour," said Dwyre, who puts much of the blame for lack of minority hiring on the recession.

Whatever the reasons, Wilbon believes the media's hiring record for black sports columnists is atrocious. The 28-team NFL takes heat for having only two black head coaches, but as Wilbon noted, "Seven of 1,600 is a whole lot worse than 2 out of 28." And among cities with professional teams in any sport, "There are black general managers; there's only one black sports editor."

If that wasn't the case, Garry Howard[15] might still be the deputy sports editor at the *Philadelphia Inquirer* instead of the sports editor at the *Milwaukee Journal Sentinel.* When *Journal* managing editor Marty Kaiser[16] offered Howard the sports editor's job, he felt inclined to turn it down because he enjoyed working at the *Inquirer* so much. But the more Howard thought about it, the idea of becoming the only black sports editor in a major city "just blew me away."

Kaiser, who came to the *Journal* in February 1994 from the *Baltimore Sun,* said he didn't set out to hire a black sports editor. Things just worked out that way. "I heard some good things about Garry's editing skills and the more I looked at him the more I was surprised he wasn't a sports editor already, so I put the rush on him to come out here," Kaiser said.

"As soon as I met him I wanted to hire him. I said I want someone who knows how to edit, that top writers really respect. I want somebody who is fired up about running a sports department. I want somebody I can enjoy being around. His name kept coming up over and over again. I did not realize there was not a black sports editor at a major newspaper. I think Garry told me when he came out for an interview."

Until there are more black sports editors, Justice Hill,[17] who holds that position at the *Fort Wayne Journal Gazette,* believes there won't be major inroads in the hiring of African American sportswriters. "The last guy I hired, a black guy, had been trying to get hired for 3 years," Hill said. "All he needed was an opportunity. Not a handout, but a hand."

One of Hill's big fears is that more black candidates for sports editor's jobs will repeat his frustrating experience with a midsize paper in the Northeast. Hill interviewed for its sports editor's job, then found that his competition was a white candidate who, on credentials alone, had the job locked up. Hill's rival already had been a sports editor at two other papers—including one in a major league city—had been a managing editor, and was a personal friend of the editor who was doing the hiring. "Why go through this charade, except that they couldn't hire until they had a black in the pool," Hill said. "I had no problem going for the interview, but don't bring me in if you know I'm not going to get the job. Why waste my time? Why waste your time?"

Even more depressing than the lack of black sports journalists is the virtual absence of black baseball beat writers. In 1994, even the National Hockey

League—which has just a handful of black players—had three black beat reporters, three times as many as Major League Baseball. Befitting its reputation as the national pastime, Major League Baseball remains the most prestigious sports beat; in addition, Jackie Robinson's breakthrough was the symbolic touchstone of racial integration in America. So receiving almost no opportunity to cover baseball is the ultimate insult for black sports journalists.

"I think it's a travesty," said Art Thompson III[18] of the *Orange County Register,* who could rightly say he was born to be a baseball writer. Only problem is, he can't get an editor to hire him as one. "I was born in San Francisco and raised on the Giants, and my grandfather [L. C. Thornton] used to take me to the games, starting when I was in kindergarten," Thompson said. "One of my goals was to have him see me covering baseball, because that's how I learned to read. . . . He died in 1990 and I really took that hard because I never got a chance for him to see me in that capacity."

Thompson grew up reading "The Sporting Green," the *San Francisco Chronicle's* sports section, and a few years ago he got a chance to meet his boyhood idol at Candlestick Park. No, not Willie McCovey, but Bob Stevens, who had covered the Giants for the *Chronicle* when Thompson was a child.

"I met him and I was genuinely touched," Thompson said. "Here was a black guy telling a white guy that he was one of my idols. I sat with him a couple innings and just told him who I was and all my memories of when he was writing about Orlando Cepeda, Willie Mays, and Jim Ray Hart."

In 13 years of writing for daily newspapers, Thompson, 39, has covered prestigious beats such as the NFL Los Angeles Raiders and UCLA's basketball and football teams. But none compare to his lifelong dream. "I let it be known at my paper that I want to cover baseball—that it's beyond a want, that it's an obsession," he said. But before the 1994 season, his own paper hired someone from outside to cover the California Angels, and Thompson was passed over by papers in Cincinnati and Minneapolis.

Sometimes the frustration drives a black sports reporter out of the business. When Merlisa Lawrence began working for the *Pittsburgh Press* in 1990, one couldn't have found a more enthusiastic young writer. She covered major college sports and loved the writing, the competition, the crowds, the excitement, and the socializing.

In addition, she was talented, as evidenced by this lead she recalled writing about a basketball game in which Duquesne kept challenging for the lead against the University of Detroit but never could quite get ahead. "It was as if Detroit was a coy lover, and Duquesne the handsome young suitor. Duquesne seemed to enjoy the chase more than the capture," she said.[19] Yet just 4 years later, Lawrence retired from sportswriting at the age of 28.

In the interim, the *Press* folded and Lawrence joined *Sports Illustrated,* which had recruited her. As a reporter, Lawrence's principal duties were checking facts and gathering notes and quotes for staff writers who would craft the stories. But she expected to soon be writing frequently.

That never happened. "I came up with story ideas and I hustled, but they [management] just didn't care," Lawrence said. So she turned her attention to her second major interest in journalism, interactive communications, but she believes she was bypassed for a position related to new technology.

Throughout her time at *Sports Illustrated,* Lawrence found some solace by talking to Roy Johnson, the only black senior editor in the magazine's 40-year history until he left to become a senior editor at *Money Magazine,* in August 1994.

"Roy would say, 'Come around to my office,' and I would tell him the horrors of the day," she said. "Not that he would give me great advice, but he would listen." And afterward, Lawrence felt, "I'm not crazy."

In June of 1994, Lawrence submitted her resignation, making sure her letter said she quit "due to a change in marital status and a lack of opportunity." She plans to write freelance articles mostly about nonsports topics. "*Sports Illustrated* has soured me on [the sports] part of the business," she said. "I don't mind proving myself to an audience, but not to the people who hired me."

The broadcast media is equally guilty of racially slanted hiring and promoting, as evidenced by the fact that in 1993 Paul Olden of WFAN in New York—he announces the New York Jets games—was the only black play-by-play or color announcer for an NFL team.

Although NFL teams have final approval on announcers, Greg Aiello said most of the power over that decision is held by the radio stations that broadcast each team's games. What does the paucity of black NFL announcers say about station owners and managers who do the hiring?

"I just think it's a sad testimony of where we are," said Spencer Tillman. He believes the prevailing attitude is that African Americans "can't articulate what happens in the course of the game although we cause what happens on the field. Maybe it just says people are more comfortable with white, middle-aged, play-by-play announcers. . . . That is a position of authority—it's representative of control."

The Newhouse School of Communications at Syracuse University has become famous for its ability to turn out noted sportscasters, with Bob Costas, Hank Greenwald (play-by-play announcer for the San Francisco Giants), and Marv Albert (the New York Knicks announcer) among them. The school's chairman, Don Edwards,[20] completely discounts the notion that radio and television stations are reluctant to have a black person announcing their games. "We're past that point in television land," he said. "We're long past that point in acceptance. It's not a question at all. . . . You're talking 1960s and 70s mentality."

As an example, Edwards noted that Darren Horton, a Syracuse graduate and black sports anchor at WFLD-TV in Chicago, is a rising star who reached a major market in just a few years. "I don't know where he's going next, but he's a first-class talent and he should be rolling," Edwards said. But Edwards —despite his extreme optimism—also acknowledged that the overall progress for blacks and women will be slow.

Thirty years ago, he said, neither group was being trained as announcers. Consequently, "What we're seeing now are the [white] guys in their 40s and 50s." Now that blacks and women are in broadcast journalism programs, "You're going to see in the next 25 years an emergence of female and African American sports talent that is going to be a major change."

In the next 25 years? That may be encouraging to the little Emmitt Smiths and Shaquille O'Neals of the sports world who are currently bouncing balls in their cribs. But today's current black athletes will wear out their knees long before that evolution occurs.

And comparing the number of white and black former athletes and coaches who leap from the playing field into the broadcast booth, one must question Edwards' race-is-not-a-factor view of sports broadcasting. There certainly is no dearth of retired black athletes who could be announcers—if offered the same opportunities as white former NFL stars Phil Simms, Matt Millen, and Howie Long or former NBA coaches Doug Collins, Hubie Brown, Matt Guokas, and Dick Versace.

On the production side, there is almost no black presence; the 2:31 ratio of producers-directors at ABC and Fox is typical. "We see [black announcers] on camera, but decisions are made behind the scenes, and that record has been absolutely atrocious for a long period of time," said sportscaster James Brown. "I have never seen an African American head of a sports division at a network. I have never seen an executive producer who is African American, and in terms of producers, I have worked with a grand total of one." That covers Brown's 16 years as an announcer.

Kimberly Belton,[21] a former Stanford basketball star who is ABC Sports' only black producer-director, said he believes the key problem is that the door to television is through word-of-friend-or-relative.

Most often, young people get into sports production as errand runners— or "go-fors"—during games. They get hired by production assistants or college sports information directors, more than 90% of whom are white. Because "likes attract likes," Belton said, blacks often get left out of TV's entry-level jobs.

To counter that when he is producing college basketball and football games, Belton suggests that production assistants ask the host school's Black Student Union or communication department if there are some African Americans who would like to be runners.

How do the production assistants respond? "They say yeah," he said, "but some do it and some don't."

Black athletes are well aware of the disparity between their numbers and the numbers of white journalists recording their achievements and failures on the field. "There's a general distrust [by the athletes], reflective of mainstream society," Tillman said. "I'm not sure all of them have sat down and pondered why they feel the way they feel, but inherently there is something to distrust there."

In fact, there is so much distrust that Garry Howard, the *Milwaukee Journal Sentinel* sports editor, said he knows black athletes who have nicknamed the media, "the White Mob, the White Face, because they don't even think from the beginning that they'll get a fair shake."

## SOLVING THE SCARCITY PROBLEM

The lack of black sports journalists is so blatant and has existed for so long, that one wonders what must be done to resolve the problem. One thing is for sure. It's a matter of divvying up the power within the sports media, and as Tillman said, quoting philosopher Ryan Holt Nieber, "Privileged groups rarely give up their privileges without great and strong resistance."

Marty Kaiser, Sandy Bailey, and Leon Carter believe change must come from the bottom up. Kaiser and Howard of the *Milwaukee Journal Sentinel* agree that newspapers must cultivate black sportswriters by encouraging local high school students to be agate clerks or prep writers. Kaiser noted that at the *Baltimore Sun,* two of his best sports staffers—Mike Davis and Mike Preston—were Baltimore natives who began as part-time agate clerks.

At the college level, Bailey, of APSE, and Carter, head of the NABJ's Sports Task Force, have joined with the Freedom Forum media foundation to develop the Freedom Forum Sports Journalism Institute, a summer program to bring aspiring minority sports journalists into the business.

In 1993, its inaugural program, 15 college students who had some sports-writing experience attended an intense, 2-week session at Norfolk State University during which they were taught the rudiments of sportswriting and heard lectures from some of the nation's top sports reporters and editors. That summer, they wrote the conference newsletter for the APSE convention in New Orleans, giving them a chance to display their talent before hundreds of editors.

Carter believes the program provided invaluable inspiration for the students, as demonstrated by the response of a student from Marshall University during the program's closing session. "When students said what they appreciated, tears came to his eyes because it was the first time he had met an

African American sportswriter," Carter said. "He was thrilled to see a Bill Rhoden or Curtis Bunn."

All 15 students eventually received internships. "We needed a feeding process and this is marvelous," said *L.A. Times* sports editor Bill Dwyre. Before the institute began, members "talked and talked, and not much happened [about minority hiring]," Dwyre added.

Yet Bailey has been dismayed by her colleagues' lack of enthusiasm about hiring interns. "I have not found the commitment to be what I thought," she said.

Getting promoted—either to a bigger newspaper or a better beat—often is a major problem for black sports journalists. Leon Carter especially derides editors for not giving black beat writers a chance to become columnists. Instead, he said editors try to hire away established black columnists like Wilbon or *USA Today's* Bryan Burwell. "The industry does itself a disservice when it always looks at the superstars, because if Burwell or Wilbon gets hired by another paper, who's to say they'll be replaced by another minority?" Carter said.

And editors must stop the practice of making black writers only part-time columnists while requiring them to also continue beat or feature coverage. Let them be full-time columnists, just like white males have been for decades.

There's a consensus opinion that more pressure for diversified hiring in sports must come from top management. When that pressure is exerted, the results can be significant.

The *New York Times,* which until the late 1980s had three blacks on its sports staff, now has nine, including a columnist (Bill Rhoden), three NFL writers (Tim Smith, Thomas George, Mike Freeman), its national baseball reporter (Claire Smith), an NBA writer (Clifton Brown), and assistant sports editor (Kathleen McElroy).

Much of that emphasis on hiring blacks came from executive editor Max Frankel, who explained on the Charlie Rose interview show (April 14, 1994) that he "rigorously" reminded editors that "unless we're diversifying at a pace I thought was necessary, we were going to stop all hiring. And that got people's attention."

Paul Olden believes management also needs to be nudged from the outside, such as recent efforts by the Reverend Jesse Jackson's Rainbow Coalition to turn the spotlight on hiring in the sports media. "It's going to take management to be suddenly enlightened," Olden said, "and I don't hold out much hope for that without pressure being applied."

Black people also have a role in increasing their participation in the sports media. Mike Wilbon would like to see more black students—and their parents—embrace journalism as a possible profession. When Wilbon gives talks at schools, "I see wizards and they can't speak the language," he said. "Everyone wants to go into engineering or wants to go pre-med. . . . I don't think anything with reading and writing is a priority [for black students]. It has no sex appeal to us."

But Derrick Jackson believes that theory gives sports editors an all-too-easy excuse. "I think there are many black students who, if reached [in high school or college] and encouraged to get into this craft, would gleefully get into it," he said.

Kelly Carter believes that some black sports journalists need to be more open-minded to advance, either in terms of where they work or what they cover. Although she was raised in Los Angeles, she had no compunction about taking her first job with the *Iowa City Press Citizen,* even though the paper's circulation was only 16,000, few blacks lived in Iowa City, she had never been there until she started the job, and when she moved there in January 1986, "I had to buy a winter coat for the first time in my life."

But the beat, covering the Big 10, was a terrific beginning job, and Carter always kept maneuvering for a better one. Knowing that her talents could be overlooked in a small town, whenever she traveled to a big city she would try to set up an interview with the local sports editor. "It's not costing sports editors anything and you have a chance to have your work evaluated by someone else," she said.

When she visited a girlfriend in Atlanta, she had an informal interview with Van McKenzie, then the *Journal-Constitution's* sports editor. He didn't hire her but was impressed enough that when he heard there was an opening at the *Pittsburgh Press,* he recommended Kelly to its sports editor, who did hire her.

Kelly has also been flexible about story topics. In Pittsburgh, she didn't balk at covering greyhound racing or golf, two sports she knew virtually nothing about and that have almost no black professionals. In 1990, she covered Wimbledon for the *Dallas Morning News* even though "I had never been to a tennis match in my life" and all she knew about the sport was the joke, "Love meant you didn't score." But she read some tennis books, bought a videotape before the tournament, survived her first Wimbledon, and eventually made tennis a regular beat.

Derrick Jackson believes there's one other crucial factor in increasing the numbers of black sports journalists: the black athletes themselves. He says they hold the ultimate leverage against the status quo. "Black athletes could change this literally overnight," he said. "In fact, in about 15 minutes, should they ever decide enough is enough. All they have to do is pick a day, walk off the court, and you would see some serious diversity work at networks overnight. Black athletes would lose a few thousand dollars but the networks would lose millions."

But because most black athletes have white agents and financial advisers and aren't entrenched in black neighborhoods, Jackson believes the athletes won't take the initiative unless the black community pressures them. "As long as black athletes choose to have their minds chained by the fear of the loss of their salary, not much will happen," Jackson said.

## NOTES

1. Phone interview, September, 14, 1994.

2. Quotations from Bill Rhoden come from a phone interview conducted by the author, July 23, 1994.

3. Quotations from Brad Turner come from a phone interview conducted by the author, September 4, 1994.

4. Quotations from Terry Johnson come from a phone interviews conducted by the author, October 10, 1994, and May 7, 1995.

5. Quotations from Derrick Jackson come from a phone interview conducted by the author, June 22, 1994.

6. Quotations from Paul Olden come from a phone interview conducted by the author, June 29, 1994.

7. Quotations from James Brown come from a phone interview conducted by the author, September 3, 1994.

8. Quotations from Kelly Carter come from a phone interview conducted by the author, June 21, 1994.

9. Quotations from Spencer Tillmann come from a phone interview conducted by the author, May 25, 1994.

10. Quotations from Leon Carter come from a phone interview conducted by the author, May 21, 1994.

11. Quotations from Mike Wilbon come from a phone interview conducted by the author, June 6, 1994.

12. Quotations from Greg Aiello come from a phone interview conducted by the author, June 28, 1994.

13. Quotations from Sandy Bailey come from a phone interview conducted by the author, June 16, 1994.

14. Quotations from Bill Dwyre come from a phone interview conducted by the author, September 29, 1994.

15. Quotations from Garry Howard come from a phone interview conducted by the author, June 6, 1994.

16. Quotations from Marty Kaiser come from a phone interview conducted by the author, September 7, 1994.

17. Quotations from Justice Hill come from a phone interview conducted by the author, September 22, 1994.

18. Quotations from Art Thompson III come from a phone interview conducted by the author, June 14, 1994.

19. Quotations from Merlisa Lawrence come from a phone interview conducted by the author, June 14, 1994.

20. Quotations from Don Edwards come from a phone interview conducted by the author, June 16, 1994.

21. Quotations from Kimberly Belton come from a phone interview conducted by the author, June 6, 1994.

# REFERENCES

Banks, L. J. (1972, November 28). Wendell broke color line in sportswriting. *Chicago Sun-Times.*
Jackson, D. (1989, January 22). Calling the plays in black and white. *Boston Globe,* p. A25.
Thomas, R. (1982, April 20). Old racist images still haunting the NBA. *San Francisco Chronicle.*
Wilbon, M. (1993, August 3). A player, a father, a man. *Washington Post,* p. C1.

# 32

# The State of Women in Sports Media

Mary Schmitt

What is the state of women in sports media? It's a difficult question to answer, mainly because there is no comprehensive data to examine. There have been studies and surveys, scholarly works and articles, estimates, gues-stimates, interviews, and essays, but all those have produced no hard data—no actual statistics.

In one of the most comprehensive reports to date, *Women, Media, and Sport,* Pamela Creedon (1994) refers to several studies that provide the best attempts so far to quantify the situation. In the early 1970s, Creedon writes, the Associated Press estimated there were approximately 30 women in sports media, 25 of them sportswriters. By 1975, the estimate had quadrupled.

Creedon also writes about a 1988 study that looked at the sports departments of the 109 largest daily newspapers in the country. The study showed that only 63% employed women sports reporters. Of the 69 papers that did employ them, only 9% (96) of the approximately 1,061 sports department employees were women.

The Association for Women in Sports Media (AWSM) was founded in 1988 when a group of about 40 women held its first convention in Oakland. By 1993, the organization had more than 500 members with more than 100 making their way to the sixth annual convention in Minneapolis. But the organization's findings in the early 1990s indicated that only 3% of the 10,000 print and broadcast sports journalists were women.

Still, there are more women employed in the sports journalism field than ever before and the numbers keep growing. At least part of the reason can be attributed to another statistic cited in Creedon's book: Sportswriting is taught as a separate course at 55 of the nation's schools of journalism and mass communication, and about 34% of the students enrolled in those courses are women.

Some of the largest papers in the country currently employ women as sports editors: the *Chicago Tribune, Philadelphia Inquirer,* Minneapolis-based *Star*

*Tribune, Seattle Times,* and *Austin American-Statesman* among them. Women serve as assistant sports editors, columnists, investigative reporters, copy editors, graphics editors, and beat reporters covering everything from the Olympics to prep schools.

On the broadcast side, all the major networks have women anchors, reporters, or both, and women are making their marks on the nations' radio stations as well. In public relations, too, women are serving as directors of communications, media relations, or both at the team level and in the league offices.

Truly, women have made their presence felt in all areas of sports journalism. And as their numbers increase, so does their power. But that is the next struggle women in sports media face. For we have found that although we still occasionally face opposition from those we cover, many more times the biggest opposition comes from those in our offices. The very people we are supposed to turn to for support in a difficult situation outside the office are the ones who are turning on us inside the office. We have fought the locker room battles; now our battleground is the boardroom.

Of course, women in all professions and businesses are facing the same things. Glass ceilings and sexual harassment are complaints of an entire generation of women workers, many of whom agree with Anita Hill's claim that lots of men just don't get it.

There are, of course, many men who do get it and are trying to do something about it. In my 1-year tenure as AWSM president, I have fielded at least one call a month from a conscientious male sports executive looking to hire a woman for his staff. From these phone calls, I feel qualified to speak to the future of women in sports media. It lies in copyediting. I could have placed women from San Diego to Syracuse. Unfortunately, most of AWSM's membership consists of sports reporters, not copy editors, so many of those conscientious male sports editors went away disappointed. As was I.

If I was to speak to women entering the sports media field, I would encourage them to consider editing as a career. Not only is that where the jobs are currently, that also is where the climb to the top starts. Traditionally, sports editors and assistants are selected from inside the sports department. If we are to increase our power along with our numbers, this is how we must go about it. To that end, AWSM plans to add a copyediting scholarship/internship to our reporting scholarships available to college students.

As a member of the scholarship committee this past year, I had the privilege of reading the applications submitted by an incredible array of talented young women. It was difficult to select the recipients, because each of the women was a winner in her own way.

But after reviewing those entries, I have a better feel for the state of women in sports media. Despite an absence of statistics to back up my claim and despite the problems we share with other professional women, in general, I would say the situation is good and getting better all the time.

## REFERENCE

Creedon, P. J. (1994). *Women, media, and sport: Challenging gender values.* Thousand Oaks, CA: Sage.

# 33

# Gender Equity in Sports Media Coverage
## A Review of the NCAA News

Bethany Shifflett
Rhonda Revelle

$P$resently, as well as historically, gender has been dichotomized by many cultures in such a way that by connotation, if not definition, males are characterized as rational and females as emotional; where males are described as active, females are passive. This perspective can be maintained and reinforced or changed through socialization.

All influences that shape the skills, values, norms, and behaviors of individuals are part of the process of socialization. These influences can include significant others, schooling, neighborhood, religion, government, and social gatherings. Although still a point of controversy, the media appears to be one of the more potent influences (Duncan, 1990; Lumpkin & Williams, 1991; Reep & Dambrot, 1989). Certainly those in government and advertising make extensive use of the media to influence public opinion.

Studies analyzing media content suggest that with respect to gender, women are underrepresented. When women are represented, existing societal norms are highlighted. For example, prime-time television characters from 1953 to 1977 were predominantly male (36%-40% were female), and when in leading roles, women were often stereotypically portrayed as passive and not as competent as their male counterpart (Dominick, 1979). This finding is not unique. Research has documented not only underrepresentation but also the predominantly stereotypic portrayal of women (Davis, 1990; Vande Berg & Streckfuss, 1992).

Similar findings have emerged from studies of print media. Whether referring to photography (Duncan, 1990; Luebke, 1989), sexual imagery in advertising (Boddewyn & Kunz, 1991; Duquin, 1989), the disparity in sports coverage between men and women (Hilliard, 1984), or the bias built into the process of collecting and reporting information (Theberge & Cronk, 1986), researchers report that the message being communicated is that men are active/powerful/important and women are inactive/subordinate/unimportant.

Research focusing on sports magazines or the coverage of sports by newspapers and other magazines indicates that female athletes have received less coverage than male athletes (Rintala & Birrell, 1984). In fact, in a selected review of the widely read *Sports Illustrated,* Bryant (1980) reported no coverage of women, and the more extensive review (1954-1987) of this magazine by Lumpkin and Williams (1991) reported that 3,178 articles featured men compared to 280 featuring women. These researchers have also pointed out that coverage of women has generally been focused on those sports (tennis, figure skating, synchronized swimming, etc.) that convey a "feminine" image. Photographs and descriptions of women and their sports activities tend to reinforce sex role stereotypes, focus on the body, and often include sexist overtones (Duquin, 1989; Lumpkin & Williams, 1991). In analyzing Olympic Games photographs and articles, Duncan (1990) reported an excessive focus on physical appearance, poses with sexual connotations, emotional displays, and photographic groupings or angles that imply a subordinate position.

To explain this differential treatment of men and women in sports coverage, some have pointed to market forces (McGregor, 1989; Rintala & Birrell, 1984). It is assumed that a focus on men and the feminine portrayal of women is what the public wants and will pay for. However, open to question is whether this differential coverage is evident in publications, such as the *NCAA News,* that are distributed primarily as a benefit to members in an organization.

Published as a service to members, one would expect gender-balanced sports coverage because (a) market forces can be expected to have little direct impact, (b) publication does not depend on advertising revenues, and (c) the publication serves those affiliated with both men's and women's sports. Given the unique focus on men's and women's sports that this organization has and the distribution of the *NCAA News* as a benefit of membership, this article examines how equitable the coverage was in selected issues of the *NCAA News.*

Eight issues of the *NCAA News* were randomly selected for review: one fall, winter, spring, and summer issue from 1988 and 1991. All articles within these issues that focused directly on athletes, coaches, or their sport were selected for evaluation. Articles highlighting legislative action, committee reports/actions, facilities, and other topics indirectly related to collegiate athletics were not reviewed.

## CODING OF TEXT

For the written material examined, the unit of analysis was paragraphs. For each paragraph, its location, gender focused on, content, and length (in square inches) were recorded. The categories for location were (a) front page, (b) back page, (c) prime (top) on a page within the issue, and (d) other location on pages within the issue. The categories for gender were female, male, combined, and neither. For the content variable, the categories were (a) factual athletic information (e.g., facilities, statistics), (b) factual information unrelated to athletics (e.g., academic honors), (c) personal (opinions/perspectives) athletic information, (d) personal information unrelated to athletics, and (e) other. This content variable was recorded only to provide information on the type of material reviewed.

Through an iterative process, the definitions for each category were developed. Two researchers independently coded the same 15 articles sequentially. Following coding of several articles, discrepancies in coding were discussed. Based on these discussions, refinements were made in category definitions that enhanced consistency between coders. This process was replicated until good intercoder reliability (proportion of agreement) across (.81) and within each category (.77 to .85) was achieved. As part of the iterative process, validity was also examined. The type of validity relevant to this analysis was semantic validity, which is assessed by determining whether units (paragraphs in this study) classified the same belong together. For the gender and content variables then, paragraphs from a wide range of articles covering every coding category were read out of the context of the article (in clusters by category) to see if they conveyed the same type of information. Although some difficulty surfaced with the content variable, semantic validity overall was quite good. Researchers subsequently continued coding the remaining articles separately.

## CODING OF PHOTOGRAPHS

Similar information was coded in examining the photographs in each of the selected issues. Each photograph's location, gender of those in the picture, content, and size (in square inches) were recorded. The categories for the content variable differed from those for paragraphs. The categories, developed using the same process described above, were (a) competing athlete, (b) athletes in a noncompetitive but athletic context, (c) head shots of athletes/coaches, (d) head shots of others (e.g., campus administrators), (e) group photographs of others (e.g., committee members), and (f) other.

**TABLE 33.1**  Source of Information, by Year

|  | 1988 | | 1991 | |
| --- | --- | --- | --- | --- |
|  | Paragraphs | Photographs | Paragraphs | Photographs |
| Season |  |  |  |  |
| Winter | 102 | 14 | 181 | 8 |
| Spring | 102 | 22 | 300 | 23 |
| Summer | 172 | 30 | 197 | 16 |
| Fall | 261 | 24 | 110 | 14 |
| Total | 637 | 90 | 788 | 61 |

## DATA ANALYSIS

Using SPSS PC+, frequency distribution tables and cross-tabulation tables were used to summarize the data collected. To examine gender equity in coverage, allocation of space for both written material and photographs was examined by gender, year, and issue as well as by gender within each year and issue. Furthermore, comparisons by gender were made for the location of paragraphs and photographs.

## RESULTS

In all, 1,425 paragraphs and 151 photographs were examined (see Table 33.1). The type of information conveyed in the articles was primarily factual (62%). Across all issues, 297 paragraphs using 731 square inches of space were devoted to women, whereas 820 paragraphs using 1,788 square inches of space were given to men. Of the paragraphs read, 21% focused on women, 58% on men, 16% had a combined focus (e.g., male coaching female team), and 5% did not focus on men, women, or their sports. Examined separately by year, 73% of the space was allocated to men in 1988 and 71% in 1991. Additionally, some seasonal variation was observed, with considerably less space being given to women (8% in 1988 and 2% in 1991) in fall issues.

Regarding location, information on women was located most often in the body of the issue and infrequently at the top of the page. Of paragraphs located in the prime position on a page, 65% focused on men and 16% focused on women (see Table 33.2).

With photographs, a similar pattern was present, with 49 pictures using 227 square inches of space allotted to women and 95 pictures using 784 square inches of space given to men (see Figure 33.1). Separated by year, the

**TABLE 33.2** Variation in Location of Paragraphs, by Gender

| | n | Focus of Paragraph | | | |
| | | % Male | % Female | % Combined | % Neither |
|---|---|---|---|---|---|
| Location | | | | | |
| Front page | 86 | 45 | 30 | 17 | 8 |
| Back page | 93 | 63 | 17 | 14 | 6 |
| Prime on page | 701 | 65 | 16 | 13 | 6 |
| Other | 545 | 49 | 26 | 20 | 5 |

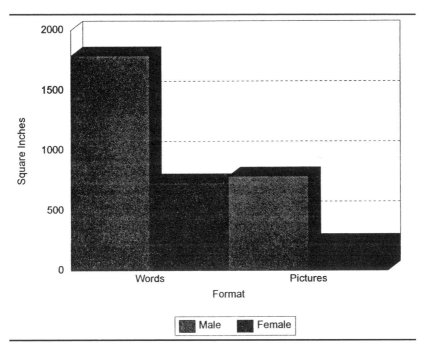

**Figure 33.1.** Summary of Words and Pictures Devoted to Male and Female Athletes in *NCAA News*

proportion of picture space for women decreased from 1988 to 1991. In 1988, 25% pictured women compared to 12% in 1991. Looking only at athletic photographs, 43% of the space pictured women in 1988 and 9% in 1991. In addition, all action shots regardless of year were of men.

With respect to location, 22% of the photographs on the front page (*n* = 18) were of women versus 61% of men, two of the three back page pictures were of women, and 33% of those found in a prime position (top of page; *n* = 76) pictured women versus 62% of men.

## DISCUSSION

A review of selected issues of the *NCAA News* found that females were underrepresented in both the articles and photographs examined. Seasonal variations were observed, with fall issues containing considerably less written coverage of women (less than 10%), regardless of the year. Perhaps the prominence of football explains this imbalance; however, there are fall sports for women, and such inequitable coverage is a disservice to those sports and their participants. In addition, whenever blocks of statistics were displayed, the men's statistics always appeared first and at the top of the page.

Because each institution must have a similar number of men's and women's sports, it was expected that representation in the *NCAA News* would be more equitable than that found in popular magazines and newspapers. In addition, because the *NCAA News* is distributed as a benefit of membership, more equitable coverage was expected on the assumption that market forces would be less influential. Instead, a similar pattern of underrepresentation was observed. Although this pattern may be, to a limited degree, influenced by the discrepancies in participation and coaching by men and women, the pattern also suggests that an unwarranted bias in favor of men's sports exists in the gathering and reporting of collegiate athletics news.

In addition to the discrepancies with respect to the allocation of space and the location of articles and photographs, there was the choice of content. One striking example was in an issue (April 1991) covering gymnastics. Photographs of the men were action shots (iron cross and handstand on parallel bars) of individuals compared to the one team shot of women hugging tearfully when they won the meet. The contrast is perhaps a reminder that a conscious effort is needed to get beyond stereotypes and to highlight the athletic element in female athletics.

Although the sampling of issues was limited and thus generalizability should be considered tentative, these findings warrant attention because the media often serves as a vehicle to frame what is acceptable, expected, and desirable. Therefore, inequitable coverage can potentially undermine the accomplishments and value of women in sports. Those reporting sports information, directing sports information offices, editing sports information, and particularly those serving as gatekeepers in the publication process can and should do better.

## REFERENCES

Boddewyn, J. J., & Kunz, H. (1991). Sex and decency issues in advertising: General and international dimensions. *Business Horizons, 34*(5), 13-20.

Bryant, J. (1980). A two year selective investigation of the female in sport as reported in the paper media. *Arena Review, 4,* 32-43.

Davis, D. M. (1990). Portrayals of women in prime-network television: Some demographic characteristics. *Sex Roles, 23,* 325-332.

Dominick, J. R. (1979). The portrayal of women in prime time, 1953-1977. *Sex Roles, 5,* 405-411.

Duncan, M. C. (1990). Sports photographs and sexual difference: Images of women and men in the 1984 and 1988 Olympic Games. *Sociology of Sport Journal, 7,* 22-41.

Duquin, M. C. (1989). Fashion and fitness: Images in women's magazine advertisements. *Arena Review, 13,* 97-107.

Hilliard, D. C. (1984). Media images of male and female professional athletes: An interpretive analysis of magazine articles. *Sociology of Sport Journal, 1,* 251-261.

Luebke, B. (1989). Out of focus: Images of women and men in newspaper photographs. *Sex Roles, 20*(3), 121-133.

Lumpkin, A., & Williams, L. D. (1991). An analysis of *Sports Illustrated* feature articles 1954-1987. *Sociology of Sport Journal, 8,* 16-32.

McGregor, E. (1989). Mass media and sport: Influences on the public. *The Physical Educator, 46*(1), 52-55.

Reep, D. C., & Dambrot, F. H. (1989). Effects of frequent television viewing on stereotypes: "Drip, drip" or "drench." *Journalism Quarterly, 66*(3), 542-550.

Rintala, J., & Birrell, S. (1984). Fair treatment for the active female: A content analysis of *Young Athlete* magazine. *Sociology of Sport Journal, 1,* 231-250.

Theberge, N., & Cronk, A. (1986). Work routines in newspaper sports departments and the coverage of women's sports. *Sociology of Sport Journal, 3,* 195-201.

Vande Berg, L. R., & Streckfuss, D. (1992). Profile: Prime-time television's portrayal of women and the world of work: A demographic profile. *Journal of Broadcasting & Electronic Media, 36,* 195-208.

# 34

## Hear No Evil, See No Evil

Sandy Padwe

From the opening sentence, it was clear that the 1993 book about the New York Mets, *The Worst Team Money Could Buy* (Klapisch & Harper, 1993), was going to be memorable. It would be memorable, however, for reasons the authors didn't envision. When the book was published, Bob Klapisch and John Harper were baseball writers for the *New York Daily News.* In their first sentence they wrote, "The worst part about sportswriting is that it kills the fan in you. Baseball writing, especially" (p. ix).

Therein lies the defining creed of many modern-day sportswriters and broadcasters: They are fans first and journalists second. How dare anything such as a labor dispute, a gambling accusation, a rape charge, a wife-beating report, or an illegal drug use allegation interfere with life between the lines? In the coaching and sports reporting mind-set, all of these things are known— by all too many practitioners of both professions—as "distractions."

*The Worst Team Money Could Buy* was a critical success. It had a breezy, kiss-and-tell style that generated lots of headlines. It also afforded both a rare peek into just how far sports journalists' ethics had plunged and a definitive look at the daily dilemma that writers and broadcasters faced as the tabloid ethic became an increasingly dominant force in daily journalism.

"On the beat," Harper wrote, "the push of the tabloid mentality often clashes with the pull of journalistic integrity. What is a story and what's not? What's fair and what's unfair? The tug of war is constant. It's easy enough at times to quote out of context, twist it just enough to warrant a back-page headline. You won't last long in the clubhouse making a practice of irresponsible reporting, but there are more subtle decisions to make on a day to day basis, and many are born out of desperation for a story" (Klapisch & Harper, 1993, p. 132).

"... Where do you draw the line in relationships with players? It's not hard to become friendly with many of them, especially when they're young and impressionable. You stroke their egos in print and in person, and the invisible barrier disappears quickly. It can be unhealthy as well as unethical, but then, the demands of tabloid reporting supersede the laws of journalism" (Klapisch & Harper, 1993, p. 198).

Sports journalism is not improving, but the tabloid mentality isn't the only reason. Conflicts of interest abound. Journalists get too close to sources. And too many journalists censor what they, or one of their editors, view as unfit to print. A prominent network sports anchor, who asked to remain anonymous, said that if the various coaches now serving as analysts ever decided to tell what they really know on the air, there would be complete chaos in pro and college sports. There are other reasons sports journalism is not improving. The freebie syndrome is alive and well. Just check the free food available in any press room or any press box or check the spreads for the media at most press conferences. Super Bowl week still is the champion of the freebies; an enterprising and hungry writer or broadcaster could get through the week without having to pay for one meal. And then there are the free pens, the free briefcases, the free coffee mugs, and all sorts of free merchandise available from the corporations who want a slice of the Super Bowl merchandise market. The closest rival to Super Bowl week is National Basketball Association (NBA) All-Star weekend, another grandiose tribute to the powers of dozens of publicity people; sports journalists—is that an oxymoron?—can leave an event such as the Super Bowl or an NBA All-Star game looking like a race car driver with all that advertising over their uniforms. The sports media people have their NBA or National Football League hats, their league duffel bags, their league golf shirts, or a sweater or some other piece of clothing from one of the league's sponsors or advertisers who represent the league and private business.

There are other reasons why sports journalism cannot break from the "toy department" syndrome. The networks own the sports they are supposed to cover, and other news-gathering organizations often find themselves in business with the leagues and sports about whom they are supposed to report. *Sports Illustrated,* for example, has been a sponsor of the Olympic Games for more than a decade. And when the magazine published special commemorative issues early in 1995 for the University of Nebraska's championship football season as well as for Penn State's perfect season, the magazine had a full-page advertisement under the headline, "*Sports Illustrated* Inside Authentics Exclusive." A fan could get videos, caps, workout shorts, sweatshirts, T-shirts, and hats from the magazine and its business partner. The universities, in effect, also were business partners with *SI.*

Where do conflicts of this sort and many others leave a sports journalist? It was ironic that when baseball writers, especially those from New York, were faced with covering a possible rape by three New York Mets players in 1991 that the *New York Post* and other papers sent cityside reporters to Florida, where the Mets were training, to help cover the story. The *Post*'s Andrea Peyser, the epitome of the overly aggressive tabloid journalist, was one of those reporters. Harper, who was with the *Post* at the time, wrote in his book: "Peyser was crusading for truth. She was also selling papers, and her editors wanted more. She wrote a column denouncing the baseball writers for covering up for the players' sexual habits, refusing to report the truth" (Klapisch & Harper, 1993, p. 63). Harper then chastised Peyser for not understanding that a baseball writer would not last on the beat if he or she reported what America's role models were doing when their wives weren't around.

Peyser (1992) wrote a column in the *Post* that said, in part, "Sorry, guys. It's time to take off the white gloves. You asked for it.

"You sportswriters. You know who you are. The ones who coddle and suck up to athletes, gratefully lapping up scraps of information tossed your way— genuflecting in the light emanating from ballplayers, many of them spoiled, 20-year-old millionaire boys with pornographic minds, sixth-grade vocabularies and good throwing arms.

"You're accomplices to crime.

"You told us Pete Rose was a hero even as he betrayed every kid who looked up to a ballplayer.

"And you winked at Magic Johnson's masculine prowess while all the while he was packing a lethal weapon in his shorts.

"You call yourselves reporters?" (p. 17).

Who even knows what the future will be like on the sports pages and on the TV sportscasts now that "new media" is here. All the forecasts predict a radical change in coverage and approaches to coverage. Sports will have to adapt, but few people in the profession have answers about what the sportswriter or sportscaster of the 21st century will be like.

Will he or she be better than many of the so-called golden-agers of the 1920s and 1930s who were full of overblown verbiage but who seldom asked why there were no blacks playing in Major League Baseball or why women's athletics were almost invisible with the exception of golf and tennis?

Will the new sports journalist be better than several of the irreverent types such as Stan Isaacs and Larry Merchant who wrote in the early 1960s and who first began to crack some of the myths and stereotypes surrounding athletes? And will some be like the actual reformers of the late 1960s and early 1970s such as Robert Lipsyte, David Burgin, Ira Berkow, George Kiseda, and Howard Cosell who wrote or broadcast story after story about the effect that sports had on American society? They were among the first to look into racism and sexism in sports as well as to ask why authoritarianism and military mind-set had such deep roots in the sporting establishment.

Many of those journalists drifted into other parts of the media and when they left sports, the pressure they brought on the sporting institutions ended, and sports journalism, with a few exceptions, regressed to the passive state that existed well into the mid-1990s.

Perhaps the most revealing piece about the sports media before Klapisch and Harper's time came in Michael Sokolove's 1990 book, *Hustle,* about Pete Rose's downfall and his banishment from baseball.

Those who watch the *Sports Reporters* program on ESPN on Sunday mornings are familiar with Bill Conlin of the *Philadelphia Daily News.* He has an opinion on everything, including how sports journalism should be covered. Any intelligent reader of Sokolove's book knows that Conlin hung himself and his profession to a degree when he talked about the Rose case, which may represent sports journalism's all-time low. "Most of us are not comfortable with covering things like the Rose scandal and do not like it," Conlin told Sokolove, referring to all the clues Rose dropped about his gambling for several years. "The reason a lot of us went into sports in the first place is so we didn't have to deal with bullshit like that" (Sokolove, 1990, p. 151). Conlin wrote a column in May of 1989 that showed how he and dozens of others were lulled by Rose into abdicating responsibility. "The media is an orchestra that Pete Rose has conducted for 26 years with a deft baton. We relay his gruff, earthy blend of raunch and reason—a jock opera— to the public with eager precision, grateful that such a famous athlete treats us with neither condescension, contempt nor impatience" (p. 151).

Sokolove (1990), who covered Rose and the Reds in Cincinnati, writes, "Not one writer in the baseball-writing fraternity did much damage to Rose. As the journalists who knew him best, they might have been expected to add something to the news coverage of the scandal. But they didn't. They stayed on the sideline and backed as far away from the actual reporting of the case as possible. 'Covering this story,' wrote Lyle Spencer, then with the *New York Post,* 'has about as much appeal as doing time' " (p. 150).

Bob Hertzel was a beat writer for the *Cincinnati Inquirer.* He was also the coauthor with Rose on two books. In 1977, Tim Sullivan, Sokolove writes, was a reporter for the *Inquirer's* sports section. Sullivan told Sokolove, "[Rose] and Hertzel were very close. They ran together a lot. They went to the track together." Asked by Sokolove to comment on his relationship with Rose, Hertzel replied, "There's nothing I could say that would help him, and I would like to help him. If I can't help him I'm not talking" (Sokolove, 1990, p. 141).

Hertzel, of course, isn't the only writer or broadcaster to do a book with an athlete. One of the benefits of being close to players and teams is that if the team wins a championship, there will always be publishers waiting with hefty contracts for first-person books. Athletes and teams turn to favored writers to get these one-sided books done, and the writer often comes away with a significant contract for the work. This has become such big business that the ethical lines become completely blurred. Big-name agents often represent major athletes as well as the writers and athletes. So if an athlete gets himself into trouble at any future time, the agent can go back to his business associate—the writer or editor—and prevail upon that person not to write anything negative. This doesn't happen only with athletes in team sports, either. Athletes in tennis, golf, and other individual sports also have high-priced ghostwriters, and more often than not, these authors cover the athlete and the sport regularly. It isn't exactly public service journalism at its best.

When the movie *Cobb,* about Detroit Tigers Hall of Famer Ty Cobb, came out at the end of 1994, the story of freelance writer Al Stump's whitewash of Cobb in a 1961 biography was the subject of several columns and stories. Stump, according to the *New York Times* (Sandomire, 1994), had to write a sanitized version of Cobb's raucous life in 1961. "Disputes over how to portray controversies in Cobb's turbulent 74-year life were settled by Doubleday, the publisher, in favor of the man voted first into the Hall of Fame" (p. 15). Stump did write a magazine article after Cobb's death, revealing the real story, and in his new book about Cobb, the *New York Times* says, "Stump has resurrected what he excluded from the earlier volume and combined it with additional reporting" (p. 15).

The ethical questions in sports journalism don't end with books. Writers and broadcasters have taken the concept of a weekly notes column to new lows. Many of these practitioners are part of a network that supplies each other with weekly information, some of which may be correct, some that may be wrong, and some that may be self-serving. Sharing information doesn't seem to bother a lot of sports editors and news directors.

Nor does the practice of print journalists serving as experts for the various networks bother these same editors and news directors. Talk about blurred lines. There often have been times when print journalists have scooped their own publications, raising the question of where the journalist's allegiances lie and when and where information will be discussed.

But then, this is only one more example of the new order in sports journalism. Who cares if the gossip that originates in Cleveland and winds up in Boston is correct? It serves a need. And who cares about the origin of the information that has been traded? Did it come from someone with questionable ties to a source or a team? The flip side is just how much isn't being printed and for what reason. How many stories were written or broadcast in 1989 when O. J. Simpson's private life became public after his wife beating hit the police blotter? Where were all the reporters and broadcasters who used to hang with the Juice? With few exceptions, they took a seat at the end of the bench on this one. "It's private," is the time-honored refrain when it comes to matters such as wife beating. But how long had it been going on? Who in the press knew what, and who didn't print it or air it?

And why didn't they? Answer that question and you will understand how the sports media work. Don't be fooled by the concept of flagpole journalism being practiced by a lot of papers, magazines, and networks who will do one big story every 6 months or so after publication or airing. They run it up the flagpole and say, "See how responsible we are. Look at what we did."

And then for the next 6 months they have their license to focus on games only, leaving the real world to the front of the paper.

## REFERENCES

Klapisch, R., & Harper, J. (1993). *The worst team money could buy.* New York: Random House.

Peyser, A. (1992, March 23). Sportswriters play hypocrisy game too. *New York Post,* p. 17.

Sandomire, R. (1994, November 30). Cobb's ghostwriter sharpens his pencil. *New York Times,* Sec. B, p. 15.

Sokolove, M. Y. (1990). *Hustle: The myth, life, and lies of Pete Rose.* New York: Simon & Schuster.

# PART VI

# Sport in the International Arena

## Introduction

When Atlanta became host of the world's greatest sports event—the Centennial Olympic Games in the summer of 1996—the joy was spontaneous and unabated. However, Atlanta, like all previous host venues, has not been without problems. In the past few years, particularly 1994 and 1995, there has been continuing controversy surrounding the city's planning for the Games.

Residents of poor neighborhoods have been displaced to build Olympic facilities, and the homeless have been cleared off the streets. What message does this communicate? For nearly 30 years, one message has been clear: The Games are for the pride of the nation; the poor and homeless are the shame of a wealthy nation. It happened in Barcelona, Seoul, Los Angeles, and even Moscow. What responsibility should Georgia and the federal government take to show that America isn't going to ignore the issue of poverty that plagues every nation in the world? What did Spain, Korea, and the Soviet Union do? They tried to cover up the shame without regard to future consequences for the poor. The 2-week hiatus from real life, whether it be in Atlanta or Seoul, is just that.

The exuberance of this grand moment does help most to forget what life is like for so many across the globe. There were serious riots in Seoul, South Korea, and increasing tensions with North Korea. Although the Games eventually served to pacify the violent activity, the media had the opportunity to direct the world's attention to the political crisis. Perhaps the greatest significance of the Barcelona Games was the appearance of South Africa in the Olympics for the first time in 32 years. South Africa represented a new kind of team—integrated and chosen without shackles of apartheid as that country was on its way to freedom.

In the first chapter of this section, Richard Lapchick describes the political history of the modern Olympic Games, clearly showing that politics and sports have been intertwined throughout the modern history of the Games. The International Olympic Committee has been confronted with controversies and conflicts ranging from potential boycotts to military unrest in participating countries. The past six decades of the Olympics have seen politics and sport inextricably mixed. By explaining the historical context of the modern Olympic Games, the political entanglement is as clear as it was dominant in the days leading up to each of the individual games.

South Africa had endured a long history of apartheid, a systematic degradation, segregation, and discrimination of blacks by a minority of whites. The abhorrent system caused millions to be killed, tortured, or imprisoned because their skin color was not white. Richard Lapchick describes the predicament of South Africa in his article "Under Africa Skies." He recounts his visits to South African townships of Soweto and Alexandra and the city of Johannesburg with a delegation of National Basketball Association players, coaches, and officials. The mission of the trip was to use sport as a positive vehicle for change in a country crushed by apartheid. The visit also marked the end to the U.S. sports boycott of South Africa, which Lapchick helped lead for two decades.

The next article in this section chronicles the inauguration of Nelson Mandela, the first black President of South Africa. Mandela spent 27 years in prison with an unrelenting determination to help his people win their freedom. The article shows the critical role played by sport and the sport boycott in leading an end to apartheid.

# 35

# The Modern Olympic Games
## A Political Cauldron

Richard E. Lapchick

Sportswriters covering daily sports events give us the results. Analysts covering the Olympics give us the political ramifications. Over the past 30 years, we have witnessed a drawn-out series of political events associated with the Olympic Games. Politicians, sportswriters, editorial writers, and most of the American public have expressed shock at the mixing of politics and sports: the black American protest in 1968, the assassination of Israeli athletes in Munich in 1972, and the African boycott of the 1976 Games. The shock stopped when President Jimmy Carter called for a boycott of the 1980 Moscow Olympics. The same people who had criticized the political influence on sports were suddenly on the patriotic bandwagon. They were ready to go along with the boycott protesting the Soviet invasion of Afghanistan. By 1984, a subsequent Soviet boycott of the Los Angeles Games became all too predictable.

The 1988 Seoul Games proved to be a showcase for the Cold War. As South and North Korea experienced their own political differences, Americans and Soviets chose to side with South and North Korea, respectively. The 1992 Games in Barcelona witnessed South Africa's readmission to the Olympics as a new dawn of freedom appeared on that nation's horizon. On the other hand, Yugoslavia's participation was limited due to a raging civil war.

However, the modern Olympic spirit, from inception in 1896, has never been free from political influence. Although the political strings were initially petty, the 1936 Berlin Olympics opened a new era in which politics has vied with sports for the spotlight in the Olympic Games. This chapter is an attempt to explore the history of the modern Olympics and to analyze what it might mean for the future of international sports.

This chapter originally appeared as "A Political History of the Modern Olympic Games," by Richard E. Lapchick, in *Fractured Focus: Sport as a Reflection of Society*, Richard E. Lapchick (Ed.). Copyright © 1986 by Lexington Books, an imprint of The Free Press, a Division of Simon & Schuster, Inc. Reprinted with permission of the publisher.

## THE MODERN OLYMPICS IN
## THE EARLY YEARS: 1896 TO 1933

Baron Pierre de Coubertin helped to rekindle the Olympic flame in 1896. Historians portrayed him as motivated by the noble thought that international sports competition would move men and nations to view each other as peaceful friends. Sports could be the arena where a common understanding might be reached. In 1894, de Coubertin stated that

> the aims of the Olympic Movement are to promote the development of those fine physical and moral qualities which are the basis of amateur sport and to bring together the athletes of the world in a great quadrennial festival of sports thereby creating international respect and goodwill and thus helping to construct a better and more peaceful world. (quoted in Berlioux, 1972, p. 1)

Eventually, de Coubertin's personal correspondence revealed that the decline in the French spirit after the Franco-Prussian War was a major motivating factor in his work to rebuild the Olympic Games. He even worked behind the scenes to keep Germany out of the first Games.

However, there was at least a public commitment that international sports must be free from all government pressures. This was incorporated into the Olympic Principles. Participation could never be determined by race, religion, or politics. The late Avery Brundage, who dominated international sports for three decades as the head of the International Olympic Committee (IOC), summed up the need for such a principle as the root of the Olympic movement:

> Were this fundamental principle not followed scrupulously, the Olympic Movement would surely founder. It is essential to the success and even to the existence of any truly international body that there are no restrictions of this kind. . . . As it is, the Olympic Movement furnishes a conspicuous example that when fair play and good sportsmanship prevail, men can agree, regardless of race, religion, or political convictions. (*Speeches of President Avery Brundage,* 1969, pp. 41-42)[1]

Sportsmen have consistently chosen to espouse these principles. It has long been believed that sport is an area in which there was equal opportunity for all, based purely on the ability of the athlete while nations compete with each other for the sake of sports only. Brundage maintained, "We must never forget that the most important thing in the Olympic Games is not to win but to take part" (*Speeches,* 1969, p. 34).[2] In essence, "Sport, like the fine arts, transcends politics" (*Speeches,* 1969, p. 65).[3]

These are the ideals of sports in general and of the Olympic movement in particular. The reality has been something less than the ideal.

The opening act of politics in the Olympics took place in 1908 when the U.S. team refused to dip the American flag to King Edward VII at the opening ceremonies of the 1908 Olympics in London. The politics of international sports remained low-key for the next 25 years until the Hitler regime changed all of that very quickly.

## THE NAZIS AND THE EXPLOSION OF THE OLYMPIC "POLITICAL SPIRIT": 1933 TO 1967

In May of 1933, the German *Reichssportführer,* Hans Von Tschammer-Osten, announced the Nazi sports policy:

> German sports are for Aryans. German Youth Leadership is only for Aryans and not for Jews. Athletes will not be judged by ability alone, but also by their general and moral fitness for representing Germany. ("Reich Now Says," 1933, p. 11)

The *Reichssportführer* thus sowed the seeds that inexorably dragged politics into sports.

In June of 1933, Tschammer-Osten approved the anti-Semitic resolutions in German sports clubs, which, taken with the municipalities, controlled most of the sports facilities in Germany, making it impossible for German Jews to train properly.[4] In November of that year, Tschammer-Osten ruled that Jews could not be members of athletic governing boards, effectively removing them as sports administrators.[5]

In August of 1935, Jews were forbidden to join in the new Nazi consolidated sports clubs.[6] It was decreed that they could not compete abroad and, therefore, could not represent Germany (Mandell, 1971, p. 59).

Jews were forbidden to attend the Winter Olympic Games in Garmisch. Signs on the gates proclaimed, "Jews are not admitted."[7] (These signs were subsequently taken down after international protest.) In October, a U.S. swimming team performed in Berlin before an all-Aryan audience. A sign over the box office read, "Jews are not wanted."[8] The segregation of sports was complete, encompassing athletes, administrators, and spectators.

Protests against staging the Berlin Games were held in Canada, Britain, Sweden, France, the Netherlands, Poland, Palestine, and, of course, the United States.[9] Despite the protests, these countries eventually all sent teams to Berlin.

The loudest protests by far came from the Fair Games Committee in the United States, led by prominent public figures.[10] Other groups were involved in the boycott crusade between June of 1933 and January of 1936: 20 Olympic champions; various Jewish, Catholic, and Protestant groups; 6 U.S. Senators; 7 governors; 41 university presidents; the American Federation of Labor; the Women's League for Peace; the National Association for the Advancement of Colored People; and other civil rights groups. The American National Society of Mural Painters withdrew its exhibit in Berlin.[11] Of particular importance was the Amateur Athletic Union (AAU). Without the AAU's sanction, no American athlete could go to Berlin. In November of 1933, the AAU decided it would boycott the Games unless the Germans changed their policy immediately.[12]

*Reichssportführer* Tschammer-Osten clearly showed the importance that Germany attached to the American's participation in Berlin: "The protest of the AAU is a complete impossibility and represents the dirty handiwork of conscienceless agitators who want systematically to undermine Germany's position abroad" ("Nazis Reaffirm Policy," 1933, p. 26). If the Americans withdrew, others would surely follow, and the Games might collapse in Hitler's face. As the AAU appeared ready to finalize its decision, Avery Brundage, then president of the American Olympic Committee (AOC), stepped to center stage. Brundage challenged American athletes to meet this

un-American boycott offensive with historic American action. . . . To those alien agitators and their American stooges who would deny our athletes their birthright as American citizens to represent the United States in the Olympic Games of 1936 in Germany, our athletes reply in the modern vernacular, "Oh, yeah."[13]

He went on to say that American athletes must follow "the patterns of the Boston Tea Party, the Minute Men of Concord, and the troops of George Washington at Valley Forge. . . . Regardless of AAU action, we (AOC) are going to send a team abroad."[14]

The American protest against the Berlin Games clearly did not represent one particular ethnic or religious group but was composed of a cross section of society that transcended religious, economic, and political boundaries. More than 20,000 people gathered in August of 1935 at Madison Square Garden to ask for the withdrawal of the American team.[15] This remains the largest single group ever to come together at one time to protest a sports-related event.

The importance of sports to Hitler was shown in the press (*Der Angriff*) after the German soccer team played in London in December of 1935 amid widespread British protests. "For Germany, it was an unrestrained political, psychological, and, also, sporting success. . . . It is hardly a secret in well-informed circles that a resumption of closer contact with Great Britain is earnestly desired" ("Anglo-German Match," 1935, p. 15). The *Reichssportführer,* as early as 1933, had said that sports played an important role in international relations and he saw it as his job to improve those relations" ("Nazi Stand on Jews," 1933).

Later, when the AOC voted to participate in the Berlin Olympics despite the raging controversy in the United States, *Reichssportführer* Tschammer-Osten said that the decision marked "a turn in the international campaign of hate against Germany."[16]

As the opening of the Games neared, the official Nazi party newspaper, *Volkischer Beobachter,* revealed the propaganda value of the Games and the national exhibit *Germany.* "The exhibition will present a concrete demonstration of the National Socialist principles and program."[17]

The German government actually paid for all the sports facilities, and the army paid for the Olympic Village, which later became an army facility.[18] This contradicted Brundage's pledges—made both before and after the Berlin Games—that the Olympics were run solely by the German Olympic Committee and the IOC.

The use of the Games as blatant propaganda was highlighted by the dedication, "Germany's thousands of years of history find their ultimate meaning in Adolf Hitler. Adolf Hitler fulfills a thousand year old German dream."[19] The official Olympic poster had a map of Europe that included German-speaking sections of southeast and central Europe within Germany's borders.[20]

The Austrian team was greeted by the German national anthem.[21] The British and French teams gave the Nazi salute to Hitler at the opening ceremonies. The 100,000 spectators cheered them wildly; however, the crowd showed tremendous displeasure with the American team when they refused to salute Hitler.[22]

The victories by black Americans caused a huge furor in Berlin. *Der Angriff* attacked the AOC for bringing "black auxiliaries" to the Games.[23] An English report was circulated that the blacks had leg operations to increase their speed. The Germans claimed they were effective because of their peculiar bone structure, and the South Africans openly depreciated their achievements.[24]

The original German plans were to have no Jews associated with their Olympic team. Hitler had even asked Lewald, the head of the German Olympic Committee, to resign because of his Jewish ancestry. However, when the Americans made their first threat to withdraw, Lewald was quickly restored in an advisory capacity. It was announced in 1935 that Avery Brundage would personally conduct an investigation into charges of discrimination against Jews in Germany. The *Reichssportführer* immediately requested that the Jewish federations name 50 Jewish candidates for the German Olympic team.[25] Before Brundage undertook his investigation, he told American athletes to prepare for the Games.[26] As Brundage left Germany, Rudolf

Hess, minister without portfolio in Hitler's cabinet, ordered that Nazis could not fraternize with the Jews.[27] Many felt that this meant the end of the Games in Berlin. Brundage expressed great interest in the order as he left.

The AOC, which met with Brundage and voted to accept Germany's invitation to participate in the Games, claimed that sport was the wedge that would lead to the end of discrimination in Germany. In a setting that added irony to the situation, the AOC meeting was held in the New York Athletic Club, which barred Jewish membership.[28]

Fencing star Helene Mayer was the only Jewish member of the 477-person German team. With the threat of isolation gone, the Germans made no real compromise. In 1959, Brundage recalled the situation and analyzed it in the following manner:

> In 1936 there was an organized and well financed attack on the Games of the XIth Olympiad, because certain individuals and groups did not approve of the German Government at that time. . . . The outcome, however, was a great victory for Olympic principles and the United States was represented by one of its largest and best teams. (*Speeches*, 1965, p. 41)[29]

Brundage obviously felt that having one Jewish team member out of 477 was a worthwhile compromise. The Holocaust did not dampen his enthusiasm for the 1936 Games.

The Germans had their sports propaganda success as they rolled to an impressive athletic triumph. Nazi Germany used their sports and sports festivals as tools of propaganda so effectively that they were able to lull sportsmen and diplomats alike into believing that Germany was a respectable nation in the family of nations. After the conclusion of the Games, Brundage addressed the pro-Nazi, American-German Bund before 20,000 in Madison Square Garden:

> "We can learn much from Germany. We, too, if we wish to preserve our institutions, must stamp out communism. We, too, must take steps to arrest the decline of patriotism. Germany has progressed as a nation out of her discouragement of five years ago into a new spirit of confidence in herself. Everywhere I found Germans friendly, courteous, and obliging. The question was whether a vociferous minority, highly organized and highly financed, could impose its will on 120,000,000 people."[30]

Brundage's comments reflected the effectiveness of the propaganda. Richard D. Mandell (1971), in his study *The Nazi Olympics,* maintains that this was a major turning point for Hitler, giving him tremendous self-confidence in the international spectrum. The lesson was not lost, for other nations have used sports ever since as a vehicle for national prestige or to spotlight political causes.


## THE ISSUE OF "TWO CHINAS"

The question of "two Chinas" was addressed in the Olympics when the IOC admitted the People's Republic of China (PRC) in 1954 while retaining the membership of the Republic of China (ROC)—also known as Taiwan or Formosa. The IOC began to maneuver on this question once it became clear that the PRC would not compete with the ROC.

The controversy reached its height when the IOC ruled in May of 1959 that the "Republic of China no longer represents sports in the entire country of China" ("Olympic Body Ousts Chinese Nationalists," 1959, p. 16), and must reapply as Taiwan. It was assumed that Taiwan would not accept this and the PRC would be the only representative of all of China. However, the U.S. Department of State immediately issued a formal position on the IOC decision: "It is evident that Communist pressures have been directed to obtaining the expulsion of the Chinese Nationalists. . . . We trust that public and sports organs, both here and abroad, will recognize the Communist threats for what they are."[31] On the same day, a resolution condemning the IOC was introduced in the House of Representatives by Francis E. Dorn of New York. Representative Melvin Laird (later to become the Secretary of Defense) introduced an amendment to the bill prohibiting the use of any U.S. Army equipment or personnel in the 1960 Winter Olympic Games, to be held in Squaw Valley, California, if any "free nation" was banned.[32] When President Dwight Eisenhower condemned the IOC action, Avery Brundage suddenly advocated readmitting Nationalist China as the "Republic of China"[33] representing a complete turnaround for Brundage.

When Canada recognized the PRC in October of 1970, all ROC passports became unacceptable for entry into Canada. The Canadians informed the IOC of this fact more than a year prior to the Games. The IOC did nothing until Canada reiterated its position on May 28, 1976. Lord Killanin, then head of the IOC, did not call a special meeting of the IOC to discuss the issue but instead waited until IOC delegates gathered in Montreal 7 weeks later.

There was no reason to believe that Taiwan would compete under an Olympic banner or as Taiwan. Therefore, the IOC knew what the result would be. The American position was to be behind the compromise under the guise of a threatened withdrawal on principle. Gold has always been heavier than principle. The Americans had their threat to withdraw on the table and the American press praised the position for its idealism.

When Canada refused to admit Taiwanese athletes in 1976 as representatives of the ROC for the Montreal Games, the question was settled de facto. The Western nations condemned Canada for bringing politics into sports. In 1980, China was not an issue because of the Western boycott of Moscow. The PRC was alone in 1984 at the Los Angeles Games, and the issue was finally resolved.

## BATTLES IN POLITICAL SPORTS
## BETWEEN THE SOVIETS AND AMERICANS

An early example of America's use of sports was when the United States refused visas for East Germans to compete in the modern pentathlon world championships in Harrisburg, Pennsylvania.[34] In February of 1960, the State Department refused visas for the East German press and members of their Olympic staff to attend the Winter Olympics on the grounds that "admission was not in the best interests of the United States" ("15 East Germans Denied U.S. Visas," 1960, p. 45). No one, including major political leaders, wanted to recall that the United States had acted in the same way when the Canadians excluded Taiwan. Somehow, this condemnation of the Canadians by the United States seems hollow with the knowledge of these past events.

The Soviet Olympic Committee fought for decades for the inclusion of communist nations such as East Germany, North Korea, and Communist China, which the U.S. Olympic Committee dutifully opposed.[35] Both France and the United States refused visas to East Germans as recently as 1962.

Later in that same year, the Fourth Asian Games were marred by President Sukarno's refusal to admit teams from Nationalist China and Israel. When India implied that the Games became "unofficial" as a result, Indonesian Trade Minister Suharto broke off trade relations, and 4,000 Indonesians "raided" the Indian Embassy in Jakarta. Prime Minister Nehru accused the Chinese Communists of arousing anti-Indian feelings in Indonesia.[36] Demonstrating its pro-Western bias, the IOC chose to ban the Indonesian team from the 1964 Tokyo Olympics for not admitting Nationalist China and Israel. However, it barely mentioned the actions of France, the United States, or the Philippines (which had barred Yugoslavians).[37] The entire Arab League then threatened to boycott the Tokyo Games unless the ban on Indonesia was lifted.[38] President Sukarno left no room for doubt about his intentions, saying, "Indonesia proposes now to mix sports with politics and we are thus establishing 'the Games of the Newly Emerging Forces.' "[39] All of this was in the name of sports.

Edward Herbert, Chairman of the House Armed Services Subcommittee, said that a $2,000,000 bill for athletes was "to make the United States the most powerful nation in the world athletically."[40] In an incredible statement for a man of his position, Vice President Hubert Humphrey said,

> What the Soviets are doing is a challenge to us, just like Sputnik was a challenge. We are going to be humiliated as a great nation unless we buckle down to the task of giving our young people a chance to compete. ("Humphrey Asks Greater Sports Efforts," 1966, p. 56)

This was in reference to the unofficial team defeat (although nations are not supposed to keep a national count of victories, most nations do) of the U.S. Olympic team at the hands of the Soviet Union in Tokyo. He went on to say that we must conclusively prove that a free society produces better athletes than a socialist society. This is not to say the Soviet Union did not have a similar aim in proving that a socialist society produces better athletes than a free one—all in keeping with the tradition set by Hitler in 1936.

## RACE AND OLYMPICS: 1968 TO 1976

> I, therefore, want to make it quite clear that from South Africa's point of view no mixed sport between whites and nonwhites will be practiced locally, irrespective of the standard of proficiency of the participants. . . . We do not apply that as a criterion because our policy has nothing to do with proficiency or lack of proficiency. (Vorster, 1968, p. 68)[41]

South African Prime Minister John Vorster reaffirmed his government's position on integrated sports during the IOC investigation of South African sports. Many assumed that this statement alone would keep South Africa out of the 1968 Mexico Olympics, just as they were excluded in 1964. In a stunning decision, the IOC, meeting in Grenoble during the Winter Olympics, voted South Africa back into the Games. This was in spite of the fact that African nations had threatened a massive boycott of the Olympics if South Africa participated. The IOC apparently felt it to be an idle gesture.

This was in spite of the fact that the Organization of African Unity strongly urged the Supreme Council for Sport in Africa (SCSA) to call on its 32 member-nations to boycott the Games in protest of South Africa's apartheid policy. The SCSA did so 2 weeks later.[42] Most Socialist and Third World countries threatened to join the Africans. By March 10th, 4 weeks after Grenoble, the *New York Times* reported that only 10 nations—all predominantly white—were certain to go to Mexico.[43] Many American athletes began to pick up the idea as the American Committee on Africa (1968) tried to enlist support. This, of course, was at the height of the threatened black American boycott of Mexico. The IOC finally reversed its decision after 2 months of delay. Avery Brundage never admitted that the change was a result of the boycott or because the South Africans violated the Olympic principles. He merely maintained that the Mexicans could not guarantee the safety of the South Africans in Mexico City (*IOC Newsletter,* 1968a, p. 151).

At the end of July, Avery Brundage called Mexico, "the most stable and fastest growing country in Latin America," and claimed that "the Olympic Movement had no little part in making it so" ("Olympic Chief Sorry," 1968, p. 40). Within days of this statement, a student strike began in Mexico City that provoked the worst government crisis in 30 years. As the opening of the Games neared, 13 were killed and hundreds injured in the 3-day riot. It was an ironic scene: Olympic posters saying, "With peace, everything is possible," were plastered everywhere in the city.[44] Brundage, it seems, was slightly premature in his evaluation of the stability of Mexico, but he was not premature in saying that the Olympic Movement had helped to make Mexico what it was. One of the reasons given by the students for the riots was that the incredibly high cost of staging the Games was a national disgrace.

The Olympic-political event best remembered in America was the 1968 black American boycott initiated by Harry Edwards. When that did not materialize to the degree that Edwards hoped, he changed strategies and planned demonstrations at the Games. The best remembered photo of the 1968 Games was the clenched-fist portrait of John Carlos and Tommy Smith during the playing of the Star Spangled Banner after a presentation of medals. Their actions were followed by the gestures of a dozen other black athletes who won medals in track and field events. Sports officials were outraged at the conduct of the black athletes. A survey taken 4 years later showed that the controversy surrounding these events lingered on: Only 2% of the whites questioned felt the athletes' gestures were justified; support was not particularly overwhelming even among blacks as 57% approved.[45]

In a press conference at the close of the Games, Avery Brundage was asked what progress the Olympics had made in human relations. He replied, "Right here in Mexico, thanks to the Juegos Deportivos, the Mexicans have proved that boys and girls are able to become better citizens, as they are stronger and healthier and have acquired a sense of discipline and national morale" (*IOC Newsletter,* 1968b, p. 577). Mr. Brundage chose to ignore the riots that took strong police action to stop in time for the Games.

Brundage's most curious statement came in response to a question asking him how the Olympics could survive as long as politics continued to become more and more involved in the Games. His response was, "Who said that politics are becoming more and more involved in the Olympics? In my opinion this is not so. . . . You know very well that politics are not allowed in the Olympic Games" (*IOC Newsletter,* 1968b, p. 578). Even as sports became more and more political, men such as Brundage continued to ignore the reality. Sportswriters and the public seemed very willing to go along with the ruse until the next Olympic-political event when they could condemn the activists for bringing politics into sports as if it were the end of the virginity of a pure and angelic child. They did not have to wait long.

In May of 1970, the IOC met in Amsterdam to consider the expulsion of South Africa from the Olympic movement in protest of that country's apartheid sports policy. No nation had ever been expelled from the movement itself, and it was thought highly unlikely that the African-led plan would succeed.[46] The difference was that the South Africans had gone too far by refusing a visa to Arthur Ashe, the Black American tennis star, so that he could compete in the 1970 South African Open Tennis Championships. This had the effect of raising American political consciousness about apartheid sports.

The second precipitating event was the insistence on the part of the South Africans on going ahead with plans to send an all-white cricket team to tour Britain in the spring of 1970. There were massive plans for protest in Britain led by the Stop the Seventy Tour (STST) committee. STST had rallied 50,000 demonstrators to various rugby fields in the winter months while a South African rugby team toured Britain. Prime Minister Wilson finally canceled the tour to avoid the certain conflict.

When the South Africans were expelled in May of 1970, what was really remarkable was that South Africa, with all the evidence and seemingly the majority of world opinion against them, was able to remain in the Olympic movement as long as it had.

The only explanation was that the IOC was dominated by representatives from white member-nations who did not oppose South Africa's continued good standing. The IOC, according to its own publication, *OLYMPISM,* was a self-recruiting elite: Membership on the committee was the result of election by existing IOC members. The statement, "It is customary to favor nationals of countries with a long Olympic tradition behind them" (Berlioux, 1972, p. 8) was reminiscent of the grandfather clause in the post-Reconstruction era of the South in the United States. The custom was a convenient way of excluding representatives from nations that were colonies during the period when "a long Olympic tradition" could have been formed. In fact, the first two representatives from Africa were white men: Reg Alexander of Kenya and Reg Honey of South Africa. De Coubertin commented on the nature of membership in the IOC: "The second characteristic of Olympism is that it is an aristocracy, an elite" (Berlioux, 1972, p. 10). He also added, "It is not sufficient to be an elite; it is also necessary for this elite to be a chivalry" (p. 2).

Of the representatives from nonwhite nations, 61% were admitted to the IOC after 1960. However, this meant only a minor change in the racial composition of the IOC because the nonwhites had only 33% of the voting power on the IOC in 1970. To achieve their 67% control, it was necessary for

11 of the predominantly white nations to have two or more representatives on the IOC. Moreover, of the national Olympic committees (NOCs) without an IOC representative (which, in effect, means they are powerless), only 12.4% were from predominantly white nations, whereas 87.6% were from emerging nations whose majority populations were people of color (*Olympic Directory,* 1969).

To the idealistic sportsperson, sportswriter, and fan who might feel that such statistics are meaningless because sports and the Olympic movement are above politics and race, the results of the following survey should be instructive. The information was gathered in a survey completed in the spring of 1970 in which the NOCs were asked for their position on South Africa's participation in the Olympics. Of the white nations, 68% were not opposed to South Africa's participation. However, 98% of the nonwhite nations opposed South Africa's participation without complete sports integration in South Africa.

Thus, it can be seen that the South African issue developed along rather strict racial lines. Race and politics had become an integral part of international sports.

The Africans had a firm grasp on their power by 1972. According to Abraham Ordia, president of the SCSA, the new goal was to have South Africa's neighbor, Rhodesia, expelled from the Olympic movement. The SCSA made the mistake of trying to do this by going through the back door: They made what they thought were impossible demands on the Rhodesians. They were sure the Ian Smith regime would never capitulate. Much to their surprise, Smith agreed, and the Rhodesian team arrived in Munich ready to participate under the stringent conditions put forth by the Africans. At the IOC meeting prior to the Games, the SCSA reversed its stand: The Rhodesians would have to be thrown out of the movement or there would be another boycott (A. Ordia, personal interview, May 16, 1976). The IOC complied.

The tragedy that led to the deaths of Israeli athletes in Munich cast a shadow over the Games and their future. The Montreal Olympic Village was an armed camp in an attempt to prevent new terrorist acts. Although the sports world expressed shock at the Munich terrorism, it is not altogether surprising that such a thing could happen. It has been the theme of this chapter that the Olympics have become so big and attract so much international attention that they have become the ideal stage for political actors with causes: the French, the Americans, the Nazis, the PRC, Taiwan, the South Africans, the black Africans, the Socialists, and the Capitalists. Why not terrorists?

Even with all this background, many doubted that there was any reason to fear an African boycott in 1976. After all, the threat of an American boycott over the two-Chinas issue had been resolved.

The Western press condemned the African nations who withdrew. The American press had not even mentioned that the real issue involved New Zealand's rugby team being in South Africa. With the election of Prime Minister Muldoon, New Zealand had resumed full sports relations with South Africa. The most controversy, however, had been raised by the rugby tour. Although the difference between British and New Zealand teams competing in South Africa may have been lost on the average sports fan, the essence of that difference was not lost on the world's political leaders. Prime Minister Muldoon had made it a policy of his government to compete with South Africa. No other government did this.

It had been known for months that the African nations would withdraw from the Olympics if New Zealand sent its rugby team to South Africa. The SCSA announced this decision early in the spring. The Conference of the United Nations Special Committee Against Apartheid supported the council's resolve at its May meeting in Havana. The Organization of African Unity, meeting in Mauritius, also encouraged the African teams to boycott the Games. Therefore, the statements of surprise that 24 African nations did not march in the opening parade were informed. The fact that other Third World nations joined them is no less surprising if one simply examines the history of the modern Olympics.

Viewed from the African perspective, the issue required a strong and idealistic stand. These countries sacrificed hard training, substantial amounts of money, and the prestige that comes from competing in the Olympic spotlight. South African poet, Dennis Brutus, a primary force behind the boycott, believed that the IOC deliberately dragged out the China issue to divert the attention away from the African threats (personal interview, July 5, 1976). It almost worked when it appeared that there would be no boycott. But because the IOC was so involved in the China issue, New Zealand was never put on the agenda, and nothing could be worked out prior to the Games. It can be reasonably assumed that the IOC believed that because no nation had ever actually taken itself out of the Games, the Africans would not do so and the issue would go away. As has frequently been the case, the IOC was proven wrong.

## THE COLD WAR OLYMPICS IN MOSCOW, LOS ANGELES, AND SEOUL: 1980 TO 1988

The African boycott made threats for the future seem more real. Still, for the American media, the United States was the "good guy"; it was others who had dragged politics into sports. That perception changed very quickly when

President Carter announced the U.S. boycott of the Moscow Games in retaliation for the Soviet invasion of Afghanistan.

The press sided with the president. Carter had to convince two other groups to go along. The first was the athletes. Led by such Olympians as Anita DeFrantz, many athletes resisted the pressure. An informal poll of the U.S. Olympics Committee Athletes Advisory Council indicated that most athletes wanted to compete. However, confronted by a wave of patriotism, they ultimately succumbed to the pressure. The president also cajoled U.S. allies into joining the boycott, promising incentives to developing nations, especially in Africa, if they would shun the Games. That was a tough sell, because the United States had never backed the African nations in their protest against the inclusion of South Africa in international sports. In addition, the Russians were offering their own incentives for participation.

The results of the boycott were mixed, with many European and some developing nations joining the United States. However, by making his point, Carter made it impossible for a Western leader to say that politics and sports are not to be mixed.

The Western press depicted the 1980 Games as a failure. This was debatable. Thirty-six new world records and 74 new Olympic records were set—more than in any previous Olympics. Eighty-one nations participated, more than 60,000 foreign tourists went to Moscow, and an estimated 1.5 billion saw the Games on TV. Moreover, it took 4 years for the Soviets to withdraw from Afghanistan.

Retaliation by the Soviet bloc nations in the 1984 Los Angeles Games was almost guaranteed by the events of 1980. The fact that the Soviet boycott was announced so late was also predictable. Only the rationale was clouded by the "security" issue, which was a real issue at the time. Reportedly, the Soviet press implied that the Los Angeles Games were a failure because so many of the world's top athletes were not present. However, more nations participated than ever before, more people saw the Games, and they were the first profitable Games. In America, they were depicted as the most successful Games ever.

Many people in the international community felt that the 1988 Games should be taken away from the Seoul government because it was viewed as an oppressive right-wing regime. In addition, political unrest, including wide-scale riots in the months before the opening ceremonies, called into question the safety of the athletes.

The 1988 Seoul Olympics served as another showcase for the Cold War tensions. The Americans sided with South Korea, and the Soviets decisively joined North Korea. North Korea insisted on cohosting the Games and, simultaneously, promoted reunification of the divided Korean territories. In February of 1988, the United States refused to issue visas to a North Korean team of speed skaters because the State Department had identified the country as being in "support of international terrorism." They postulated that North Korea was directly involved in the bombing of the Korean Airlines jet in which 115 people died. The IOC stalled on a decision, probably because of controversy surrounding the downing of the plane.

North Korea denied any involvement with the plane crash and continued to press the IOC for a part in the Olympic festivities. With 115 innocent lives lost, an open invitation to North Korea did not seem likely. Chang Ung, then secretary general of the North Korea Olympic Committee, served as the leading lobbyist for North Korea's quest to play an active role in the 1988 Games. Ung said he believed that if an agreement was reached, it would help to unify the countries. A lack of agreement, on the other hand, was certain to harm relations.[47] As usual, the Olympics were viewed as having the capacity to have a powerful impact in the political arena. Although the riots stopped, the Games were held, and the press hailed the peaceful spirit of athleticism. Ultimately, North Korea boycotted the Seoul Games and did not cohost any of the Olympic events.

## BARCELONA: SOUTH AFRICAN PRESENCE
## AND YUGOSLAVIAN CONFUSION

Prior to the 1992 Olympics in Barcelona, the main topic of international sports was whether or not South Africa would participate. Nelson Mandela, as the new president of the African National Congress, recognized that South Africa was among the world's most sports-conscious countries. That is why the sports boycott was such an effective lever against white South Africans. South Africa's readmission to international competition became a reality as South African athletes competed for the first time since 1960. But this was a new South African team that was chosen on merit and was integrated. The South African flag, anthem, and symbol of the springbok were not used because they represented symbols of the apartheid regime.

Sam Ramsamy, the new South African Olympic Committee president, led the fight to drop the symbols of opposition against strong white opposition. There was also some internal black South African opposition to ending the boycott so soon. However, Mandela, supported by Ramsamy, believed that this would be the one arena where black South Africans could rightfully choose to end sanctions. As this chapter was being completed, Mandela had become president and Capetown was a primary candidate to host the 2004 Olympics.

The civil war that raged in the former Yugoslavia left doubts as to whether Yugoslavia would participate in the 1992 Olympics. The United Nations (UN)

Security Council ordered sanctions against Yugoslavia on May 30, 1992. These sanctions were imposed by the UN after it had identified Yugoslavia, which consisted of the republics of Serbia and Montenegro, as the aggressor in the current Balkan war. The goal of these sanctions was to end the bloodshed in Yugoslavia. The sanctions also included a requirement that all member nations of the UN deny the Yugoslavians the right to compete internationally.

Despite these sanctions, the IOC invited Yugoslavia to the Games on July 9. Juan Antonio Samaranch, head of the IOC, proposed that the Yugoslavians compete in individual events and use the neutral Olympic flag and anthem. Spanish authorities said that they would not issue entry visas to the Yugoslavian athletes as a result of the UN sanctions.

The question of Yugoslavian participation rested in the hands of a UN Security Council sanctions committee. The committee was to review how Yugoslavia would compete in team sports and not be identified as a nation. At the same time, the former Yugoslavian republics of Bosnia-Herzogovina and Macedonia petitioned for inclusion in the Games.

On July 21, the UN Security Council agreed to allow Yugoslavia to participate in the Summer Olympics. The conditions for their participation were that athletes compete only in individual sports without national identification. They were not allowed to participate in team sports or in any ceremonies with the Yugoslavian flag or national anthem.

The Yugoslavian Olympic Committee accepted the IOC's conditional invitation to the Games, agreeing to compete only in individual sports. Their team entries, which included water polo, men's and women's handball, and men's and women's basketball, were excluded. The places of their team entries were to be filled by runner-up teams from qualifying tournaments. Bosnia-Herzogovina was granted a provisional membership by the IOC and was invited to participate. Macedonia was also invited to participate in the Games.

Although the political involvement has consistently been decried by the world of sports, the self-proclaimed idealist, Avery Brundage, must share much of the blame. He, too, had frequently viewed the role of sports in international politics as being far more important than it is in reality. In his own unique historical perspective, Brundage largely attributed the downfall of Ancient Greece and Rome to an improper sports outlook:

> Twenty-five hundred years ago the Greeks made a breach in the city walls to receive their home-coming Olympic champions. A city with such heroes for citizens needed no fortifications. When they began to give large special awards and prizes, however, they created a class of athletic loafers instead of heroes. The Games were finally abolished and the glory of Greece departed. (*Speeches,* 1969, p. 10)[48]

the Romans did not descend into the arena, which was left to professionals, gladiators, grooms, etc. They were spectators, not participants, and lacked the discipline of sports training. Eventually a victim of her own prosperity, Rome fell to the barbarians, the hard and tough Goths and Vandals, invaders from the North. (*Speeches,* 1969, p. 22)[49]

The lofty role that Brundage saw fit for modern sports, as led by the IOC, was revealed in his speech to the 62nd IOC Session in Tokyo in 1964:

The Olympic Movement is a 20th Century religion, a religion with universal appeal which incorporates all the basic values of other religions, a modern, exciting, virile, dynamic religion, attractive to Youth, and we of the International Olympic Committee are its disciples. (*Speeches,* 1969, p. 80)[50]

Even after all of this, the sports world will probably always remain ready for a sublime Olympics. Naïveté is still in its ascendancy in the IOC. In 1959, George Orwell said of international sport, "It is bound up with hatred, jealousy, boastfulness, disregard for all rules and sadistic pleasure in witnessing violence—in other words, it is war minus the shooting."[51]

Although the reality is not quite that negative, politics is and has always been part of the Olympic movement. If we want to change that—and many do not—then a large-scale overhaul must begin. But the time for expressions of astonishment, wonder, and shock should have passed many years ago. We have known the reality; now it is ours to face.

## NOTES

1. Speech to the 55th Session of the IOC in Munich, May 23, 1959.
2. Speech to the 53rd Session of the IOC in Sofia, September 22, 1957.
3. Speech to the 60th Session of the IOC in Baden, October 16, 1963.
4. See the *New York Times,* June 13 and August 27, 1933.
5. See the *New York Times,* November 23, 1933.
6. See the *New York Times,* August 12, 1935.
7. See the *New York Times,* October 21, 1935.
8. See the *New York Times,* October 21, 1935.
9. See the *New York Times,* November 5 and November 22, 1933; August 26 and December 28, 1934; March 18, October 4, November 12, and November 16, 1935; March 9, March 13, March 31, May 10, May 17, June 16, and June 20, 1936.
10. See the *New York Times,* October 11, 1935.
11. See the *New York Times,* May 31 and June 6, 1933; August 12, September 3, and September 27, 1934; July 22, July 31, August 5, August 23, September 1, October 4, October 16-27, November 26, November 27, and December 1-4, 1935; January 4 and January 25, 1936.
12. See the *New York Times,* November 21, 1933
13. See the *New York Times,* December 4, 1935.
14. See the *New York Times,* December 4, 1935.
15. See the *Times* (London), August 12, 1935.
16. See the *New York Times,* September 30, 1934.

17. See the *New York Times,* April 23, 1936.
18. See the *Times* (London), May 31, 1936.
19. See the *New York Times,* July 18, 1936.
20. See the *Times* (London), July 18, 1936.
21. See the *Times* (London), August 1, 1936.
22. See the *New York Times,* August 2, 1936, and the *Times* (London), August, 3, 1936.
23. See the *New York Times,* August 6, 1936.
24. See the *New York Times,* August 7, 1936.
25. See the *New York Times,* June 28, 1934.
26. See the *New York Times,* August 11, 1934.
27. See the *New York Times,* September 19, 1934.
28. See the *New York Times,* September 27, 1934.
29. Speech to the 55th Session of the IOC in Munich, May 23, 1959.
30. See the *New York Times,* October 5, 1935.
31. See the *New York Times,* June, 1959.
32. See the *New York Times,* June 4, 1959.
33. See the *New York Times,* August 1, 1959.
34. See the *New York Times,* September 17, 1959
35. See the *New York Times,* March 17, 1961.
36. See the *New York Times,* September 3, 1962.
37. See the *Times* (London), February 8, 1963.
38. See the *Times* (London), February 21, 1963.
39. See the *Times* (London), October 29, 1963.
40. See the *New York Times,* May 23, 1966.
41. Address to Parliament, April 11, 1967.
42. See the *Times* (London), February 27, 1968.
43. See the *New York Times,* March 10, 1968.
44. See the *Times* (London), September 26, 1968.
45. Survey conducted by the author in August 1972 in the following cities: New York; Philadelphia; Washington, DC; Denver, CO; Norfolk, VA; and Los Angeles.
46. See the *Star* (Johannesburg), May 14, 1970.
47. See the *New York Times,* February 8, 1988.
48. Speech to the 48th Session of the IOC in Mexico City, April 17, 1953.
49. Speech to the 51st Session of the IOC in Cortinna d'Ampezzo, January 23, 1956.
50. Speech to the 62nd Session of the IOC in Tokyo, October 6, 1964.
51. See the *New York Times,* October 4, 1959.

# REFERENCES

Amateur status in Olympics "Hypocrisy." (1963, October 29). *Times* (London), p. 10.
American Committee on Africa. (1968, April 10). [Unpublished data].
The Anglo-German match: Sport and politics. (1935, December 6). *Times* (London), p. 15.
Berlioux, M. (Ed.). (1972). *Olympism.* Lausanne, Switzerland: International Olympic Committee.
15 East Germans denied U.S. Visas. (1960, February 7). *New York Times.* p. 45.
Humphrey ask greater sports efforts. (1966, May 23). *New York Times,* p. 56.
*IOC Newsletter* (No. 8). (1968a).
*IOC Newsletter* (No. 15). (1968b).
Mandell, R. D. (1971). *The Nazi Olympics.* New York: Macmillan.
Nazis reaffirm policy of discrimination in new order affecting Jews in athletics. (1933, November 23). *New York Times,* p. 26.
Nazi stand vague on Jews in sport: Von Tschammer-Osten, commissar leaves status unsettled in formal interview. (1933, August 6). *New York Times,* p. 4.

Olympic body ousts Chinese nationalists. (1959, May 29). *New York Times,* p. 16.

Olympic chief sorry for S.A.: Disappointed at attitude of dissident countries. (1968, July 31). *Star* (Johannesburg), p. 40.

*Olympic directory.* (1969). Lausanne: International Olympic Committee.

Reich now says status of German Jews in next Olympics has not been settled. (1933, May 29). *New York Times,* p. 11.

*The speeches of President Avery Brundage, 1952 to 1968.* (1969). Lausanne: International Olympic Committee.

Vorster, J. (1968). *Report of the IOC Commission on South Africa.* Lausanne: International Olympic Committee.

# 36

## Under African Skies

Richard E. Lapchick

It has been a long and deeply personal and emotional odyssey that started in September of 1992 with my first trip to South Africa, a country that dominated my life for more than 20 years in spite of my never having been there. It culminated in the last days of August 1993 when a contingent from the National Basketball Association (NBA) and the Players Association (NBAPA) spent 5 days in South Africa, officially ending the U.S. sports boycott of the apartheid regime. It was a boycott I helped to start in the 1970s and helped to maintain for nearly two decades.

That boycott resulted in keeping a number of athletes from competing internationally. Allies of the anti-apartheid movement boycotted Olympic Games, Commonwealth Games, and other assorted major international events. Those South African athletes who could afford to were forced to compete for other countries. Others simply had their talents atrophy without international competition. It was a high price to pay, but the rewards are now being harvested as South Africa inches closer to its first democratic elections.

In this context, the new National Olympic Committee of South Africa asked me and my colleague, Kunle Raji, to help develop programs to use sports to rebuild the nation and help heal racial wounds inflicted on that society by apartheid. We called the program TEAMWORK South Africa. The new Olympic Committee, which brought South Africa back into international sports, is headed by my dear friend, Sam Ramsamy. Sam lived in exile for nearly two decades as the international leader of the boycott of South Africa sports.

When Kunle and I went in September 1992, everyone was talking about the Dream Team. They wanted us to bring the NBA to South Africa. I told them it was unlikely, but in December I met with NBAPA Executive Director

A version of this chapter originally appeared in *The Sporting News*, September 27, 1993. Reprinted by permission.

Charles Grantham, who was very enthusiastic. I also met with various NBA officials, and they committed to seriously consider it. Eight months and two trips later, NBA Commissioner David Stern and Charles Grantham led a 20-person delegation of players (Dikembe Mutombo, Alex English, Bob McAdoo, and Mike Bantom), coaches (Wes Unseld and Alvin Gentry), and various NBA officials who arrived in Johannesburg amid the worst 2 months of violence in that country's recent history.

Security arrangements were made by the NBA, the State Department, and the African National Congress. The South Africans were extraordinarily generous in this regard even though they were certain we would be safe. It turned out that we always were.

The players and coaches gave clinics for kids and coaches that were very well received in a nation where basketball has become the number two sport but is still new and played mostly by whites. Although whites attended the clinics, most of the participants were black.

Whatever our group gave, we got much more in return. What we got was the opportunity to bear witness to both the enormity of the oppression blacks have lived under and the brightly burning faith they still have that a multiracial democracy is not only desirable but also possible. The people are proud that they have survived the oppression and that they can actually see the day when blacks will finally lead this land of contradictions.

We took the NBA delegation to the township of Alexandra. The dust blows across the town, filling your eyes and nostrils. Alex is Johannesburg's first African township. The 1 square mile of Alex is home for 500,000 "registered" residents. There are closer to 1 million.

As we drove through the streets of Alex, we saw shanty after shanty. The corrugated steel buildings, where 3 to 12 or more people could live in a 10' × 10' area, surround what exists in the townships as the only sports facility built and run by the people. That facility is an oasis, a retreat from the political oppression and recent street crime that dominate the lives of most blacks. The people embrace sports to forget their oppression and to help their children avoid the drugs, robbery, and gang violence that make everyone—including blacks—feel unsafe.

We took them to Soweto where 2.5 million registered residents live in South Africa's largest African township. We visited the school where students began their revolt in 1976 that resulted in nearly 1,000 children being killed by police. That revolt put the forces of history in motion and eventually set the stage for the release of Nelson Mandela. We passed his house and that of Bishop Tutu. You could see the images being created on the faces of our group. I knew they were images that would be indelible.

Sam Ramsamy and others see the rapid development of sports and the integration of Africans in sports at all levels—from the schools to clubs to the national and international levels—to be one area where sanity can return more quickly.

Such a priority is being placed on this that Nelson Mandela hosted us for dinner. In the midst of all the killings, of negotiations leading to a new constitution and to elections next April, Nelson Mandela carved out an entire evening to be with the NBA, the NBAPA, and its players. Dikembe Mutombo told him that he had waited for 7 hours to see him when he first visited the United States in 1990. Now he was less the 7 feet away across the table. David Stern and Charles Grantham offered Mr. Mandela any assistance they could give when he returns to America in October. They made it clear that this trip was the beginning of a long relationship.

I had dreamt of being with Sam Ramsamy in South Africa ever since meeting him in the 1970s. Here we were with him as the president of the National Olympic Committee of South Africa. Nelson Mandela has been a hero of mine since 1963 when he went to prison. Here we were with him for dinner in his own land.

However, the biggest victory lies ahead. Mandela is more than 40 percentage points ahead of his nearest rival in the polls to become South Africa's first democratically elected president (see Chapter 37).

On those dusty fields of Alexandra and Soweto, surrounded by the signs of the most wretched poverty, the violence, and the hatred that whites have heaped on them, blacks talk of a free South Africa where power is shared with whites. They see sports as a way to build that future. Sport will possibly have played a more important role in integration there than it has in any other nation, even the United States.

Meanwhile, those fields of dust in the townships will continue to occupy the time of so many South African children until they find their fields of dreams in a free South Africa.

# 37

## The Role of Sports in the Destruction of Apartheid

Richard E. Lapchick

The new flag of South Africa blew in the breeze. The government buildings where black South Africans had cleaned floors and served coffee were about to pass into the hands of a black-led government. The troops and military hardware that had been used to oppress blacks were set to be placed under the command of President Nelson Mandela. The inauguration was about to commence.

I dreamed I would be in South Africa when Mandela became head of state. Although, I doubted I would ever see that day, the time had come, and I was there.

Mandela acknowledged that sports played a significant role in his triumph. In his first speech after the election results were in, he called on all the sportsmen and sportswomen of the world to come to South Africa after being asked to stay away for 30 years.

Mandela ignored the diplomatic parties on the night of his inauguration and went directly to Ellis Park Stadium to speak during halftime of a soccer match between South Africa and Zambia.

No South African, black or white, had to wonder why a man who had gone from prisoner to president in 4 years could consider sports as a subject to deal with at a moment of such monumental proportions. South Africans knew the importance sports had played for decades in keeping the hopes of blacks alive and in letting whites know that the world considered the apartheid regime a pariah state.

Mandela heard of overseas protests against apartheid on playing fields in England, Australia, and New Zealand as far back as the late 1960s as a prisoner on Robben Island. South Africa was excluded from the Olympic Games in 1964. Although some nations continued to play against Springbok teams that had come to represent apartheid, South African athletes found themselves increasingly shut out of international competition in rugby, cricket, track and field, soccer, and swimming. The sports boycott of South Africa was one of the first signs that the international community would eventually isolate South Africa.

Mandela had once been a competitive boxer. Many of his fellow political prisoners had been athletes themselves. While imprisoned, they held the Robben Island Olympics each year to buoy their spirits. Dan Moyo (now deputy to the president of the National Olympic Committee of South Africa, Sam Ramsamy) himself spent 10 years in prison. Moyo told me how the prisoners would create their own Olympic flames for their competition.

Mr. Mandela made the value he placed on sports clear as soon as he was released from prison in 1990 by helping to form a new National Olympic Committee. Mandela and his African National Congress (ANC) called for an end to the sports boycott even as they insisted on maintaining all other international sanctions.

South Africa officially resumed its place in the international community of sport at the 1992 Olympics in Barcelona when the ANC determined that sports sanctions should be the first to be lifted. As the South Africa team, absent for 32 years, entered the Olympic Stadium, the television cameras zoomed to Nelson Mandela in the stands. The tradition, of course, was for the cameras to go to the head of state. For most South Africans, disenfranchised throughout their lifetimes, this recognition of Mandela was preliminary victory.

At the soccer match, President Mandela told the nearly all-black crowd of 65,000 that the embodiment of the spirit of reconciliation was represented by always playing both anthems: The ANC's national anthem, "Nkosi Sikelele Afrika," was sung at Mandela's inauguration along with the apartheid regime's anthem, "Die Stem van Suid-Afrika," a musical symbol of the oppression suffered by so many for so long.

The 30-year sports boycott was a high price for South African athletes to pay. The standards of a generation of runners, swimmers, cricketers, rugby, and soccer players had atrophied. But today, at last, the rewards are being harvested.

The plans to rebuild South Africa place sports in center stage. Ultimately, sports will possibly have played a more significant role in integration there than it has in any other nation.

# PART VII

# The Beauty of Sport

## Introduction

$R$eaders could easily come away with a rather pessimistic view of sport after reading some of the previous chapters. Without question, sport is plagued by many of the same issues confronting our society. The media attention afforded to professional and college sports has fostered an ever growing cynicism toward athletics as a whole because of a few sensational incidents. Whereas in the 1980s there was a tendency for sportswriters to glorify sports and a reluctance to critically examine the problems associated with organized athletics, the past 10 years has seen the pendulum swing to the opposite extreme. Focus on violence, crime, gambling, drugs, and strikes has all but drowned out the many positive acts performed by coaches and athletes that are worthy of mention. Furthermore, the negative stories are written without a filter to explain the context.

I wanted to conclude this book with some of the very inspiring sport stories that I have become familiar with over the past 10 years. Since forming the Center for the Study of Sport in Society, I have had the opportunity to meet people affiliated with sport who embody the finest human qualities that our nation has to offer. Their efforts fail to make the headlines and are often overshadowed by stories considered more "newsworthy." It is my dream that these individuals will brighten our perspective and lift our hope for the future of sport in today's society. This section commences with in-depth profiles of

Ernestine Bayer, Reneldi Becenti, Bill Bradley, Lawrence Burton, Alan Page, Rachel Robinson, Bob Shannon, and Vivian Stringer.

Following this chapter is a tribute to Reggie Lewis, a professional basketball player for the Boston Celtics, who tragically died of a heart attack at the age of 27. The direct cause of his death was widely questioned in 1995 by the media. There were charges that he used cocaine and this led to his death. His family and local doctors strongly denied this. In spite of this controversy, I believe that his example and leadership on and off the court as well as serving as an outstanding member of the community proved that athletes can be role models to children and adults. His funeral brought together thousands of people from all racial backgrounds. Reggie transcended racial issues in Boston and in the nation as a whole.

Winning football games and helping save the lives of children form an unbeatable game plan for success. Tom Osborne, the University of Nebraska's head coach, and Willie Stewart, a coach at Anacostia High School in Washington, DC, are champion coaches both on the football field and within their respective communities. As leaders and mentors, they share a common positive attitude and an ongoing concern for the welfare of their players in their different environments.

Muhammad Ali, arguably the most recognizable person in the world, is a hero in sport and in society. Because he has achieved the highest standard of excellence in the boxing ring and has touched lives with his compassion, he was honored by Northeastern University as its first and sole inductee to its Sport and Society Hall of Fame. "The Greatest" captures Ali because he possesses the finest human qualities outside the ring.

The final chapter in *Sport in Society: Equal Opportunity or Business as Usual?* is a story about Darryl Williams, who fell victim to an incident of racial violence when he was shot during a football game in Charlestown, Massachusetts. In his survival of this life-threatening situation, Darryl demonstrates true heroism. Although confined to a wheelchair, he has returned to school to obtain a college degree and is a spokesperson to inner-city school children in Boston, sharing his horrifying experience, which ultimately inspires these children to end any form of violence.

# 38

## Hope

Richard E. Lapchick
Mary Frances Anderson

Hope gives us all inspiration and confidence. These individuals have demonstrated the power that hope has for a community. A common characteristic of these leaders is their athletic spirit, which manifests itself on and off the playing field. They each have a strong sense of social responsibility and have given themselves to others, particularly children, to better our society. They are the forerunners of many positive sports figures who will serve as role models in the future.

### ERNESTINE BAYER

Ernestine Bayer is rowing's matriarch. Although now in her 80s, her love for rowing remains vibrant. During the summer, she can be found on the Squamscott River, near her home in Stratham, Maine. In the fall, she still competes in regattas.

Bayer began working for women's right to row in 1938 when she founded the Philadelphia Girls Rowing Club (PGRC), marking the beginning of the modern women's competitive rowing movement. There were 14 original members who paid $25 in annual dues. Although her individual efforts opened the sport of rowing to women, Bayer attributes much of her success to her husband, Ernest Bayer. As a participant in the 1928 Olympics and a silver medalist, he taught Ernestine the technique and skills that brought him to the pinnacle of rowing.

Combining her skills with sheer determination, Bayer began teaching hundreds of women from the PGRC's boathouse. Throughout the 1940s, 1950s, and 1960s, her enthusiasm and passion made her an ideal instructor for young women interested in rowing. Bayer rowed in the first women's race in 1938, which was composed of the same members of her Philadelphia Club and scored a victory. Nearly 30 years later, in 1967, she took the first American women's eight to compete in Europe, where they proved they could compete against international crews. Bayer also served on the first U.S. Women's Olympic Rowing Committee, which sent rowers to the Montreal Games in 1976. She was also instrumental in the initiation of the rowing program at the University of New Hampshire. Her daughter, Tina, rowed at the University of New Hampshire. Tina now serves as her mother's coach.

Bayer's list of accomplishments is extraordinary. In 1993, the Amateur Athletic Union nominated her for the Sullivan Award, which honors the country's top nonprofessional athlete. She received the U.S. Rowing Medal from the U.S. Rowing Association for lifetime achievement in October of 1992. At the 1992 Head of the Charles Race in Boston, which is considered by many to be the nation's most important rowing competition, she won the 60-and-over division. When considering Bayer's strengths as a rower, it is equally important to realize that she loves the sport and enjoys the spirit of competition.

Although her efforts to establish competitive rowing programs for women in the 1930s were met with resistance, she revolutionized the sport and ultimately led American women's rowing to a 1984 Olympic gold medal. Although the awards are meaningful to Bayer, she treasures the invitation by the gold medal team to row with them as her greatest honor.

Bayer's courage is an example to all people, especially athletes. She has allowed neither age nor gender to become insurmountable obstacles in her quest for success. Bayer uses her physical, mental, and emotional energies to their highest potential, thus serving as an outstanding role model and an inspiration.

## RYNELDI BECENTI

Ryneldi Becenti is a Navajo and former student-athlete at Arizona State University where she was one of only three Native American women in the nation playing Division I basketball. As an athlete, she made her dreams turn into reality through persistence, hard work, and a determination to win. As a young woman, Becenti reaped the benefits of her father's guidance and coaching. In addition, she met the challenges of playing basketball with her four brothers. She never gave up.

Becenti is the first Navajo to show "the People" that it is possible to learn the Anglos' ways and still return home, thus paving the way for a number of other Navajo athletes. Like Ernestine Bayer, she is both a role model and a source of inspiration. Becenti first attended Scottsdale Community College, where she played for 2 years. She then enrolled at Arizona State University with an athletic scholarship. Because of her talent and success, hundreds of Native Americans came to support her at basketball games throughout the season. During Becenti's career at Arizona State, attendance at women's games doubled.

Becenti ran the offense for the Arizona Sun Devils. She led the team in scoring (13.2), assists (6.9), steals (85) and 3-point attempts (135). As a junior, she led the Pac-10 in assists and steals. She also had the only triple-double (i.e., double figures in three of four categories: points scored, rebound, assists, or steals) in the nation in 1991-92. Her season high was 30 points as a senior, and she scored in double figures 20 times and had three double-doubles. Ryneldi's statistics are so impressive because they show that she is a team player. On the floor, she actively looks to make the best play for the team, not for herself. Her coach described Becenti's court sense as "better than anyone I've ever seen." Playing and starting in all 29 games during that same season, Becenti simultaneously proved her leadership and became well liked and highly respected by her teammates. While competing at the highest level on the basketball court, Becenti also performed well in the classroom. Balancing time between practice and studies, she majored in sociology and graduated with her degree after completing her athletic eligibility.

The public admires Becenti as a basketball player. However, she is also a remarkable young woman who has a strong sense of giving back to others by sharing her talents. Since her graduation from Arizona, Ryneldi has created opportunities for Native American children by hosting special basketball camps and teaching them to replicate her skills. Her lessons reflect her leadership in the Navajo community.

Becenti emulates courage, too. Even after her mother died during her freshman year in college, she still challenged herself to achieve her goals and perform to the best of her abilities. She gives hope that we can face the most difficult of problems and still find meaning and happiness in life.

In November of 1994, Becenti signed a contract to play professional basketball in Sweden.

## SENATOR BILL BRADLEY

In 1979, Bill Bradley was sworn in as a member of the U.S. Senate and became the nation's youngest senator at age 35. In his first 15 years of service in the Senate, he has received prestigious assignments and been mentioned seriously as a presidential candidate.

Senator Bradley appreciates the true merit of education, especially for today's youth. As a college and professional athlete, Bradley practiced self-discipline both on the playing field and in the classroom. While attending

Princeton University, he epitomized the term *student-athlete.* His performance on the court earned him the honor of All-American. Despite offers to
become a professional basketball player, he opted to become a Rhodes
Scholar. Later, Bradley played for the New York Knicks and helped lead them
to their first National Basketball Association World Championship. In 10
seasons, he performed in 742 games, scoring well over 9,000 points. Nearly
20 years after his retirement, he remains among the top 10 all-time Knicker-
bocker career scoring leaders. He was elected to the Basketball Hall of Fame
in 1983. His experience and example have made him a powerful force
emphasizing the importance of education for today's student-athletes.

Senator Bradley introduced the Student Athlete Right-to-Know Act. The
act called for the graduation rates of all National Collegiate Athletic Association (NCAA) institutions to be made public at the close of each year,
particularly to parents of prospective student-athletes. Although never passed,
it prompted the NCAA to publish graduation rates. Bradley succeeded in
leading the passage of the Student Right-to-Know and Campus Security Act,
which mandates publication of graduation statistics for all students. In particular, schools are required to distinguish between athletes and nonathletes
in addition to specifying the particular sports within each school as well as
the race and sex of the students. His leadership and initiative on behalf
of student-athletes continually demonstrates his commitment to academic
excellence.

He has been a sponsor for legislation for National Student-Athlete Day and
has acted as honorary cochair of National Student-Athlete Day since it's
inception. Bradley believes that it is wonderful to be a good athlete, but it is
more important to receive an education. His philosophy stems from his
conviction that individuals who get a meaningful education will have full
lives.

As a government official, Bradley has been regarded as a leader in race-
related issues. His eloquent candor, honesty, and sensitivity on this issue have
motivated other legislators to listen to his voice for expanded civil rights. In
an interview with *Black Issues in Higher Education* ("A Revealing Conversation," 1995), Bradley said, "The American city needs physical rejuvenation,
economic opportunity and moral direction, but above all, what it needs is the
same thing every small town needs: the willingness to treat another person of
any race with respect you show for your brother or sister, with the belief that
together you'll build a better world than you would have ever done alone, a
better world in which all Americans stand on common ground." Bradley's
proven leadership has brought racial issues to the forefront of the Senate's
agenda, forcing it to take a serious look at economic, political, and social
implications of racism in society.

## LAWRENCE BURTON

Lawrence Burton graduated from Purdue University where he was an All-American flanker as a member of the football team. In his senior season, he caught 38 passes and ran for over 700 yards. He was also a star sprinter on the track team. When he participated in the 1972 Olympic games, he finished fourth in the 200 meter event. Burton tied the world record for the 60 yard dash at 5.9 seconds and won the NCAA 200-meter run. Playing two sports at the highest level in college is an outstanding accomplishment.

His quickness and speed on the track made him an ideal receiver in the National Football League. Burton played professional football as a wide receiver for the New Orleans Saints after they selected him as their number one draft pick. He later went on to be a member of the San Diego Chargers, who won their first division title in 14 years and reached the playoffs.

After his retirement from professional football in 1980, Lawrence Burton joined a new team of "family teachers" in Omaha, Nebraska, at Boys Town. Burton's interests in the lives of troubled youth actually began when he took an off-season job working with young people in a New Orleans Police Department program. It was as if he received a calling when he realized that these children needed him. His work there as a counselor to troubled youth led to a lifelong commitment. Burton now inspires the youth to set their goals high and strive to accomplish them.

A mentor, role model, and friend, Lawrence Burton shows his colleagues and the world the value of giving back to the community through service to those in need. Burton and his wife, Ida, have devoted their lives to being family teachers, which is part of the reconstructed Boys Town approach that puts kids in need into everyday family situations.

After serving as an instrumental figure in lending assistance and friendship to hundreds of children, Burton moved back to California to expand on the principles and practices of Boys Town. He formed an emergency residential care program that gives immediate help to children confronted by abusive behavior. Burton's vision is to educate the children, provide activities for them, and offer counseling and intervention. His mission has seen such far-reaching effects that over 400 children are cared for at 17 different sites all over the nation.

During his 15-year tenure at Boys Town, he raised his own 3 children and had as many as 10 foster children in his house each year. Burton's motto has been, "If you can make one kid better now and if he has kids and they have kids . . . it is something that grows and grows."[1] Burton has made a difference in thousands of lives of American youth.

## JUSTICE ALAN PAGE

Alan Page had been a professional football player for 14 seasons when he was voted Most Valuable Player in the National Football League. It marked the first time the honor was ever bestowed on a defensive lineman. In 1988, he was inducted into the Football Hall of Fame. Playing for the Minnesota Vikings and the Chicago Bears, he went to four Superbowls and nine consecutive Pro-bowls.

He earned his Juris Doctor from the University of Minnesota Law School while he was still playing professional football, a rare achievement. He managed to balance the academic demands of law school and the athletic pressures of professional football. He demonstrated that it is possible to earn a degree, play a sport, and go into the professional world to build a career. In 1985, he was appointed to the attorney general's office for the state of Minnesota and in 1987 became assistant attorney general.

He understands the needs and dreams of American children of different races. Although Page was a fierce competitor on the field, off the field he is compassionate about the needs of American citizens, especially to aspiring young African American male athletes.

Like Senator Bill Bradley, Alan Page believes in the power of education. He reaches out to young children, offering them hope that they are capable of succeeding and learning. Page feels that someone has to take that first step forward and provide leadership, guidance, and continuity. By establishing the Page Education Foundation, he facilitated assistance with postsecondary education to minorities and other disadvantaged youth. In addition, he organized the Kodak/Alan Page Challenge, a nationwide essay contest encouraging urban youth to recognize the value of education.

Within his community, he goes to elementary schools and talks directly with fourth graders. He has visited an astounding 45 American cities, communicating the message to have a positive attitude while inspiring youth to reach their respective potentials.

Page will not accept "no" for an answer and remains relentless in his pursuit to make this world a better place for our children.

## RACHEL ROBINSON

Rachel Robinson is the wife of the late Jackie Robinson, the first African American to play in Major League Baseball. She created a foundation, named appropriately after her husband, in 1973 to honor him and to make a difference in the lives of others. Rachel Robinson remains a beacon of hope despite trying circumstances. Both her son and her mother died within a year and a half of

Jackie's death. She simply has not let her spirit be defeated. Athletes and nonathletes alike can draw strength from Rachel's perseverance.

It took tremendous personal integrity for Jackie Robinson to break baseball's "color barrier" in 1947. Having shared in these struggles, Rachel Robinson truly appreciates their importance. Through the Jackie Robinson Scholarships, she keeps the memory of his achievements alive and inspires hundreds of young people to face the challenges in their own lives with the same spirit of determination.

The Jackie Robinson Foundation offers scholarships—4-year grants of $5,000 a year—to help expand educational opportunities for young people. In 1994, 117 college students were benefactors of the scholarships. Since the program was founded, 359 other students have received scholarships. Participants have an impressive graduation rate from college. More than 300 Robinson scholars have obtained their degrees, including Elaine W. Steward, an attorney and assistant general manager for the Boston Red Sox. Steward is the highest-ranking black female in Major League Baseball. In Robinson's words, "The program's a success because it's a comprehensive package of support. It includes summer jobs and career development and gives the students experience that they wouldn't get otherwise."[2]

In addition, the foundation closely monitors the hiring practices of Major League Baseball to encourage the employing of minorities. Rachel Robinson took action by meeting with both the National League President and Commissioner in 1991 to vocalize her stance that fairness and equality should be not only a reality but a practice. Robinson also helped create a sports management degree program at St. John's University in the early 1980s, enabling students in higher education to pursue a career path in the sports world. Robinson has not only kept the dreams of her husband alive, but she has also built new dreams. Her determination to create opportunities continues to be strong, and she is a true inspiration.

## BOB SHANNON

Bob Shannon went to work at East St. Louis (Missouri) High School in 1971 and immediately noted the horrible conditions and deterioration of the area. East St. Louis represents one of this country's most glaring examples of urban collapse. Half of its 41,000 residents are unemployed and 75% receive public assistance. In this environment, Bob Shannon coaches the highly successful East St. Louis High School football team. In a city where too many men wind up on the streets, in jail, or dead, Shannon has sent well over 100 of his players on to obtain college scholarships.

As a coach, Shannon wants his players to dedicate themselves to reaching their full athletic and academic potential. He motivates, inspires, and challenges them with a goal for his team while keeping each individual's potential in mind. His positive attitude is potent on the playing field and in the classroom, where he often stresses the importance of making sacrifices early in life so one can enjoy life later as an adult.

Shannon makes things happen. By giving African American young men the opportunity to play ball, he has provided them with a paved escape route from the streets of East St. Louis, an area notorious for gang activity and drug abuse. The football field is their safe haven. Moreover, he has introduced a new way of life to these youth, one in which they set personal and team goals that they achieve by applying techniques learned on the field. By instilling self-confidence and self-discipline in his players through rigorous athletic training, Shannon has created champions.

He has devoted his life to helping his student-athletes accomplish their dreams. In an environment where consistency and role models are often absent, Shannon has spent 24 years coaching at East St. Louis High School, the last 16 as head coach. His teams have won the state championship six times while winning an astounding 88% of their games. *The Sporting News* has named Shannon the High School Coach of the Year five times. Coach Shannon has provided these youth with a solid foundation, and he continues to build on the strengths of the team.

## VIVIAN STRINGER

Vivian Stringer is the head women's basketball coach at the University of Iowa where she runs one of the most successful basketball programs in the country. Her teams have won a remarkable 81% of their games, and her record of 509 wins is the third highest among coaches of women's teams. In 1994, after Stringer's 500th victory, the University of Iowa created an endowed athletic scholarship in her name—the first named after an active coach. Prior to the 1994-95 season, Stringer was ranked Number 3 on the active coaching list, and in her 22 years she has accrued a remarkable winning percentage of .912. Perhaps the most impressive thing about Stringer is her style of teaching. She is an excellent mentor because she sincerely cares about each and every one of her players while devoting a great deal of time, energy, and emotion. As she works with her players, she takes a personal interest in them. At the same time, she expects them to produce results on the court.

Stringer's peers have twice voted her National Coach of the Year. In 1991, she coached the United States to a bronze medal at the Pan American Games. She also holds the distinction of being the only women's coach to take two different teams, Cheyney State and Iowa, to the Women's Final Four. No less impressive than Stringer's athletic accomplishments is her commitment to education: Over 90% of her players have graduated during the 11 years that she's been a coach.

Since the tragic death of her husband in 1992, Stringer has been the single parent of three school-age children. She represents the essence of perseverance. Like Becenti and Robinson, Stringer has experienced the loss of a loved one but has successfully managed to be the finest mother and coach. Stringer carefully protects her time with her family, scheduling basketball practices at 6 a.m. to keep her evenings free to be with them. It should be noted, too, that as an African American woman, she serves as a key role model to minority women seeking a future at the highest levels of sports.

## NOTES

1. Quotation from Burton's acceptance speech at the Giant Steps and Excellence in Sports Journalism Awards Banquet, November 10, 1993.

2. Quotation from Robinson's acceptance speech at the Giant Steps and Excellence in Sports Journalism Awards Banquet, November 2, 1994.

## REFERENCE

A revealing conversation with Senator Bill Bradley: Decoding race and politics. (1995, January 12). *Black Issues in Higher Education.*

# 39

## Reggie Lewis
### An Incredible Tribute to a Remarkable Man

Richard E. Lapchick

It was at once one of the saddest and one of the most hopeful days I can remember. Reggie Lewis was being buried, leaving Boston for the last time.

The sadness was obvious, overwhelming, and devastating. Reggie had been taken from us at such a young age; we would no longer see that grace and brilliance on the court. His workmanlike style helped him go from being sixth man on his high school team to being captain of the Celtics and the heir apparent to Larry Bird. Gone also would be the brilliant smile that could light up the Shelburne Community Center as readily as it did the Boston Garden. Missed more than anything would be his presence in the community where he remained one of its people until the day he died.

The hope came from the outpouring of love bestowed on Reggie and his wife, Donna. The first few days were filled with innuendoes about medical opinions and taking risks. Who was to blame? Was it Dr. Gilbert Mudge, who said Reggie could play again? Did Reggie himself make a terrible choice?

Story after story ran until the Celtics' unprecedented news conference during which players and officials simply poured out their hearts, tears flowing, in front of the nation. The regal Celtics in staid New England were suddenly as real and human as you and me. This seemed to change the mood all around. At the end of the news conference, it was announced that Reggie's funeral would be in Matthews Arena at Northeastern University. His last moments with us were going to be in the community he loved at the university where Boston started its love affair with Reggie. It captured everything to have his body lie in state at Northeastern, not at the state Capitol or in the Boston Garden. The people of Boston took over the story.

Like so many others, I had the good fortune to cross paths with Reggie a few times at Northeastern. After he collapsed in April, I sent him a copy of a

---

A version of this chapter originally appeared in *The Sporting News,* August 16, 1993. Reprinted by permission.

book I wrote and a note of encouragement. But it was not the casual way I knew him that moved me but how deeply he touched the people who knew him both intimately and casually. I have spent the last 25 years working in the area of race relations. The day of Reggie's funeral was the most extraordinary interracial event I have ever witnessed. And it took place in Boston, where you don't see too many interracial events. I remember going to hear the Boston Symphony for the first time with my good friend Tom (Satch) Sanders. Having recently arrived from New York, I said I was worried that I wouldn't find him in the crowd. He smiled his wry smile. He and his daughter were two of four African Americans in the hall. That turned out to be typical of Boston "events," which are nearly all white or all black.

Not so on August 2. I sensed it the night before when driving through Boston. I saw many stores with the number 35 or signs that read "Reggie" in the windows. I got to the arena early to help out. By 10 a.m., the street was filled with orderly and saddened groups of men and women, boys and girls, blacks, whites, and Latinos. There were octogenarians and infants. People were in suits and ties, shorts and T-shirts. There were those who were well-known and those who weren't. Those who weren't were there because Reggie remained one of them. He never got bigheaded and distant. Police estimated that 15,000 passed the coffin by the time the funeral started at 1 p.m. Matthews Arena, which baked in the glaring sun, was filled with 7,000 who sat stunned and teary eyed during the 2 hours of tributes. It was incredible.

After it was over, a large but private group gathered to go to the graveside service. It was family and friends, NBA stars and officials, and Northeastern University people. We lingered outside of the arena for what seemed like a long time. No one wanted to move. Perhaps we wanted to preserve our last moments with Reggie.

Finally, we piled into a group of buses and a handful of cars for the ride. The moment seemed to be broken by the wave of relief from the air conditioning that hit our drenched bodies and the cold drinks that the bus driver handed to everyone. Casual conversations about Reggie and the day started. So did the buses.

Then the biggest miracle began as we hit the streets of Boston. The streets around the university, which sits on the Roxbury border, were filled with people. They were waving at us holding signs that read "We love you Reggie," "We'll miss you Reggie" and, simply, "35." I put on my sunglasses to hide the tears. This was no ordinary love affair. This was passion for a man who transcended race and class.

There were boys with their fathers, holding Celtics caps over their hearts; mothers caressing their infants; boys clubs filling a block with signs about Reggie. Houses and apartments were decorated with Reggie Lewis jerseys;

car antennas had "35" flags flying at half-mast. There were people in business suits and homeless men standing side by side.

An estimated 10,000, mixed with every category of humanity, lined the streets all the way to the cemetery. There were blacks on Latino streets, Latinos on black streets, and whites on every street in Roxbury. I would bet that some of those whites had never stepped on the ground in Roxbury before that Monday afternoon.

One man, an athlete, helped us transcend all the issues that separate us. They say it has never happened before in Boston. I know I have never seen it.

There were many NBA players there all day and many more around the nation watching the news reports. Perhaps Reggie's greatest legacy will be that he showed that to be truly loved by people, no matter how high your star rises, you need to be one of them and remain among them.

We all went back to Northeastern, which held a private reception for those who went to the cemetery. Everyone was talking about this incredible tribute. I really hope there is an afterlife so Reggie saw this outpouring.

I went over to pay my respects to Donna Harris Lewis. She was comforting the entire crowd with her strength, no doubt reinforced by the day's events in the face of such tragedy. She remembered the book I had sent and said, "Reggie never had the chance to read your book. Now I will have to read it for him. I will."

I hope the power of the events August 2 makes us all say, "I will" help carry on the legacy of this beautiful man. We'll miss you terribly, Reggie, but you will live on in our hearts. We love you.

# 40

## Tom Osborne and Willie Stewart
Two Coaches Linked by Commitment

Richard E. Lapchick

Tom Osborne and Willie Stewart were among the winners of the 1994 Giant Steps awards, given by Northeastern's Center for the Study of Sport in Society in Boston. The awards are given annually to individuals and organizations that exemplify the ideals and provide the support necessary for youth to fully realize and work toward their academics potential. Osborne and Stewart are winning football coaches. On the surface, the similarities seem to end there.

Osborne leads the nation's top-ranked team at Nebraska, where he has become America's third-winningest active Division I-A coach during his 22-year reign. He has the luxury of a fully funded program that provides excellent compensation for his staff, wonderful facilities, and a recruiting budget that would make most coaches envious. Lincoln, Nebraska, serves as a wholesome and safe environment for young boys who want to become men alongside the cornfields of America's heartland.

On the other hand, Stewart leads Anacostia High School in Washington, D.C., where the streets are a more vicious competitor than any opposing team. He has won six city championships in 12 years, but many wonder what keeps him at Anacostia. Stewart and his assistants work for low pay; his players wear uniforms and shoes he received from the University of the District of Columbia.

Although they coach in different worlds, Osborne and Stewart share something else: an uncommon concern for the welfare of their players and their communities.

In Osborne's case, he saw firsthand how easy it was for a Division I-A program to build broad bodies with little concern for advancing intelligent minds. In the 1960s, Osborne, then a graduate assistant coach, became Nebraska's first academic counselor and began to strike a balance between

A version of this chapter originally appeared in *The Sporting News,* December 19, 1994. Reprinted by permission.

academics and athletics. Thirty years later, 82% of his student athletes who complete their eligibility graduate. This is especially significant considering that 49% of football players graduate nationally.

Cornhusker players don't merely get by; Nebraska leads the nation in every category of major national academic awards. Of Osborne's players, 43 have been named GTE Academic All-Americans. Nebraska has had more National Collegiate Athletic Association Top Six Award winners than any other school.

Osborne does not forget his athletes who leave for the National Football League before they finish their degrees. Instead, he stays after them to come back to complete what they started. Six former Cornhuskers returned to graduate in 1994 alone.

But the campus, even next to the cornfields, sits in an increasingly dangerous world for children. Nebraska athletics has the nation's most expansive school outreach program, reaching 50,000 young people in 1993-94 with messages about making responsible choices about school and drugs. Osborne and his wife, Nancy, established an endowment in 1991 that provides scholarships to students who have gone through his Husker Teammates Program, which matches Husker football players as mentors with at-risk junior high school students. Sensitizing and educating his student-athletes, Osborne is helping save lives in the community.

Stewart is even more direct in saving lives, and his task is urgent. In the last year, four of his players have been shot, one of them fatally.

Stewart drives his players from the worst neighborhoods to school in the morning and home from practice at night. He makes sure they study to overcome the long odds society has laid down for Anacostia students to graduate and go to college. Stewart, who has regularly turned down more lucrative college offers, recognizes the dearth of African American male role models for inner-city youth.

"These are the kids who need the guidance, not the college kids," Stewart says. "You can't save everybody but I still try."[1] Of the 17 graduating seniors on last year's football team, 8 received college scholarships. These young men learned the importance of academics from their mentor. Furthermore, Stewart inspired them to realize that success in athletics comes with a sense of responsibility—they need to come back to help others.

Osborne and Stewart may come from worlds apart, but somehow they learned similar values. Hundreds of young men have benefited. Osborne and Stewart are true heroes of sport.

As part of the award ceremony and the center's 10th anniversary celebration, the center launched its Sport in Society Hall of Fame to honor people from the world of sports who make an especially significant contribution to society, one that extends far beyond the game itself. Muhammad Ali was rightly the sole inductee.

Ali watched, awaiting his turn, to be inducted. Moved by the entire evening Ali reflected on Osborne and Stewart: "That's what coaching should be all about." Coming from "The Greatest," perhaps this was the highest accolade of all.

*Author's Postscript: In the 1994-95 season, Nebraska won its first national championship in the Orange Bowl and Anacostia won its seventh city championship.*

## NOTE

1. Quotation from Stewart's acceptance speech at the Giant Steps and Excellence in Sports Journalism Awards Banquet, November 2, 1994.

# 41

## Muhammad Ali
### The People's Champion, Once and Still

Richard E. Lapchick

The headlines rang out recently that George Foreman had regained the heavyweight championship at 45. A generation of people in their late 40s saw hope that growing old might not matter so much.

But hope was already in abundance in Boston before the fight. Muhammad Ali had come to town to be the first inductee into Northeastern University's Sport in Society Hall of Fame and to receive an honorary degree. When Ali is around, nothing else matters. Fourteen years after he stepped out of the ring, Ali is still the people's champion.

This is a man who enraged many white Americans when he changed his name from Cassius Clay after embracing the teaching of Elijah Muhammad. Ali stepped into the political maelstrom surrounding the Vietnam War by refusing to be inducted into the Army and became a symbol of hope for antiwar activists and a symbol of hate for so many others. He seemed to be a fixture on the barricade of race and war that separated Americans.

Now, more than anyone I can think of, Ali transcends any remaining barriers. I was able to spend parts of 3 days with him and watched children and old people come to him—blacks and whites, men and women, Catholics, Muslims, and Jews. He received doormen as he received chairman of the board, making one and all feel better than before they met Muhammad Ali.

With this unique man, age, race, sex, religion, geography, and class have no meaning. He is above it all because he walks with the people. His pace may be slower as a result of having Parkinson's syndrome, but nobody near him was bothered. You may have to lean to hear what he has to say, but that is a good excuse to get closer to him to hear him speak. It is always personal and memorable.

A version of this chapter originally appeared in *The Sporting News*, November 21, 1994. Reprinted by permission.

There was a time when he traveled with a large entourage. Now he moves with his wife Lonnie, their son Assad, and Howard Bingham, Ali's closest friend. Bingham was also receiving an award in Boston for his brilliant and artistic photo essay, *Muhammad Ali: A Thirty Year Journey.* It is family and friends. He does not need an entourage. As soon as the elevator door opens, an entourage is forged. Wherever he is, people come. Ali does magic tricks to make people smile. But he is the magic; no tricks are necessary.

How strong is his magnetism? My 5-year-old daughter, Emily, was 20 feet and 50 people away when Ali gestured for her to come. Emily had not met him at that point, and I was sure her shyness would keep her at her mother's side. But this was Muhammad Ali, and she ran to him, leaped into his arms, and accepted his kiss with a broad smile.

In my 49 years, I have never asked for an autograph. I now sit under two signed boxing gloves. This was Muhammad Ali.

Has his mind been dulled by Parkinson's syndrome? Twenty-four hours after meeting my kids, he said to me, "You have three beautiful children. But in 10 years, that Emily is going to cause you a lot of trouble." Muhammad never misses a chance to make you feel good. Never. You could be alone with him in a small reception or in a huge banquet hall—Muhammad Ali takes the time to make you feel unique.

After a long evening, Ali asked to be inducted into the Hall of Fame at his table. There wasn't a dry eye in the room. Northeastern President Jack Curry, in conferring the honorary degree on Ali, was at his best:

> With a unique blend of speed, power and poetry, you became the people's champion. . . . For you, brute force took second place to grace, agility, and finesse. Although you danced lightly in the ring, out of the ring you have stood firmly on principle, displaying unwavering devotion to the ideals of peace and justice, crying out against the cruelty of war . . . and imploring our children to search for purpose in their lives. Whether standing your ground against a close-minded nation during the tempestuous 1960s or matching physical skills with young, strong challengers to your boxing supremacy, you have countered all opposition with inexhaustible talent, courage, and independence. In recognition of your commitment to the unity and equality of all people and because of your tireless work to improve the lives of the children and the poor of the world, Northeastern University is privileged to confer on you the honorary degree, Doctorate of Public Service.

Before President Curry could move toward Ali's table, Ali literally burst to the stage to receive the degree. The 650 people in the audience were again on their feet happily cheering. He leaned into the microphone, proclaiming, "Now you can call me Doctor." Ali is not a one-in-a-million figure but a once-in-a-lifetime person. "The Greatest" is just that, a magic man, who was, and still is, the champion. There are no pretenders and no challengers.

# 42

## Darryl Williams
### The Ultimate Role Model

Richard E. Lapchick

National Student-Athlete Day is celebrated around the country each April. It is a day set aside to celebrate the good that student-athletes do in their schools and communities. Although, his playing days are long since over, no one has given more back or paid a higher price than Darryl Williams.

His playing field experiences had to be applied to the game of life at a premature time. Having survived a life-threatening situation, he has since become a voice for the human rights of all people. Darryl represents the spirit of self-empowerment and forgiveness that is so desperately needed if we are to go beyond the hatred that caused his victimization.

Fifteen years after the attack, young Boston student-athletes know about Darryl Williams. Darryl was a 15-year-old from Roxbury making his first varsity football start. He caught a pass that gave his visiting Jamaica Plain High School a 6-0 halftime lead over Charlestown High. September 1979 seemed like a good time for Darryl. He had visions of going to the National Football League. As Jamaica Plain gathered in a huddle before the second half, three snipers finished his dreams. Darryl's career was over, but at least his life was saved. His fate that day was probably the product of the court-ordered busing that had placed Boston on national television as a center of racial hatred and violence.

Darryl Williams returned to Charlestown 11 years later. "I don't understand why people do the things that they do." he said. "I think they were trying to kill somebody black. Why? Why?"[1]

After the attack, which nearly killed him and left him without the use of his arms and legs—after all the broken promises of medical and financial support—Darryl looks at life with an attitude that surprises many people. Most, blacks and whites alike, assume that he probably hates whites. Not

A version of this chapter originally appeared in *The Sporting News*, April 11, 1994. Reprinted by permission.

Darryl, who says, "I'm not going to blame every white person because three whites shot me. There are bad whites and bad blacks. I can't hate a whole race of people because some are bad."

Darryl dreams of and works for something else. "My dream is to live in a world in which racism doesn't exist anymore, just have racism be a bad, bad distant memory. Because if we don't start getting ourselves together, trying hard to get rid of that poison which is racism, we won't have anyone else to blame but ourselves. We can just look in the mirror and say, 'Well that's the person who did it.' "

Darryl is Boston's—and perhaps America's—best example of a living hero for the cause of racial equality. Having paid a heavy price for his platform, Darryl brings his inspiring message to thousands of Americans. Many are student-athletes who see how quickly the sports dream can end. But that is not what Darryl communicates to them. His very presence symbolizes hope for meaningful life after sports.

In many ways, he reminds me of lesser-known Nelson Mandela, who emerged from 27 years in prison full of love instead of hate, reaching out instead of turning away. Darryl Williams, now a student at Northeastern University on a special presidential scholarship and an employee in the Massachusetts State Lottery, reaches out every day. Darryl treasures the fact that he is a student again. "I consider myself blessed to have such good friends to support me and will always remember Northeastern President John Curry for awarding me a scholarship. My fellow students at Northeastern have been very helpful and reassuring. I feel at home and believe that anything is possible."

The student-athletes that we recognized on National Student-Athlete Day give our country hope at a time when the lives of many of our youth are mired with despair. No one gives more hope than Darryl Williams. These student-athletes have direction and purpose and see there is reason to believe in themselves. America should be very proud of them. But none more than Darryl Williams.

*Author's Postscript: Darryl Williams now is a regular member of Project TEAMWORK, the Center for the Study of Sport in Society's highly acclaimed violence prevention program.*

## NOTE

1. Quotations from Darryl Williams are from an interview with Williams conducted by the author in April 1994.

# Conclusion

Richard E. Lapchick

For years, I have been asked if the term *student-athlete* is an oxymoron. Many are ready to believe that you can be a student or an athlete but never both. I think we are more ready to believe that now that 60% of our Division I basketball scholarships go to African Americans. It fits the national stereotype many whites maintain that African Americans are less intelligent.

I entered the sports scene in 1982 as a full-time critic. I believed that the sports world was racist and sexist and that it universally exploited athletes. My credentials for this assessment were actually meager. I was the son of a star (he played for the Original Celtics and coached St. John's and the Knicks for 30 years) who happened to have a social conscience. Beyond that, I merely had closely followed such issues in the media. However, I was doing a lot of research and was writing the first of five books that would look at these issues in American sports.

My early analysis was simple. There were good guys and bad guys. The former were presidents and athletes; the latter included owners, coaches, and athletic directors.

The creation of Northeastern University's Center for the Study of Sport in Society and my appointment as its director gave me the platform to address these issues. In addition to this, it unexpectedly placed me in the middle of the worlds of presidents, coaches, and athletic directors on a regular basis.

A funny thing happened to me on the way to the platform. I discovered that there were as many coaches and athletic directors committed to the concept of the student-athlete as there were presidents.

In the pros, owners and athletes both pursued the dollar with equal vigor. In the complex new world of big-money college sports, many had lost a vision of how to win, generate revenues, and educate at the same time. The rapid expansion of television in college sports, of the commercialization of bowl games, and the riches of the National Collegiate Athletic Association's men's Final Four led a handful of schools and those who administered and coached in their programs to become greedy, cheat, and cut corners. Some others slipped into the trap of trying to compete with outright cheaters, and perhaps, inadvertently fell into their patterns. For me, the worst result was in the plummeting graduation rates for student-athletes in the revenue sports. At the highest levels of college sports, players were sure they would make the pros. Concentrating on athletics became the key to their futures. If coaches didn't insist on their going to class, tutoring, and study halls, then why should they?

In the early 1980s, coaches believed they were hired to win games and fill stadiums. No one's contract said anything about how many athletes graduated. Without anyone measuring them, graduation rates were generally assumed to be quite high. On the other hand, coaches knew that if they did not win, they could be fired. There was no tenure to protect them. In the 1980s, there was a 25% turnover of coaches each year.

Back to my father. He believed he was at St. John's for life. There was no other college for him. He couldn't resist what became a 10-year stint with the Knicks, but then he returned to St. John's when I was 12. He came home from the first day of practice at St. John's and went upstairs to change. We lived in a big old house in Yonkers, New York. He had not come down for 2 hours, so I went up to see him. Here was this towering man in tears. I had never seen any man cry, but there was my father in pain.

He told me that he found out that his players were not going to class and were getting passed through the system. The recognition was devastating. He prided himself on his personal relationship with his players and would ask them about summer jobs, their girlfriends, or what they wanted to do in life. For the first time, he recognized that he had never asked them about what they were majoring in, if they would graduate, or anything related to school. And he was working for an educational institution.

On the following day, he and his assistant, Lou Carnesecca, put together a daily mandatory study hall for all players. That was the late 1950s, and I believe it was the first of its kind. Graduation rates have been extremely high at St. John's ever since.

I share that story to say that we can't expect coaches to do something until they somehow understand that it is part of their responsibility. Today, most coaches recognize that they are educators. That knowledge has resulted in graduation rates steadily increasing over the past decade.

That brings us back to the question of whether the term student-athlete is an oxymoron. That was easy to assume when graduation rates were low. However, it was always an illusion. The real oxymoron is *dumb jock*. The tragedy has been that because society believed that there was such a thing, athletes came to believe it as well. Sometimes the lack of expectation led to a self-fulfilling prophecy, and athletes neither sought nor received an education.

Today, that stereotype has been shattered. Wherever expectations have been raised, most athletes have struck a new balance between academics and athletics. Whether it was no pass, no play at the high school level or Proposition 48 in college, our young people have proved that if we ask them to go to the next level academically (and let them know we believe they can), they will do so.

Moreover, an increasing number of coaches and athletic directors have become partners with presidents in trying to strike that balance between academics and athletics. To be sure, there are still cheaters without conscience, but many increasingly view themselves as being part of the educational mission of universities. Without the opportunity to work with them, I might never have learned that.

Now that I have, I truly believe that all of us who have historically viewed ourselves as adversaries—presidents and athletic directors, faculty and coaches, students and student-athletes, owners and players—must move toward working together to effectively resolve problems. I believe we have made strides on the college level that have not yet been achieved at the professional level where labor conflicts in baseball and hockey in 1994 and 1995 left many fans wondering what they had been cheering about for so many years. It is obvious that we still have a long way to go to achieve equal opportunity and to stop doing business as usual.

# Suggested Readings

## Race in Sport

Abdul-Jabbar, K. (1983). *Giant steps.* New York: Bantam.

Archer, R., & Bouillon, A. (1984). *The South African game: Sport and racism.* London: Zed Press.

Ashe, A. R., Jr. (1989). *A hard road to glory: A history of the African-American athlete* (3 Vols.). New York: Warner.

Axthelm, P. (1970). *The city game.* New York: Harper & Row.

Chalk, O. (1976). *Black college sport.* New York: Dodd, Mead.

Coakley, J. J. (1994). *Sport in society: Issues and controversies* (5th ed.). St. Louis, MO: C. V. Mosby.

de Broglia, C. (1970). *South Africa: Racism in sport.* London: Christian Action.

Edwards, H. (1969). *The revolt of the Black athlete.* New York: Free Press.

Eitzen, D. S. (1993). *Sport in contemporary society: An anthology* (4th ed.). New York: St. Martin's.

Eitzen, D. S., & Sage, G. H. (1993). *Sociology of North American sport* (5th ed.). Madison, WI: Brown & Benchmark.

George, N. (1992). *Elevating the game: Black men and basketball.* New York: HarperCollins.

Gilmore, A-T. (1974). *Bad Nigger: The national impact of Jack Johnson.* Port Washington, NY: Kennikat Press.

Hain, P. (1971). *Don't play with apartheid.* London: Allen & Unwin.

Jarvie, G. (1991). *Sport, racism and ethnicity.* New York: Falmer.

Jordan, P. (1971). *Black coach.* New York: Dodd, Mead.

Lapchick, R. (1986). *Fractured focus: Sport as a reflection of society.* Lexington, MA: Lexington Books.

Lapchick, R. E. (1987). *On the mark: Putting the student back in student athlete.* Lexington, MA: Lexington Books.

Lapchick, R. E. (1991). *Five minutes to midnight: Race and sport in the 1990s.* Lanham, MD: Madison Books.

Lapchick, R. E., & Slaughter, J. B. (1989). *The rules of the game: Ethics in college sport.* New York: Macmillan.

Olsen, J. (1968). *The Black athlete.* New York: Time-Life Books.

Orr, J. (1969). *The Black athlete.* New York: Lion Books.

Peterson, R. (1970). *Only the ball was white.* Englewood Cliffs, NJ: Prentice Hall.

Ragosin, D. (1983). *Invisible men: Life in basketball's Negro leagues.* New York: Atheneum.

Ribowsky, M. (1994). *Don't look back: Satchel Paige in the shadows of baseball.* New York: Simon & Schuster.

Robinson, J. (1972). *I never had it made.* New York: G. P. Putnam.

Ruck, R. (1993). *Sandlot seasons: Sport in Black Pittsburgh.* Champaign: University of Illinois Press.

Rust, A., Jr. (1976). *Get that Nigger off the field.* New York: Delacort.

Tygiel, J. (1983). *Baseball's great experiment: Jackie Robinson and his legacy.* New York: Oxford University Press.

Wielgus, C., & Wolff, A. (1980). *The in-your-face basketball book.* New York: Everest House.

## Gender in Sport

Beran, J. A. (1993). *From six-on-six to full court press: A century of Iowa girl's basketball.* Ames: Iowa State University Press.

Boutilier, M., & San Giovanni, L. (1983). *The sporting woman.* Champaign, IL: Human Kinetics Press.

Bouton, B., & Marshall, N. (1983). *Home games: Baseball wives speak out.* New York: St. Martin's/Marek.

Burton Nelson, M. (1991). *Are we winning yet? How women are changing sports and sports are changing women.* New York: Random House.

Burton Nelson, M. (1994). *The stronger women get, the more men love football: Sexism and the culture of sports.* New York: Harcourt Brace.

Cahn, S. K. (1994). *Coming on strong: Gender and sexuality in twentieth century women's sport.* New York: Free Press.

Coakley, J. J. (1994). *Sport in society: Issues and controversies* (5th ed.). St. Louis, MO: C. V. Mosby.

Creedon, P. J. (1994). *Women, media, and sport: Challenging gender values.* Thousand Oaks, CA: Sage.

Eitzen, D. S. (1993). *Sport in contemporary society: An anthology* (4th ed.). New York: St. Martin's.

Eitzen, D. S., & Sage, G. H. (1993). *Sociology of North American sport* (5th ed.). Madison, WI: Brown & Benchmark.

Fornoff, S. (1993). *Lady in the locker room: Uncovering the Oakland Athletics.* Champaign, IL: Sagamore.

Gerber, E. (1974). *The American woman in sport.* Reading, MA: Addison-Wesley.

Gregorich, B. (1993). *Women at play: The story of women in baseball.* New York: Harcourt Brace Jovanovich.

Guttman, A. (1991). *Women's sports: A history.* New York: Columbia University Press.

Hall, M. A., & Richardson, D. A. (1984). *Fair ball: Toward sex equality in Canadian sport.* Ottawa: Canadian Advisory Council on the Status of Women.

Ingham Berlage, G. (1994). *Women in baseball: The forgotten history.* Westport, CT: Greenwood.

Johnson, S. E. (1994). *When women played hardball.* Seattle, WA: Seal Press.

Kaplan, J. (1979). *Women and sports.* New York: Viking.

Klein, A. M. (1993). *Little big men: Bodybuilding subculture and gender construction.* Albany: State University of New York Press.

Lapchick, R. (1986). *Fractured focus: Sport as a reflection of society.* Lexington, MA: Lexington Books.

Lapchick, R. E. (1987). *On the mark: Putting the student back in student athlete.* Lexington, MA: Lexington Books.

Lapchick, R. E., & Slaughter, J. B. (1989). *The rules of the game: Ethics in college sport.* New York: Macmillan.

Lenskyj, H. (1986). *Out of bounds: Women, sport and sexuality.* Toronto: The Women's Press.

Messner, M. A. (1992). *Power at play: Sports and the problem of masculinity.* Boston: Beacon.

Messner, M. A., & Sabo, D. F. (1990). *Sport, men, and the gender order.* Champaign, IL: Human Kinetics Press.

Messner, M. A., & Sabo, D. F. (1994). *Sex, violence and power in sports: Rethinking masculinity.* Freedom, CA: Crossing Press.

Mewshaw, M. (1993). *Ladies of the court: Grace and disgrace on the women's tennis tour.* New York: Crown.

Meidzian, M. (1991). *Boys will be boys: Breaking the link between masculinity and violence.* New York: Doubleday.

Miracle, A., & Rees, C. R. (1994). *Lessons of the locker room: The myth of school sports.* Amherst, NY: Prometheus.

Oglesby, C. A. (1978). *Women and sport: From myth to reality.* Philadelphia: Lea & Febiger.

Parkhouse, B. L., & Lapin, J. (1982). *Women who win: Exercising your rights in sports.* Englewood Cliffs, NJ: Prentice Hall.

Twin, S. (1979). *Out of the bleachers: Writings on women and sport.* New York: Feminist Press.

## Athletic Uses and Abuses

Andre, J., & James, D. N. (1991). *Rethinking college athletics.* Philadelphia: Temple University Press.

Bailey, W. S., & Littleton, T. C. (1991). *Athletics and academe.* New York: Macmillan.

Brown, P. B. (1992). *My season on the brink.* New York: St. Martin's.

Burnett, D. (1993). *Youth, sports and self-esteem.* Indianapolis: Masters Press.

Cady, E. H. (1978). *The big game: College sports and American life.* Knoxville: University of Tennessee Press.

Coakley, J. J. (1994). *Sport in society: Issues and controversies* (5th ed.). St. Louis, MO: C. V. Mosby.

Cole, L. (1989). *Never too young to die: The death of Len Bias.* New York: Pantheon.

Cosell, H. (with Whitfield, S.). (1991). *What's wrong with sports.* New York: Simon & Schuster.

Denglinger, K., & Shapiro, L. (1975). *Athletics for sale.* New York: Thomas Y. Crowell.

Durso, J. (1975). *The sports factory.* New York: Quadrangle.

Eitzen, D. S. (1993). *Sport in contemporary society: An anthology* (4th ed.). New York: St. Martin's.

Eitzen, D. S., & Sage, G. H. (1993). *Sociology of North American sport* (5th ed.). Madison, WI: Brown & Benchmark.

Feinstein, J. (1993). *Play ball: The life and troubled times of Major League Baseball.* New York: Villard.

Fleisher, A., Goff, B., & Tollison, R. (1993). *The National Collegiate Athletic Association: A study in cartel behavior.* Chicago: University of Chicago Press.

Frey, D. (1994). *The last shot: City streets, basketball dreams.* Boston: Houghton Mifflin.

Funk, G. B. (1991). *Major violation: The unbalanced priorities in athletics and academics.* Champaign, IL: Leisure Press.

Goldstein, J. J. (1983). *Sports violence.* New York: Springer-Verlag.

Gorman, J., & Calhoun, K. (1994). *The name of the game: The business of sports.* New York: John Wiley.

Graham, P. J. (1994). *Sport business: Operational and theoretical aspects.* Madison, WI: Brown & Benchmark.

Hoch, P. (1972). *Rip off the big game.* New York: Anchor.

Hoffman, D., & Greenberg, M. J. (1989). *Sport$biz.* Champaign, IL: Leisure Press.

Horrow, R. B. (1980). *Sports violence.* Arlington, VA: Carrollton.

Joravsky, B. (1994). *Hoop dreams.* Atlanta: Turner Publishing.

King, P. (1993). *Inside the helmet: A player's-eye view of the NFL.* New York: Simon & Schuster.

Koppett, L. (1994). *Sports illusion, sports reality.* Chicago: University of Illinois Press.

Lapchick, R. (1986). *Fractured focus: Sport as a reflection of society.* Lexington, MA: Lexington Books.

Lapchick, R. E. (1987). *On the mark: Putting the student back in student athlete.* Lexington, MA: Lexington Books.

Lapchick, R. E. (1991). *Five minutes to midnight: Race and sport in the 1990s.* Lanham, MD: Madison Books.

Lapchick, R. E., & Slaughter, J. B. (1989). *The rules of the game: Ethics in college sport.* New York: Macmillan.

Lock, T., & Ibach, B. (1982). *Caught in the net.* New York: Leisure Press.

Mullin, B. J., Hardy, S., & Sutton, W. A. (1992). *Sport marketing.* Champaign, IL: Human Kinetics.

Quirk, J., & Fort, R. D. (1992). *Pay dirt: The business of professional team sports.* Princeton, NJ: Princeton University Press.

Rooney, J. F. (1980). *The recruiting game: Toward a new system of intercollegiate sports.* Lincoln: University of Nebraska Press.

Sage, G. H. (1990). *Power and ideology in American sport: A critical perspective.* Champaign, IL: Human Kinetics.

Sammons, J. T. (1990). *Beyond the ring: The role of boxing in American society.* Chicago: University of Illinois Press.

Sands, J., & Gammons, P. (1993). *Coming apart at the seams: How baseball owners, players, and television executives have led our national pastime to the brink of disaster.* New York: Macmillan.

Scott, J. (1971). *The athletics revolution.* New York: Free Press.

Scott, J., & Walton, B. (1978). *On the road with the Portland Trail Blazers.* New York: Thomas Y. Crowell.

Simon, R. L. (1991). *Fair play: Sports, values, and society.* Boulder, CO: Westview.

Simson, V., & Jennings, A. (1992). *Dishonored games: Corruption, money, and greed at the Olympics.* New York: S. P. I. Books.

Simson, V., & Jennings, A. (1992). *The lord of the rings: Power, money and drugs in the modern Olympics.* London: Simon & Schuster.

Smith, C. F. (1992). *Lenny, Lefty, and the chancellor: The Len Bias tragedy and the search for reform in big-time basketball.* Baltimore, MD: Bancroft.

Smith, M. D. (1983). *Violence and sport.* Toronto: Butterworth.

Sommers, P. M. (1993). *Diamonds are forever: The business of baseball.* Washington, DC: Brookings Institution.

Staudohar, P. D., & Mangan, J. A. (1991). *The business of professional sports.* Chicago: University of Illinois Press.

Strasser, J. B., & Becklund, L. (1991). *Swoosh: The unauthorized story of Nike and the men who played there.* New York: Harcourt Brace Jovanovich.

Tatum, J., & Kushner, B. (1979). *They call me assassin.* New York: Everest House.

Taylor, W. N. (1991). *Macho medicine: A history of the anabolic steroid epidemic.* Jefferson, NC: McFarland.

Thelin, J. R. (1994). *Games colleges play: Scandal and reform in intercollegiate athletics.* Baltimore, MD: Johns Hopkins University Press.

Voy, R. (with Deeter, K. D.). (1991). *Drugs, sport, and politics.* Champaign, IL: Leisure Press.

Whitford, D. (1993). *Playing hardball: The high stakes business for baseball's new franchises.* New York: Doubleday.

Wolff, A., & Keteyian, A. (1991). *Raw recruits: The high stakes colleges play to get their basketball stars—and what it costs to win.* New York: Simon & Schuster.

Yaeger, D. (1991). *Undue process: The NCAA's injustice for all.* Champaign, IL: Sagamore.

Zimbalist, A. (1992). *Baseball and billions.* New York: Basic Books.

## Stereotypes, Myths, and Realities About Athletes

Araton, H., & Bondy, P. (1992). *The selling of the green.* New York: HarperCollins.

Ashe, A. R., Jr. (1989). *A hard road to glory: A history of the African-American athlete* (3 Vols.). New York: Warner.

Bailey, W. S., & Littleton, T. C. (1991). *Athletics and academe.* New York: Macmillan.

Baker, W. J., & Carrell, J. M. (1981). *Sports in American society.* St. Louis, MO: River City.

Ball, D. W., & Loy, J. W. (1975). *Sport and social order.* Reading, MA: Addison-Wesley.

Ballinger, L. (1981). *In your face! Sports for love and money.* Chicago: Vanguard.

Blanchard, K., & Cheska, A. (1985). *The anthropology of sport: An introduction.* Hadley, MA: Bergin & Garvey.

Boyle, R. (1973). *Sport: Mirror of American life.* Boston: Little, Brown.

Cantelon, H., & Gruneau, R. (1982). *Sport, culture and the modern state.* Toronto: University of Toronto Press.

Coakley, J. J. (1994). *Sport in society: Issues and controversies* (5th ed.). St. Louis, MO: C. V. Mosby.

Curry, T., & Jiobu, R. (1984). *Sports: A social perspective.* Englewood Cliffs, NJ: Prentice Hall.

Dolson, F. (1982). *Beating the bushes: Life in the minor leagues.* South Bend, IN: Learus.

Edwards, H. (1973). *Sociology of sport.* Homewood, IL: Dorsey.

Eitzen, D. S. (1993). *Sport in contemporary society: An anthology* (4th ed.). New York: St. Martin's.

Eitzen, D. S., & Sage, G. H. (1993). *Sociology of North American sport* (5th ed.). Madison, WI: Brown & Benchmark.

Gruneau, R. (1985). *Class, sport, and social development.* Amherst: University of Massachusetts Press.

Guttman, A. (1978). *From ritual to record: The nature of modern sports.* New York: Columbia University Press.

Harris, J. C. (1994). *Athletes and the American hero dilemma.* Champaign, IL: Human Kinetics.

Hart, M., & Birrell, S. (1981). *Sport in the sociocultural process.* Dubuque, IA: William C. Brown.

Hoberman, J. M. (1984). *Sport and political ideology.* Austin: University of Texas Press.

Kahn, R. (1973). *The boys of summer.* New York: New American Library.

Kramer, J. (1969). *Farewell to football.* New York: World.

Lapchick, R. (1986). *Fractured focus: Sport as a reflection of society.* Lexington, MA: Lexington Books.

Lapchick, R. E. (1987). *On the mark: Putting the student back in student athlete.* Lexington, MA: Lexington Books.

Lapchick, R. E. (1991). *Five minutes to midnight: Race and sport in the 1990s.* Lanham, MD: Madison Books.

Lapchick, R. E., & Slaughter, J. B. (1989). *The rules of the game: Ethics in college sport.* New York: Macmillan.

Leonard, W. M. (1980). *A sociological perspective of sport.* Minneapolis, MN: Burgess.

Lineberry, W. P. (1983). *The business of sports.* New York: H. W. Wilson.

Lipsky, R. (1981). *How we play the game—Why sports dominate American life.* Boston: Beacon.

Lipsyte, R. (1976). *Sportsworld: An American dreamland.* New York: Quadrangle.

Loy, J. W., Kenyon, G. S., & McPherson, B. D. (1981). *Sport, culture, and society.* Philadelphia: Lea & Febiger.

Loy, J. W., McPherson, B. D., & Kenyon, G. S. (1978). *Sport and social systems.* Reading, MA: Addison-Wesley.

Messner, M. A. (1992). *Power at play: Sports and the problem of masculinity.* Boston: Beacon.

Messner, M. A., & Sabo, D. F. (1990). *Sport, men, and the gender order.* Champaign, IL: Human Kinetics Press.

Messner, M. A., & Sabo, D. F. (1994). *Sex, violence and power in sports: Rethinking masculinity.* Freedom, CA: Crossing Press.

Michener, J. (1976). *Sports in America.* New York: Random House.

Mihalich, J. C. (1982). *Sports and athletics: Philosophy in action.* Totowa, NJ: Rowman & Littlefield.

Miracle, A., & Rees, C. R. (1994). *Lessons of the locker room: The myth of school sports.* Amherst, NY: Prometheus.

Mitchell, R. G. (1983). *Mountain experience: The psychology and sociology of adventure.* Chicago: University of Chicago Press.

Nixon, H. L. (1984). *Sport and the American dream.* New York: Leisure Press.

Rentzel, L. (1972). *When all the laughter died in sorrow.* New York: Bantam.

Rozin, S. (1979). *One step from glory: On the fringe of professional sports.* New York: Simon & Schuster.

Russell, B. (1966). *Go up for glory.* New York: Berkley.

Russell, B., & Branch, T. (1979). *Second wind: Memoirs of an opinionated man.* New York: Random House.

Scott, J. (1969). *Athletics for athletes.* Hayward, CA: Otherways.

Scott, J. (1971). *The athletics revolution.* New York: Macmillan.

Smith, C. F. (1992). *Lenny, Lefty, and the chancellor: The Len Bias tragedy and the search for reform in big-time basketball.* Baltimore, MD: Bancroft.

Snyder, E. E., & Spreitzer, E. (1978). *Social aspects of sport.* Englewood Cliffs, NJ: Prentice Hall.

Telander, R. (1989). *The hundred yard lie: The corruption of college football and what we can do to stop it.* New York: Simon & Schuster.

Tutko, T., & Bruns, W. (1976). *Winning is everything and other American myths.* New York: Macmillan.

Williams, P. (1994). *The sports immortals: Deifying the American athlete.* Bowling Green, OH: Bowling Green State University Popular Press.

Yiannakis, A., McIntyre, T., Melnick, M., & Hart, D. (1979). *Sport sociology: Contemporary themes.* Dubuque, IA: Kendall/Hunt.

## Media and Sport

Blain, N., Boyle, R., & O'Donnell, H. (1993). *Sport and national identity in the European media.* London: Leicester University Press.

Fornoff, S. (1993). *Lady in the locker room: Uncovering the Oakland Athletics.* Champaign, IL: Sagamore.

Fountain, C. (1993). *Sportwriter: The life and times of Grantland Rice.* New York: Oxford University Press.

Helitzer, M. (1991). *The dream job: Sports publicity, promotion and public relations.* Athens, OH: University Sports Press.

Koppett, L. (1994). *Sports illusion, sports reality.* Chicago: University of Illinois Press.

Naven, E. (1994). *Diamonds are a girl's best friend: Women writers on baseball.* Boston: Faber & Faber.

Oriard, M. (1993). *Reading football: How the popular press created an American spectacle.* Chapel Hill: University of North Carolina Press.

Whannel, G. (1992). *Fields of vision: Television sports and cultural transformation.* London: Routledge.

## Sport in the International Arena

Archer, R., & Bouillon, A. (1984). *The South African game: Sport and racism.* London: Zed Press.

Coe, S., Teasdale, D., & Wickham, D. (1992). *More than a game: Sport in our time.* London: BBC Books.

de Broglia, C. (1970). *South Africa: Racism in sport.* London: Christian Action.

Espy, R. (1979). *The politics of the Olympic Games.* Berkeley: University of California Press.

Gilbert, D. (1980). *The miracle machine.* New York: Coward, McCann and Geoghegan.

Griffiths, J. (1979). *Sport: The people's right.* London: Writing and Readers Publishing Cooperative.

Guttman, A. (1992). *The Olympics: A history of the modern games.* Urbana, IL: University of Illinois Press.

Hain, P. (1971). *Don't play with apartheid.* London: Allen & Unwin.

Hoberman, J. M. (1984). *Sport and political ideology.* Austin: University of Texas Press.

Hoberman, J. M. (1988). *A whole new ball game: An interpretation of American sports.* Chapel Hill: University of North Carolina Press.

Horrell, M. (1968). *South Africa and the Olympic Games.* Johannesburg: South Africa Institute of Race Relations.

Johnson, A. T., & Frey, J. H. (1985). *Government and sport: The public policy issues.* Totowa, NJ: Rowman & Allanheld.

Lapchick, R. (1975). *The politics of race and international sport: The case of South Africa.* Westport, CT: Greenwood.

Lapchick, R. (1986). *Fractured focus: Sport as a reflection of society.* Lexington, MA: Lexington Books.

Leaver, J. (1983). *Soccer madness.* Chicago: University of Chicago Press.

Lowe, B., Kanin, D. B., & Streak, A. (1978). *Sport and international relations.* Champaign, IL: Stipes.

Lucas, J. (1980). *The modern Olympic Games.* New York: A. S. Barnes.

Lucas, J. (1992). *Future of the Olympic Games.* Champaign, IL: Human Kinetics.

Macintosh, D., & Hawkes, M. (1994). *Sport and Canadian diplomacy.* Montreal, Canada: McGill-Queen's University Press.

Mandell, R. D. (1971). *The Nazi Olympics.* New York: Macmillan.

Newnham, T. (1975). *Apartheid is not a game.* Auckland, New Zealand: Graphic Publications.

Newnham, T. (1978). *A cry of treason: New Zealand and the Montreal Olympics.* Palmerstown North, New Zealand: Dunmore.

Pickering, R. J. (1978). *Cuba: In sport under Communism.* London: C. Hurst.

Prouty, D. F. (1988). *In spite of us: My education in the big and little games of amateur and Olympic sports in the U.S.* Brattleboro, VT: Vitesse.

Riordan, J. (1977). *Sport in Soviet society.* Cambridge, UK: Cambridge University Press.

Schaap, D. (1976). *An illustrated history of the Olympics.* New York: Ballantine.

Seagraue, J., & Chu, D. (1981). *Olympism.* Champaign, IL: Human Kinetics.

Simson, V., & Jennings, A. (1992). *Dishonored games: Corruption, money, and greed at the Olympics.* New York: S. P. I. Books.

Sugden, J., & Bairner, A. (1993). *Sport, sectarianism and society in divided Ireland.* London: Leicester University Press.

Sugden, J., & Tomplinson, A. (1994). *Hosts and champions: Soccer cultures, national identities, and the World Cup in the USA.* Aldershot, UK: Ashgate.

Ungerleider, S., & Golding, J. (1991). *Beyond strength: Psychological profiles of Olympic athletes.* Eugene, OR: Brown & Benchmark.

## The Beauty of Sport

Coakley, J. J. (1994). *Sport in society: Issues and controversies* (5th ed.). St. Louis, MO: C. V. Mosby.

Horrigan, K. (1992). *The right kind of heroes.* Chapel Hill, NC: Workman.

Thompson, J. (1993). *Positive coaching: Building character and self-esteem through sports.* Madison, WI: Brown & Benchmark.

# Index

# About the Editor

**Richard E. Lapchick** brought his experiences as a civil rights activist, scholar, and author to Northeastern University where he is founder and director of the Center for the Study of Sport in Society.

Since its inception in 1984, the center has attracted national attention to its pioneering efforts to ensure the education of athletes from junior high school through the professional ranks. The center helped form the National Consortium for Academics and Sports (NCAS), a group of over 115 colleges and universities that have adopted the center's programs. To date, 7,937 athletes, 3,351 of which have graduated, have come back to NCAS schools after their eligibility expired. Nationally, the NCAS athletes have seen more than 2,308,322 students in the school outreach program. Lapchick serves as president and chief executive officer of NCAS.

He was the American leader of the international campaign to boycott South Africa in sports for more than 20 years. In 1993, the center launched TEAM-WORK-South Africa, a program designed to use sports to help improve race relations and help with sports development in postapartheid South Africa. He was among the 200 guests specially invited to the inauguration of Nelson Mandela.

A prolific writer, *Sport in Society: Equal Opportunity or Business as Usual?* is his eighth book. He is currently working on his ninth book and is a regular columnist for *The Sporting News.* He serves as an adviser to the Reverend Jesse Jackson and the Rainbow Commission on Fairness in Athletics and to the players associations of the National Basketball Association, the National Football League, and Major League Baseball on the issue of racial hiring practices in sports.

Considered among the nation's experts on sports issues, he has appeared numerous times on *Nightline, Good Morning America, Face the Nation, The*

*Today Show, ABC World News, NBC Nightly News, the CBS Evening News,* CNN, and ESPN. He is the recipient of numerous humanitarian awards including the Ralph Bunche International Peace Award. He is listed in *Who's Who in American Education, Who's Who in America,* and *Who's Who in the World* and was named in 1993 and in 1994 by *The Sporting News* as "one of the 100 most powerful people in sports."

Lapchick received a B.A. from St. John's University in 1967. He earned a Ph.D. in international race relations at the University of Denver and in 1993 was named that school's outstanding alumnus. Before coming to Northeastern, he was an Associate Professor of Political Science at Virginia Wesleyan College and a Senior Liaison Officer at the United Nations. In 1994, he received three honorary doctorates, from Bridgewater State College, the University of Nevada, Reno, and Northeastern University.

The son of Joe Lapchick, the famous Original Celtic center who became a legendary coach for St. John's and the Knicks, he is married and has three children.

# About the Contributors

**Dean F. Anderson** is Professor and Chairperson of the Department of Health and Human Performance at Iowa State University. He received his B.A., M.A., and Ph.D. in physical education from the University of Minnesota. While an undergraduate, he lettered in track. He has served as both a high school and college track and cross-country coach. He has published and presented nationally and internationally in the areas of sport sociology and sport social psychology. His sports articles have been in published in journals such as *International Review of Sport Sociology, Sociology of Sport Journal, Journal of Sport & Social Issues, Journal of Sport Behavior,* and *Perceptual and Motor Skills.* He has served as Chairperson of the Sociology of Sport Academy in the American Alliance of Health, Physical Education, Recreation and Dance (AAHPERD).

His research interests have focused on sports career socialization, sexism, and racism in sports, sports fan behavior, children's sports, and exercise adherence behavior. He belongs to the North American Society for the Sociology of Sport, AAHPERD, and the National Association for Physical Education in Higher Education. He relaxes by going fishing, doing wood-working, and reading mysteries.

**Mary Frances Anderson** of Houston, Texas, graduated cum laude from the University of Oklahoma n 1994 with a B.A. in letters. Currently, she is an editor of Richard Lapchick's forthcoming book *The Bosnian Boys: It Was Never a Game.* She is also a research assistant at the Center for the Study of Sport in Society. Chapter 38 in this volume, "Hope," is her first publication.

**Alison Bass** has been a staff writer for the *Boston Globe* since July 1987. She currently covers mental health and human behavior for the "Health and

Science" section and daily pages of the *Boston Globe.* She has also written cover stories for the *Globe Sunday* magazine, ranging from articles on the origins of violence to the stresses of dual-career families. Prior to coming the *Globe,* she was a senior editor and writer from 1982 to 1987 at *Technology Review,* a science and technology policy magazine published by the Massachusetts Institute of Technology. She worked as a staff writer for the *Miami Herald* from April 1980 to November 1982 and was a reporter for two other newspapers previous to that. In the late 1970s, she also worked in public relations for the Massachusetts Eye and Ear Infirmary. She graduated from Brandeis University in 1975 with a B.A. in English literature.

**Jeffrey R. Benedict** is Director of Research at the Center for the Study of Sport in Society and Lecturer at Northeastern University. He has written "Male Student-Athletes Reported for Sexual Assault: A Survey of Campus Police Departments and Judicial Affairs Officers" (*Journal of Sport & Social Issues,* May 1993) and completed a 2-year case study, *Athletes and Rape: How Sport Culture Complicates the Establishment of Consent,* on the use of the consent defense in cases of acquaintance rape involving professional athletes. He received his bachelor's degree in history from Eastern Connecticut State University and a master's degree in political science from Northeastern University.

**Debra E. Blum** graduated from Duke University in 1987 and completed a brief stint the following year as a researcher and reporter at United Press International. She then began working at the *Chronicle of Higher Education,* as a reporter, covering such issues as collective bargaining on campus, academic freedom, and scientific fraud. In 1993, she became senior editor for the athletics section of the *Chronicle.* Each week, she writes and edits articles on subjects such as honesty and dishonesty in sports programs, efforts to wipe out gender imbalances, the conflicts between academic standards and box office concerns, sports as a sociological force, and the important issues in college athletics and the people who try to cope with them. Originally from the suburbs of Philadelphia, she lives with her husband, a patent attorney, in Washington, DC.

**Suzanne Halliburton** graduated from the University of Texas in 1983 with a degree in journalism. After 2 years at the *Beaumont (Texas) Enterprise,* covering labor issues and small-town politics, she joined the sports staff of the *Austin American-Statesman,* where she has worked since 1986. She covered the final 3 years of Tom Landry's legendary regime with the Dallas Cowboys and has since covered most of the University of Texas teams. Her current assignment is the Olympics. Her first big series was a report on the

number of women suffering from eating disorders on UT's nationally domi-
nant swim teams. Her specialty since then has been investigative and enter-
prise reporting. She has won national awards from the Associated Press Sports
Editors, the Women's Sports Foundation, and the Center for the Study for
Sport in Society. Her work has been featured in *A Kind of Grace* and
*Contemporary Sports Reporting.* She currently resides in Austin.

**Byron Hurt** is the training specialist for the Mentors in Violence Prevention
(MVP) project, which attempts to raise awareness about men's violence
against women, at Northeastern University's Center for the Study of Sport in
Society. As a scholarship student-athlete, he played quarterback on the Northeastern University football team. He also served for 2 years as the editor of
*The Onyx Informer,* Northeastern's black student newspaper. He interned at
three Boston television stations (WBZ-TV, WHDH-TV, and WCVB-TV) and
wrote for the *Quincy Patriot Ledger.* He created, produced, and directed the
Northeastern University black senior video yearbook, a 50-minute documentary film about the hopes, dreams, and aspirations of African American
graduating seniors at Northeastern and the trials and tribulations of being an
African American college student at a predominantly white New England
university. The black senior video yearbook, titled *Moving Memories,* was the
first video yearbook in the history of Northeastern University.

   He is the 1994 recipient of the prestigious Echoing Green Public Service
Fellowship Award. As an Echoing Green Fellow, he is currently producing
and directing a documentary film on black masculinity in America as well as
designing an educational outreach curriculum to accompany the film. His
work has appeared in several publications, including the *Boston Globe.*

**Jackson Katz** is a nationally renowned speaker and activist on the issue of
men's violence against women, masculinity, media, and sports. A former
football, basketball, and track athlete, he was the first man to earn a minor in
women's studies from the University of Massachusetts at Amherst. He holds
a master's degree in education from Harvard University and lectures and
conducts training at colleges and universities, national conferences, prep
schools, military academies, and high schools and middle schools nationwide.
He is the creator of the Mentors in Violence Prevention (MVP) project, the
nation's first large-scale attempt to enlist collegiate and professional athletes
in the fight against rape and all forms of men's violence against women. Based
at Northeastern University's Center for the Study of Sport in Society, this
pioneering project encourages men and boys to redefine masculinity and
consider active rather than passive bystander behaviors.

   He is the author of numerous articles on topics such as "The Construction
of Violent White Masculinity in Advertising," "Rethinking Private Pleasure:

Men and Pornography," and "Sports and Masculinity." His educational slide shows include *My Gun's Bigger Than Yours: Images of Manhood and Violence in the Media,* and *Fighter Pilots and Draft Dodgers: The Marketing of Presidential Masculinity, 1972-1992.* He has appeared on numerous television programs, including ABC's *Good Morning America,* the *Phil Donahue Show, Montel Williams,* and the *Jerry Springer Show.*

**Donna A. Lopiano** is Executive Director of the Women's Sports Foundation. According to *The Sporting News,* she is listed No. 43 of the 100 most influential people in sports and *College Sports* magazine ranks her No. 31 among the 50 most influential people in college sports. She received her bachelor's degree from Southern Connecticut State University and her master's and doctorate degrees from the University of Southern California. She has been a college coach of men's and women's volleyball and women's basketball, field hockey, and softball. As an athlete, she participated in 26 national championships in four sports and was nine-time All-American at four different positions in softball, a sport in which she played on six national championship teams. She is a member of the Softball Hall of Fame and the Texas Women's Hall of Fame, among others.

She previously served as the University of Texas Director of Women's Athletics, as the President of the Association for Intercollegiate Athletics for Women, and as a Trustee of the Women's Sports Foundation. She currently serves as a member of the Advisory Board of the Center for the Study of Sport in Society, as a Title IX consultant, and as an Ethics Fellow of the Institute for International Sport. A prolific writer and speaker, she is considered by most to be a champion of equal opportunity for women in sport and the ethical conduct of educational sport.

**Sandy Padwe** is one of the nation's most respected sports journalists. He is now Assistant Professor at the Graduate School of Journalism at Columbia University and a consultant to ESPN. He graduated with a B.A. in journalism in 1961 from Penn State University. He is a former winner of the Headliner Club Sportswriter of the Year award, which he won prior to becoming a sports editor. He wrote for *Newsday* and the *Philadelphia Inquirer.* His career as an editor began at *Newsday* in 1973 when he was named Deputy Sports Editor. Four years later, he moved to *Sports Illustrated* as a Senior Editor, where he became the Investigations Editor. He joined the *New York Times* in August of 1980 as Editor of *Sports Monday* and became Deputy Sports Editor in April of 1981. He returned to *Sports Illustrated* in January 1985. He left the magazine in July 1994 to work at Columbia full-time. He has also served as a Fellow at the Institute for International Sport at the University of Rhode Island.

**Rhonda Revelle** is head coach for softball at the University of Nebraska, Lincoln.

**Shelly Sanford Rothman** obtained a bachelor of journalism from the University of Texas at Austin, and a juris doctorate from St. Mary's University in San Antonio, Texas. She also attended the University of Texas School of Law while interning at the Supreme Court of Texas. She has an environmental, general litigation, and sports and entertainment law practice in Houston, Texas.

**Gary A. Sailes**, Ph.D., is Associate Professor of Sport Sociology in the Department of Kinesiology at Indiana University. He currently serves as chair-elect of the Sport Sociology Academy of the National Association for Sport and Physical Education, a major association of the American Alliance for Health, Physical Education, Recreation and Dance. He has published extensively in the area of race and sports, focusing on the African American athlete. He has led two congressional sessions on Capitol Hill that investigated the treatment of African American intercollegiate athletes. He also consults with university and college athletic departments in the counseling of minority student athletes. He is founder and director of the Indiana Sport Education Foundation, which hosts an annual workshop bringing together professional and college athletes, educators, agents, business professionals, parents, and high school athletes to discuss issues relevant to educational success in college and beyond. He is currently working on a book titled *Chasing the Dream: African American Males and American Sport.*

**Mary Schmitt** is a general assignment reporter/columnist in the sports department of the *Kansas City Star*. She previously has worked for the *St. Paul Pioneer Press*, the *Eugene Register-Guard*, the *Milwaukee Journal*, the *Minneapolis Tribune*, the *Washington Post* and the *Milwaukee Sentinel*, covering professional, college, and amateur sports. She has a journalism degree from Marquette University, which won the NCAA basketball championship when she was a senior in 1977. She lists former Marquette coach Al McGuire as the sports personality who most influenced her career.

**Ed Sherman** is the Associate Sports Editor of the *Chicago Tribune*. For 13 years, he covered Major League Baseball, pro football, and college football. He was the president of the College Football Writers Association in 1994-1995. As a writer, he specialized in in-depth reporting, probing beyond the surface of sports. A series on membership policies at golf clubs was cited by the Associated Press. Another series, "The Passing Game," written with Barry Tempkin, on athletics and academics in college sports, won numerous awards, including the 1994 Excellence in Sports Journalism Award for print media from the Center for the Study of Sport in Society at Northeastern University. He is a 1981 graduate of the University of Illinois. He has been at the *Chicago Tribune* for 14 years. He is married and lives in Highland Park.

**Bethany Shifflett** is Professor at San Jose State University in the Department of Human Performance. She has a doctorate and a master's degree from the University of Iowa and a bachelor's degree from Southern Connecticut State College. Her professional experience includes 13 years coaching gymnastics, teaching K-12 and at the college level, and 8 years service as measurement and evaluation specialist at the college level. She belongs to the American Evaluation Association, The American Alliance for Health, Physical Education, Recreation and Dance (AAHPERD) Research Consortium, the National Council of Measurement in Education, and the AAHPERD. Her service activities include software development, peer review for *Research Quarterly,* AAHPERD, and Western Society for Physical Education of College Women (WSPECW) conference papers, and service at the university and state levels in the capacity of academic senator. She has received the University Meritorious Performance and Professional Promise Award and a Young Scholar Award from the Western Physical Education Society. She also works as a research design and analysis consultant to San Jose State University's Educational Opportunity Program, Santa Clara County Juvenile Probation Department, and Monterey County (Salinas) PATTERNS program.

**Donald Siegel** holds a B.S. from Brooklyn College, an M.S. from the University of Massachusetts, and an Ed.D. from the University of North Carolina at Greensboro. He has taught at Smith College for the past 20 years and is currently professor and coordinator of its graduate program in exercise and sports studies, which specializes in coaching education. He teaches courses and has published papers in the areas of sport psychology, sport sociology, motor learning, and computers. He was a collegiate basketball athlete, currently plays tennis recreationally, and has been a nationally ranked squash player.

**Barry Temkin** received a B.A. with honors from the University of Wisconsin —Madison, in 1970 and an M.A. in history from the University of Chicago in 1971. Presently, he is a high school sports columnist and feature writer for the *Chicago Tribune,* a position he has held since June 1988. Until that time, he was high school sports coordinator for the *Tribune* since August 1986. He also served as assistant sports editor from September 1983 to August 1986. He received a first-place award from the Associated Press Sports Editors for investigative reporting and a Peter Lisagor Award for public service from the

Chicago Headline Club for "The Youngest Professionals," a *Tribune* series he coauthored in 1991. He also won a Peter Lisagor Award for sports journalism for the "The Passing Game," a series he coauthored in 1993, which received the 1994 Excellence in Sports Journalism Award for print media from the Center for the Study of Sport in Society at Northeastern University.

**Ron Thomas** has been a sports journalist for the last 22 years, covering mostly professional basketball and football along with writing feature stories. Throughout his career, he has had a special interest in racial and historical aspects of sports. After graduating from the University of Rochester with a bachelor's degree in political science, he earned a master's degree from Northwestern's Medill School of Journalism in 1973, then became a prep writer at the *Rochester Times-Union.* In 1975, he became the Big Ten beat reporter for the *Chicago Daily News.* When the *Daily News* folded in 1978, he was hired by the *San Francisco Chronicle* where he remained for 15 years, except for a 2-year stint, from 1982 to 1984, as *USA Today*'s first NBA writer. At the *Chronicle,* he covered the Golden State Warriors and San Francisco 49ers for a total of 11 years and in 1980 wrote an award-winning series about the lack of black managers and coaches in professional sports. Since leaving the *Chronicle* in 1993, Thomas, along with his partner Mike Brown, has worked on projects for their company, the Sports Institute, which specializes in racial, gender, and media issues in sports. He returned to daily journalism in February 1995 as a sportswriter/copy editor with the *Marin Independent Journal* outside San Francisco.

**Lawrence A. Wenner** is Professor of Communication and Director of the Graduate Program in Sports and Fitness Management at the University of San Francisco. Since 1992, he has served as Editor of the *Journal of Sport & Social Issues.* His books include *Media, Sports, and Society* and *Television Criticism: Approaches and Applications.*

**Stanton Wheeler** is Ford Foundation Professor of Law and Social Sciences at Yale Law School, where he has taught since 1968. After teaching at Harvard and the University of Washington, he was a full-time staff member at the Russell Sage Foundation from 1964 to 1968 and a consultant to the foundation until 1982. He has been a Fulbright Research Fellow at the Institute of Criminology and Criminal Law at the University of Oslo, Norway, and a Fellow at the Center for Advanced Study in the Behavioral Sciences in Palo Alto, California. In 1985, he took a 2-year leave of absence from Yale to become the first Director of the Amateur Athletic Foundation of Los Angeles, a creature of the financial success of the Los Angeles Olympics in 1984.

His early scholarly work focused on delinquency and prisons, the latter part of a more general interest in institutions that process people. More recently, he directed a program of research, titled Yale Studies in White Collar Crime. He is the coauthor of two volumes in that series, *Sitting in Judgment: The Sentencing of White Collar Criminals* and *Crimes of the Middle Class* (1988 and 1991, respectively). He is currently working on issues involving intercollegiate athletics and on a cultural history of brass music. He has a B.A. from Pomona College and an M.A. and Ph.D. from the University of Washington.

**Raymond Yasser** is Professor of Law at the University of Tulsa College of Law. He is a recipient of the university's most prestigious teaching award, having been named Outstanding Teacher of the Year in 1993. He teaches in areas of torts, trial practice, and sports law. His research interest is mostly in the area of sports law, where he has published widely. He is the coauthor of the nation's most widely used sports law book, *Sports Law: Cases and Materials* (with Goplerud and McCurdy). He has also served as Chair of the Association of American Law Schools Section on Law and Sports and has represented numerous professional and amateur athletes.